P9-CPW-200

Also by Ellen Stern

Best Bets

The Very Best from Hallmark

Once Upon a Telephone (coauthor)

Sister Sets (coauthor)

Threads (coauthor)

Gracie Mansion

THE BIOGRAPHY

ELLEN STERN

Skyhorse Publishing

Skyhorse Publishing books may be purchased in bulk at special discounts for sales promotion, corporate gifts, fund-raising, or educational purposes. Special editions can also be created to specifications. For details, contact the Special Sales Department, Skyhorse Publishing, 307 West 36th Street, 11th Floor, New York, NY 10018 or info@skyhorsepublishing.com.

Visit our website at www.skyhorsepublishing.com.

10 9 8 7 6 5 4 3 2 1

Library of Congress Cataloging-in-Publication Data is available on file.

Cover design by 5mediadesign

Print ISBN: 978-1-5107-5940-4
Ebook ISBN: 978-1-5107-5941-1

Printed in the United States of America

For Peter

"If you live long enough, everything happens."
—Al Hirschfeld

CONTENTS

HIRSCHFELD

AUTHOR'S NOTE

In 1987, I interviewed Al Hirschfeld for *GQ* magazine. The profile ran, he liked it, and that was that. We never saw each other again. But I held on to my notes.

In 2011, when his widow sold the town house where he'd lived, worked, and hosted so many starry soirees, I rediscovered the copy of his book *Show Business Is No Business* that I'd asked him to inscribe that afternoon twenty-four years before. This is what he'd written:

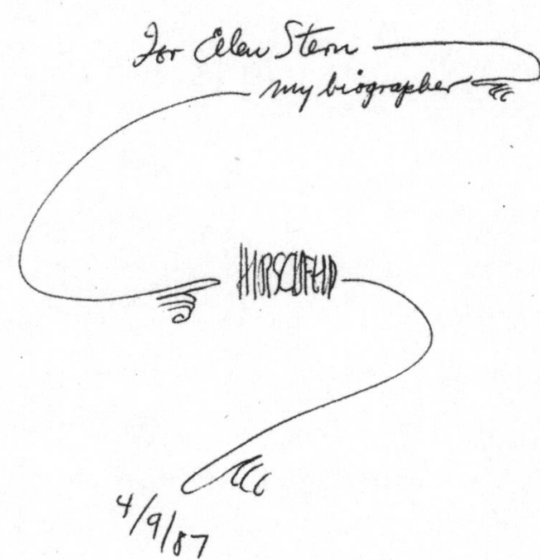

So here goes.

AT THE TOP

On the fourth floor of his Ninety-fifth Street town house, a bearded fellow is in a barber chair. Perched on two small pillows and a torn green leather cushion, his slippered tootsies parked on an iron footrest supported by two phone books, the artist is at work. This is his studio. It is where he does several drawings a week, several hundred a year, ten thousand in a lifetime. It is his refuge when things go right and things go wrong. "I spend most of my time here," he says. "I just visit downstairs."

Attired in his blue jumpsuit, Al Hirschfeld ponders the product before him: a pencil sketch of Merman, Mostel, or Bernstein that will, when he puts ink to it, capture the essence of Merman, Mostel, or Bernstein fit to print in *The New York Times*, the *Herald Tribune*, *TV Guide*, *Vanity Fair*, the *Brooklyn Daily Eagle*, *The American Mercury*, or *Seventeen*. The swirls, the curls, the ginger, the bounce!

The windowsill is a garden of dusty plants, and the linoleum floor is cracked, but the room is in deliberate disarray. He knows where—among the bookshelves, mountains of drawings, mounds of reference materials, piles of magazines, tubes and boxes and envelopes—things are. The green walls are tacked and taped with the unfinished sketches, drawings, and posters he keeps close (Anita Ellis in the spotlight, Sonny and Cher in color, George Burns, Pavarotti) and signs: TOW-AWAY ZONE NO PARKING . . . VIETATO FUMARE . . . REMEMBER: IT WAS AN ACTOR THAT KILLED LINCOLN. The bulletin board is festooned with yellowed clippings, letters, snapshots, and cartoons.

The slanted top of the old oak drafting table, picked up at an auction years ago, is scarred by years of slicing his own triple-ply, cold-pressed illustration boards before he started having them custom-cut. No matter the size of the published drawing, the original is done on a board measuring twenty-one by twenty-seven inches. Antique wooden boxes contain the Gillott crowquill pens and Venus B pencils, rulers and knives, electric eraser. Jars of Higgins black India ink share the space with brushes in glasses, cans, and jars, while others dangle dancingly from hooks. Hirschfeld draws by daylight, skylight, and a lamp over his head—relic of a Cincinnati department store and installed by his friend Abe Feder. The phone is close at hand, since he's listed in the book and grabs it when it rings.

The Koken barber chair, a product of St. Louis, entered the scene in the 1930s. He considers it the most functional chair in the land. "It goes up and down, it turns around, it becomes a chaise longue," he says. Lee Shubert, who kept a barber chair in the office so he could be shaved twice a day, used his for a nap. Sweeney Todd, on the other hand, used his for Stephen Sondheim.

A crony will flop on the couch to schmooze, but outsiders take the captain's chair with its time-worn blue cushion. These are the sitters, here to be immortalized. Unlike the stars of stage, screen, and bandstand he observes in their own habitats, these are the designers, composers, and orthopedists who come to be Hirschfelded on their own dime.

They're disappointed. They expected communion. For them, the encounter is history; for Hirschfeld, it's business. He's genial but brisk, attentive but uncommunicative. The visit goes too fast, allows too little. "Al simply looked at my father, did a couple of squiggles, then took the paper and turned it over. That's all I saw him do," says Ted Chapin, recalling the day he accompanied his father, Schuyler Chapin, New York's former commissioner of cultural affairs, to be drawn. From squiggles to immortality, just like that.

"I thought he was going to sketch me when I went up there," says the Broadway lyricist Sheldon Harnick, "and I was surprised that instead of that he took Polaroids."

"Is there anything in particular you'd like me to do? Do I sit in a certain way?" the composer Maury Yeston asks. "Oh, no, absolutely not," says Hirschfeld. "We just have a conversation and I do my work."

To be welcome in this sanctum, so close to the artist who has illustrated Broadway so well for so long, is an honor in itself. To be seen by the eyes and sketched by the hand of the man who has drawn so many hotshots and hambones is intoxicating. A Tony is swell. A Hirschfeld is better.

1
MEET HIM IN ST. LOUIS

He first appears on a Sunday, as well he should.

June 21 is the first day of summer, the longest day of the year, and the date most often assigned to *A Midsummer Night's Dream*. But the setting of Al Hirschfeld's birth is no bank where the wild thyme blows, where oxlips and the nodding violet grows. It's a steamy back bedroom in St. Louis.

Blocks away from the two-family brick house on Evans Avenue, preparations are relentlessly underway for the Louisiana Purchase Exposition, originally scheduled to open this year but nowhere near ready, no matter how much pomp attended Teddy Roosevelt's dedication in May. It is 1903.

While the *St. Louis Post-Dispatch* boasts of exposing corruption at the post office, the *Globe-Democrat* offers a solution for overcrowded trains, and the *Republic* glorifies a dead cardinal, a sweating midwife brings forth the Hirschfelds' boy. While East St. Louis, across the river, remains awash after a mud levee slid into the Mississippi two weeks ago, baby Albert slides into the world and is swaddled.

He is the third boy for Rebeka and Isaac Hirschfeld. The first, Alexander, is eight. Milton is a year and a half. All three are named for Isaac's late mother, Mildevine Alexander Kirschbaum Hirschfeld. It's a pretty extensive tribute, because there are now two Als.

Alexander has claim to "Al Hirschfeld." Young Albert is "Babe."

Rebeka is Russian, Isaac is American. She's been imported to St. Louis by her younger brother, Harry, a tailor. Quite a force in immigration, he's also brought their parents to settle in the Jewish quarter and live the Orthodox life. Harry keeps a close eye on everyone and lives a few doors away with his wife and five children.

As tailoring threads through the history of Jews without the means to do more, it threads through this family on both sides. Isaac's father and Babe's grandfather, Marcus Hirschfeld, came to New York from Prussia in 1867 and found his way to Albany. A twenty-seven-year-old tailor sailing from Hamburg on the *Teutonia*, he'd left his bride and infant daughter behind until he could afford to bring them over in May 1869.

In Albany, Mildevine became Malvina, and Marcus ran a tailor shop, moving the family from home to home, always upward, Broadway to South Pearl, to Arch, to Broad.

Isaac, their first child born in America, was born on Broadway.

Other than more space for the growing brood, the greater incentive might have been a one month's concession, meaning a month's free rent with every move. The Hirschfelds' most impressive stop was the little brick house on Catherine Street directly across from the splendid Schuyler Mansion. Not only did George Washington sleep here, but so did Alexander Hamilton, while wooing Schuyler's daughter.

The Hirschfelds attended services at the Romanesque Temple Beth Emeth, where Isaac Mayer Wise, the father of Reform Judaism in the United States, took the pulpit. He introduced such unorthodox practices as praying in English and German as well as Hebrew and allowing men and women to sit together. Too much too soon—he was soon out.

Marcus kept sewing. But Isaac, his oldest son, had no interest in joining him, so he left home to become . . . a cowboy. In 1892, he hitched to a Texas town so resourceful that toads were employed to wipe out roaches in the corner saloon. The Albany City Directory listed Ike that year: "removed to Marshall, Texas." Why Marshall? A mystery unlikely to be solved, but there he was. And with few skills in most things, least of all cowpoking, he was forced to rely on the family trade.

Despite little affinity for it, he got set up with his own needle, and the locals brought him their duds. He had no knack, but they kept coming. One day, the sheriff brought in his dress suit and said he'd be back for it later. Lickety-split, Ike hung a sign on the door, OUT FOR LUNCH, skedaddled to the station, and headed north.

Wherever he had it in mind to end up, he stopped at a St. Louis boardinghouse on Carr Street. There he bumped into the newly arrived Bekie Rothberg. She spoke only Russian and Yiddish. He didn't. She was plump and warm and twenty. He was a slim twenty-five. Or twenty-six. However they communicated, sparks flew, love bloomed, and in January 1894 they were married.

The midwife who delivers Al Hirschfeld probably doesn't speak English too well either, so while she's good at birthing, she's not so hot at reporting. More than a month after Hirschfeld is born, a clerk enters the birth date into the St. Louis registry—not as June 21, 1903, but as July 25.

This, for keeps, is Al Hirschfeld's official birth date, the one he'll be compelled to use on passports and other legal documents for the rest of his life. And not only that. The name is misspelled: "Hirschfield."

Downtown, and out of their reach, is theater—plenty of it—at the Olympic, the Imperial, the Gayety. There is opera and vaudeville. And finally, in 1904, there is the Louisiana Purchase Exposition, known as the World's Fair. Like everybody else, the family Hirschfeld joins the hullabaloo. Pulled along in a wagon, baby Babe licks Milton's ice cream cone and nibbles Al's hot dog and gets his fingers sticky with "Fairy Floss," the maiden name of cotton candy, which goes for twenty-five cents the box.

At one, he's round-faced and puckish with dark curls and a strong gaze. He gawks at pygmies and contortionists, Apaches and ostriches, glass weavers and cow milkers. On "the Pike"—a thrilling arcade of fantasy and reenactment—he sees a bullfight and the Galveston Flood. Under the dome of Festival Hall, he takes in the world's largest pipe organ; in Machinery Gardens, a band concert; ragtime at the Grand Basin; and on every lip a new song called "Meet Me in St. Louis," written for the occasion.

For his first two years, Hirschfeld resides on Evans Avenue without electricity, gas, or running water, except for a pump in the kitchen and a privy in the yard. "I come from a very poor background," he'll later say when explaining his resolute work habits, "and the business of paying the room rent is not imaginative. It stays with me forever."

Over the next seven years, the family will move five times—just like the St. Louisan Tennessee Williams, whose family also skips from flat to flat, and David Merrick, who ends up hating the place so heartily he won't even fly over it.

Mom is the family force. In 1908, she runs a confectionery on the ground floor of the house at Goodfellow and Page, selling penny candies and ice cream, smokes and soda pop, and probably in-and-out calls, because a private telephone is a rare bird in these parts. Pop is listed in the city directory as a tailor, cutter, even a cigar salesman—which puts him behind the counter of Bekie's shop—but his primary contribution to the family's support is tending the boys.

Babe and Milton are at Dozier, a grammar school on Maple Avenue, a block from home. Big Al has a job. They get around on foot or by horse-drawn streetcar; the electric tram costs a nickel in any direction. Ike rides a bike and joins the local branch of the Columbia Wheelmen. As always, the former cowpoke does what he likes, taking things at his own speed.

When a fire breaks out one night, Ike's in bed while Mom's yelling and trying to throw the mattress out the window. "Take it easy," he says, placing his hand on the wall. "It isn't even warm yet."

Bekie's parents won't come for dinner, because she won't keep kosher. She goes to shul on the high holy days, lights Sabbath and *yahrzeit* candles, and uses the Passover matzo for ham sandwiches. "She had her own religion," Hirschfeld recalls. "She made up her own laws as she went along, and we all followed them."

In 1911, she leads the family to Kensington Avenue, into a redbrick, semidetached house with flanking bay windows. They're in the downstairs flat.

In *Meet Me in St. Louis,* as moviegoers well know, Judy Garland lives in a pretty house on a pretty street and in "The Boy Next Door" sings, "I live at 5135 Kensington Avenue, and he lives at 5133."

Hirschfeld lore, perpetuated by his family and factotums, claims that Garland's address is Al Hirschfeld's address. That when he was doing the poster campaign for the movie, the songwriters were so charmed to hear this that they put it into the song as an inside joke.

In fact, Judy Garland's address in the movie belongs to the writer Sally Benson, who lived there with her own family until 1910 and later celebrated it in a five-part series—"5135 Kensington"—in *The New Yorker*.

But Hirschfeld is not the boy next door, nor the boy in the house. He's the boy across the street. At 5124.

New neighborhood, new school. Now he and Milton attend Clark Public School, an imposing redbrick elementary on Union Boulevard. Erected in 1907, the place is named for William Clark, the Clark half of Lewis and. Here young Hirschfeld learns the day's basics, including arithmetic, geography, and cursive writing—but mostly he draws.

A pen-and-ink drawing, known as the earliest Hirschfeld work of art, is said to be a portrait of Clark. But it's not. The building looks like a school all right, but authorities in the St. Louis public school system don't recognize it.

Whatever the subject, he keeps drawing. "It never occurred to me I could do anything else," he'll say years later. It's all he wants to do. Rebecca (she has now anglicized her name) sees the gift and takes him to the museum in Cass Gilbert's sumptuous Palace of Fine Arts built for the World's Fair. She also enrolls him in a Saturday-morning children's class at Washington University's School of Fine Arts.

As she stands, now behind her counter at Stix, Baer & Fuller, the city's foremost department store, she thinks about Babe's obsession. And when she takes her break in the employees' sitting room, she becomes friendly with a portrait artist named Charles Marks.

From genteel salons to the Missouri State Fair, Marks shows his work around. He'd come to St. Louis from New York when he was twenty-one, studied at the School of Fine Arts, and established an artistic photography firm with a partner in 1890. "They make high-class oil, pastel and crayon portraits a specialty and aim to do this at popular prices, counting no work as well performed that is not satisfactory to the sitter," explained a city guide of the time. Now at Stix, Baer, Marks is producing display cards and price tags. After Bekie shows him Babe's drawings, he agrees to give him lessons and takes him out sketching every Sunday.

And he urges her to get out of town, gloomily predicting that otherwise her talented Babe will be forever stuck in St. Louis, turning out the same display cards and price tags at the same store. So whether it's faith in his future or merely keeping a step ahead of the landlord, Bekie pulls Albert and Milton out of school in October and takes them all—Ike and the three boys—eastward.

In 1912, the Hirschfelds hit New York.

2
MANHATTAN TRANSFER

From Pennsylvania Station they walk to Sixth Avenue and board the No. 39 streetcar. With no destination but the future, they ride it to the last stop, Amsterdam Avenue and 193rd Street . . . and nearly trip over the edge of Paradise. This is Fort George Amusement Park—or Paradise Park—a sprawling wonderland overlooking the Harlem River, where kids run free and the mother of Lillian and Dorothy Gish runs a candy-and-popcorn stand. But no stopping now. First there's a roof to find.

The pilgrims straggle south through orchards and fields. When Bekie sees a two-story frame house to rent on 183rd Street between Audubon and Amsterdam, she grabs it. The upper floor costs four dollars a month. Within days, she gets herself a job at Wertheimer's, a department store on West 181st Street, while Pop enrolls Albert and Milton at PS 132, a redbrick elementary on Wadsworth Avenue.

This is rural terrain in 1912. Mom buys her fruits and vegetables at Willie Serana's farm on Broadway at 181st—right where the Blue Bell Tavern once stood, doing a brisk bed-and-bar business during the American Revolution, and where the Coliseum Theatre will arrive in 1920, doing brisk show business with the Marx Brothers, W. C. Fields, Eddie Cantor, Gertrude Berg, and Harold Lloyd. In the meantime, there's the Wadsworth Theatre nearby, offering photoplays and vaudeville.

Vaudeville's sweeping the country, and anyone with a modicum of flair—or a mama with a dream—wants to shine. And thanks to an expert named Frederic La Delle, anyone can. "I hope you will be a credit to the stage as well as to yourself," he states in his mail-order primer, *How To Enter Vaudeville*. "Special talent is not necessary for acting any more than it is for any other profession," he assures suckers, making the art of freak acts and "chapeaugraphy," bell ringers and barrel jumpers, trick cyclists and knife throwers seem a cinch. Even for handcuff, chain, and trunk acts, he adds, "No experience or special ability is required."

Tell that to Harry Houdini.

Martin Beck won't. Beck's the boy who discovered young Ehrich Weiss disentangling himself in a St. Paul saloon and became his manager. Now they're top of the heap. Weiss, famous for his Chinese water-torture cell escape and underwater box escape in the East River, has become Houdini. Beck, now a big shot on the vaudeville circuit, has just built the Palace—the jewel in Keith-Albee's crown, the house every headliner has to play. Later, Beck will build another theater on Forty-fifth and name it for himself.

Al Hirschfeld enters the world of Broadway in 1914, when he sees his first musical at the Casino Theatre, a Moorish Revival fairy-tale castle at Thirty-ninth Street. For a lad of ten, *High Jinks* is a jolly introduction. The score, by Rudolf Friml and Otto Hauerbach (later Harbach), is frothy; the setting is France in springtime. "It begins with a laugh, ends with a frolic, and is punctuated by a considerable amount of rollick in the course of its three acts," states *The New York Times*.

Once again taking advantage of a rent-free month, the Hirschfelds move to a six-story apartment building at Audubon and 178th, with the added income of two young German boarders. While Mom's at the store, Alexander is selling men's hats, Albert and Milton are memorizing state capitals, and Pop is feeding the birds.

Ike's not the provider. He's a bachelor at heart with a Houdini-like yen to escape. And one day, he does. Kissing the family goodbye, he takes off for Boston—by streetcar, no less, one after the other—so the story goes. It takes him a week! And then he comes back, where Mom holds things together and moves them all once again, now a block south, to 598 West 177th Street. The new place has an elevator operator, switchboard operator, canopy, and doorman. The rent is fourteen dollars a month, and that's it for moving. She and Ike will remain there for the next fifty years.

Al remembers that "all the kids in the neighborhood always came to our house. We never went to theirs. My father taught them how to shoot crap, pitch pennies, play ball." In winter, Ike takes them skating in Van Cortland Park. At Christmas, he dresses as Santa and crawls in from the fire escape. In ball season, he umps their games. Before long, he becomes a starter at the trotting races on the Harlem River Speedway, as close to pistol packin' as this buckaroo will ever get.

For a fellow who will eventually spend so many years on a barber chair, fourteen-year-old Al Hirschfeld is a bundle of get-up-and-go. He plays stickball in the street and catcher for a semipro sandlot team called the Altheas. Also on the team: Lou Gehrig (who lives over on Amsterdam Avenue and is two days older). Another playmate is pretty Dorothy Wegman, who later will remember the neighborhood as "a village in itself. One need go no farther than a few streets to get all the essentials of living." One of the essentials for her is a Howard Simon, who hopes to earn enough clerking at the art store to study at the Art Students League.

Baseball is in the air, around the corner, on Cracker Jack baseball cards. At the new Polo Grounds on the Harlem River, the boys sneak in to watch the New York Yankees. Hirschfeld loves the game and thinks about a future, but when his catcher's hand swells up, he kisses the game goodbye (Gehrig goes on) and starts playing with clay instead.

Upon graduation in January 1918, Hirschfeld's eighth-grade colleagues sign his autograph book, variously addressing him as Albert, Al, Babe, and Hirshy. "May your future be as bright as an Edison electric light," writes William Dreesen, another ballplayer. "Roses are red, / Violets are blue, / When it comes to fun, / Thats you," scrawls an Irving. "May your artistic abilities be magnified to success," adds a Charles. And from Mom: "To my darling baby—I wish you all the luck in the world and I hope you will always be honest and upright and that you will make me happy and proud of being your Mother."

Not to worry.

Gehrig enters the High School of Commerce, starring on a baseball team that will beat a Chicago high school team in 1920, where he's *noticed*. Dorothy Wegman becomes a commercial artist and then a dancer in the *Ziegfeld Follies*, where her name becomes Dorshka and Al Jolson pursues her to no avail because her stage door Johnny is still Howard Simon. But before long, she'll marry writer Samson Raphaelson, whose short story "The Day of Atonement" will become *The Jazz Singer* (with Jolson).

Hirschfeld enters the Vocational School for Boys at Fifth Avenue and 138th Street. And while his peers are diagnosing carburetors and laying tile—and his brother Big Al has become a foreman at a hat factory—young Al takes up printing, engraving, art, and his newest enthusiasm, sculpture. Even if he doesn't know where it will lead.

"I was the most naïve boy in the whole world," he recalls. "I had great confidence in myself—the ability to see and translate it onto paper. But I didn't know where to go with this. I didn't know how to become a sculptor. I had no connections of any kind. I did this for my own gratification. Where the hell do you go with sculpture?"

Downtown, he's told, to a factory making architectural elements used for decorative moldings. There he sees artists designing rosettes and leaves to be turned out by the yard. "I was absolutely amazed," he says, "the way they would take a tool and swish around in that Plastolene or clay, and out would come a rose or something." And "My God!" he thinks. "This is not what I want out of life."

What he wants isn't yet clear, but excitement is a part of it. And what with moving pictures, the circus, and vaudeville stirring things up all around, he becomes a vaudeville kid gazing down from his twenty-five-cent seat at the Palace on Ed Wynn and Nora Bayes, Lillian Russell and Will Rogers, Bert Williams and Bobby Clark, and always Houdini. His fascination will endure, and one day he visits Houdini in his dressing room, watching the magician swell his wrists before they put the handcuffs on him, awed by the muscle control.

Meanwhile, Milton has hit the road with a friend to look for work. His letters to Mama often mention his health, which means it has not been good. "I am as sound as a rock and am feeling fine," he assures her from Buffalo in May 1918, "so you shouldn't worry." A few days later, big news from Detroit: "I've got some job!" he writes. "We are having a great time and thank God that we are both well, and a doctor is always around the place in case anyone gets sick." He adds a PS: "Gee you ought to be out here Babe you would never want to come home." And a few days after that: "I am still feeling fine and we are going to go further still and we won't come back until we have made good and learn to be men."

This doesn't work out too well. By autumn, Milton is back in New York as an office boy and not feeling fine at all. Influenza is poisoning the air and the lungs of the war-worn city. Movie houses close, new releases are put on hold. Seven plays in the theater district close in one night. The prices of lemons and oranges go up, and sales in ladies' dresses go down. When the plague first appeared in the spring, it was considered a three-day fever. Now it's ferocious, and it grabs Milton. His body aches, his cough is relentless, he has a fever of 104. Mom and Pop are helpless to stop his rapid collapse. For young Al, this is a terrible theft—losing a brother he has never been without.

At 10:00 p.m. on October 3—the day after *The New York Times* announces the discovery of a new vaccine—Milton dies of bronchopneumonia. He is sixteen, one of fifty million people in the world lost to the epidemic, one of thirty thousand in New York.

From this time on, Al Hirschfeld has a profound fear of illness.

3
POSTER BOY

Howard Simon has been taking a night class in drawing at the National Academy of Design. This sounds good, so Hirschfeld joins him, biking down to Amsterdam and 109th Street. He takes an "antiques class" for one term in which he draws classical sculptures and produces a plaster sculpture of Abe Lincoln's head. But at sixteen, he needs a job. By day, Simon is working as a gofer in the art department at Goldwyn Pictures. This also sounds good.

Al has heard of Goldwyn, everybody's heard of Goldwyn ("Samuel Goldfish and the Selwyns, latest partners in the film business, combined names and called their enterprise the Goldwyn Picture Corporation," wrote the young drama reporter George S. Kaufman of the *New-York Tribune* when the company started up in 1916. "Why not the Selfish?"). The office is at 485 Fifth Avenue, and Hirschfeld makes tracks.

There he finds Lionel Reiss, Goldwyn's art director—a serious painter, and only twenty-five himself—who hires him as a gofer and brush cleaner for four dollars a week. He also meets Howard Dietz, Goldwyn's new publicity director, a Columbia dropout who has an instinct for icons. Although some say it's Lionel who was responsible for the lion created as a logo, it was Dietz. Was he inspired by the marble lions, Leo Astor and Leo Lenox, guarding the New York Public Library across the street? No. He was inspired by the lion mascot of Columbia University. In September 1917, *Polly of the Circus* was the first Goldwyn picture released under the lion's silent roar. Some Goldwyn print ads now feature the lion lying in profile above the famous legend "Ars Gratia Artis."

As for Dietz, wit and wordsmith, he's "neither warm nor tactile," remembers Jonathan Schwartz, whose father, Arthur Schwartz, will become Dietz's longtime songwriting partner. But Howard has an eye.

One day in the office, after finding some crumpled Hirschfeld drawings in the wastebasket, he gives the kid a shot, and soon sixteen-year-old Al is working on ads and lobby cards for such Goldwyn fare as *The Great Lover*, *Edgar's Little Saw*, *Hold Your Horses*, *Don't Neglect Your Wife*, and even *The Cabinet of Dr. Caligari*. He's beginning to make it.

But he's soon risking the wrath of Reiss when he and Mom take off for St. Louis to visit the relatives. Having a good time there, he writes to the boss and says he'd like to stay another couple of weeks. "Take as long as you want," Reiss swiftly replies. "There's no great need for you to come back." And when he does, another kid is cleaning his brushes.

Finding work is not a problem for feisty young Al. So he signs on with Stark & Cowan, a music publisher on West Forty-sixth Street, as a song plugger. The publisher gives him studio space, and while he gives it art for its sheet music, that's just the start. Most pluggers sit at the piano in a department store, playing the sheet music they're handed, wooing the ladies to buy it. Young Gershwin does it, Harry Warren, Jerome Kern. And now Al Hirschfeld does, too. But no spinet for him. Al does his singing, tapping, and uke-plucking on the night boat to Albany—a naughty one-night-stand-ish venue for girls, gambling, and hooch. A pleasure cruise that answers the question of the current pop song "Why Do They All Take the Night Boat to Albany?" from the 1918 musical *Sinbad*.

Hirschfeld's musical offering is hard to summon up. One can only try to imagine him warbling, "You know for you I would die / But never ask me to try"—the song being "Scandinavia (Sing Dose Song and Make Dose Music)"—with a *Svedish* accent.

Back on land, he moves on to Universal Pictures for seventy-five dollars a week. At seventeen years old, that's a lot of clams. When he tells Reiss, Reiss cocks a skeptical brow. Hirschfeld's comeback includes an offer: if he can't prove to Reiss that the job is legit by showing him his paycheck, he'll treat Reiss to lunch. But if he *can* prove it, lunch is on Reiss. A good lunch. Deal? Deal. Sure enough, the next week he shows up with the check, and it's lunch time. Reiss has lost his appetite, but okay, where does Hirschfeld want to eat? At the Astor, of course, where Hirschfeld orders the fanciest stuff he can.

Before long, he's moved on to the Selznick Corporation for the same money, but this time with a contract. Selznick is an extravagant dynasty sired by the high-living Lewis J. Selznick—a man Hirschfeld greatly admires, with an ability to "guess right"—and operated with his short-fused son, Myron, and intellectual son, David. With productions booming on both coasts, the New York office fills two floors at 729 Seventh Avenue and another at 501 Fifth Avenue. Broadway's dotted with blue-bulb electric signs blazing the slogan SELZNICK PICTURES CREATE HAPPY HOURS, the *Saturday Evening Post* runs pages of full-color ads, and Hirschfeld is doing the illustrations for ads, posters, brochures, lobby cards, and other components of these splashy publicity campaigns. His drawings of Theda Bara, Rupert Hughes, Betty Compson, Owen Moore, and Elaine Hammerstein are everywhere.

Hirschfeld and David Selznick become fast friends, and he sketches David at twenty, wearing a bow tie, glasses, and a toothy smile. He's now Selznick's art director, for $250 a week. He's eighteen.

Through Selznick, he meets Sam Marx, an office boy in the export department at Universal, shipping canned prints from a gated storage room on the tenth floor at 1600 Broadway. And through Marx he meets Gordon Kahn, a young writer on a gossip sheet called *Zit's Weekly*, a snappy compilation of Broadway goings-on (much of it culled from *Variety*). Marx and Kahn become Al's close friends for life.

And he remains close to his kin in St. Louis, getting out there when he can. On a visit in 1921, he goes over to the art museum, his former home away from home. In Sculpture Hall, he meets a genial gent with whom he finds great rapport as they stroll along discussing art. It's a memorable afternoon.

When he returns to the city, Mom asks if he remembered to look up his old art teacher, Charles Marks. No, says Hirschfeld, "I hadn't the least idea where to look for him." Mom tells him Marks is the fellow in charge of the desk at the City Art Museum. The front desk! "I spent a whole afternoon with him and didn't know it," Al realizes. "I'll have to write him and tell him he was my first teacher."

But Marks never sees the letter. "A skidding truck on an icy street, a day and a night of suffering, and then the end," recounts the *Globe-Democrat*. And in January 1922, Charles Marks, sixty-three, a prominent painter and member of the St. Louis Artists' Guild—who showed in a 1916 exhibition at the City Art Museum, worked at the front desk, and has been making ten dollars a month for printing signs there—is buried at Mount Olive Cemetery.

With resources aplenty, Hirschfeld doesn't deny himself. Through the years, he'll have an ongoing love affair with the automobile. It starts with a Stutz. A red Stutz Bearcat, the cat's meow. Everybody wants one—"a Stutz as low as a snake and as red as an Indiana barn," as Scott Fitzgerald puts it—and he takes the boys for a ride. One night, it's Sam Marx and a guy named Bernie. As Al drives like a bat out of hell, Marx bounces along next to him, noodgy and nail-biting. When he can't take any more, he leans over and snatches the key, leaving Al to maneuver the car to the curb. He pulls Al out, shoves him into the back seat with Bernie, and grabs the wheel. Now they're breezing down Broadway, and *pow!* there's a ruckus behind him. Al and Bernie are pushing and punching and screeching at each other. Marx keeps going.

The fury stops. Sudden silence. Good, Marx figures, they've calmed down. A few minutes later, he turns around to see what's what, and there's Al, serenely watching the world go by. No Bernie. Where's Bernie? "Oh," says Al with a shrug. "He fell out a couple of blocks back."

Sometimes Al will take the car down in the morning and go home on the subway, forgetting where he parked. Other times he just forgets. When drivers store their open-top cars for the winter, he takes his to the used-car showroom on the ground floor of his Washington Heights apartment house. When he goes to reclaim it in April, not only is the car gone, but so is the showroom, and has been for months. He's been going in and out of the building every day without noticing.

The boys frequent an eatery called Three Steps Down in a Greenwich Village brownstone. The cafeteria-restaurant-garden on West Eighth is run by the Strunsky girls and Mascha, the mother. Albert Strunsky, the father, is an emperor with property all over the place.

"There were two great cultural forces," Village legend Maxwell Bodenheim has observed, "which collided with each other and sought to occupy the intellectual vacuum which is charitably called the bohemian mind. They were Gertrude Stein, who ruled the Village by remote control from Paris, and Albert Strunsky, the Village landlord, whose benevolent despotism extended beyond the frontiers of Sheridan Square."

The Strunsky girls make melodious matches. Daughter Emily marries Lou Paley, a schoolteacher and wordsmith who's written lyrics for forgotten musicals and a couple of songs with his friend George Gershwin. When the Paleys host their Saturday-night salons in their Eighth Street flat, George, who adores them both, works the piano. Leonore Strunsky marries George's younger brother, Ira, the lyricist. And niece Lillian is married to James Englander, the head of publicity at Selznick Pictures—which is how Hirschfeld gets here.

Three Steps Down is a home-cooking place, and it operates on a homespun system. A slice of roast beef is a dime, vegetables are a nickel apiece, the apple pie is dandy. One of the sisters sits at the door. You tell her what you ate, she tells you what you owe. And if you don't have it on you, you bring it in later.

For a Stutz owner, Al isn't much of a spender, and he has his own system. He comes in every day and writes the menu on a blackboard over the counter—in return for lunch.

Lewis J. Selznick, suffering from overexpansion, has an idea. How about if Al does the art-directing as a freelancer? They make a deal in which he can hold on to the Selznick account and take on new clients. Collecting assignments from other studios as well, Hirschfeld rents two floors in a bay-windowed brownstone at 51 West Fifty-third. The Selznick art department, with nine artists, occupies one floor. Hirschfeld takes the other.

Why he brings nine cocker spaniels into his bachelorhood around this time is unknown. But he does, naming the mother Peanuts and her puppies Walnut, Pecan, Cashew, and so on. Nuts! When he goes out in the evenings, he parks them on the roof, and angry neighbors toss shoes and tin cans at their howling.

Marx and Hirschfeld go into business together with two of Al's Selznick artists—Al's old friend Howard Simon and another named Laurence Chaves. Marx is the salesman, and while he isn't very good at it, the team gets along by selling drawings to ad agencies and magazines.

In 1923, with Selznick in diminishing health and his company in the hole, the studio releases the last of its crop, *Rupert of Hentzau* and *The Common Law*, as prestigious "theatre pieces." The plan is "you had to be there at a certain time, and they were going to charge box-office theatre prices," Hirschfeld recalls. But it's a bust. The bankers close in and release them as ordinary pictures.

Rupert, the sequel to *The Prisoner of Zenda*, opens in July at the Strand. Broadway windows and subway stations get decorated, and the theater features a lobby display of "clever pen and ink drawings made by Al Hirschfeld, art director for Selznick, of the entire cast," as the company gazette remarks. But reviews are mild, hopes are dashed, and soon Selznick is paying Hirschfeld with a "trade acceptance," which gives him half his salary and a promissory note for the rest. Unfortunately, L.J. goes bankrupt, and his company folds.

Once again on the loose, Hirschfeld and Marx rent a studio in Greenwich Village. But first they have to escape the uptown lease and their battle-axe landlady. The plan they devise, more slapstick than strategy, is to sneak into the studio in the middle of the night, take the furniture, drawing boards, brushes, paints, and everything else they can get their hands on, and sneak out. In their opinion, this should break the lease. Doesn't mean the landlady will agree.

A new day dawns, and Hirschfeld goes to work—not to the new studio they've just rented downtown, but to the old studio they've just vacated. Head in the clouds, dreaming his dreams, he walks in and notices the place is empty. Everything's gone! Quick as a shot, he reacts with a shout. Help! he cries down the hall and out the window. We've been robbed! And in runs the landlady, fists flying.

Next on the scene is a process server.

4
FLO

The 1920s are roaring, and Al is in their midst. His circle expands. New York is a party mecca for young artists, and Carl Van Vechten is the consummate host. A man-about-town, he cherishes dance, jazz, opera, art—all the arts—and has various abilities, from writing novels, criticism, and a history of the house cat, to reviewing music and dance for the *Times*, to photographing his famous friends, to making significant matches among them. But none is so stimulating as his interest in Black culture.

A dandy undaunted by his bulk, he gussies up in silk shirts and bracelets and everything but bells on his toes. Gay when he wants to be, he nonetheless maintains a long-running marriage to Fania Marinoff, a Russian actress, while nurturing the exotic and the oppressed. (Langston Hughes is one such favorite.) With his odd features—beady eyes, snow-white hair, and buck teeth once compared to "squares of broken crockery"—Van Vechten knows everybody, so everybody shows up at his flamboyant duplex on West Fifty-fifth, where everybody meets somebody.

Nearly as starry as the parties thrown by Condé Nast and his *Vanity Fair* editor Frank Crowninshield, Van Vechten's soirees are populated by a slightly artier crowd, including those infatuated with the Harlem Renaissance, so close to his heart. "Carl was giving us parties to meet his Negro friends, who somewhat scandalized me by their outspokenness," Alice B. Toklas writes of evenings spent there with George Gershwin, Theodore Dreiser and H. L. Mencken, Knopfs and Fitzgeralds, flappers with rouged knees, poets with promise.

Van Vechten is very fond of Ralph Barton, the caricaturist du jour who often draws dear "Carlo" and illustrates the jacket for his new novel, *The Tattooed Countess.* Barton usually arrives with his wife, Carlotta Monterey (who will divorce him in 1926 and marry the increasingly important Eugene O'Neill in 1929, the same year E. E. Cummings marries Anne Minnerly, who's also divorced from Barton). Another is Alexander King (né Koenig), a Viennese artist and writer, who also knows everybody. And yet another is Miguel Covarrubias, the eighteen-year-old caricaturist recently arrived from Mexico.

In such a convivial world, Al Hirschfeld meets characters who will populate his life henceforth. One of them is Covarrubias. Hirschfeld is in need of space, as is he, so in 1924 they take a studio together in a six-story building at 110 West Forty-second Street. Hirschfeld commemorates the occasion with two pencil sketches of his workmate at the drawing board (one is now at the National Portrait Gallery, the other is at the Library of Congress).

Through Van Vechten and his crowd, Hirschfeld and Covarrubias become enchanted by Harlem and its players, spending night after night in the dance halls and speakeasies of "Darktown." Prohibition (that would be the Volstead Act) went into effect in January 1920, in order to save the populace from wicked spirits. Avoiding the law lends a larky mystique—knocking on secret doors, sipping gin from teacups—and as they toast their swift-moving lives, the boys sketch up a storm on matchboxes, napkins, and the "membership" cards that gain a guest admission.

"Miguel influenced me more than I did him," Hirschfeld often says, with everlasting grace. "His technique consisted of elimination and simplification." His ideas have impact as well. Covarubbias's drawings of "the New Negro" appear in *Vanity Fair's* December 1924 issue and many issues to follow, as well as in his book *Negro Drawings*. Hirschfeld's revelers, cruisers, and jammers will show up in a tribute to Harlem in 1941. And in the mid-1960s, Hirschfeld's series for *Playbill* called "Unlikely Casting"—in which he depicts Barry Goldwater and Lyndon Johnson in *Waiting for Godot*, Ethel Merman and Ernest Borgnine in *Private Lives*, Zero Mostel as Peter Pan, Jimmy Durante as Henry Higgins, Bert Lahr as Lear—comes straight out of Covarrubias's "Impossible Interviews" of the 1930s, pitting such unlikelies as Greta Garbo vs. Calvin Coolidge, John D. Rockefeller vs. Joseph Stalin, and Aimee Semple MacPherson vs. Mahatma Gandhi in *Vanity Fair*.

The quintessential chorus girl of the 1920s is a long-stemmed beauty coveted by barons and bankers, imitated by salesgirls, envied by debs. Most delectably displayed in the *Ziegfeld Follies*, that shimmering evolution of the vaudeville show, she has been selected and tutored by Florenz Ziegfeld Jr. to join a congregation of gorgeous showgirls in complicated costumes descending sumptous staircases on elaborate sets. Ziegfeld is a gossip's god, and these are Ziggy's Girls.

He naturally inspires copycats. George White's *Scandals* is scandalous, Earl Carroll's *Vanities* more so. And his performers require endurance and armor from head to toe. The effete Carroll favors an alabaster look, and after having their bodies shaved by Carroll's personal barber, the girls smear those bodies with a milk-white concoction (and if one gets sunburned, her skin turns purple so she can't go onstage). False eyelashes are so expensive, the girls apply black mustache wax to each eyelash with a toothpick.

Costumes are so heavy, so complex, they have to be lowered from the ceiling. There are no flimsy fabrics, no way to cheat on weight. Even the hats are dangerous. Imagine the horror of feeling your skirt pull down as you ascend a staircase because you haven't held the dress high enough to lift your foot—while holding a steel umbrella in one hand—as the girls behind you fall like dominoes. Imagine rain falling over a revolving stage covered with soaring glass pyamids you have to climb, holding a flashlight, in a blackout number. It's so grueling that girls often buy another girl's night off.

On the heat-struck night of July 5, 1923, the *Vanities* opens at the Earl Carroll Theatre with Peggy Hopkins Joyce in chinchilla, the comic Joe Cook, and songs by the willowy and self-admiring Carroll himself, because he's too chintzy to pay other songwriters.

On New York's stages, Romanticism is losing its appeal. The book musical is shoving the operetta aside. Brave new drama by brave new playwrights is poking *Florodora* in the petticoat. But Earl Carroll insists he's not reacting. "We haven't changed a thing," he protests on September 25, 1924, in response to complaints about the dancer Kathryn Ray as a swinging pendulum in the "Counting the Hours" number, with only a sequin band around her waist, "and won't if we can help it."

By October 30, he'll be in the lockup, threatening a hunger strike as he awaits trial for exhibiting nude paintings of three chorus girls in the theater lobby.

"Poisoned Self," shouts the front page of the *Daily News* on November 1, 1924. "Chorus Girl in Taxi Drinks Poison," says the *New York Evening Journal*. "Show Girl Silent as Suicide Fails," announces *The World*. "Why did pretty Florence Allen, member of the cast of 'Vanities of 1924,' attempt suicide?" asks the *Daily Mirror.* "Was it because of her shattered romance? Or because of her 3-year-old baby?"

"Please do not ask me why," says pretty Florence Allen, as the tears roll down. "I have so many, many troubles." Enough, apparently, to have guzzled some Lysol in the back of a cab after leaving the Club Richman on West Fifty-sixth Street. "I had driven a block when I heard a groan," the taxi driver tells the *Mirror* (although the *News* reports it as a scream). "She was on the floor with a bottle of poison in her hand."

In the *Journal*'s report, the doll says she wants to ride around a bit before going to bed; the driver starts toward Central Park and sees her put the bottle to her lips. Whatever the brutal facts, ink is splashed with gay abandon, and the specifics don't matter very much.

In these giddy, limelit days, there's a romance to suicide—surely enhanced by the death by mercury chloride of Olive Thomas, former Ziegfeld girl (and girlfriend), at the Paris Ritz a few years earlier. (Dorothy Parker milks the theme, in poetry and at lunch. "She was 'Suicide Sadie,'" the Round Tabler Marc Connelly says years later.) In any case, two weeks after Flo Allen's adventure, another Earl Carroll girl named Clay Long gives it a try in a gas-filled room. Hers, too, is "the cry of a baffled soul, hurt and puzzled," sympathetizes the *New York Evening Graphic*, but alas, she succeeds.

Whatever Flo's story, the hack calls a cop and they hustle her to Roosevelt Hospital where, says *Variety*, she is saved by "stomach pumps and antidotes." From her hospital bed, she confides in an anxious press. "Perhaps some day the real truth will become known." Then, "Let me alone. I'm awfully tired."

Upon hearing the news, Earl Carroll announces from his cell in the Tombs that he'll cover the hospital charges. He assures Flo that her place in the chorus will be waiting for her upon her return, and sends over fifty dollars with a cheery note.

"Why would such a beautiful woman try to commit suicide? You'd think she'd have everything to live for," Al Hirschfeld says to his friend Alex King, eyeing her in the paper. And King says, "Why don't you go over and see if she'd like some company?"

Hirschfeld hotfoots it over.

Poor Flo. "A shattered romance?" Maybe. "A three-year-old baby?" Absolutely.

Florence Allen is the former Florence Hobby of Bloomfield, New Jersey, born in 1902. Married to a Pennsylvanian named Norman Ellwood Conard, she gives birth to a daughter, Renee Mae, on December 12, 1921.

But if you see yourself as a star and your bumpkin hubby doesn't, and you move to New York anyway, leaving him and your baby with his parents in Upper Darby, Pennsylvania, so you can give it a shot . . . well. The girls in *Vanities of 1923* include flossies galore—Florence Gillingham, Florence Ames, Flo White, Flo Tempest, and then, later in the run, Florence Allen, as a replacement dancer.

It's not the splash she hoped to make. And on October 30, when the *Evening Graphic*'s front page blares, "Quits Screen to Love Baby"—referring to Leatrice Joy, who's just given birth to a daughter and vows to renounce movie stardom—the unfulfilled Flo can't help but notice. The next night, she sips the Lysol.

For Hirschfeld, however, life is peachy. At twenty-one, he's attractive, persuasive, a success. His hair is coffee-brown, his chin clean-shaven, his eyes big and brown, his eyebrows important. In a photo from 1924, he's also nattily dressed, in tweed jacket and bow tie. Blond and blue-eyed, Flo's a knockout with a sob story. In a jiffy, she's discharged and they're in love. She probably mentions her daughter somewhere along the way, but Al's not interested in anybody's daughter, so that's that. Flo doesn't insist. The daughter stays in Pennsylvania, and Flo stays put.

Hirschfeld doesn't mind that she spells her name Allen in the *Vanities* playbill and Allyn on her envelopes, that she gives her middle name sometimes as Marie, sometimes as Ruth. He doesn't care that she's a year older than he, that she's superstitious about black cats and salt over the shoulder and the number thirteen. Al's smitten. Inspired by the name Conard, he whimsically tells friends that Flo's grandfather, a fellow named Coney, founded Coney Island.

Flo has been living with the *Vanities* stage manager (and his family) on West Fifty-first Street. When Al and Covarrubias give up their studio, Covarrubias moves down to the Village, and Al moves to a studio at 44 West Fifty-first, a few blocks east. He and Flo hit chop suey joints, chophouses, Childs. He paints a watercolor of her in a sheperdine *Vanities* costume à la Marie Antoinette at her Petit Trianon.

In January 1925, Flo leaves town on the *Vanities* tour. Al pines. "An empty bottle stands where a full one had stood but an hour ago," he writes to her in Boston, having just returned from the Illustrators' Ball in a snowstorm. "The old town looks as tho it had a two foot blanket of mashed potatoes spread over it." Worse, he recently caught a screening of *Bad Company*—a silent "starring Madge Kennedy and Flo Allyn," as he puts it, "but didn't like it—tho I will say you did look beautiful."

As Flo travels on, city to city, Al moves home to Washington Heights. Working for George Bonte in the art department at Warner Bros., he allows himself five dollars a week and turns the rest of his salary over to his stiffed Selznick artists. Nights he spends playing poker with Sam Marx and Gordon Kahn . . . except for the nights they spend in speaks listening to swing. Or riding the rails to Knowlton, Canada—a quaint village in Quebec, of all places—where he and Kahn savor some off-site hanky-panky.

Alas, poor Flo, his very own chorus girl, is suffering from the grippe and "Kleig eyes," the result of staring into the spotlights from her position atop the big clock on the *Vanities* set. He can't join her, because he's "doing a lot of caricatures for the dailies," he writes.

The first of these for Warner Bros.—a twofer showing Syd Chaplin (Charlie's brother) in *The Man on the Box* and Irene Rich in *My Wife and I*—is published in *The World* on April 12, 1925. These are his first published caricatures.

He's being careful here, steering clear of exaggeration other than squaring their chins and widely parting their hair, and the drawings are gentler than those of the office gang. "Nobody's safe at 1600 Broadway when Al Hirschfield's [*sic*] around," notes *Brass Tacks*, the Warner Bros. newsletter. "He has taken a dreadful itch to caricature people and what he makes you look like reminds one of a bad dream come true." Frank Spicker in the art department draws Hirschfeld as "the Culprit," with crosshatched chin and pen in hand, reading the words "I Never Shave It's Cheaper."

5

AN AMERICAN IN PARIS

Love, *la grippe*, and Warner Bros. are soon left behind. Paris calls.

"Good-Bye Al, Best Of Luck!" It's September 1925, and *Brass Tacks* bids him adieu. "Al Hirschfield [*sic*], one of the mainstays of the art department, quits the office at the end of this week and leaves in a few days for that gay Paree," the story goes, accompanied by George Bonte's caricature of Hirschfeld in smock, spats, and beret, standing before an easel with palette and dripping brush. "There," it says, "he will continue his art studies, and things."

Thanks to the generosity of his uncle Harry Rothberg in St. Louis, Hirschfeld travels with an endowment of five hundred dollars. "He proposes to study at Julian's, in the Rue de la Grand Chaumiere," the article continues—although Académie Julian and Académie de la Grande Chaumière are two different schools.

On October 1, Hirschfeld sails from Pier 57. The SS *De Grasse*, a glossy two-funnel steamer new to the French Line's transatlantic fleet, completed her maiden voyage a year ago—a maiden voyage on which Hirschfeld will later claim to have sailed. Not up to the *Mauretania* in speed or status, her indoor pool and promenade deck have still managed to attract such passengers as Basile Kibalchich, director of the Russian Symphonic Choir; Mrs. John Ringling, wife of the circus owner; Mrs. Maxfield Parrish, wife of the artist; and John Philip Sousa Jr., son of the "march king." On his voyage, Hirschfeld meets Marcus Aurelius Goodrich (who will become a journalist, screenwriter, and husband to Olivia de Havilland), and Goodrich gives him the name of his favorite hotel in Paris.

He docks at Cherbourg on October 9, cables Mom and Flo that he's arrived, and catches the boat train to Paris. As planned, his pal Howard Simon is at the Gare Saint-Lazare to meet him on this cold and rainy Friday night. Simon's been in town since June. He takes Hirschfeld to his own hotel, a seedy little place in the Latin Quarter, and Al is disconsolate. There's no bath. His room, up six flights of rickety stairs, has torn wallpaper, a single lamp, and neither closet nor chest for him to unpack his trunk.

In later years, as the theater works its magic on him, Hirschfeld will dramatize his arrival to a fare-thee-well.

"So I arrived there," he says, "and no Howard Simon. And I don't speak French. I didn't know what to do, so I show this paper with the hotel name on it—Hotel Blois—and got into the cab with my bags, and it's raining, and he takes me to this hotel, deposits me in front of the hotel, takes the bags out, and I'm left on the sidewalk. It didn't look like a hotel at all, but there was a sign saying HOTEL. And I pulled the bell chain, and waited, and I pulled again. And by this time, I'm soaking wet, and standing there in the rain with my bags. And a man comes to the door in a nightgown. And I made gestures showing him that I want a room, and so on. And he writes down on a piece of paper the number of the room, and points upstairs. And I start up the stairs."

(At another time, he'll amend it further, having Marc Goodrich not just jot down the name of his hotel but take him there. In fact, neither version is quite right, since the Hotel de Blois is in the Rue des Plantes, not in the Latin Quarter.)

"I had never been a drinking man up to that point," the tale goes on, "but I decided I'm going to get drunk, and spend all my money, and the hell with it, and get out of here as fast as possible." He walks around the corner and finds "a little bar called the Select." He orders a beer. "There's a fellow standing next to me who looked vaguely familiar," he says. "Had a Borsalino hat on, a big cape and a mustache. I look at him closely, and it's Howard, my friend. I said, 'What happened to you at the station? I mean, you don't realize what I've been through.' He said, 'I didn't realize you were coming over this week. I thought it was the next trip.' One of those things."

Within moments, he meets two Brits at the bar, a painter and a poet. They stay up all night, go carousing around Montmartre. In the morning, back at the Dôme with coffee, they decide to find a studio together. They go to an art shop, where a bulletin board offers a listing of availabilities, and soon they're en route to a distant block.

It doesn't really happen that promptly, since his first letter to Mom and Pop says that he vows to find a studio as soon as he can. "I shall not be content until I have one. Have not done any work yet and shall not do so until I get settled."

And he hears from Flo. "Oh, Al," she writes in a nine-page letter, "I feel as tho we did something contrary to Fate. I'm perfectly sure we should have taken our maiden trip together"—and with reason. Rushing across Seventh Avenue in front of the Earl Carroll Theatre, she catches her toe in the car track and falls flat in the midst of traffic! But survives.

But apparently more is afoot. Almost blithely she refers to a health problem that appears serious, with few details. It can't be an abortion, because she'll be able to go to the hospital in a month after "a few more treatments" to be sure she's "ready." Then what? "I understand I can go to a women's hospital and get a free operation and only have to pay my two weeks board so I can do it for a hundred," she writes without further ado.

Fine by Al, who since the death of his brother Milton maintains a deliberate ignorance of matters medical.

She calls him Babe, and she calls her baby Babe, too—complaining that her husband and daughter have been to visit one of her friends, and "they never mentioned me. I think they took Babe to see her just to make me envious."

Meanwhile, in Paris, he's unsettled in every way, including language (speaking not a word, he mimes along with gestures and sketches). "Howard is as much use to me as a one armed sparring partner," he complains to Flo of the perpetually loyal Howard Simon. "Have not seen him in 2 days." With no heat in his fleabag, he has to sleep in "the cave" of Le Select, one of the cosier cafés on the Boulevard Montparnasse.

While young artists and writers are living *la vie bohème*, Hirschfeld sulks. Nothing amuses him, not even a street parade to celebrate the Medical Students' Ball. "Women, at least a hundred of them, some partly nude, others entirely stripped marching, dancing and singing in the pouring rain," he adds, aghast. "Women here are rotten to the core, looking and morally." To illustrate the point, he encloses a drawing of "he & she on the Boulevard Montparnasse in front of the Café Du Dôme"—the man in a cape sucking a meerschaum, the woman in fringe and turban smoking a long-holdered Gauloise. Not so different from the familiar characters and affectations of Greenwich Village, but here they have a wicked allure, and tease his pen.

Meanwhile, he builds a nest. He, Roger Furse, and Francis Musgrave—the painter and the poet—take a five-room bungalow with mullioned windows, pitched roof, and skylight at 172 Rue de Vanves, a cobblestoned street in the 14th arrondissement. It's "a long, narrow thoroughfare," notes a travel writer of the day, "studded on either side by tenements, the ground floors of which provide shops of the what-not sort—just as many another Paris street does. Along this thoroughfare are installed the boucherie, the crémerie, the boulangerie, the mercerie, here and there a small café, or bistro; and less frequently a curiosité shop." On the next block, a small shingle-roofed shop sells saucepans and watering cans. L'Hôpital St.-Joseph and its chapel are directly across the way. It's a half-hour walk to Le Select, ten minutes by bicycle.

They sign an eight-year lease for 2,500 francs a year, making his share thirty-three dollars. Coffee in his district is twenty-five centimes, and a prix fixe dinner is six francs, or twenty-four cents, with a carafe of wine. All he has to do is knock out one picture every now and then, and on fifty dollars a month, he figures, he'll get by. "I was shopping today for a bed and other bare necessities and had the damnest time with the frogs, making them understand what I wanted," he writes to Flo. "Went into one store and drew a picture of a bed, and he brought me a jewel box."

Montparnasse has become such a draw it's inhabited by more Americans than many of the French would like. Every artist comes here. Unlike Montmartre, all dressed up in jazz, this is style-free and easy. A perfect life.

But frugal. Hirschfeld, Musgrave, and Furse live less like the Three Musketeers than the Three Bears. Three chairs and three beds, with a blanket apiece and no sheets or pillowcases. His steamer trunk as dining table, one coatrack, two potbelly stoves, a coffeepot and frying pan, four plates, six forks, six knives, and six spoons. "God knows what we're going to put in the other 4 rooms," he writes to Flo. "Oh, I almost forgot the 3 electric bulbs and 2 broken gas mantels." The studio has stone floors, so they buy eight rugs, which barely do the job, and winter is just around the corner. Meanwhile, "it's raining cats and dogs and has been for 4 days.

"This studio is without equal. It is absolutely funnier than Steeplechase at its best. To top all of this, there is no hot water, and it will be 3 weeks before the gas is turned on. This leak which has just sprung in the roof is the finishing touch to a near architectural masterpiece. The doors separating the rooms have a knob on but one side. If by accident (which I always do) one closes the door, you must jump out the window and enter by the front door walk through the apartment and then get back where you started."

But "am getting to like Paris more each day," he writes.

And "am growing a beard."

Back in the homeland, Flo has been writing up a storm. Not just letters, but short stories. If Zelda Fitzgerald and Zora Neale Hurston and Dotty Parker and Edna Ferber can do it, why not Flo? She wants his opinion of "Not Wanted," one such fling with fiction. "Very well written," he pens from Paris, "but a horrible end. Let's hope it turns out differently. Have read it but once as I hate to think of resigning myself to its moral or conventional fate." Her words are lost to history, but his words suggest all manner of distress. In any case, he supports her wish to write . . . and give up the stage! "Am glad you have not mentioned even a slight desire to go back in show business," he tells her. "Hope you fulfill your every desire."

Fulfilling his own, Hirschfeld enrolls at the Académie de la Grande Chaumière, just off the Boulevard Montparnasse. Alexander Calder, another student there, remembers that "there were no teachers, just a nude model, and everyone was drawing by himself." So Hirschfeld and Furse, both twenty-two, discuss the idea of posing models in their own studio. On another bulletin board along the boulevard, the boys find the names of models who will cook and *sleep in*. But they cost money. So for his *croquis* class, where he's learning the quick sketch, Hirschfeld's models run more toward rug peddlers and peanut vendors.

But nothing, it seems, is more essential to the young artist than the right café. The Brits and Americans seem to favor the Dôme, as they have since it opened in 1898, although Hemingway and Lewis have moved on, considering it too talky and touristy. The Russians (and Picasso) prefer La Rotonde, the biggest and brassiest. Others cling to the Dingo, the Falstaff, and La Closerie des Lilas—to Café de Flore and Les Deux Magots on the Place St. Germaine. "Each one had their own little place where they'd sit around til 2 o'clock in the morning solving world affairs and the whole history of art," Hirschfeld will remember, although he himself moves from one to another.

The café is the perfect forum for every smoky argument, every significant affiliation, every pose. "I don't care what you *did*. If your hobby was to engrave on the top of a pin, you would find at least five people around the corner who were interested in the same thing. There was an ambition to write the great American novel or paint the great American picture—but everybody shared their interests. There was no competition."

Hirschfeld scribbles most of his letters from a café, mostly the Dôme and mostly to Flo, whom he will variously address as Dear, Dearest, Chérie, Darling, and Dahlink! At his Dôme away from home, he sits on a cane-woven chair talking arty with Howard Simon (whose book of woodcuts and drawings is about to be published). This is also where Grant Wood tells Simon he's had enough Paris and is going back to his small town in the West to paint real people.

In the evening, when work is done, they drift over from their ateliers and academies in neighboring blocks, and from At the Sign of the Black Manikin, Edward Titus's bookshop-gallery around the corner on the Rue Delambre. Titus is married to Helena Rubinstein, which makes it possible for him to publish such provocative works as *Lady Chatterley's Lover* and

Kiki's Memoirs—the autobiography of the neighborhood's It girl, with an introduction by Titus's friend Ernest Hemingway.

Huffing and puffing all over the scenery, Hemingway is the bull in the bookshop, the bully in the ring. He's on view at most cafés, bistros, bars, and the American Club, where he goes to box. Hirschfeld knows that he always boxes guys smaller than he so he can beat the living daylights out of them. "Not one of my favorite fellows," he recalls.

The season is on. The 1925 Autumn Salon exhibits thousands of new canvases, Chaplin arrives in *The Gold Rush*, George Antheil offers an industrial-pitched jazz ballet called *Mécanique* while George Gershwin's music is everywhere, and *parfumiers* are pushing makeup for men. Meanwhile, out on the Rue de Vanves, Hirschfeld continues with his face design and writes to Flo that he liked Bonte's caricature of him in *Brass Tacks* because it was "very funny and a good likeness as I have a 4 days growth and my beard is beginning to get past the unshaven state. Shall have my photo taken as soon as it becomes a definite beard."

His hands are numb from the cold, but not so numb that they can't produce comical sketches of the street cleaner, the postman in his military gear, the waiter with his clownish feet, the policeman with his wide mustache, and the studio. He also paints a beautiful watercolor of the backyard with its tool-shed—or outhouse—and garden wall.

"Never felt better in my life," he writes to Mom. "I love Paris, it sure is all that it is famed for." And in postwar Paris, it's famed for everything—art and jazz, costume and dance, innuendo and innovation. The Exposition Internationale des Arts Décoratifs et Industriels Modernes—a spectacle of avant-garde art, architecture, fountains and furniture, jewelry and perfumes that will come to be labeled "Art Deco"—is on display from the esplanade of Les Invalides to the entrance of the Grand Palais. "More than ten million people have attended which, by the way, if you have been there, you will know, has been nine million nine hundred thousand too many for comfort," Janet Flanner reports in *The New Yorker*. As for other forms of amusement, there are some 180 movie houses, and wouldn't it be something to wander into a picture he's drawn the ad for?

In November, he meets the publicist for the Folies Bergère, who takes him backstage. "They put on a thoroughly artistic, novel and disgusting performance," he writes primly to Flo. "The chorines are entirely different than those of American shows. One merely tells the usher which girl he wants and she immediately becomes his property during intermission for 500 francs. The show girls are beautiful or rather they could be if they'd wash. Nude scenes become a bore after the first 50 scenes and the comedians dress like clowns and laugh at their own jokes."

When he hears from her, he's ecstatic. When he doesn't, he's stung. Time and again, she mentions the mysterious hospital procedure she's considering, and he seems incurious. Or afraid. After Milton, now Flo? In fact, her letters mostly make him jealous.

"Please keep away from Bway parties," he implores. "If you do go to them or rather if you feel you must go to them—Don't write me about them. I can't bear the thought of you being pawed and sought after by those fellows"—because all along, Flo, like many a flirty flapper, has been mentioning dinner dates, cabaret dates, this one and that one. "When I came to the part about your being up all night at a speakeasy," he writes, "I blushed—I could have screamed. So, please honey, for that reason—if none other—do not write me about them. I have thought of you out of that class—let me keep thinking that way. It has the same effect as plunging a knife through a painting."

Meanwhile, the clothes Hirschfeld lugged over in the trunk are of no use whatever. At the suggestion of his impractical father, he's brought a cutaway coat and striped trousers. Pop's *beau idéal* is Alphonse in the American comic strip, *Alphonse and Gaston,* Hirschfeld says. "I noticed people were staring at me. They thought I must be a diplomat on his way to an embassy reception, or maybe Adolphe Menjou on holiday from Hollywood." So he goes to the Galeries Lafayette and buys a corduroy suit and a pair of sabots, those wood clogs familiar to peasants and cherished by artists. "No one pays any attention to your dress over here," he writes, "and these are much warmer than ordinary shoes." The Hirschfeld beard, while still in its formative stage, suffers a minor setback when he lights a cigarette over an oil stove.

History records that Abraham Lincoln grew his beard for a stronger image. Sophocles, Melville, and Freud had their own reasons. And then there's Hirschfeld, who will amuse friends and interviewers through the years with his excuse: no heat in the studio, solid ice in the tap, impossible to shave. It's just as likely he's growing a beard because he's an artist in Paris in the 1920s, wearing corduroys and clogs, and this is part of the uniform.

In the studio, Musgrave is now a poet, of sorts. "He only wrote poetry when he got drunk," Hirschfeld remembers, "one of those things." After studying for a spell at the Institut National des Langues et Civilisations Orientales, Muzzy has emerged a linguist. "He learned to say 'Your fly is open' in every language in the world. He'd stand in front of a café and yell it out in every language he knew. You could tell what part of the world these people came from when their heads looked down. It was a kind of lunatic time."

The boys re-wallpaper the studio, and it looks worse than before. "It's all on cockeyed," he grouses to Flo, "and we didn't have enough paper, so ¼ of the big wall is nude. Can't get the paste out of my hair and won't be able to for some time. Ruined a good pair of shoes by dropping one in the bucket of paste. The place smells like a glue factory. The damn stuff won't dry. You can move the paper about, on the wall. You can slide or adjust it any shape or position you desire." But Paris, oh Paris. "There is nothing like it. It's infinite in beauty."

They buy a potbelly stove, which eases the chill but not the heart. Picturing Flo as he lies atop his solitary bed in pajamas, smoking robe, and slippers, a half-lit pipe clenched in his teeth, he's sipping champagne and feeling sentimental. "It is very warm and I can think of nothing but you," he writes.

In his correspondence, he uses a graceful cursive and signs "Al" in the same style. But on the backs of his envelopes, he now makes a change. In October 1925, he starts writing his name in elongated thin-stroke letters—HIRSCHFELD—like those used by Hal Phyfe, a theatrical illustrator of the day. He kinda likes the look.

While New York is playing hide-and-seek with Prohibition, Paris is just playing. In November, Hirschfeld and friends drop into a Russian cabaret for dinner and vodka, then to Montmartre—"the Times Square of Paris," he explains to Flo. At 2:30, he hails a cab and makes a deal with the driver to take him home for fifteen francs, and the driver agrees. Upon delivery, however, the driver changes his mind and insists on twenty-five, which Hirschfeld doesn't have. The driver reaches into his back pocket, and Hirschfeld smacks him in the snoot. The driver falls back into the cab, and Hirschfeld goes to his studio door.

"Felt something tickling my spine," he writes, "and turned around to behold the angriest Frenchman I ever want to see, automatic in hand." A cop appears, marches Hirschfeld into the studio, and there is Roger Furse, sound asleep. The driver wakes Furse and points the gun in *his* face, demanding payment. Furse leaps out of bed and makes out a check (a bum check) to the driver, and away he goes.

"Chauffeur Draws Gun to Collect Extra Fare, So Client Writes Check," reads the headline in a Paris paper the next day. "A new, practical method is by way of being adopted by more enterprising taxi drivers for collecting their full fare when the passenger complains of the exorbitant rate charged him, according to the experience of Mr. Al Hirschfeld, American artist," the story relates. "Mr. Hirschfeld, who confesses that his French is rather thin and meagre, argued limpingly," it says, "but failed to make himself understood.

"'Vingt-cinq!' shrieked the taxi driver, flashing two 10's and a 5 on the fingers of his expressive hands.

"'Fifteen!' shouted Mr. Hirschfeld, white with rage." As this version has it, he calls the cop, who listens and walks away. And with the gun at his gut, Hirschfeld gestures that the driver follow him into the studio, in which no Roger Furse appears to be resting.

"The menacing gun gave the American a queer feeling as it tickled the sensitive small of his back," the tale goes on. "Once in the studio, however, the painter made out a check for 25 fr., which the Jesse James driver accepted, putting up his gun and departing without a murmur. The question in Mr. Hirschfeld's mind now is: Will the driver be so naïve as to try to cash the check."

It's fun making the papers, so he entices the *Herald* critic over to the studio. A few days later, his portrait of a Left Bank artist shows up in Arthur Moss's column, "Over the River." Moss covers the art scene for both *The New York Times* and the Paris *Herald*, traveling the *académie* and gallery circuit, seeking new talent. His is a well-read column, and having one of your paintings appear in it (with your name spelled right) is a coup. "Too bad that Al Hirschfeld's canvas can't be reproduced in color," Moss writes, "as he managed to catch the exact shade of Bob Shaw's pink beaver." (In this context, a beaver is a beard.)

The money is dribbling away. Just in time, Furse's sister comes to town and takes them to Tour d'Argent for duck. Thence to the Théâtre des Champs-Élysées for a performance by Pavlova, the Dôme for coffee, Harry's Bar for drinks. "Paris," he reminds Flo once again, "is paradise to me. Do you think we shall ever be in Paris together. It would be marvellous. You would love it, honey, so much that I am afraid you should never want to see New York again." In closing, he writes that the jade she gave him upon his departure still dangles from his watch chain . . . and always will.

With all the goings-on during this first visit to Paris, in none of his letters does Hirschfeld mention the doyenne of expatriates, Gertrude Stein, at 27 Rue de Fleurus —which he would, if he were to meet her. In later years he does, noncommitally. "It was a great place to get warm in the winter," he says. "Great food. It was a pleasant place to be invited to every now and then or, if you were in the neighborhood, to drop in. There was no formality connected with it." And "you knew you would be fed."

The rosier Hirschfeld is, the bluer is Flo. Her literary career having hit a snag, she's still looking for work, but he can't help asking about the upcoming medical event. "Haven't you enough money to go to the hospital? Please don't tell my folks what you are doing"—whatever it is she finds necessary to fix her body and further her career. "I am sure they shall be disillusioned as I told them you would never return to theatricals."

As winter blows in, Hirschfeld looks south. "Paris in the winter is for connoisseurs of melancholy," Irwin Shaw has said, and that's not Al Hirschfeld. So, as he recalls it, "I decided that I've got to get someplace and get a little sunshine. And I made this announcement at the Dôme one night. I said, 'Anybody wants to come with me is welcome. I'm going on a painting tour, and I'm going to get some sun. I don't know where I'm going, but . . . south.' Well, the next morning, two fellows showed up."

"I had never met either one before. But they knew me from around the Dôme."

They are Victor Thall and James ("Mac") Macmullen, both Americans, both also in their early twenties. Like so many in his set, Thall—who has studied at the Art Students League and Julian's—claims to know Hemingway and Fitzgerald. In his own view, he's considered something of a darling because he has money and can buy the drinks.

On December 9, Hirschfeld sends Flo a little map of their proposed route—south through Avignon and Marseille to Spain, Africa, Italy, and back to France—which adds up to some five months, if the money holds out. He's exhilarated. "Imagine the thrill of arriving at Casablanca to be greeted by Arabs, Camels, a colorful landscape and a warm climate." He's really fired up. The trip will cost about $250, he figures, financed by Mom. "Hot patookie!"

Then not so hot. Bekie has cabled him it's off. "Am on the verge of exploding with temperament, soreness, meaness and all my other lovely qualities," he writes to Flo days later. "I am leaving even if I have to work on a Camel ranch," he rages, as if stamping his feet on the cold stone floor.

And on to Flo herself. "What the devil is happening to you? You make me imagine all sorts of things. Your ideals are gradually shattering to the ground. Please, please, don't let me think of you as a weak show-girl seeking nothing but good-times, parties and all the rest of the artificial things that make B'way, Broadway. Let me think of you as you resolved to be. Your letter telling me that you joined the forces of 'The Caravan Club' came as a shock to me but as I have explained in a previous letter your cancer is your own to do with as think best." *Cancer*! The ailment! "Am sorry to ask this many times asked and unanswered question again, but I must. When are you having your coming out party or stomach removal festival or something like that? If any?"

Whenever, the malady seems not to have cast a shadow on her datebook. "There is no excuse for getting drunk however and certainly none for doing it so often," he chides. "Your last three letters tell me of the awful head the next morning, etc. If you care for me a little bit I should imagine you could give all this up. Why do you deliberately hurt me in this way. You must know that I take objection to it. The holidays are almost upon us. I have never experienced the thoroughly disgusted, disheartened and blue spirit which I now possess. Am sore at the world. Sorry I can't write you any news or a note of my activities but my mind is tonguetied." He considers tearing up her photograph. But then, nonetheless, "Love & kisses from your sweetheart frothing at the mouth."

While he awaits a visa to Morocco, Hirschfeld catches more of the sights and most of the shows—Mistinguett at Moulin Rouge, the Dolly Sisters at Casino de Paris, Hasoutra at the Apollo. With a new friend, an American millionaire, he hits the Perroquet, Harry's Bar, the Mirador, Jacks, Pigalle, and Joe Zelli's Royal Box on the Rue Fontaine.

Within, Zelli's "royal boxes" are planted along the balcony so joy-seekers can survey the action below while sipping champagne and gabbing on inter-table telephones. Some walls of the long, pillared dance floor are mirrored. Others are decorated with caricatures of celebrities drawn by an Italian artist called Zito. Zito has until recently belonged to Josephine Baker, the exotic creature from St. Louis who just stormed Paris in *La Revue Nègre*. Her revue has her stripped down to feathers while performing what Scott Fitzgerald calls "her chocolate arabesques" against sets designed by none other than Al's friend Miguel Covarrubias.

"Inside Zelli's it was crowded, smoky, and noisy. The music hit you as you went in," says Hemingway. That music is Black jazz and Argentinian tangos—unless it's Hirschfeld and Furse tapping and uke-playing their hearts out, says Hirschfeld.

All this while he's been claiming he's too broke to send his love a Christmas present. But now he comes through. Shaving off the beard and mustache he won't need where he's going, he sends his "proudest and most precious possession. Enclosed please find one beard." And there, wrapped in tissue, is a packet of holiday trimmings. Red whiskers.

6
LINES IN THE SAND

Al, Thall, and Mac do depart on Tuesday, January 5, taking the train south from Paris to Barcelona. There, Hirschfeld finds the cigarettes pricey and the señoritas unimpressive, and he has nothing to wear. The caps came off the paint tubes in his suitcase so his suit resembles a palette, one suitcase falls apart, and he loses another in the crush boarding the boat from Cádiz—in traditional Hirschfeld style—not realizing it's missing until the boat has left the pier.

Landing in Tangier after a rough crossing, Al and Vic guard the bags while Mac scouts for lodgings. Three hours later he returns, and with a throng of willing Arabs carrying their baggage, they parade to the hotel, which they consider merely a stopover. Until the next day, when they miss the boat. At the American consulate, they learn that Vic's passport expired six months ago. Summoning their most persuasive palaver, they convince the consul that their only objective in going to Fez is to paint it. The official agrees not to send Vic back to the States and fines him ten dollars.

The "three Rover boys," as Al calls them, travel to Rabat and to Fez. Hirschfeld's first take is harsh. "Millions of Arabs, camels, snake charmers, carpets—roughly it is an enlarged Barnum & Bailey circus in the streets," he writes to Flo. "The rainy season has just ended here and the heat is almost unbearable. The so-called noble Arab is, without exception, the dirtiest living human in the world. Their homes are made of mud and straw. They sleep with their animals, pigs, camels and goats." Hotels are booked with French troops here to aid the Spanish fight the Berbers in what's known as the Rif War. "The war or rather the armies are waiting until June to resume fighting," he adds. Gloomily, he closes. "Write me often and many," he implores. "I'm very lonesome in this dirty, cannabalistic, syffeletic and beautiful town."

He shares other observations with George Bonte and the gang back at Warner Bros. "The street scenes are an unending procession of camels, donkeys, Arabs, arches and flies. It takes one about two days before he realizes there is no circus in town. Saw 'The Midnight Alarm,' a Vitagraph picture, at the only picture house in Fez. I was the only white man in the house. Women do not attend the theatre. Tea is served between each part, and one cup is the portion for five people. Having been informed that to refuse a drink of tea is compared to stealing a man's wife in America, I partook and haven't felt the same since."

But he assures Flo there are attributes to be found. "While walking back to the hotel after painting all day, the Grand Pasha (of which there are many) passed me by, riding a beautiful white Arabian horse; his white silk burnoose flying in the wind, gold boots and spurs, silver trappings on this horse and followed by his slaves on foot. That's a picture you can find nowhere but here."

As for other pictures, he's making lots—charcoals, watercolors, and etchings of the marketplaces, musicians, even the weather. None of this, however, distracts him from Flo's health. "Are you going to the hospital Jan 25?" he wonders—and, because January 25 is also her twenty-fourth birthday, he sends her a jade pin that the appraiser at the consul's office has assured him is a perfect stone.

While sketching in a café one day, he chances upon an American sculptor whose name he was given in Paris and makes a dinner date with the man and his wife. This is a lucky break, it turns out, because he "knows all the Pashas, Sultans and other such funny people. So, I shall probably get some good inside dope on Arabs and their homes." Until he does, he encloses in his letters a couple of delightful sketches—one of "African Lindy waiter" balancing two teetering trays, another of "Charleston Arab," a robed figure with his right leg in a flapper's kick.

"I suppose by this time you have visited the hospital," he scribbles the next week. "Write me the result of it all. How long were you confined in bed? I'm thinking of you and hoping for you, honey. I long to have you stroke my hair while I serenade Insufficient Sweetie to you, somewhere on 51st St. Them was ye happy days."

Before leaving Fez, Hirschfeld buys a couple of carpets and a trunk to replace the suitcase that died. The boys journey on, by car and train, to Oujda and Algiers (where the new trunk is misplaced for three days). He looks up a doctor friend of a friend to show him the town. They drive around in the doc's Minerva, then dine at his home—"superbly arranged with magnificent Kairanan tapis and Oriental carpets of every description. Brassware, trinkets, guns and curios of every sort." He also has "a most charming wife and some 10 or 15 Arab slaves who at a single applaud jump from apparent nowheres to serve his simplest command."

Thence to villages in the Sahara accessible only by camel. One of which he rides.

Many of which he smokes. In Tunis on Valentine's Day, they join up with sailors from an American destroyer docked nearby. "They sure looked good to see. We spent the evening with them, raising hell and creating much excitement for

Tunis. Imagine speaking American to someone that understands it. It was a great thrill."

Onward to Carthage, and the boys arrive at an archaeological candy store. "Bits of marble, mosaic, Roman pottery and old coins are lying about and we have temporarily become amateur *excavateurs*," he exults. "None of the ruins have been touched by restorators and one may cart away all he can carry." Doing his part, Hirschfeld encloses a Carthaginian coin he picked up at the base of a Roman column.

At sunrise he misses Flo mightily, and finds the nights "mysterious and unending." But the days are full of paint and wonder. When he returns to his hotel, he tacks his sketches to the wall but after dinner indulges in anxiety, imagining Flo "in all sorts of disagreeable circumstances and situations," he writes.

He's become obsessed "with the idea of a terrific storm raging outside, trees being uprooted and a heavy rain beating against the window pane. Looking out the window assures me of a perfect tropical evening, lifeless trees and the quiet stillness in the air as calm as an Indiana farm on a summer's evening. This may be the ravings of some nut, maybe I am that, but seriously I am convinced of some tangible change which I feel intensely and describe foolishly.

"I suppose by the time you are in receipt of this letter, the operation is a thing of the past. Were your expectations fulfilled ? ? ? ?"

She continues to skirt the issue, and Hirschfeld continues to probe, politely. "Judging from your letter," he writes a few days later, "you seem to treat the hospital event very *lightly*. The gent who said, 'Women are life's mystery,' merely scratched the surface. I have made a promise to myself, not to advise you or quarrel unnecessarily over this, as you no doubt know my attitude by this time! Do what you think best, honey, and here's hoping you're right. Only please give it careful thought—Must you be sick to appreciate the sensation of being well?"

When she again diverts his curiosity to complain of "Kleig eyes"—now on a movie set—he is further troubled. "Glad to hear you are getting picture work and have taken more than a fancy to it," he writes gently. "I am not happy because it is picture work, but, because it is not without heart in it, that is the admirable quality."

Back in Europe, it's April in Nice. When Hirschfeld and Thall are pedaling around, sketchbooks on their backs, brushes in their baskets, one of them has a brainstorm! Why not drop in on Matisse, who lives nearby? According to Thall, not known as a terribly reliable reporter, Matisse arrives home just as they appear. When he sees their art supplies, he invites them in and asks to see their drawings. Sadly, what Matisse sees in Hirschfeld's work will remain forever unknown because Thall's mention is all that survives.

Back in Paris—which Hirschfeld tells Flo he likes "better than New York by far"—he's accrued a good batch of watercolors and drawings, and sketches to be used later for bigger paintings. He gets them framed for an exhibit he hopes to have when he gets home.

Arthur Moss's report in the Paris *Herald*, however, shows interest in another matter. "Al Hirschfeld, returning beaverless from a long tour of Spain, Italy and North Africa, has a perfect excuse for the surrender of his hirsute ornaments," he writes. "He discovered that the principal industry of North Africa is the raising of beavers, and after seeing thousands of them he felt that they were blots upon the landscape; hence the sacrifice of his own. Competition kills 'em. Al is soon leaving the

Quarter again, next trip Westward bound, to exhibit his paintings in New York City."

He crates his bulky goods—the litho press he's bought, the baskets and rugs, the octagonal Moroccan coffee table inlaid with mother-of-pearl. When American Express comes to pick it all up, the concierge won't let him leave until the rent is paid. He walks to the Dôme without a franc in his pocket. Furse and Musgrave are in London, but he finds a friend who takes him to find the building agent on the Right Bank. In desperation, he gives the agent the watch Uncle Harry gave him for his bar mitzvah, and the agent gives him a note to the conciege to release the baggage. He checks it in at the Gare Saint-Lazare and returns to the Quarter—where, lo, his friends present him with the watch! They've taken up a collection, paid his rent, and retrieved it.

"All I remember is getting very drunk that night," he later recalls, "and waking up in that train in a compartment with two nuns." He passes out on the floor, they plant a lily on his chest, and, he adds, "That was my exit."

7
HIS INFINITE VARIETY

Home on the *Leviathan*, he sails straight into Flo's arms. It's May 1926, and Hirschfeld's back in town. To commemorate his return, Gordon Kahn goes lyrically overboard in "The Broadway Diary of Samuel Eppis," the somewhat precious column he writes for *Zit's*. "Later to come upon Albert Hirschfeld, excellent fellowe, whom I had not seen this twelfemonth, ever since he did set sail upon a barkentine to the Afrique to limn with pigments upon canvas pictures of sunsets in Tangiers; stray curs in Fez and savages in Morocco. Quaffed full two beakers of java-brew iced while he did recount of his travails among the ferocious hill-men called Riffs who evince a hatred so strong for white men, more especially Castillians and French, that they do slay them with muskets upon sight."

Through his ever-growing circle, the twenty-three-year-old Hirschfeld is meeting playwrights, thespians, Round Tablers. Unlikely as it seems, he and Eugene O'Neill frequent swing joints and speaks, from Fifty-second Street to Harlem, together.

Hirschfeld and Covarrubias hit Harlem as well—and what a throbbing landscape it is. Joints big and small—Small's Paradise, the Savoy Ballroom, Connie's Inn, Bentley's Clam House, the New Coal Bin, the Alamo Café, the Cotton Club—spangle the avenues. Barron's is so exclusive that "only light-skinned Negroes could get in," remembers one such famous expat called

Bricktop (who runs a hot cabaret in Montmartre), "unless you happened to be someone special like Jack Johnson or the great Negro comic Bert Williams." Limousines pull up to unload gents in jackets and ties, dames in ermine and pearls, luminaries such as Al Jolson, strivers such as Lucille Le Sueur (the incipient Joan Crawford).

The cakewalk, the bunny hug, the turkey trot, the Charleston, the black bottom! For Al and Miguel, this is heaven on earth, paradise in a paint box—"a scene of blazing color," the uptown author Claude McKay rhapsodizes. "Soft, barbaric, burning, savage, clashing, planless colors—all rioting together in wonderful harmony."

Hirschfeld is back promoting movies for Warner Bros.—Dolores Costello in *Old San Francisco*, Louise Fazenda in *Finger Prints*, Irene Rich in *The Honeymoon Express*, George Jessel in *Private Izzy Murphy*, the first Jason Robards in *White Flannels*, the first Rin Tin Tin in *While London Sleeps*, the first Robards and Rin Tin Tin together in *Jaws of Steel*—and on August 5, 1926, the company introduces Vitaphone at Warners' Theatre on Broadway. After some shorts featuring the Philharmonic Orchestra and operatic soloists comes *Don Juan*, a John Barrymore swashbuckler and the first feature film to use synchronized sound effects and full score (but no spoken dialogue). Hirschfeld draws ads for the picture, knows this is a beginning, although silents will be golden for a few more years.

And excitement is all over town. From the Velodrome up on 225th Street—a vast wooden stadium for amateurs and pros, where Hirschfeld suffers "a terrible wood burn" when he's thrown from his bike and slides down one of the steep banks—to Madison Square Garden on Eighth Avenue, six-day bicycle races have become an enthralling sport. The professional events at Madison Square Garden are wildly popular—the Jazz Age descendant of America's turn-of-the-century bicycle mania and forerunner of the exhausting dance marathons to come. The moneyed show up after the theater, after the opera, instead of either. It's big stuff. Here's Flo Ziegfeld, Texas Guinan, Jed Harris! There's Herbert Fields, who's written a musical about it called *The Girl Friend* with Rodgers and Hart! The spectacle is lit like a circus, as Alexander Calder's painting *Six Day Bike Race* depicts.

And in the stands together: Al Hirschfeld and Eugene O'Neill.

Still at Warner Bros., Al takes a studio at 128 Washington Place and throws his rugs on the hardwood floor. Here he deals with a fireplace installed over the veto of the fire department, a wet spot on the ceiling, loose floorboards, a landlady looking like a hand-carved umbrella handle, and the smell of burning mattresses, as he describes it.

And he's picked up a companion, for painting time. A photograph shows Hirschfeld and his old studio mate Covarrubias posing together before the hearth, both wearing smocks and leather shoes (no sabots here). At night, he goes back to Flo.

Leaving his office on Broadway and Forty-eighth after work, he walks down the Great White Way as hubbub circles the *Times* building and the regulars take position—the pencil sellers and flower women on the corners, beggars under the canopies, shadowboxers before the dance halls, evangelists and pamphleteers rousing the rabble. It's on to Chinatown or Dreamland, Barnum & Bailey or the Flea Circus at Hubert's. It's a time of ballyhoo.

Everything's a show. Even within the walls of Frank E. Campbell's Funeral Church on Broadway, where the bigs and smalls of entertainment are treated with kid gloves, from Rudolph Valentino in his ten-thousand-dollar casket to "Zip, What Is It?" a prominent member of P. T. Barnum's freak show, whose grieving colleagues include Count Graf, the Human Art Gallery; Joe Cramer, the Rubber-Neck Man; Alphonso, the

Human Ostrich; Ajax, the Sword Swallower; Gus Birchman, the Human Claw Hammer, and Jolly Irene, the Fat Lady (occupying most of a pew).

With Campbell's, who needs Coney?

Thanks to his visibility through movie land, Hirschfeld is being wooed by publicists fond of seeing their clients depicted in clever ways. Soon before Christmas of 1926, he's invited by the Theatrical Press Representatives of America to submit a cover design for the program to be handed out at its annual benefit. No pay, but the exposure didn't hurt Howard Chandler Christy, who did the cover the year before.

A few days later, Dick Maney calls. He's a rising press agent who started as an advance man for Flo Ziegfeld's beloved, Anna Held (known, probably thanks to Maney, for bathing in milk), and "a very literate guy," Hirschfeld remembers, "one of the few press agents capable of writing a complete sentence." He invites Hirschfeld to join him for a run-through of a show at Chanin's Forty-sixth Street Theatre. It's a double bill of French comedies. Neither is new, but both have been Parisian hits, and both are written by Sacha Guitry, the French actor who's appearing in them with his wife, Yvonne Printemps. First comes act two of *Deburau*, a verse play about a nineteenth-century French clown. Then comes *Mozart*, with a score by Reynaldo Hahn. Mozart is played by the feminine Printemps. Baron von Grimm, his jealous sponsor, is played by Guitry.

Perhaps in awe, perhaps in order to stay awake, Hirschfeld doodles this bewigged and bespectacled character on the slip he's holding. Maney sees it, grabs it, and tells Hirschfeld to copy it onto a clean piece of paper so he can get it over to the *Herald Tribune,* where he knows a few guys.

A career is born.

The drawing appears in the *Trib* on Sunday, December 26, 1926, the day before the show opens. It is Hirschfeld's first published theatrical caricature.

In January 1927, Hirschfeld is back in St. Louis for the opening of his exhibit at Newhouse & Son, a gallery on North Kingshighway Boulevard. He's not here because he wants to be. Characteristically, he sent his paintings to the gallery with the titles separately, and the gallery couldn't put them together.

The exhibit opens on January 17, with twenty watercolors and six black-and-white drawings from his jaunt through North Africa. "Some of the strongest and most charming of his things in the Newhouse gallery bear the titles, 'Market Scene, Fez,' 'Oranges, Tunis,' 'Water Hole, Carthage,' 'Moorish Café, Tangiers,' 'The Docks, Tunis,'" writes the art reviewer for the *St. Louis Globe-Democrat*. She especially likes *Ponte Veccio, Florence*, and comments that "his drawings are exceptionally strong and direct."

But by the end of the two-week run, he's sold only two paintings—*Market Scene* for $150 and *Store* for $75. After deducting a third for his share of the expenses, he comes out with next to nothing. But the show will move on to Chicago and New York, and hopes are high. Meanwhile, the gallery ships the rest of the work back to him in New York, unscathed, which he regards as a victory. "That was considered a successful show in those years," he says, "if you got the pictures back without the frames being broken."

He offers a watercolor to the art museum. "It would please me very much if this picture, through the St. Louis Museum of Fine Arts, might give to some others only a small portion of the pleasure which the works of more important artists gave me when I called St. Louis home," he writes to the director. *Tunis* shows a steamer being coaled at a wharf with small boats in the foreground. "The watercolor was not too bad," he recalls. "And I was beginning to believe that I was really Hirschfeld." The picture is accepted and officially acquired in February.

But such generosity isn't a frequent occurrence. In May, the Newhouse people have a request. Sending him two prints each of two watercolors, they ask him to sign them on the back, "giving them a little personal note by perhaps mentioning the conditions under which they were painted, etc. This will add considerable interest to the pictures and will aid in their sale."

Hirschfeld returns one print of each. "The endorsements were received this morning," replies the gallery lady, "and are interesting beyond my expectations." She sends him two more prints, "since the others undoubtedly went astray."

Howard Dietz, having graduated from Goldwyn to Metro-Goldwyn-Mayer as director of publicity (while also contributing lyrics to Broadway shows, most notably *Dear Sir* with music by Jerome Kern), gives Hirschfeld a contract for some twenty thousand dollars a year. It's not exclusive (after the fall of the house of Selznick in 1924, he vowed never again to work for any one company), but it's lucrative, what with illustrations for *The Garden of Allah*, *Bitter Apples*, *Love* (Garbo's first go at *Anna Karenina*), *Lovers*, and *Tillie the Toiler*. "I was a great movie buff," he says. "I lived in the movies."

At lunches with the MGM art department, he meets John Held Jr., whose mores-pricking cartoons of collegians, club ladies, and kissy-poo coquettes have long lit up *Life*, *Puck*, *Judge*, *Vanity Fair*, *The Smart Set*, and *The New Yorker*—and who will forever receive his praise. Flappers, flivvers, "that's all Johnny, not Fitzgerald," he says. "That whole Jazz Age was Johnny."

It's 1927, Hirschfeld is now in a studio at 3 Sheridan Square, and by summer the place is *hot.* "I used to work in my shorts," he recalls, "and I would put a pen to paper, and it permeated that paper, like putting ink into an inkwell." The Rivoli up on Broadway has introduced air-conditioning to a grateful movie public, but playhouses are yet to follow. "I think they had a fan blowing over ice in the theater, which cooled it off when you came in," he goes on. "But the ice melted, and by the time the intermission came you were perspiring again, and by the time it was over you were ready for a bath."

The whole neighborhood's hot. Barney Gallant, Gene O'Neill's old roommate, runs the Greenwich Village Inn two doors away with the biggest dance floor around, and there are hideaways by the bottleful. "Tearooms" punctuate the landscape like dandelions in spring.

Hirschfeld finds the milieu almost like Paris, abounding in hangouts such as Hubert's Cafeteria, the Pepper Pot and Kopper Kettle, the Bat and Crumperie, and his particular favorites such as the Jumble Shop and Romany Marie's. The speakeasies are smoky with jazzists and scholars, hams and scamps roasting and toasting themselves as they did in Montparnasse. "It was not a state law, it was a federal law," he recalls, "so the state paid no attention to it, which made everybody a lawbreaker. And that brought in a whole gangster era. Nobody seemed to pay much attention to it, because they never killed civilians, they killed each other."

But artists are good company. Alex King introduces him to De Hirsh Margules, a long-haired, beret-wearing, Romanian-born watercolorist and poet known in the Village as "the Baron." King, Baron, and Hirschfeld spend hours together, spooling out opinions. Margules and Hirschfeld have painted in Paris and North Africa—where King and Covarrubias once lived together. King and Margules have also been to Bali, where King has illustrated travel pieces glorifying the island, and their enchantment strikes Hirschfeld.

Alexander Calder, who's been leading a parallel life sketching *la vie* of Montparnasse, the horse shows at Madison Square Garden, and the sideshows of Coney Island, has also become a friend. Hirschfeld still dabbles with clay, Calder with wire. For the studio, he gives Al a sculpture he's made of Helen Wills, the tennis player. The piece is life-size, and every time Hirschfeld comes in, the sculpture "somehow seemed to catch my fly," he remembers. And where is it? "When I moved out of there, I just left it."

At twenty-four, he's making the rounds, lugging his portfolio, joining his confreres on the "mourners' bench" at the New York *World* (where the drama critic Alexander Woollcott chooses the art for his page), waiting to be seen so his work will be seen. Since his debut in the *Herald Tribune* with Guitry, he's been getting keen assignments from the editor Arthur Folwell, the critic George Goldsmith, and the reporter Marcus Goodrich (from the Paris trip). He'll appear in the *Trib* for years to come. Folwell, both jovial and acerbic, has been around the journalistic block, and as drama editor, he's become a magnet for every illustrator in town.

"The editor was not an easy man to see," recalls Don Freeman, an artist making the same rounds as Hirschfeld, toting a similar portfolio. "There was already a waiting room full of artists anxious to have their stuff in print. One by one they went in and had their moment with the editor, reporting, as they came back with long faces, the same story. They could leave their work if they wanted to do so but he couldn't promise to use any of it; space in the paper was scarce and, furthermore, he wasn't running an art magazine!" To Freeman, who's here to audition a drawing of Shubert Alley, Folwell looks "more like Mr. Pickwick than the monster I had imagined him to be." A monster he is not, although he doesn't bother with small talk or even good news, and to Freeman's amazement the drawing shows up in Sunday's paper.

He and Hirschfeld, who meet here and there on the circuit, become pals for life. Freeman's a trumpeter, he's played with jazz bands, and he's good.

One day Folwell assigns Freeman a drawing of the stage show at the new Roxy. It's his first time inside the fabulous movie palace, and the press agent shows him around. When Freeman meets Fred Waring down in the pit, the maestro suggests he observe from the seat of the mighty Wurlitzer because the organ won't be used for the stage show. From there, Freeman will be out of the way and get a good view. Freeman pulls out his pad and pencil, the lights go down, and he goes up. The press guy has pushed the wrong button, and Freeman is riding an ascending organ!

"But it was too late. The organ by now was completely off on its own, ascending into space!" he remembers. "Just as I thought we would go through the ceiling, the organ stopped. I was now suspended in mid-air and, to say the least, the center of attention." The audience loves it. "Thus ended my first and only appearance at the Roxy. I was never offered a return engagement, although the press agent and Fred Waring and his entire orchestra were splitting their tuxedos as I landed back in the pit." Such is the life of a young illustrator.

Al's making money. In addition to the movie work, he's drawing enough for the *Trib*, *The World*, and a rag called *Beau* to send Mom to Europe on a grand tour in June.

Things are moving so fast now pals are calling him "Flash."

8
BABE IN THE WOODS

Knock-knock. It's Western Union. January 1928, and Hirschfeld gets a telegram:

> WOULD LIKE A DRAWING OF HARRY LAUDER TWO COLS 4 ½ INCHES DEEP DELIVERY NO LATER THAN TUESDAY —SAM ZOLOTOW NEW YORK TIMES.

Dick Maney's been touting Al to Zolotow for a year now, and Lauder, an aging Scottish vaudevillian, is making his annual farewell tour. He'll be appearing at the Knickerbocker Theatre for four weeks doing some of his "New and Old Song Characterizations."

At the *Times*, Zolotow, like Ziegfeld, is famous for sending telegrams. Dick Maney is famous for helping his friends. Al draws Lauder in a kilt and argyles, with a cigarette in his mouth, a crooked stick in his hand, and, oddly, what seems to be a star of David—a six-pointed star—on his chest. The picture appears on page 4 of the *Times* the following Sunday, January 29, 1928.

The *Times* wants more, too. Soon Hirschfeld gets another telegram requesting a picture of Zelma O'Neal in *Good News*, and on goes this impersonal arrangement with assignments for three-, four-, and five-column drawings. He develops a routine—seeing a performance or rehearsal, then going backstage to sketch the actor. When the drawing is done, he delivers it to the gent at the front desk in the lobby.

Meanwhile, his theater work for the *Herald Tribune* continues, with Lester Lonergan in *A Free Soul*, Aline MacMahon in *Maya*, Guy Robertson in *Lovely Lady*. Some are singles of the actors, some of the cast. His *Grand Street Follies* covers the entire front page of the Drama section.

And his friend Sam Marx is now the editor and sole writer of *New York Amusements*, a free guide to theatrical goings-on, so Hirschfeld picks up work there, too. Between April and June, he draws a number of Broadway entertainers, including Ed Wynn in *Manhattan Mary*, Billie Yarbough in *Keep Shufflin'*, Billy B.Van in *Sunny Days*, Eric Dressler in *Excess Baggage*, Reginald Carrington in *The Skull*, Jane Cowl in *The Road to Rome*, Effie Shannon in *Her Unborn Child*, Will Mahoney in *Take the Air*, Gus Shy in *Good News*.

He does the artwork for an MGM comedy called *Honeymoon*, starring Polly Moran, Harry Gribbon, and Flash the Dog. (Another Flash.)

He does *Blackbirds of 1928* for both the *Times* and the *Trib*—a single of Bill "Bojangles" Robinson for the *Times*, the full cast for the *Trib*.

Much in demand, his theatrical caricatures have become more regular and more prominent, and as successful as he is in other settings, it is theater for which he is becoming best known. And why theater? "Because the papers all had a drama section," he says. "They all had them—the *Tribune*, the *World*, the *Telegram*, the *Telegraph*, the *Brooklyn Eagle*, the *Sun*. It was not uncommon in the twenties to have eight or nine drawings in one drama section," in addition to publicity photographs and the charcoal drawings based on them. Little wonder his snappy, precise drawings pop off the page.

"Every Monday you'd find twenty, thirty artists in the drama department," he remembers, all of them hanging around waiting for someone to look at their portfolios. With fourteen papers on the stands, there's plenty of work. And with all the plays, photoplays, vaudeville and burlesque, there are plenty of pages to fill.

Of all the illustrators on the playing field—including William Auerbach-Levy, Paolo Garretto, Irma Selz, and Aline Fruhauf—it's the well-established Al Frueh, now gone from the entertainment pages to *The New Yorker* (where he had a cartoon in the very first issue), whom Hirschfeld calls "the master." Frueh is renowned for his economy of line, as in his caricature of George M. Cohan—with hat, stick, and no face—drawn for *The World* in 1922. But *the master*? "Hirschfeld was a very self-effacing man," observes the drama critic Martin Gottfried. "Hirschfeld is a lot better than this guy, but this guy happened to have been the first celebrated one, so in a way he opened the door to Al."

Hirschfeld brings something new. He calls them caricatures. Sometimes. More often, he says that caricature "implies a critique or criticism and is a derogatory term. So I don't refer to my drawings as caricatures. I prefer to think of them as 'character drawings,' and I would feel more comfortable being classified as 'characterist' if there is such a word or school."

Amid the flurry, Al makes a move he's been putting off.

He and Flo have billed and cooed for almost four years now—except for his intermission in Paris and North Africa—and she wants to settle down. He wants to show her Paris, as people in love are wont to do. And Russia, as young liberals of the time feel compelled to do. And Persia, to paint. So why not put it all together and make it a honeymoon?

In April, giving her name as Florence Marie, she files for divorce from the long-abandoned Norman Conard. On July 13, the divorce is granted, and that day she marries Albert Hirschfeld—giving her name as Florence Ruth. They provide the same address: the Hirschfeld family home on West 177th Street. The groom is twenty-five and an artist. The bride is twenty-six and a "writer."

The ceremony takes place in the new Park Central Hotel on Seventh Avenue and Fifty-fifth Street, with Big Al as one of the witnesses. Officiating is Leonard J. Rothstein, a Reform rabbi currently in residence, having departed his pulpit in St. Paul (after explaining to his flock that he could not vote for Calvin Coolidge).

The Park Central is no Ritz-Carlton, but it has its moments. The bootlegger Arnold Rothstein goes to glory in Room 349 when he's gunned down after refusing to pay up after a poker game. Later, the mobster Albert Anastasia checks out, too—in the barbershop, where, getting a shave and a haircut, he's blasted to smithereens.

"Dear Mom," the bride writes to Bekie, at sea on the *Ile de France*. "So far we've had a marvelous trip. I haven't felt better in my life and Babe is the same"—even after winning at the horse races and, mistaking the ten-franc note for an empty cigarette pack, tossing it overboard. "Just like him, isn't it?"

Roger Furse has sent a congratulatory five-pound box of candy, and Uncle Dave from St. Louis a fruit basket so splendid it would take a page to describe it, so she doesn't. Apparently, Al hasn't sprung for top notch. "We went up to First yesterday," she reports from her third-class cabin. "I didn't feel a bit envious of them. They are very dull. We see much more activity and color down here." And speaking of color, her groom, who plays shuffleboard every day, is "sunburned to the shade of lobsters."

In Paris, his early studio mate Musgrave meets them at the station and takes them to the Hôtel Odessa, where he's booked them a room. Together they see the old familiar places—the bistros, galleries, cafés. They attend Bostock's American circus at Luna Park. They gape at the Eiffel Tower, the Tuileries, and so on. One afternoon, Al takes his bride on a sentimental journey to the old studio out on the Rue de Vanves, but with their limited French neither can convince the concierge they're there to look at it, not rent it. After paying a call on the editor of the Paris *Tribune*, they stop at the Russian consul to see about their visas, for Hirschfeld is tantalized by the "Russian Experiment."

"I believed then that that was the salvation of the world," he remembers. "I thought the better distribution of money and equality should be straightened out in some way, and the only ones who were doing it, it seemed to me at that time, were the Socialists and Communists. They had at least a platform to try to distribute the wealth of the world. I was tremendously impressed with what was going on there. It seemed to me that that was the hope of the world."

Al buys a Russian dictionary. Flo learns the alphabet and thinks she'll be able to read signs, and "at night we study Russian in bed and laugh ourselves sick over the pronunciations," she writes. But she's not laughing in the morning. She can't rinse the shampoo out of her hair, and her foot is bothering her so she can hardly walk. She even finds eating a bother. "Meat in one place and coffee and desert in another—and they never have just what I have a yen for."

He's not with his confreres at the Dôme this time around. He's with a restless wife, already tired of sightseeing and shopping. To buck her up while they wait for their visas, Al takes her on the town. One evening they attend the *Revue des Ambassadeurs* at the *café-concert* of the Hôtel de Crillon—already painted by Degas and Lautrec and now to be drawn by Hirschfeld. They wear their party clothes, mostly (Babe discovers he packed no black socks so has to wear green ones).

The extravaganza features the comical Buster West, the singers Morton Downey and Florence Gershwin, a few songs by her brothers (including "The Man I Love," which she introduces here) and others by the up-and-coming Cole Porter. Buster West is an "eccentric dancer." Noble Sissle, the singer and composer (of 1921's *Shuffle Along* with Eubie Blake), has thrown together a band (including Sidney Bechet) to fill in for two months between Fred Waring's Pennsylvanians and Ted Lewis and His Orchestra. Hirschfeld's depiction of West and Sissle onstage, with Sissle's orchestra in the background, is published in the *New York Herald Tribune* on August 19, for which he's paid sixty dollars.

They pick up knickknacks at a flea market: two pieces of copper for 290 francs—"Immense big things and very old," says Flo. Babe gets a shave (the *beard*?) and a haircut, his first since July. They stay up until dawn, stopping in at an Apache dance hall near Les Halles, strolling through the market, having onion soup. She keeps Mom posted on all the "dirt," then explains that "dirt is Broadway slang for news. I explain that 'cause I don't think you're up on Broadway slang."

On August 25, they pick up their visas, and at dawn on September 4 they're at the Select with their baggage—of the sixty pounds they're allowed, forty are art supplies—where they sit around drinking coffee and studying their Russian until the Dôme opens, for oatmeal. Thence to the bus for Le Bourget, the field where Lindbergh landed the previous year. Al is exhilarated, Flo jittery.

It's an eight-passenger plane—and their first. "The motors started a terrific racket and in a couple of minutes I looked out and saw we were well off ground," she writes to Al's pal Mac (the third musketeer on the trip to North Africa) and his wife. "For about two minutes I was too scared to look and see how Al was taking it. After that tho we looked at each other and smiled. Nothing had happened and we were off." They land at Cologne, lunch on the field, and take off for Berlin, where they spend days thanks to a mix-up with the bus and so forth—before leaving . . . immediately to return with engine problems. But after many bumps and grinds, they land in Riga. Then Smolensk and then, finally, Moscow.

Al will remember the flight with Lady Astor aboard. In fact, when the Lady goes to Moscow, it's by train, not plane, in another year, and with George Bernard Shaw, not Al Hirschfeld.

The lady he does fly to Moscow with is Flo.

"We knew we were going by plane a week ago but I didn't want to tell you as I knew you'd worry," she writes to Mom, sparing the details. "We've been so excited over it I could hardly keep from telling you. Imagine, instead of six days steady riding on a dirty uncomfortable train we ride less than twenty hours in comfort. What a trip. I wouldn't have missed it for anything."

They check into the Lux. Hirschfeld's friend William Gropper, the socialist painter and political cartoonist whose work has appeared in the *Herald Tribune* as well as in the more liberated *Liberator* and *New Masses*, is just back from a tour of the Soviet Union with authors Sinclair Lewis and Theodore Dreiser to celebrate the tenth anniversary of the Russian Revolution. So Gropper knows just where to stay. The Lux isn't luxe, he's told Al, but it's convenient, and the best place to meet real people. He and Flo will be happy there. Only rich tourists stop at a grand hotel.

Known in the 1920s as a headquarters for foreign Bolsheviks, the Lux has its advantages, but it also has "the character of an overcrowded tenement, an overflow of untidy perambulators in the lobby, pervasive and peculiarly unpleasant food smells, slatternly housewives, cooing and quarreling audible in the corridors," reports Eugene Lyons, Moscow correspondent for United Press International.

The hot water is sufficient for tea, a shave, and washing one pair of stockings, but not for a bath, and Flo wants one. It's their first brush with the language problem. Babe consults his dictionary and asks a waiter for hot water. Many waiters later, there are many incomprehensible explanations, but still no water. Nor is there food, since the hotel restaurant doesn't open until next week. In the meantime, "we buy buns and cheese and tomatoes, cold meats, bread, grapes and such" for breakfast and lunch in the room. For dinner, they go out. "Food is good and cheap and we have a lot of fun ordering," Flo writes cheerily. "Everyone in the restaurant comes to our table trying to understand what we want."

To Al, the Russian epic will become another piece in his repertoire to render again and again. With every telling, with every new listener, it may emerge verbatim or with added details and detours (and without Flo). Here's how it goes:

After landing in Moscow and giving the name of his hotel to the bus driver at the airfield, he is delivered to the sidewalk with his luggage. At first sight, he finds the Lux like "a little French provincial hotel," which surely romanticizes it more than it deserves. He enters the lobby and notices that there's no front desk nor even a bellboy in sight. Alas! Despite his diligence with the dictionary (and his lifetime with a Russian mother), he speaks barely a Russian word. Even worse, he has no money because he wasn't allowed to bring any rubles into the country. What he has are American Express checks. Once he makes his presence known, somebody takes him upstairs to show him a room. Not until he unpacks does he discover that there's no running water—just a copper tank in the corner with a little spigot at the bottom. The tank will be filled with clean water every morning, and the spigot will let it trickle out. But here he is, it's about 7:00 in the evening, and there's no restaurant in the hotel either. Out he goes to find one. Not an easy task in the Soviet Union when you have no money and don't know where you are. As a result, he doesn't find one and decides to go to sleep with his growling stomach and wait until morning.

The sun rises, and so does Hirschfeld. He moistens his face and hits the street. First stop, a bank to get some rubles. But no. It's a bank holiday. He's empty, he's hungry, he hasn't had a bite since yesterday. Back at the hotel, he tries to explain his plight to the porter, but he's no help because he understands nothing but Russian. Doesn't even speak French or German. Not that Al does either, but he thinks he could at least make himself understood. So he figures he'll just wait another day (apparently still without nourishment). The next morning he returns to the bank, and it's *still* a bank holiday. Two days in a row! This is ridiculous, he concludes. He's famished!

He comes up with a solution. He suddenly remembers the name of a "Dr. Hammer," who took himself off to the Soviet Union years ago and opened a pencil factory there. (That would be Armand Hammer, who, after graduating from Columbia Medical School and visiting Russia for the first time in the early 1920s, has turned his interest from curing typhus to trading American grain for Russian furs, producing asbestos in the Urals, and becoming a pencil manufacturer, and is making billions more in liquid markets such as bourbon and oil.)

Somehow Hirschfeld has ascertained that in Russian the H becomes a G—that his name would become Girschfeld, and Hammer would become Gammer. He looks it up in a phone book under G and, sure enough, finds a listing for Dr. Gammer. Naturally encouraged, he then decides to try his luck with the pronunciation and with Russian numerals.

He makes the connection, somebody answers the phone, and he asks for *Vrach* Gammer. The other voice says something, which Hirschfeld doesn't understand. Seconds go by, and he tries it in English. "Are you Dr. Hammer?" The answer is "Yes." He explains his quandary. He says he hasn't eaten for thirty-six hours. He says he has no money, and it's a bank holiday, and there's no restaurant or dining room at the Lux.

Dr. Hammer has good news. He's hosting a party at the moment, and there are a lot of correspondents and other fellas Hirschfeld probably knows. So why doesn't he come over? Hirschfeld, ecstatic, asks how to get there, and Hammer tells him. There's a line of *droshkies* in front of the hotel, so just hail one and say to the driver, "'*Vrach* Gammer.' Everybody in Moscow knows me and knows where I live." Wonderful.

Hirschfeld hails a droshky and tells the driver, "*Vrach* Gammer." The man looks blank and asks a lot of questions in his tongue, to which Hirschfeld keeps insisting, "*Vrach* Gammer, *Vrach* Gammer." The driver calls over a couple of other drivers, and they too have no idea what the bushy-browed lunatic is hollering. *Oboy*, thinks Hirschfeld, *I'm in a real pickle*. He goes back into the hotel and picks up the phone again, but this time it's not so easy. The operator won't connect him and she too starts asking a lot of questions. Since he doesn't comprehend a syllable, Hirschfeld hangs up. And picks it up once more. On the third try, he reaches Dr. Hammer again, tells him what's been happening and mentions that nobody in Moscow seems to know him or where he lives. "I'm stranded! I'm starving!" he cries. "You're dealing with a wild man! You've got to send for me!" And Armand Hammer says he'll send somebody right over to pick him up.

Which he does. A sleek auto pulls up to the Lux, and Hirschfeld is delivered to a lavish thirty-room mansion, renowned as a haven for privileged American visitors. And there he meets people who will become good, devoted friends. One is Eugene Lyons, the UPI reporter; another is Walter Duranty, Moscow bureau chief of *The New York Times*. And then there's a Russian tenor named Sergei Radamsky, who will become an even greater pal, and a player in other tales to be told.

Russian doors are starting to open.

9
TO RUSSIA WITH LOVE

While back in Manhattan the artist Don Freeman is loitering in theater lobbies hoping to pick up discarded ticket stubs, Al Hirschfeld's press credentials are unlocking Moscow. Box seats for *Carmen*! A Soviet movie set! Supper at the Grand Hotel! Passes to a different play every night, including a Russified *Desire Under the Elms*! The city's jammed, Flo writes home, and their street "always looks like Broadway at theatre time." But a little more decrepit. "Evidently the revolution did a lot of damage," she notices, "and they haven't gotten around to repairing it yet."

She's quite an observer. "The people dress in anything and everything. Some wear hats, some bandanas and some a rag. You see one person with a nice suit and shoes and the next one may be a woman barefooted, with feet cracked from exposure, a man's army coat on her and very little else. Half of the women have bobbed hair held back with a comb like they do on the East side. Some look like they never think of dressing but just put on anything they find around the house. Others dress neatly and nicely, use a lot of makeup, bleach their hair and wear earrings like ours. You never saw such contrast."

What Hirschfeld sees are the poets gathering in Red Square to recite their poems, and a satirical magazine called *Crocodile* (*Krokodil*) with smart antigovernment drawings. "That was a transitory time," he recalls. "There was a great surge toward education, in a country where aristocracy didn't speak the language. They spoke French, they didn't speak Russian." Nor do the Hirschfelds, who keep Al's dictionary handy.

One evening, they spark a battle between two *droshky* drivers competing for their patronage. One grabs Al's right coat sleeve, the other his left, both yelling, with Al in the middle, also yelling. The winner drives them to their destination with Al in a daze, Flo in a tizzy, and all three of them laughing.

Thanks to the intervention of Sergei Radamsky, they're able to rent an apartment in his building with a bedroom, sitting room, foyer, kitchen, bath, and maid for a hundred rubles a month (which Flo describes on a snapshot as "our Russian Town House"). All that's missing is a double bed. They dine well—duck, pea soup, "bayguls"—but not well enough to keep the chill at bay. "I think we're going to freeze to death," Flo writes in late September. By the time the maid builds a fire, "it's bedtime and we don't need it."

What Al needs are visas and permits to paint and take photographs. Not only do such licenses cost rubles, but they're good for only a month! He's furious.

But within weeks, he's sending work to Folwell at the *Herald Tribune*, which shows him absorbing Russian graphics and personalizing them. *The Blue Blouse*, published in the *Trib* on October 21, 1928, depicts the creator and actors of a politically satiric outfit called Blue Blouse, a postrevolutionary movement that has spawned troupes in Japan, Germany, England, and Czechoslovakia. Hirschfeld is fascinated with theater-by-ferment—or ferment-through-theater—which will interest him all his life.

He's also providing the words with the art. "The Blue Blouse was organized at the Moscow State Institute of Journalism in 1923 by B. Youjanin, its present director, and was originally intended as a sort of spoken newspaper," he writes in his review of the revue. "I went prepared to see a show of some kind. Instead I found myself ushered into a meeting of the Taxi and Droshky Drivers' Union of Moscow." When the stage is cleared of the committee's desk and chairs, the performance begins, with folk dancing and acrobatics, songs and skits. "For sheer entertainment and color a Blue Blouse performance rivals many of the more elaborately staged revues one sees on Broadway."

He draws and reviews the neorealistic Kamerny Theatre, its work and theories, in a piece to appear in November. The Kamerny "stands for acting first," he writes, and "maintains its own training school, wherein it aspires to develop a super-actor who shall be able to play any role, with the reasonable exception of opera and ballet."

In a drawing that illustrates the importance of his role here, he presents the *Trib* with a graceful composite portraits of eight leading lights that is given an ungraceful headline, "Directing Minds of the Russian Cinema and Theater, Drawn From Life." Thanks to an interpreter, it seems that he and Flo have met and interviewed the foremost directors of theater and film, including Alexander Tairov, Vladimir Nemirovich-Danchenko, Esther Schub, Sergei Eisenstein, and Vsevolod Pudovkin—and even Anatoly Lunacharsky, the commissar of culture and education. Flo, as collaborator, tells Mom that they've hired the interpreter for ***their interviews***, because she's writing some of the articles to go with Al's art! "We've worked hard here."

Her groom confirms it. "Flo has been writing articles on the theatre," he informs Uncle Harry in St. Louis, "and I have been doing the drawings to accompany them."

The one-column piece to the right of Hirschfeld's artwork on page 4 of the *New York Herald Tribune* is a straightforward report on upcoming film production. "Moscow is about to have its own Hollywood. The foundation of a large studio and a 'movie' colony covering 150 acres, has been laid at Lenin's Hills on the outskirts of Moscow," it begins. The byline: Florence Hirschfeld.

So too the piece accompanying his drawing of *Princess Turandot* at the Vakhtangov Theatre, for the *Trib*, and the piece with his picture, "Drawn from Life at the Moscow Art Theater," depicting Stanislavsky and his actors.

Shivering aplenty and finding warmth only in fur, Al writes Uncle Harry that "Flo has proved herself a great companion—travelling 3rd class all the time." Complaining nonetheless, he adds that "the food here is lousy and the mice are large," but "this is more than compensated for by the beauty and color of the place."

To his friend Mac, he writes that "these trick stoves which heat a square patch of enameled tiles are useless. The tiles are supposed to retain the heat, well, they do, to the exclusion of everything else in the room. We stand against them all day and if we step three feet away from them it is like going outdoors in a blizzard. You remember how we felt before leaving Paris on our trip to the south—that is exactly how I feel now.

"I have not made a watercolor yet—what with spending every night at the theatre (gratis) and getting interviews all day—and doing caricatures—and then there's the weather—so you see my time is if not well spent—at least spent. However, I am doing my caricatures a bit more seriously than I am accustomed."

He invites fan mail. "If you like them," he tells Mac, "would appreciate your dropping a line to the *Trib* & telling them so. It may create a little interest." He signs his letter with a self-caricature, his eyes staring out from a hedge of hair, beard, and mustache: "no shave or haircut for the last 2 months—and still going strong." Adds Flo, "And don't think this drawing of him is exaggerated for it isn't. He's in paradise, hasn't shaved since the first week in Paris. But nobody cares in Russia—not even I."

Radamsky is going on tour, and they throw a party for him in their apartment. Flo is taken with the Russians' passion for American dance music, especially the Charleston. Even Al is kicking up his heels. "Mom, your son is dancing like a fool," she writes, "and I can hardly think for the racket he's making. What a nut he is."

But by late October, the pleasure is wearing thin. "When I leave here I don't want to see another theatre," he writes home. "We go every night and believe me I'm fed up with it. They treat us very nice here and on one occasion they announced us from the stage and we had to take a bow. Funny people these Russians." The *Trib* has provided cachet, but he's had enough.

"Babe wants to go south for a while so he can paint," Flo writes. "So far he's only had time for caricatures."

She herself wants to go south so she can cure her cold, her toothache, and her painful foot . . . and buy a double bed.

On the train to Kharkov, Al and Flo pool their rubles to make an immediate purchase for their third-class quarters. "We bought mattresses and pillows and sheets the minute we were on board and when we saw the nice clean things they gave us we felt quite comfortable," she reports, "especially since we had a nice roasted chicken with us and other good things to eat." At every station they run out and refill their new teakettle with hot water.

After arriving at their hotel, after painful discussions with the wrong people, they finally meet a Mrs. Berman who speaks English, invites them to dinner, and offers to help them find Aunt Hanna, the stepsister of Bekie Hirschfeld and Harry Rothberg.

"Imagine it, Mom, we never expected to find her alive!" But alive she is, this long-lost relation, nearly buried in a basement next to a bakery. Hanna recognizes Babe from a photograph and goes on and on in Kharkovian, punctating her baffling babble with strange little noises, as the helpful Mrs. Berman tries to translate. "She is a tiny little thing and quite old—says she's sixty-five but must be more," writes Flo. Her husband and children are dead, and for thirty-eight years she's lived alone in this dark cell with its stone floor, rags for rugs, single bed, and barrels of pickles and pickled tomatoes that she sells on the street, although there's also a china closet with four fancy plates and a wine decanter. She has no coal, so uses a one-plate kerosene stove. She has no toilet, so uses an old cooking pot in the woodshed. And if she's ill, "no wonder," adds Flo. "She doesn't eat enough to keep a canary alive."

Over tea, she relates a tale of woe, involving stolen gold rubles and the twenty dollars Uncle Harry sent last winter. Babe hands her fifty dollars on the spot. Next day, they return for lunch, and "poor soul she's gone out and bought meat cakes and wine and cake and tea," Flo writes. And she tells them about Bekie—what a beauty she was, how she was called "Rifky" and "Rookel," and how a gypsy told her when she was two years old that she'd have luck and go to another country to marry. Hirschfeld is captivated.

When they leave, she gives the young couple a small pillow covered with a case Bekie made when she was fifteen, four silver wine cups for them, and two for Bekie. She hugs Babe tight and tells him he has his mother's eyes and hands. When they tell her they want to take a snapshot, she becomes flustered and won't remove her bandana.

Leaving Hanna hunched on the doorstep, they move on to Yalta, a resort they consider "the prettiest bit of Russia" yet. Free from hunger and cold, Babe rushes to the balcony to sketch, savoring the first nontheatrical vista he's seen in weeks. Forty-five million miles from Broadway, he's working with newfound enthusiasm. In this seaside paradise set between the Black Sea and the Crimean mountains, where Chekhov wrote *The Cherry Orchard*, Hirschfeld paints fruit stands and palaces.

Here, too, Flo's aches and pains subside, which is no surprise in a place well stocked in sanatoriums. She writes to Mom, "Tell Pop I make good use of the big pocket he put on my coat. I don't carry a purse so I stuff the pocket with dictionaries, gloves, hankies, cigarettes, make up and candy and what not."

By the end of October, they're on the *Pestel*, sailing to Georgia, to ports unknown, and having a glorious time—especially because caviar is plentiful and the ship's doctor comes up with a remedy for Flo's foot. They arrive in Tiflis (the future Tbilisi) for a big November 7 holiday and enter a town decorated "with oodles of red and pictures everywhere of Lenin and Marx." Between oodles and canvases, Hirschfeld buys himself a pair of Caucasian boots and has his first haircut and shave in four months. Flo has her first bath in three weeks. And then there's all that laundry! Of such events are letters written.

As Mickey Mouse sails onto the screen in *Steamboat Willie*, Mr. and Mrs. Al Hirschfeld are winding through snowcapped mountains on dark Persian roads to the light of caravan campfires and the sound of camel bells. As their driver brings them into Tehran through a huge mosaic gateway, they pass men seated on carpets, drinking tea and strumming odd instruments. And, eureka! The hotel has a double bed!

The weather is perfect here in mid-November, the streets a-bustle with open shops selling "piles of queer pottery and gay materials and strange fruits and the funniest breads. Rolled out as large as a dresser scarf and as thin as paper," Flo observes. "Both men and women dye their hands a bright red and it's quite the fashion for men to henna their hair and beards—an orange henna—weird looking. Even the white horses have their feet and tails and manes hennaed and wear bright blue bead necklaces."

The cafés are patronized only by men, who sit smoking pipes and sipping tea, listening to Persian songs. Women on the street, hiding behind black veils, look her up and down. "Don't think many women come here," she adds. And a lot fewer now, after a movie theater for women burned to the ground two weeks ago—the work of "a party of men opposed to such liberties for women," says the *Chicago Daily Tribune*.

Hirschfeld has come to paint, but painters are unfamiliar in these parts, so on his first outing he's escorted by four policemen. To no avail. He's mobbed by gesticulating natives, so he gives it another try in another neighborhood. He's rather jolly about it. Hirschfeld loves an audience. "Lot of fun working here," he writes to his pal Mac a week later. "I have a policeman call for me every morning at 9 oclock and bring me back for lunch—he appears again at one and deposits me back in my hotel at 5. His official job is beating away the people. Some service, huh? The reason for all this attention is because the natives are quite fanatic and object to being photographed or painted. Something like Marocco only they mean business here. The American Consul was killed about 6 months ago for photographing a baptismal."

In order to safeguard this American artist, the authorities insist on providing an escort. "So they showed me a photograph of the Police Department of Teheran, about 30 fellows on a photograph. And they asked me to pick one out," he later tells friends, "so I picked out a likely-looking fellow with a tremendous mustache, like Chester Conklin." The man speaks no English but remains at Hirschfeld's side as he sets up the easel and sets to work. "He had a little whip with him, and anybody who would stand behind me would get a hock with this whip."

Somewhere along the way, he and Flo meet Amin Ghanima (or Ghanima Amin, being referred to in their letters as both "Mr. Amin" and "Mr. Ghanima")—a fellow later identified by Hirschfeld as the Singer sewing machine concessionaire for Persia—who drives them around from bazaars to cafés to the ruins of Babylon. "It's nothing short of a miracle the way we've found someone who practically adopts us every place we go," oohs Flo.

"The color is not quite as vivid as N. Africa or the costumes quite as spectacular," Hirschfeld writes to Mac. "The hat is something like a brown derby without a rim. The souks are very much like Tunis—all cement covered," he says of the marketplaces. "They are very much larger, however. Today I walked for 3 hours in one direction without reaching the end. They are inexhaustable and practically impossible to work in. The other day I sat myself down and the usual crowd gathered—except in this case the crowd was more than usual—I had seven policemen with me but they were helpless. The crowd gathered like they do at Times Sq. during the world series. One ass fell through a show case and the store keeper tried to soak me for a new glass. It was too funny to try & describe. All the cops shouting and beating the people away. Burros, camels, men with carpets, others with bundles on their backs big enough to hold a Ford," he goes on. "All watching the great man at work.

"The cops by the way look like the soldiers of a 'Flit' ad"—Flit being the popular insecticide whose ads are drawn by one Theodor Seuss Geisel (Dr. Seuss's maiden name).

And thence to Baghdad. "The place is a fairyland of color," Flo writes. "My eyes aren't big enough to see everything. I've read at least a hundred stories of Bagdad and I'm thrilled to death to see it."

Hirschfeld paints the town. In the first week, he turns out ten watercolors, although he's destroying as many as he paints. "He is so happy to be working after not being able to do a thing in Moscow except of course the caricatures," Flo says, then, "I wonder if they're appearing and if my stories are too. I doubt the latter. Gee, I'll get a thrill that'll probably kill me if I see my stuff with Babe's. The suspense is terrible." In the meantime, she watches a set-to between Arabs ("looking just like the sheiks we see in the movies"), admires the perpetual pageant, and gets her nails done by the manicurist to the Queen.

Scrapping plans for Cairo, they decide to return to Paris and have Al's pictures framed. They arrive at dawn.

It's Christmas Day, and no room at the inn. Alas, the weary travelers from the East, exhausted after six days in an auto, eight days on a boat, and one day on a train, are compelled to while away seven hours at the Dôme until they can check in. Which gives them a chance to read the papers and catch up on their mail. Gleefully, Flo learns that her articles have indeed been published with Babe's pictures in the *Trib*! "Don't we make a great team?" she writes exultantly to Mom. "Hot dogs."

10
THE *TIMES* OF HIS LIFE

Ah, Paree!

"Hirschfeld, a young American artist who has made a name for himself as a theatrical caricaturist in New York, but whose true vocation is the art of painting in water-colors, is one of those who has heard the call of the East—that is to say, of the old East which is still holding out against the Western flood that is inexorably leveling men and manners all over the world," writes B. J. Kospoth, city editor and Jacques of all trades for the *Chicago Tribune*'s Paris edition, on January 13, 1929. "He has just returned to Paris from a six months journey which took him through Russia, Persia and Mesopotamia, and is showing the pictures that he painted on the way, often under considerable difficulties, at the Galerie Havard Frères on the Boulevard Montparnasse, before taking them with him to the United States."

Georges Bal at the *Trib* is especially taken with *The Arab*, which he calls "a remarkable study of human physiognomy," and *Le Café Arabe à Bagdad*, depicting "the halt of the caravan at the gates of the city, with the kneeling camels, and the view of the picturesque street with old houses ornamented with moucharabis."

Kospoth suggests that Hirschfeld's watercolors would make a beautiful album. "They are the work of a capable and sensitive artist, who deserves being taken seriously, and who has excellently performed his part in fixing for future generations the features of the Orient which are unveiling themselves only to be consumed by our devastating gaze."

The voyagers sail home on the *Paris*, arriving in New York on January 23, 1929—and their journey makes the next day's *Times*, in which Hirschfeld humors the reporter. "'I went to Teheran to paint the Shah,' Mr. Hirschfeld said, 'but unfortunately he had to go south. He is a fine man with modern ideas. I am afraid the Mullahs will get him. They are an unclubby lot.'"

A week later, the *New York Evening Journal* displays two watercolors and two Hirschfelds. Both wearing pinky rings, Al and Flo are shown examining a robe of Resht embroidery they picked up in Persia. They've also brought back a hand-carved wooden statue of a woman holding two spears, with a snake coiled atop her head, and "a Persian beggar's outfit," which Hirschfeld tells a reporter "consists of a large wooden pot, beautifully carved, to hang from the beggar's arm by heavy silver chains, and a metal cane, the head of which is a replica of a man's face with two horns. The awesome looking cane is carried by the mendicant for the purpose of 'scaring away evil spirits.'"

Not to be undone by the downtown press, two Washington Heights papers run pieces—one identifying the famous young couple as Mr. and Mrs. David Hirschfeld and providing an incorrect address. Mr. Hirschfeld "has put upon canvas and into sketch books much of the picturesqueness that his eyes beheld," and Mrs. Hirschfeld—described in one piece as "a free lance journalist," and in the other as "a dramatic critic"—is planning to write a book, accompanied by her husband's illustrations, based upon her "careful account of their impressions and reactions."

Mr. Hirschfeld mentions his beard (which the *Times* describes as black and one of the gazettes describes as brown). The reporter discloses that "their eyes are still blinded by the blaze of color that means Damascus" and that "it will take some time before they are able to settle down to the rather staid and regulated life of Washington Heights." Not likely.

With or without the editorial collaboration of his spouse, Hirschfeld has been working on a book about the Russian theater, with hundreds of drawings of the actors, directors, and productions. He has even persuaded Lunacharsky, the culture commissar, to write the foreword. Soon after his return, he takes the manuscript and drawings down to Boni & Liveright—the estimable house famous for publishing Dreiser, Trotsky, and even Al's friend Alex King, who's done the illustrations for O'Neill's *The Emperor Jones*—and leaves it with the publisher Albert Boni.

Boni & Liveright is the name of the firm all right, but Boni left ten years ago and set up his own shop. Whichever place he submits it, Hirschfeld hears nothing. After three weeks, he calls Boni.

Hirschfeld: "The secretary said, 'Mr. Boni is in Europe.' And I said, 'When is he coming back?' She said, 'He'll be back in a couple of weeks.' And I said, 'Please have him call me.'

"So when he came back he called me, and I said, 'Well, what about the book?' He said, 'What book?' I said, 'Don't you remember?' I said, 'Listen, I'm coming down to see you.'"

Years later, telling the story to Studs Terkel, he says, "I was a young man then, and I had a black beard." Telling the same story to the art director Steven Heller, he says, "I had a red beard and was kind of startling-looking."

Whatever its color, the beard, at least, makes an impression.

"I came into his office and I said, 'Do you remember me?' He did. 'I left my book here with all the drawings.' He said, 'Well, it must be around here someplace. We'll find it.' He called me and said, 'We can't find it. You're sure you left it here?' I said, 'Absolutely.'

"They combed the place, and they never did find it. And nobody stole it, because not one of those drawings ever showed up across all these years. I don't know *what* happened with it. The cleaning lady must have just tossed it out or something. It was just one of those unfortunate things. But that was a year down the drain, with that thing. It was impossible to do it over again, so I forgot it. The only ones that survived are the ones that ran in the *Tribune*."

His arrangement with the *Times*, where he has still not met anyone upstairs, has gone on for almost two years when he's at the Belasco one night in 1929. At intermission he bumps into the ubiquitous Dick Maney ("who seems to be some kind of a spiritual advisor or something," Hirschfeld chuckles). While they're chatting, a stranger strolls over and joins the conversation. "You fellows know each other," Maney says.

Hirschfeld and the stranger stare at each other, whereupon Maney introduces him to Sam Zolotow.

Zolotow, a genial, barking, cigar-chomping news chomper, came to the *Times* in 1919 as an office boy. Soon he was adding to his income as the office bookie. Then he was publishing the *Advance Theatrical Guide*—or "the *Zolotow*"—a weekly mimeographed sheet providing dates for impending Broadway shows that became indispensable to the industry. In the mid-1920s, he started a messenger service, delivering items from hot tickets to lost keys. But most significantly, he's been an unshakable legman, bringing in the day's theatrical info to George S. Kaufman, the drama editor (and writer, collaborator, or director of such as *The Royal Family*, *The Front Page*, and *Animal Crackers*), who decides what gets into the *Times*.

"You're the most mysterious man on the paper," Zolotow tells Hirschfeld. "Nobody's ever seen you." Hirschfeld says, "Well, I've never tried to get past the doorman." Zolotow says, "Next time, come up and meet the fellas in the drama department." So Hirschfeld does and meets Kaufman and J. Brooks Atkinson, the elegant young theater critic.

He now moves to the Sherwood Studios at 58 West Fifty-seventh Street, a large brick-and-stone building wrapped around the southeast corner of Sixth Avenue. "I got fed up with the Village," he recalls. "It became a tourist trap, with people throwing up on the stoop." But more than that, West Fifty-seventh is a smart and arty stretch and quite the place to be. Painters and sculptors, decorators and composers populate this airy crosstown street on both sides, featuring Carnegie Hall, Steinway Hall, the Russian Tea Room, and the Art Students League.

Al and Flo settle in studio 35, along with their curios and Al's increasing collection of phonograph records. They throw dinner parties, host Wednesday-night soirees, have dinner with Mom and Pop every Friday, see Big Al and his family from California.

Less occasionally, they see Flo's little girl from Pennsylvania. Renee Conard, now eight, resides with her father, stepmother, and half sister. When Flo's in the mood, she's brought to her by train.

"She absolutely adored Al Hirschfeld," says Michele Dabbeekeh, Renee's daughter. "She'd sit and watch him draw, just quiet as could be. She said he was very kind to her, and she always said very nice things about him. She really enjoyed her visits to New York when she was visiting the two of them, all good memories for my mother."

But Renee is an interruption for Flo, whose maternal yearnings or pangs of remorse seem to cause her no grief. "My grandmother was probably very selfish. It was all about *her* and wanting to get into show business," says Dabbeekeh. "My grandmother loved to travel—I know that she'd been to Russia and all over—and I think it was all about *her*."

Hirschfeld and Gordon Kahn are lunchtime regulars at Dave's Blue Room, a deli on Seventh Avenue at Fifty-second, described by habitué Milton Berle as "the big hangout for people in this business, and also the Syndicate boys and the detective squad, before we all switched over to Lindy's." But early on, when proprietor Dave Kleckner is still hungry for business, Hirschfeld and Kahn come up with a gimmick. Instead of handing out free bean sandwiches with every beer, they suggest, he should make a meat sandwich so thick he "could tout it as a 'meal in your hand' and charge a dollar for it," remembers Gordon's son Tony. It goes on the menu as the "Fresser's Special."

Next comes the Hellinger Happiness sandwich for a dollar, named for another regular, the Broadway columnist Mark Hellinger. Dave's no dummy. Coddle the customer, name a sandwich after him, make him yours for life as they do over at Reuben's. Once he has names between the bread, Dave decides he wants them on the wall, too, as they do over at Sardi's. No sooner does Dave ask than Hirschfeld delivers, sending over a batch of caricatures he did for *New York Amusements*—of Reginald Carrington, Ed Wynn, Billie Yarbough, Billy B.Van,

Eric Dressler, Jane Cowl, Effie Shannon, Will Mahoney. Dave gets the performers to sign them, wraps them in green wood frames, and hangs them up. And again, Hirschfeld gets a free lunch.

Meanwhile, his output for MGM promotes the films, the stars, even the newsreels—showing up on the one-, three-, six-, twenty-four-, and forty-eight-sheet posters attached to surfaces from theater display cases to the sides of buildings. His posters for King Vidor's *Hallelujah*, the "all-talking all-singing all-negro drama," sing out in resplendent color. So do his Laurel and Hardys, two stooges he sees as the number 10—Laurel being the 1 and Hardy the 0. In an ink and collage, he tucks them under a quilt. "I sewed that myself," he says, with a laugh.

When Howard Dietz and the composer Arthur Schwartz write the score for *The Little Show*, starting them off on their longtime collaboration, Hirschfeld's drawing for the *Times* includes Fred Allen, the juggler turned comic (and soon to be radio star), a favorite friend Hirschfeld descibes as "a cantankerous sourpuss with a heart of gold." In 1927, he married one of Flo's best friends, Portland Hoffa, a co-chorine from the *Scandals*, *Follies*, and *Vanities*. When Fred's at work, Portland comes over to the Hirschfelds' to play poker.

Otherwise, Al and the gang drive out to Coney Island. In town, they hit the jazz joints, the clubs, and gyp joints that call themselves clubs: the Dizzy Club, the Encore Club, the Stag Club, the Onyx Club, Jimmy Durante's Club Durant, and one Ming Soy. Hirschfeld's at them all. He's even at the Hotsy Totsy Club in the wee hours of July 13, 1929, when part-owner "Legs" Diamond and an associate eliminate a couple of "stout waterfront fighters" (as the *Trib* descibes them) at the bar—and is presumably in the crowd "staggering and tumbling down the stairs into Broadway" as the unconscious are dragged out, "some of them the casualties of terror and alcohol, others of bullets and blackjacks."

Albert Hershfield vs Variety Inc.

Al Hirschfeld is irate (or pretends to be) and sues *Variety* for libel. This is the offensive material from the showbiz bible's front page of October 23, 1929:

> Beards for young men may be coming into fashion. Half a dozen Broadwayites under 30 have grown hirsute adornments in the best Civil War style.
>
> Opinion among the disciples of hanging gardens seems to be that whiskers bring dignity and importance to the wearer and may help financially.
>
> Broadway's best known youthful beard-wearer is Al Hershfield, who does art work for theatres and film companies. Al admits that before he got the beard idea he struggled without success, couldn't make an impression and was generally discouraged.
>
> But once his boyish face became a landscape he began to click, to get commissions. People asked him who he was, noticed him with interest and found him talented.

Hirschfeld laughs and calls it *insane* . . . until Portland Hoffa's brother-in-law, a lawyer named Hershkowitz, urges him to take a shot at legal action and see how far it'll go. On October 28, 1929—a day before the stock market crashes and *Variety* reports "Wall Street Lays An Egg"—Hershkowitz serves it.

On November 6, in the "Literati" column on page 60, *Variety* slaps back at the summons served "when one Albert Hershfield said he felt badly, about $100,000 worth, because 'Variety' had said on its front page that Al was hiding behind a bush." As a final thrust: "Herschfield is indirectly connected with the theatre. That's probably why he wanted publicity. He got it, beard and all."

The case begins. Al takes the stand.

"'Is it not a fact that you, Mr. Hirschfeld, make your living by ridiculing people? That you make cartoons of them—vicious cartoons of them?'" he recalls of the opposition's question. "For the tiniest fraction of a second, he had me," he says. "But, adopting the suave manner of Osgood Perkins, I ployed, 'Mr. Driscoll, I am not a cartoonist, vicious or otherwise; I am a caricaturist. I consider my work satirical, not comical.'

"Mr. Driscoll seemed stunned by this brilliant repartee and quickly changed his line of attack. 'Perhaps you would be good enough,' he purred, 'to tell us the difference between satire and comedy? That is . . . if I am right in assuming, uh, that there is a difference and that you could explain the difference to us ignoramuses?'"

Whether the ignoramuses get wise or not, the case drags on, and the sealed verdict of November 17, 1932, reads, "The Jury say that they find a verdict for Defendant [*Variety*]." Years later, Hirschfeld claims that the jury found *Variety* guilty and awarded him damages of six cents.

It's a better story.

11
BALI HIGH

Al's output and income remain strong in papers and magazines, and in 1930 and 1931, he's making steady deposits in their joint account at the Corn Exchange Bank on Broadway and Fifty-fifth. Roger Furse, en route to a designing career, comes to town and takes a studio on West Fifty-seventh Street, just down the block, and Francis Musgrave arrives predictably pence-less. His brief visit makes the society page of the *Los Angeles Times*. "Francis Musgrave (perhaps better known as the Goat Man of Montparnasse) . . . found himself broke in New York recently," a columnist writes. "He just won an automobile in one of those title-guessing contests and promptly sold it to someone who could afford gas. Now he's back in his favorite Paris café."

In fact, Mussy is living in a two-room flat far from the Dôme with a parrot and a sweetie named Kay, and he's clutching at straws. Although he's doing the occasional book or theater review for the *Times* or the *Boston Evening Transcript* and will appear in the first issue of *The New Review*, he writes to Al for money. As if on cue, Hirschfeld almost simultaneously produces one of his most eloquent lithographs, *Art and Industry*, of an artist and his dog begging on the pavement outside the British Museum.

In New York, his old friend Howard Simon is on the upswing, with an exhibition of drawings and woodcuts at the Civic Club.

His work is being published in quarterlies such as *The Print Connoisseur*, and he's illustrating fine book after fine book, including *Jews Without Money*, the fierce and poignant novel by Michael Gold (né Itzok Isaac Granich) about his childhood on the Lower East Side. A proud Communist and literary critic, Gold is also editor in chief of *New Masses*, the radical gazette, which was born in 1926 with a wallop of wit and indignation.

In a lighter vein, Gordon Kahn's in Hollywood, working for Sam Marx on the MGM lot. (Overnight, Marx has become Irving Thalberg's story editor.) Kahn's letters to Hirschfeld are studded with boyishly vulgar references, but tender just the same. He misses the lights of old Broadway and the friends. "Sometimes, when I'm putting on the feed-bag I think of Flo's cooking, than which there is nothing whicher," he writes. "I'd give the whole Brown Derby's commissary for one slab of roast beef the way she makes it." He has a place where, he adds, "your oil sketch of me hangs prominently. It's admired by everybody who looks at it." This includes a schoolteacher named Barbara, whom he marries in May.

Hirschfeld thirsts for a project. He misses the old saloons, and nowadays speakeasies fill the bill. So, even as Prohibition lingers on, he submits a proposal for *Favorite Recipes of New York Barmen*. An editor at E. P. Dutton is somewhat interested—but how about some "reading matter" to go along with the pictures? Hirschfeld enlists Kahn, and together they knock out a roundup of their favorite joints and barkeeps, with patter on the chow, décor, and clientele.

Here are Dan of Bill's Bar, Bill of the Stonewall, Philip of the Bath Club, Carlos of the Tony's, Jimmy of Jack's, along with drink recipes elegant and toxic. "Let nobody dare say it was not well-researched," Hirschfeld will remark years later of their hangouts uptown and down. "Every single spécialité de la maison was tried over and over by my pal Gordon Kahn and me until we passed out testing it for our reading public." In his drawing of Jack's, he puts Kahn on a bar stool.

But he lets Kahn drop. "I got my listing of the speakeasies from police headquarters," he'll later reveal, first-personing the research and writing and knocking his pal from the tale. "They had 75,000 speakeasies listed in Greater New York City. And I went around to quite a few of them and did drawings of the bartenders and the clientele and put together a book. I remember going to Jack and Charlie's, which later became 21, and there was Jimmy Walker, our mayor; police commissioner, Supreme Court judge, all breaking the law. It was a silly time, but an exciting time."

Manhattan Oases will come out in October 1932. Prohibition will go out in December 1933.

In the fall of 1931, Hirschfeld sends word to those who need to know where he is, illustrated by a dark-haired, dark-bearded, single-browed, one-eyed, bow-tied self-portrait.

The Depression is on, and while it's not affecting Hirschfeld or his income, the mood is grim and he wants to get out of town. In preparation, he's been reading up on the South Seas, gearing up for a romantic place to paint. Empowered by a "To Whom It May Concern" letter from the drama editor Arthur Folwell—introducing Hirschfeld as a member of the *Herald Tribune* staff and appreciating any courtesies extended to him—Al and Flo leave New York, drive cross-country to California, and sail off for Tahiti.

Whatever Gauguin saw here, Hirschfeld does not.

The "arrival of the 'S. S. Monowai' of the New Zealand Steamship Company at the Tahitian port of Papeete every twenty-eight days," he recalls, "was the big social event of the island," and he's repelled by the rumrunners, gangsters, "pimply-faced natives," and visitors who transform themselves into shirtless "artists."

To the rescue: Miguel Covarrubias. He and his wife, Rosa—recently married at the country home of Alex King—are honeymooning in Bali, the Indonesian island that will become his paradise. And not just his.

"Miguel had written to me extolling the virtues—climate, food, people, music, art, theater, dance—of Bali in response to my misanthropic account of life in Tahiti. The 'colorful' natives of Tahiti (playing Portuguese ukeleles and singing Hawaiian songs written in Tin Pan Alley by Irving Berlin) seemed imported from Central Casting," Hirschfeld goes on. "He would write from Bali, telling me what a beautiful place it was, and I would tell him what a stink-hole Tahiti was, and he wrote that if I ever got over to his part of the world, he'd leave his bicycle, dishes, and all the rest for me."

Hastily, Hirschfeld makes a deal. In exchange for a couple of watercolors, he and Flo can hop the next freighter to New Zealand. Another picture gets them to Sydney, then across the Great Barrier Reef to Makassar, and finally aboard a steamer to Bali. By this time, Covarrubias has left, but he's asked a friend—a representative of KLM, the Dutch steamship line—to meet the Hirschfelds at the dock.

Ninety miles later and deep into the bounty of Bali, the Hirschfelds arrive at Belaluan and the sprawling household of Prince Gusti Alit Oka. Here, within Gusti's walled compound, they take possession of their hand-me-down pavilion—and Covarrubias's knives, forks, bicycle, and houseboy—for fifteen dollars a week. It's perfect, and exactly what he hoped for. "The food was great; the people, the music, everything about it made it the last paradise," he will later recall. "Miguel had seen that, and he was right."

It's Shangri-la, awakening things in him he doesn't know are there. With his training, talent, and ability to react to what's happening before him, everything clicks.

He types up a vocabulary list of the Malay-Balinese words he knows he'll need: *matahari* for "sun," *bulan* for "moon," *tuan* for "gentleman," *daging* for "meat," *nasi* for "rice." *Penna hitam* is "the black pen." *Warna apa dinding?* means "What color is the wall?"

Meanwhile, the missus is bending to the customs of the country. Here, where a wife belongs to her husband, where her duty is to care for her lord and master, the *Vanities* girl is doing her darndest. After Al grills some critter on the fire, Flo takes the greasy pan down to a stream to wash it in cold water.

The Hirschfelds spend close to a year here, a year of endless summer, discovering misty lakes, active volcanoes, rosebushes twenty feet high, tree trunks covered in orchids, stepped rice fields of quilted green, witch doctors, and screeching monkeys—and inheriting a Russian-born German émigré named Walter Spies, who has built a bamboo house in Ubud, a museum, and an aquarium. A musician and painter himself, Spies is Bali's best booster and tour guide. So much did Covarrubias absorb from him that he, Covarrubias, is now working on a socioanthropological history to be called *Island of Bali*, and to become a bestseller.

Even he himself is surprised to find that "although the artist is regarded as a preferred member of the community," Covarrubias writes, "there is no separate class of artists, and a sculptor is simply a 'carver' or a figure-maker, and the painter is a picture-maker." In other words, there is no word for "artist." But Hirschfeld does his picture-making nonetheless, not only with paint, but also with his 16-millimeter camera. Schooled in the ways of silents, he prints up signs to introduce the scenes he shoots: "Legong: A legendary story done in dance" . . . "The Topeng . . . about 200 masks are used (dance for sick children)" . . . "Cock Fighting—The Balinese National Pastime—In the event of both roosters being killed all bets are off." His subjects wear feathers, fans, the hair of shaggy beasts. He shoots monkeys, markets, Flo chomping on tortoise meat. All very theatrical.

Let metropolitan primitivism run wild in Harlem and Paris. Hirschfeld finds his in Bali.

And he finds his *line*.

"The Balinese sun seemed to bleach out all color, leaving shadows, so that things became black and white. Everything was pure line. The people became line drawings walking around," he remembers. "I knew that my life would never be the same."

And then, as if utopia weren't ducky enough, in paddles Charlie Chaplin. He and his brother Sydney are on a cruise of the Orient when Syd suggests stopping off on Bali. They arrive at the dock by rowboat. Sometimes Al recalls going down to meet the boat because he and Chaplin have known each other since the early Pathé days, but it's more likely they know *of* each other—and with Hirschfeld on paper, Chaplin on screen (now a soaring star after *The Kid* and *The Gold Rush*), how could they not? Other times he says, "I met him ten years ago on the island of Bali," and "before the day was over we became fast friends."

The Chaplins move on to the Bali Hotel in Denpasar and are invited to dinner that evening at the Hirschfeld pavilion. "Our landlord has a pig that he'd like to roast and we have a hundred and fifty pound turtle that has lived long enough," Flo writes (as Al undoubtedly dictates). "We shall eat to the tunes of a Balinese orchestra and fifty or so natives inhaling rice."

After dinner, the four take a stroll, and the night is "dark and sultry. Not a breath of air stirred," Chaplin recalls, "then suddenly a sea of fireflies, acre upon acre of them, raced over the rice fields in undulating waves of blue light. From another direction came sounds of jingling tamborines and clashing gongs in rhythmic tonal patterns. 'A dance going on somewhere,' said Hirschfeld. 'Let's go.'"

Winding through a group of natives, they come upon two ten-year-old girls dressed in embroidered sarongs and tinsel headdresses, swaying in a religious *legong*, dancing to the music of a gamelan orchestra. Chaplin is drawn to a *garuda* dance, in which the main character wears wooden wings. He rushes up, picks up a wing, and does a dance of his own. The natives scream with laughter.

"I told the compound, all the people in the little district where I lived, that he was a very famous man and a comedian and so on, in movies," Hirschfeld remembers. "They didn't know what movies were like because there was no electricity on the island of any kind, so they'd never seen a movie. It's probably the only spot in the world where he was not known. In the most remote sections of China they knew Chaplin, but in Bali they didn't know him." As Covarrubias puts it, "To the Balinese, Bali is the entire world."

Intrigued, Chaplin decides to carry out an experiment, to see if his comedy is universal. In progressive accounts, Hirschfeld remarks that Chaplin performs for five houseboys or seven houseboys; or, later, it's a crowd. Sometimes he recalls Chaplin wearing a pith helmet, other times a toupee. Whatever's he's wearing, Chaplin puts it on and lets it spring off his head, and the natives howl with laughter. They then toss their turbans in the air. "That was the experiment," Hirschfeld says. "He had wanted to see if the Balinese would laugh at his pantomime. They did."

By the end of it, Chaplin has acquired a new identity, because the Balinese "have a difficult time with European names," Hirschfeld says. "I was 'the bearded man,' my wife was 'the beautiful lady,' and he was 'the funny man.'"

Chaplin is having such fun he drops out of the tour. "The ship went off without him," Hirschfeld says, "and he stayed with me."

But not for long. After three days, the funny man contracts dysentery and is shipped off to a hospital in Singapore. But before he leaves, he buys some watercolors, providing Hirschfeld and the missus with enough lucre to get back to New York and live well for the next six months.

And those watercolors keep on traveling. They go with Chaplin to Hollywood, where he marries Paulette Goddard, then with her to Switzerland when she marries Erich Maria Remarque, the German author of *All Quiet on the Western Front*, a savage bestselling novel about the angst of young German soldiers during and after World War I (and soon followed by the Oscar-winning movie version). And then, because Remarque has a great collection of his own with little room for Balinese landscapes, they go on the market.

The year 1932 brings Bali to Broadway. On December 4, Hirschfeld's drawing of Fanny Brice and George Jessel, headlining a stage show at the Paramount, runs in the *Trib*. Two other characters accompany them—their shadows. Such is the influence of the culture and its shadow puppets.

12
THE GIRLFRIEND

The first issue of *Americana* has recently appeared, and 1932 is a poor time to launch any magazine, especially one brimming with left-wing satire. Hirschfeld will remember being the coeditor with Alex King, but King's widow, Margie King Barab, says not, and he's been off in Bali anyway. The masthead shows King as editor with the militantly antimilitant caricaturist George Grosz and the writer-critic Gilbert Seldes as associates. No mention of Al, although, upon his return, he's soon available—as artist, adviser, and photography stylist.

"We would pose photographs—a pregnant woman looking at a stork in the zoo, or a kid shining shoes at the base of a Lincoln statue for Lincoln's Day, that kind of foolishness, you know—and occasionally retouch a photograph . . . the Statue of Liberty holding a pawnbroker's three balls," he remembers. "Alex did most of the drawings, and every now and then I'd do a drawing for them, but I spent most of my time thinking up ideas for photographs."

An early statement on the editorial page declares: "We are not Republicans because . . . the present office holders have dismally failed in leadership and intelligence and because the moneyed oligarchy that runs and ruins this country is animated by stupid and shameless greed best exemplified by the Republican party. As for Mr. Hoover personally, we rest content by presenting the record of his flabbiness and incompetence." And "We are not Democrats because . . ." and "We are not Socialists because . . ." and "We are not Communists because . . ." and then: "We are Americans who believe that our civilization exudes a miasmic stench and that we had better prepare to give it a decent but rapid burial. We are the laughing morticians of the present."

Other contributors include such writers and artists as Theodore Dreiser, James Thurber, E. E. Cummings, William Steig, Will Cotton, Covarrubias, and Eugene Fitsch (with whom Hirschfeld took an etching class at the Art Students League for an evening term in 1927). But King is most of it, using different styles and signatures to fill the pages. If the pages even get filled. "They were given a page to do whatever they wanted," Hirschfeld says. "Ten dollars. And if they didn't feel they wanted to do anything, they could leave the page blank. It was that kind of a thing."

King is an acquired taste. Hirschfeld is devoted to him, his Viennese accent, his peculiar humor. The ambitious, glamorous Clare Boothe Brokaw, a rising star at *Vanity Fair*, values his savvy and sensibility. But not everyone does. Helen Lawrenson—the acid-inked writer and inamorata of Condé Nast—recalls that "King, who did a piece or two for *Vanity Fair*, although he was never on the staff, as he later claimed, was an exuberant, verbose little man who was not the best raconteur of his time but was indisputably the most persistent, to the point where, frankly, when we saw him coming, we would groan."

But Al and Alex share a political view, which often takes them left of the beaten path, although "I think Al was more involved than Alex was," remembers Margie.

Americana will be published on and off for something more than a year, during which Hirschfeld provides frequent opinion. In July, he contributes a wood carving called the *Woodin Nickel*, an oak caricature of FDR's multifaceted treasury secretary. Not only is William H. Woodin a moneyed adviser who's been appointed to solve the Depression, but he's also a composer of orchestral pieces and, more regrettably, *Raggedy Ann's Sunny Songs*.

In August, when Covarrubias gets a glorious full-color spread in *Vanity Fair*, displaying Hollywood's deities on the beach at Malibu, Hirschfeld produces a black-and-white cartoon called *Germany Speaks*. In this spare line drawing, a barrel-chested von Hindenburg is holding Hitler drawn as a dachshund on a leash as a stereotypically stooped and bearded Jew comments, "Aw, stop squawking, she's just a harmless bitch." In November 1933, he produces *Inflation*, showing Hoover's swollen head atop a skeleton, puffing a cigar.

Despite the magazine's attitude, or because of it, *Americana* soon folds or, as Hirschfeld prefers to say, is acquired by Condé Nast. "They felt that we were taking circulation away from *Vanity Fair*, which was floundering, and so they offered everybody jobs on *Vanity Fair*," he claims. "Alex became an associate editor, Cummings went there—he wrote about burlesque," and more political articles and caricatures come to *Vanity Fair* at *Americana*'s demise.

Hirschfeld, who's wanted to break into *Vanity Fair* anyway, now gets his chance—with a spread in November 1933. "The Supreme Bench" shows the "nine old men" of the Supreme Court aged and dozing. (When he reprises the mighty justices in a 1937 lithograph, he'll make them even more crotchety.)

And his output in the papers remains steady. The way the payments work is that he's paid by the producers of the shows he draws, through their press agents—fifteen dollars per column width in the Manhattan papers, twelve dollars in the *Brooklyn Daily Eagle*. So he comes up with a scheme, doing his *Eagle* drawings in a pennant shape so exaggerated that one picture might be eight columns wide.

"Dick Maney said, 'I'm not paying for the last three columns. There's nothing in there, it's just an empty space!' Hirschfeld recalls. "I also had a design for a circle thing, a pie. This was a swindle of the most horrifying kind," he says, delightedly. "I had a lot of fun."

But not at home. In September, he gets an eviction notice, and he disappears. Home with Mom? Back to Paris? The New York City Directory lists no Al or Flo in 1933 or 1934, separately or together. These are the years they split.

Why?

"I guess it would be my grandmother," says Michele Dabbeekeh. "Guessing off the top of my head, she got bored with him."

"He was a very intense guy," says Frances Hershkowitz, daughter of Artie the lawyer. "He was always *on*, and she just couldn't take it anymore. She left Al. That's what Portland said. He was very demanding, and she couldn't give her whole life to this man. It just was too much for her."

"I do know that Flo was the one who left," agrees Margie. "And Al won her back. And then he was the one who left. He couldn't bear the fact that she'd left him and not vice versa, and he wooed her back and then *he* left *her*."

"He was going to go on some trip, and she didn't want him to," remembers another family friend. "He wasn't angry; it was just something he was going to do. But to show how annoyed she was, she shaved off all her hair, which he said was one of her good features. He went on the trip anyway. And when he came back, he expected some kind of big 'Oh, my darling, you're back!' but she was doing something and didn't even look up. That was sort of the catalyst. The hair gone and not even looking up when he came in."

Years later, another curious friend will say, "You seemed so different. Why did you two get married?"

"Well," Hirschfeld will reply, "because everyone told me *not* to."

"And why did you break up?"

"Well . . . I don't like to see a woman drunk."

Whatever the reason, in 1935 he's back, thirty-two and Flo-less.

During this period, his pals are also on the move. Victor Thall, his former co-traveler, is residing at what he calls "a Federal Forestry Camp" in Banning, California. He's in this lockup for bindle stiffs after riding the rails to Los Angeles, hoping to make his move in movie land.

Once he was nabbed, it was this or jail. No luck, no money, no nothing—including the pregnant wife and the baby he's left behind. When he hits New York and glimpses the daughter who's been born while he's off finding himself, he plans to drop in on Hirschfeld.

When he shows up, he's a mess, weighing 117 pounds. As he later relates in his poetic way, "I had malnutrition, intestinal poisoning, colitis, both eyes black, my nose half broken from being beaten up, and I was taken into a delousing machine and I got out of this delousing machine, my wet body fell against the metal and all the skin of my buttocks was ripped off and pasted against the steel, and that's how I rode from Texas to New York. And I came to Al Hirschfeld's apartment and I walked in with this costume of the rover with my bundle over my back, and his jaw literally dropped . . . and I just turned around and unbuttoned my trousers and turned around in my bare buttocks, and he fainted. That's the sight I was."

Meanwhile, wandering another landscape, Howard Simon is marking trails artistic and marital. With his new wife, Charlie

May Hogue, a sculptress he met in Paris, he's now homesteading in the Ozarks. His etchings and woodblocks have swerved from penniless Jews to hatchet-wielding hillbillies as he produces a rugged body of work reflecting the mountain life he's come to love. He's showing his work at the Smithsonian in Washington and illustrating children's books written by his bride.

Al's career continues its climb, too, building a bigger following, and his line becomes ever more surgical. When more of the theater world moves up from Herald to Times Square, and honky-tonk flavors the district, Hirschfeld does the opposite. As Broadway adds on to itself, Al is subtracting.

By the mid-1930s, he realizes he's so good at this people are looking like his caricatures rather than the other way around. His ads and posters for the Marx Brothers in *A Night at the Opera*—including a collage of cotton, tinfoil, scouring pad, pipe cleaner, and sheet music—are so good that MGM's makeup department tries to reshape Groucho's mop of hair into what Hirschfeld has made it: two winglike triangles flying out from a center runway. Before Hirschfeld, the brothers just look like a loony threesome. After Hirschfeld, they look like Hirschfelds.

In 1935 he's living alone in a luxurious fifteen-story building at 405 East Fifty-fourth Street, between First Avenue and the East River—just a block away from menace, what with the East Fifty-third Place Gang hanging around the waterfront, next to the fashionable River House. These tenement toughies are bait to Sidney Kingsley, who's written a new play called *Dead End* and renamed them the Dead End Kids (featuring eleven-year-old Sidney Lumet as one of them). With a set so graphic that the kid actors actually dive into the East River (the orchestra pit), the drama will open at the Belasco and be drawn by Hirschfeld for the *Brooklyn Eagle*.

And there's another gangster bringing excitement to the block as well. Lucky Luciano parks his yacht nightly at the end of the street when he comes to see his doll, in Hirschfeld's building. Gay Orlova is a blond showgirl in a ground-floor apartment. As one of "The Most Beautiful Girls in the World" recently seen in Earl Carroll's *Murder at the Vanities* (and drawn by Hirschfeld in the *Herald Tribune*), the Russian Orlova paints her walls black so she can more easily snooze through the day.

It's about now that Hirschfeld meets a brunette singer-danseuse who wants to be Sarah Bernhardt. Paula Laurence (née de Lugo) is nineteen or twenty or twenty-one (she's not saying); Al is thirty-two. With her heavy-lidded eyes, arched eyebrows, and prow-like profile, she's "quite a very special beauty," says the restaurateur Jean-Claude Baker, "and you can use the word 'beauty.' Almost like a goddess." She's a breezy gossip, a catholic reader, opinionated and sharp, fun to have around. She's also nuts about Al and claims him as her first lover.

But a hausfrau she is not, so Hirschfeld hires a cook named Dan. A cook, a manservant, a domestic helper or helpmate for his well-being is always a necessity. A man of ritual, Hirschfeld the host enjoys designating certain nights for certain people. Among them are Fred Allen and Portland Hoffa, on every Tuesday for Chinese. Friday belongs to Mom, and usually Pop. Everyone loves Mom. If dinner's not dished up in Washington Heights, it is on East Fifty-fourth, where she makes a huge meal for Al's friends who come to feed, then to play cards. Brother Al from California—Big Al, Small Al, they have so little in common—occasionally turns up. He doesn't get a special night.

Another habitué is George Braidwood McCoy, a screwy radio host and sidewalk interviewer who goes by "the real McCoy." A Damon Runyon creation of his own devising, he has a résumé more colorful than any palette. As Hirschfeld describes him, McCoy has "a life saver's physique, a policeman's face, an allergy to money, a great capacity for friendship and an insatiable appetite"—with credits ranging "from life guard at Coney Island to Al Smith's bodyguard on his presidential tour, from salesman for the Chick-Chick Easter Egg Dye Co. to New York's accredited No.1 gate-crasher." Now he's sleeping on Al Hirschfeld's couch once a week.

Perkins Harnly, another member of the circle and an *Americana* alumnus, doesn't sleep on the couch. Harnly sleeps in a coffin (but not at Al's). Hirschfeld has no idea why this character also likes cocooning himself in carpets that cover the floor, climb the walls, and upholster the ceiling. But he's spellbound. Harnly is a prolific illustrator for the WPA's *Index of American Design*, and his watercolors include *Garage of Funeral Parlor* and *Dentist's Operating Room*.

"He was wildly gay and from Nebraska," adds Margie King Barab. "He was celebrity crazy, and crazy about Mae West. He was always drawing buildings that had bosoms, balconies, and things, like Mae West."

Al is amused, not judgmental. Crackpots and clodhoppers bring laughs to his nights—and fodder to his folktales.

Gordon Kahn is around, when not suffering the vagaries of Hollywood. Brooks Atkinson (who's dropped the *J.* from his byline) shows up with his wife, Oriana. Vic Thall comes to mooch. Don Freeman and his wife, Lydia, drop in, and so do Artie Hershkowitz and Lastone Hoffa (Portland's sister). As for Paula, she's *always* around. Years later, Margie Barab will say that "she sort of moved in on him," and that "his clan of male friends weren't too fond of her."

She isn't exactly living with him, but she has a place in every room and a view to his pleasure. So when the barbershop in her Aunt Ethel's office-building arcade closes, Aunt Ethel suggests that Al take the barber chair, which she considers the most comfortable chair a man can have. Al likes the idea and pays a mover ten dollars to lug it up.

Other than manipulating the levers on that chair, he doesn't exercise. His workouts entail little but lifting his right hand and shifting his gears. At the board, behind the wheel, he is a still life. But not his art. Dipping a crow-quill pen into India ink, he traces his pencil sketches inch by inch by inch until the line loops, swoops, and *flies*. He draws; he's always drawing. As long as the sun shines. "I have very little truck with New York," he says about his meticulous schedule. "I don't go out during the day at all."

His focus is fierce, and he can do the drawings no matter how persistent the distractions. Paula and the pals, Mom and Pop, food and drink, doorbells and thunderstorms—nothing interrupts the flow of his pen. And then, when the work is done, he wants a reaction, from anybody around, from the cook to the postman to the very best friend. He's open to other eyes and willing to try even the most intricate change. If he agrees with it, fine. If not, he stays his own course.

Don Freeman, also covering the theater, soon concocts a more personal outlet. In 1936, he publishes the first issue of *Don Freeman's Newsstand*, defining it as "Reports from a Roving Sketchbook all Around the Town—news not found on the 'front page.' New York's own cast of characters in color and black and white from the original plates." Filled with his own lithographs—of street musicians, hoboes, doormen, backstage Broadway, Columbus Circle (where he lives)—this is quarterly as gallery, a paean a-brim with inside references. The articles and sketches are guest written by actors and artists he comes across, but mainly by his friends and about his friends—including Hirschfeld, Paula, Roger Furse, and his old pal William Saroyan, from California. Issued intermittently through the next five years, *Don Freeman's Newsstand* will vary in size but not in personality.

For a special theater number, Freeman draws a portrait of Hirschfeld in his barber chair, with inks and brushes nearby, a phone on the chair behind him: "Al Hirschfeld—caricaturist, traveler, collector of masks and sculpture, hot record connoisseur, intense enjoyer of life, humorist, keeper of open house to multifarious friends, lithographer, and drum beater." In another issue, he runs a portrait of Paula—holding the playing card of herself as the queen of hearts, drawn by Al.

13
AND READ ALL OVER

But in August, Hirschfeld sails away. "There was always a rumor that he went on that trip to get away from her," says Michael Sommers, a drama critic who's known her for years. "Paula was intimidating. She could just cut you in *half*," adds Joel Kaye, a wit-about-town who's also known her for years. "She had *too much* personality," adds the artist Gray Foy.

But there is a more compelling reason to leave town: a return to Russia. "I was so enthusiastic about the Soviet theater that they thought I was enthusiastic about the Soviet government," Hirschfeld recalls, and he is invited to cover the Russian Theatre Festival. He tells Konstantin Umansky at the Soviet embassy in Washington that he himself can do very little, that the important fellow at the *Times* is Atkinson. So could Atkinson and his wife come too? *Da.*

When Babe takes off, Paula takes charge. Before the *Normandie* has left the dock, she's clearing out the apartment and getting the phone disconnected. While he's heading to Leningrad, she's packing his paints and brushes, films and camera equipment, Balinese masks and drums, clothes and toothpaste. She sends the couch and big chair to Alex King, the rugs to be cleaned and stored. Mom comes for the silver. Paula pays his bills, deposits checks from the *Times* and the *Eagle*. She takes his records to her family's home in Flatbush, where she plays his Armstrong, Cleo Brown, and Bali records on her Victrola.

As the Depression releases a panacea of movies—Busby Berkeley kaleidoscopic musicals, Deco-decorated penthouses, screwball, madcap, escape—glossy magazines, from *The Saturday Evening Post* to *Vanity Fair*, fairly ignore the situation. *Vanity Fair* editor Frank Crowninshield, still going for silk-stocking ads, refuses to acknowledge it, Hirschfeld recalls: "And this is when people were on breadlines, Hooverville from 72nd Street north. But he would not look at it, didn't want to hear about it."

The theater world faces it full-on, nowhere more fully than with the WPA's Federal Theatre Project. In 1936, John Houseman produces *Horse Eats Hat*, adapted from a French farce and directed by a young Orson Welles. Paula plays Agatha Entwhistle, the female lead.

It's a grueling rehearsal schedule, but Paula still has a foot in the door on Fifty-fourth Street. And before the place is emptied of everything, that's where she goes. "The sleepy elevator man. 12E. Good night. Key. Light. Door slam. The ghost of you hovers and sighs over the packing cases, way up on the wall where the masks used to be," she writes to Al. "My heels clack-clack on the bare floors echoing. Warm bath. Delicious. Mustn't fall asleep yet. The bed is a cloud. How dark and still. Sleep. Oblivion."

As Hirschfeld and Atkinson pull into Moscow, she watches the movers pull out. "12E is just a memory now," she writes on September 10. And sends him a laundry list:

Bed cover cleaned . . . $1.25
Car put in dead storage . . . $16.12
Rent & electricity . . . $95.73
Ties cleaned (47 of them) . . . $2
Five shirts laundered (found in paper parcel in studio closet) . . . 85 cents

Telephone bill (call to Long Beach made by Sergei Radamsky) . . .40 cents

Electricity . . . $3.50

Tips ($1 each for 2 moving men, $1.50 for man who takes litho stone) . . . $3.50

Her devotion continues through Hirschfeld's absence, with frequent updates on bills, payments, and savings. Although he's been producing mountains of work and earning good money for the 1930s, his bank balance in October is $402.10.

While Al is analyzing the labor situation in Red Square, Paula spends Labor Day weekend with the Kings at their house on Greenwood Lake in Orange County, New York—with a roaring fire, lots of books, a noisy bridge tournament, and Mom Hirschfeld's blintzes, cheesecake, and corned beef and cabbage. In the other room, King is working on *Nightwatch in Syria*, his play about the day of the crucifixion. Soon he'll start on his next, a farce about an artificial-flower tycoon whose wife joins a dance troupe. "He does all the proletariat artists up brown," Paula writes, having been promised the wife role.

In Moscow, Hirschfeld is at the Metropole, and he sees how the city has changed. Not only does his old hotel have a new facade and his old apartment have new windowpanes, but the people "seem more Russian than before. They seem to stand out against their new architectural background like a Gypsy waiting for a Fifth Ave bus," he writes to Mom. The city is "grotesquely expensive," and he's already spent thirty dollars on a week's cigarettes.

Then there's the Theatre Festival. It's a *dud*. On opening night—which Hirschfeld and the Atkinsons attend with Harold Denny, the *Times* correspondent—the performers include singers, saber twirlers, flame throwers, Kazatsky dancers. When their interpreter explains that these aren't professional performers but subway workers and folk artists, Atkinson is impressed.

Back at the typewriter, he reports in the *Times* that other than a splendid production of *Eugene Onegin*, the week has been a grim disappointment. "Russian dramas are not written or produced to please the artistic sensibilities of a New York theatergoer," he writes. "Only a Communist or social revolutionary can wax fat on the diet of proletarian heroism that was served up night after night in the festival."

Hirschfeld feels the same and says so in an article he writes for *Stage* magazine that will appear the following May. He describes how Oriana was barred from the studio of the Moscow Art Theatre because she refused to check her coat, while he and Brooks were locked inside. He runs through the festival's events, which disappoint him, especially when "the much overrated Meyerhold (whose direction resembles on old movie projected at ten times its normal speed) presented his staccato thespians in a miserable thing called *Woe to Wit*." And he wraps it up by deciding that the real theater of Russia is seen not on the stage but in the streets.

"It all deteriorated, it all fell apart. It was like a different planet in '36," he says, comparing it with the place he visited in 1928, a year before Joseph Stalin slashed into the dictatorship. "And Stalin, big rotogravure portraits of him hanging in the streets, kissing babies. None of that existed before, none of it. It was, I'd thought, a whole new beginning of something, it all seemed so exciting. And then suddenly it became corrupt like everything else."

When the festival moves on to Leningrad, taking two trainloads of theater enthusiasts with it ("the goddamnest bunch of collective and individual bores the western world has to offer," Hirschfeld writes to Mom), the two *Times* men stick around in Moscow to see what's cooking at the Moscow Art Theatre, and they are rewarded. Not only is *Dead Souls* lively, but a Russian translation of *The Pickwick Club*—a "discursive bundle of humors," as Atkinson puts it—is so inspiring he thinks it could work in New York.

But it's Hirschfeld's view that piques the greater interest. In his accompanying picture, he has drawn four characters, including a puffy Pickwick stuffed into a chair. For extra fun, he has printed PAULA running up Pickwick's right boot. Naturally, she has noticed. "Darling: Your Times drawing was simply swell. And I found my name on the little man's boot immediately. How sweet you are. No one but you could think of such a thing." Others have noticed, too. "Everyone died of envy from Houseman down to the night watchman," she adds.

The Atkinsons leave for Paris, and Hirschfeld goes to London to study lithography at the County Council's School of Photo-engraving and Lithography. His class meets Tuesday and Thursday evenings from 7:00 to 9:30 and offers "original lithography and hand reproduction from the originals on polished and grained stone and metal plates for printing in monochrome and colour."

He finds a studio, hires a cook, and is so stuck on the stone that he turns down a series on London pub men for the *Daily Express*, although in October a few drawings appear of the York Minster on Dean Street, the Savoy bar in the grand hotel, and Frisco's International Club in Piccadilly (best known of the city's "coloured" nightspots). One day his name pops up in a London gossip column, where one Arthur Lawson, who writes in Western Union-ese, reports that Hirschfeld, in town after Russia, is doing lithography, "which says real work—caricaturing hobby. Too many friends, life too complicated New York settle down in peace." He adds, "Says disappointed no new plays Moscow. Acting better than New York but plays, settings, not so good."

"Dear More-so-than-ever baby," Paula writes, in *her* style. "Your London letter arrived today and London sounds frightful. Would it cost very much more to rent a flat than to live in that dreary hotel?" She urges him not to wander around with wet feet drinking cold tea. "What will you do if you get sick & 3000 miles of ocean prevents me from administering my never-failing cure?"

Only then does she share her excitement about *Horse*'s opening night—the curtain calls, flowers over the footlights, Houseman's confidence that it will run all winter, although it won't. While Gummo Marx sees it five times, Balanchine sees it every night for a week, and Marc Connelly frequently returns, *Horse* is a turkey.

She reports that Artie Hershkowitz and Lastone Hoffa are saving up to get married, even if they do make each other miserable. As for herself, "I am filled with autumn melancholia. It's raining again. Everything weeps." And when she writes him a poem in late October, it, too, weeps with melancholia.

> Now start the grey days of waiting
> The air is chilled
> Soon it will be winter
> I walk the busy streets all day
> Night finds me tired and wistful
> And probably no letter from you . . .
> Other people complicate my life
> For a brief moment I may find a respite
> In another smile
> I laugh & have a good time
> But nothing really drives away my thoughts of you . . .
> Without you
> Winter will be difficult

"I'm glad my verses pleased you so much," she writes upon receiving his praise. "If you stay away forever, I shall naturally write more of them. But when we're together I'm so busy living poetry, I have no need to write it."

When Hirschfeld invites her to join him, she declines. First of all, *Horse Eats Hat* will probably run until Christmas, and who knows what will follow. "I know you don't take my acting seriously," she writes. "But I do." In fact, she may be wrong. Blowing her own horn doesn't faze him, and his regard for her ambition is nothing like his effort to squelch Flo's.

Then she gets to the real reason. "You told me yourself, once, that we could never travel together because Flo would nab us as soon as we set foot anywhere & make a scandal & you'd have to pay her alimony the rest of your life."

In November, Al sails to France—where, to his great displeasure, Customs charges him thirty-five dollars for his radio. This time, he checks into the Lutetia on the Boulevard Raspail, tonier than he's accustomed to, because he plans to work in his room. "The smaller hotels have no elevators," he writes home, "and it would be much too much like work to carry a litho stone up five flights of stairs."

Paula writes that John Houseman is directing Leslie Howard in *Hamlet*, and she looks forward to comparing it with Gielgud's. "Howard's a surprisingly nice guy with no illusions as to his acting genius," she informs Al. "He's a shrewd little English jew with a good sense of theatre." Also, Virgil Thomson is off to Paris "to do 4 Saints in French with La Stein. I'll find out where he's stopping & do look him up & give him my regards. He's very amusing & I think you might have some fun with Gertrude."

As her letters cross the ocean, addressed to "My nearest & dearest," "My wonderful one," "Darling darling darling," "My sweet, my onion, my little white dove" and signed "La Flame," Al's pen reaches back to her. And on November 15, 1936, he delivers another visual gift. In his drawing of *The Country Wife*, an umpteenth revival of Wycherly's Restoration comedy that he sees at the Old Vic, he inserts a portrait of Paula over the mantelpiece. "It's de-licious de-lightful de-lovely (Cole Porter's new song in 'Red Hot & Blue')," she joyfully responds. *The New York Times* is not amused.

When she moves from *Horse* to *Dr. Faustus* as Helen of Troy, Paula writes to Al, "I float out on the stage & Orson (Dr. Faustus) says 'Is this the face that launched "a thousand ships. . ."' & then carries me off to rape me." The Welleses take her everywhere and let her stay with them, which she much prefers to Flatbush.

"Are your eyes really as large as I remember them?" she asks. "And do they still swim around in your head? Do your eyelashes still curl & do you still make a bridge between the saucer & the tablecloth with your coffee spoon? Do you still sit on the end of your spine & wiggle your feet when you read? How many people's eyes have you poked out swinging your key chain around? I'm sure you used your toothbrush to make spatter with & haven't brushed your teeth since about Oct. 3. Go buy another one immediately & please wash your comb this minute. You're mad & silly & sweet & I think you're wonderful & don't ever change."

Meanwhile, she mopes, getting through Thanksgiving with his parents, whereas Al's Thanksgiving in Paris, with international correspondents and their wives, is more scintillating.

"I'm glad you got to like Paula," Al writes to Mom. "I know, even though you have had the good sense not to tell me, that Paula offended you because of her possessive attitude. I have always attributed this to her lack of shrewdness which is the one quality I respect most intensely about her. Anyone with such obvious tactlessness is much too honest a person to connive."

He's coming back by January. Paula's ecstatic, "foaming at the mouth, panting, swooning, & reeling with joy." And off she goes to find him an apartment. She combs Central Park South, Sutton Place, Beekman Terrace, and Murray Hill, "and there's something wrong with every one. Not enough kitchen or not enough closets or too dark or the window ledges aren't low enough." She can hardly wait for his return, when she can spend Sundays "as every woman would like to—cooking for you & scratching your head & spoiling you in general."

And like manna from heaven, like a bearded Santa with his sack of toys (including a fragile batch of records by Django Reinhardt), Hirschfeld arrives on Christmas Eve.

14
FIDDLING ON THE ROOF

Action for Absolute Divorce. In March 1937, Hershkowitz the lawyer represents Flo the plaintiff in her action against Al the husband. He alleges that "on or about the 17th day of February, 1937, in the borough of Manhattan, City of New York, and particularly at 405 East 54th Street," he "committed adultery with a woman whose name is unknown to the plaintiff."

Flo has no immediate plans to remarry (although Paula hopes she does), and without further ado, as if the whole thing had never happened, the papers remain unfiled. No one divorces anybody, and life returns to normal.

Normal is Al raking it in from MGM—posters and ads for *A Day at the Races* ($360), *Madame X* ($100), Joe E. Brown in *Flirting With Fate* ($225)—and theater drawings for the papers. In May, he's all over the Sunday page of the *Brooklyn Eagle* with Rodgers and Hart's *Babes in Arms*—"caught by Professor 'Flash' Hirschfeld," the story notes—and in June, he does the same show for the *Trib*.

Soon he's hustling *10 Lithographs by Hirschfeld*, and he mails out a brochure with an introduction by the artist George Grosz, his former colleague from the lefty days at *Americana*. "The people in these prints, and their milieu, are fitted into a satiric pattern which owes nothing to political bias or a transiently fashionable irritation with well entrenched smugness," Grosz writes. "I see and greet in Albert Hirschfeld one of the most promising lithographic artists in this country and I hasten to recommend his fine work to all genuinely discerning print lovers." The prints, drawn on stone, include works new, recent, and socially significant. Here is the renovated version of his 1933 portrayal of the Supreme Court's "nine old men," nightclubs, Russian laborers, and the "hook shop" he visited in Paris. Prices are ten, fifteen, and twenty dollars.

The folio's a flop. He can't sell the work. No matter his intention or desire, no matter how good the lithographs, drawings, watercolors, or anything else he might produce, they're not theatrical caricatures, and that's what his audience wants.

Dr. Faustus closes in May, and Welles and Houseman turn their social consciousness to *The Cradle Will Rock*, Marc Blitzstein's opera set in Steeltown, USA. But with strikes and violence rocking the country, the WPA (Works Progress Administration) is attacked for endowing such pro-labor fare, and funds are cut. On June 16, 1937, the night of the one preview at Maxine Elliott's Theatre, the WPA says the show must not go on. Welles rushes to Washington, fruitlessly. Houseman hatches a plan.

The theater is padlocked. While cops stand out front to prevent actors and musicians from entering, ticket holders mill around.

Hirschfeld is among them.

The Cradle doesn't rock. Although the scourges in Washington have decided it's subversive and slammed it down, Welles refuses to buckle. He urges the swelling crowd on the sidewalk to be patient and stick around until he and Houseman find another house, and actors Howard da Silva and Will Geer toss them songs and dialogue.

Houseman dispatches Jean Rosenthal, his production assistant, to find a piano and keep the truckers driving until there's a theater to take the piano to. "We tried ballrooms, night clubs and Turnvereins," Houseman recalls, before finally snagging the Venice Theatre. Given their cue, the crowd starts moving en masse from Thirty-ninth Street to Fifty-eighth. Curtain is moved to 9:00, and ticket holders are urged to bring friends. "There was cheering as the voyage began—by bus, subway, taxi and (it being a fine June evening) on foot," Houseman adds.

They march into the theater—Hirschfeld among them—to see a bare stage with the curtain up. Having made it inside, they're also making history. The piano has made it here, too, and Blitzstein is sitting at it. The actors sit in the audience. Houseman gives an explanatory speech and, script in hand, so does Welles, who describes the set-less scenes and costumes. When he motions for the orchestra to start, Blitzstein plays the overture. The actors rise from their seats out front to deliver their lines. Welles invites them onstage, and up they go. It's a thrilling event, and although it breaks the back of the WPA Theatre, it gives birth to the Mercury Theatre.

Hirschfeld's at that opening, just as he's at most openings now—very often with Brooks Atkinson. Mrs. Atkinson often stays home. With the instinct of an oracle, Oriana can sense if a show is going to be worth her while. Her husband has no choice, of course, and when he returns, she loves being able to say she told him so. But Al's up for anything. By opening night, he's already seen a rehearsal or tryout and turned in his drawing, but he loves being there.

His new home is in his old neighborhood. A favorite story in the canon has him strolling along when he looks up, points, and says, "There! I'd like to live up there." *Up there* is the roof of the Osborne Apartments, a Romanesque-and-Renaissance-style building wrapped around the northwest corner of Fifty-seventh and Seventh. He goes to the front door, finds the janitor, and thereupon arranges to have a studio built for himself up on the roof.

In September 1937, he moves into Apartment 12D, which isn't exactly built for him because it already exists. (An architect's blueprint from 1922 indicates alterations on what's been there for years.) It's more shack than penthouse, but snug and sweet. From the bedroom, with its north light and a parquet floor, he has a clear view of Central Park and points north. "It was like a ship," remembers Faith Stewart-Gordon, owner of the Russian Tea Room, who would live in it years later.

His neighbors include sopranos, actors, flutists, explorers, doctors, jurists, and obscure royals. His playmates, as usual, form a menagerie. Animals, people, *characters*. Alex King gives him a seven-foot voodoo drum wrapped in banana leaves, so tall it has to be brought up on top of the elevator. Don Freeman gives him Bill Saroyan, the refugee from Fresno. When Saroyan stays at the Great Northern Hotel across the street, he's more often here—or in Harlem with Hirschfeld. They're conjuring a collaboration.

His son, Aram Saroyan, recalls that "Pop didn't have a lot of close friends, and Al was one of them." The two share hairiness, humor, hot dogs. "Every time I've had Sunday supper at Al's house he's dished out frankfurters of some kind," Pop Saroyan himself recalls. "The last time this happened he said, I suppose you think frankfurters is the only thing I eat . . . No, I said, I believe you eat other things too. Well, beans, Al said, which proved I was right."

Saroyan brings in Boris Aronson, because the young stage designer is living at the Great Northern, too, having worked his way up from the Lower East Side. One of ten children born to a rabbi in Kiev, Aronson painted, designed, and wrote books on graphic art and Chagall before arriving in New York in the early 1920s. A rather moody, intense fellow—or, as Atkinson describes him, "gloomy as Beethoven"—Aronson is also a dry storyteller, which fits him right in.

S. J. Perelman is here, too, although it's unclear just how and when he and Hirschfeld met. Perelman says it was Paris in

1932, a Javanese restaurant in the Rue Pigalle, when a fashion writer pulled up to the table and introduced her companion as the theatrical caricaturist of *The New York Times*. "Hirschfeld wants to do a caricature of you," she said. Perelman, as tight as he is tart, said nothing. "It's free," said Hirschfeld. "In no time at all—five minutes, to be exact—we were laughing and chatting away as though we had known each other five minutes," S.J. remembers.

Others put it at a Benny Goodman rehearsal in New York. Wherever, whenever, Perelman's in the picture.

And Paula's in the picture, of course. He's now drawn her twice as *Dr. Faustus*'s Helen of Troy. In the *Times,* she's soft and murky. In the *Trib*, her headdress is a spiky affair, and her shoulders look lethal.

Thanks to his flirty friendship with Clare Boothe Brokaw-now-Luce, Alex King lands a job at *Life* magazine as an editorial associate in charge of "Speaking of Pictures." He has a colorful wardrobe, colorful stories, and colorful story ideas. Hirschfeld is most intrigued by his collections of oddballs—such as the twenty-two-inch dwarf whose photograph can fit, life-size, on a *Life* spread. . .or the guy who's invented an edible picnic plate, which Al and Alex agree tastes like a cross between dog's breath and a soggy matzo . . . or the guy in a hula skirt who sets it on fire.

In August 1937, King uses Hirschfeld in *Life*. In a set of "Photo-Doodles," he defaces several famous ones via mustaches, glasses, funny hair. With broad strokes, he converts Herbert Hoover into John L. Lewis, Winston Churchill into W. C. Fields, Gertrude Stein into Albert Einstein, and so on. "Mr. Hirschfeld's doodles always have a definite artistic aim and direction," King writes in the accompanying text. "They set out to effect a profound but justifiable change in the original subject." One original subject, however, is livid. When Hirschfeld chooses to "transmute one autocrat like Harold Ross, dictatorial editor of the *New Yorker*, into another autocrat like Joseph Stalin, dictatorial rules of Soviet Russia," Ross reacts with a decree: Hirschfeld will never appear in his magazine. "This was the death blow," says Hirschfeld. "We never spoke after that."

But he's a hit at Boston University, where a philosophy professor seeks permission to use some of the "Photo-Doodles" to illustrate the psychological principle that changing a part alters the whole.

There seems no end to foolery and pranks. In September 1938, the Museum of Modern Art opens a show called *Useful Household Objects Under $5.00*. The idea behind exhibiting an adjustable towel rack, tweed brush, martini mixer, transparent hat box, wire glove dryer, and pancake turner is that good design can be bought for peanuts. Most of the one hundred objects are displayed on tables with explanatory cards beside them. Others, like hangers and frying pans, are on the wall.

Enter Don Freeman.

He calls Hirschfeld. "Al, congratulations!" he cries. "I saw your piece down at the Modern! It's great you're in the show."

"What are you talking about?"

"C'mon. Quit the false modesty. You're in the Modern. That's good. You deserve to be there."

It seems that Freeman has made a card crediting Hirschfeld and slipped it next to an ashtray. What guys!

King is not the only one taken with dwarfs. When *Snow White and the Seven Dwarfs* opens at Radio City Music Hall on January 13, 1938, Frank Nugent, the *Times* critic, calls it "a classic, as important cinematically as 'The Birth of a Nation' or the birth of Mickey Mouse."

Hirschfeld calls it something else. In a critique called "An Artist Contests Mr. Disney" that runs in the *Times* two weeks later, he praises the dwarfs—"these inspired gnomes, with their geometrical noses, flexible cheeks, linear mouths and eyes, highly stylized beards, costumes and three fingers"—but not Snow White, Prince Charming, or the Queen, "badly drawn attempts at realism." On he goes, grousing about the contrasting styles and the "staccato movements of Snow White and her cardboard lover."

Little does he know that by the end of a busy summer Snow White herself will show up on his doorstep.

15
PARTY LINES

Although Hirschfeld's political art is not lucrative, it feeds his soul. For *Ken*—a short-lived controversial biweekly produced by Arnold Gingrich and David Smart (the founders of *Esquire*), brandishing cover illustrations of menacing Moroccans, Nazis, caricatured presidents, and a political interior of commentary, photographs, and cartoons—he takes off on Hemingway's fourteen-issue coverage of the Spanish Civil War with a drawing of bulls in the stadium watching Spaniards goring each other in the ring. As a member of the American Artists' Congress—which includes hundreds of Communist Party members (of which he is not one)—he attends a rally at New York City's Town Hall and joins the call against fascism and censorship.

And for *New Masses,* the lefty weekly filled with equally momentous writing and political art, he takes some of his most acidic ink-pot shots—signing his own name where other artists fear to tread. "They were playing cops and robbers, using different names," he says, "to avoid the inquiries and so on." He caricatures the Prince of Wales, attacks isolationism and Nazism. And in January 1939, he gives the magazine *Peace in Our Time*—inspired by Neville Chamberlain's declaration of "Peace for our time"—because *The New York Times* won't run it.

It's a lithograph. And, it seems, lithography is *dangerous.*

In the 1920s, certain symbols became identified with Communist art. "The worker, for instance, was always drawn with his feet spread-eagle, like Chaplin—it was taken after Chaplin, the little man—and the capitalist was always pigeon-toed, so if you drew anybody with their feet out it was a proletarian," Hirschfeld explains. "So those symbols became identified with the Communists. And now the medium—lithography—became identified with the Communist Party.

"I did a lithograph of the British Parliament being bombed—a hole in the top of it—they're all standing around with gas masks on. 'Peace in our Time.' And I took it to *The Times* and the editor said, 'It's a Communist drawing.' And I said, 'What's Communist about it? There's nothing Communist about it.' I said, 'It's a lithograph, if that's what you mean.' He said, 'No, no, it's a Communist drawing.' He says, 'Why don't you take it to the *New Masses*?' So I said, 'Well, okay, if it's a Communist drawing, I'll take it to the *New Masses*.' I took it to the *New Masses* and they ran it, a double spread. Later on I saw the *Times* editor. He said, 'I *told* you it's a Communist drawing!' I said, 'Fine, it's a Communist drawing.'"

Hirschfeld goes on, warming to that parlay with the Sunday editor, Lester Markel. "Now we dissolve, a couple of years go by, and I get a call from the British Embassy. There's a thing at Radio City Music Hall for Russian War Relief—a very gala occasion—and they wanted to know whether they could use this drawing for the cover of the brochure and how much I would want for it. So I said, 'Nothing.' I said, 'I'm very pleased that you want to use this,' and I said, 'Please send me a copy immediately it's off the press.' Which they did. It was very beautifully printed, and it was bound in silk ribbon and so on. And I hot-footed it down to *The Times*, threw it on Markel's desk, and I said, 'Look, here's the drawing you said is a Communist drawing. Now it has the accolade of the British Empire.

It's being used for the Russian War Relief.' He says, 'England's going Communist!'"

But if anything sticks in his craw, it's Father Charles E. Coughlin, the silver-tongued, rabble-rousing "radio priest" who spews anti-Semitic pro-Fascist hatred on the air. Sinclair Lewis refigures him as "Bishop Prang" in *It Can't Happen Here* and does a dandy impersonation of him, too. For his part, Hirschfeld draws him for *New Masses* "with swastikas etched on his eyeglasses" and "a Hitler-like mouse peering from under his clerical collar." What's more, he's holding the Ten Commandments, with an eleventh attached: "Don't forget to wire your Congressman."

The drawing doesn't appear. "What happened?" he asks the *New Masses* editor. "We're sending up a delegation to see you," the editor says.

"I said, 'Don't send up any delegation, just bring the drawing out.' He said, 'Well, we can't print the drawing. It would offend a lot of Catholics.' I said, 'That's the idea. That's the whole point.' I said, 'Use the drawing or that's the last drawing I do for you.' And that's the last political drawing I did. They arrived in my studio, about seven or eight fellas. I had to forcibly get them out of the studio. I kept saying, 'Listen, you're the people who've been preaching for years that religion is the opium of the people, and now here's an anti-religious drawing, you won't print it.' But they never used the drawing.

"So that's when I realized that to do political things, you have to be able to switch with the times. You can be pro-union one day and the next day anti-union. I'm no good at that. You have to be able to switch with the times and play politics, but it's not for me. I'd much rather have the villains and the heroes made by the playwright. That's his worry, not mine. My worry is to do a decent drawing. And I stick to that.

"I just interpret what the playwright intends to say. Sometimes it works."

The New York World's Fair opens in April, and Flushing Meadows is its stage. As a prelude to this industrial celebration, Meyer Berger of the *Times* writes a portrait of "The Real New Yorker," who ain't quite the city slicker fairgoers fear. Hirschfeld illustrates the piece with vignettes from the real New Yorker's real humdrum life, from supper table to bingo night to subway—which he labels "High Jinks."

New York is a-frenzy with fair fever. Papers produce special sections; guidebooks and maps swamp the newsstands. He draws a souvenir vendor hawking Trylons and Perispheres, which are—like Laurel and Hardy, Weber and Fields, even Mom and Pop—another form of the number 10. He does *Sightseer's Map of New York* for the *Times* with vignettes of boxers at Madison Square Garden, an artist in the Village, a bassist at Lewisohn Stadium, Rockettes kicking, and so forth. (Maps have become a favorite motif, especially in summer-theater season.) In July, he delivers *Sunday in the Park*, an elaborately detailed map of weekend joy-seekers in Central Park.

Soon he hits the sticks on his annual tour of the tents—the "straw-hat circuit," on which he draws America's summer-theater offerings. One July evening, he and Paula attend opening night at the Bucks County Playhouse in New Hope, Pennsylvania. Bucks County is significant not just for the shows that play here but for the writers who write them, the directors who direct them, and the audience who attends them, many of whom—Oscar Hammerstein II, S. J. Perelman, Ruth and Augustus Goetz, Moss Hart, George and Beatrice Kaufman—have weekend homes close by. Kaufman and Hart are at their peak, having written *Once in a Lifetime*, *I'd Rather Be Right*, and *You Can't Take It With You*—the play Hirschfeld illustrated for the *Trib* and the *Brooklyn Eagle* and that was still running on Broadway when the movie opened with a campaign also illustrated by Hirschfeld.

Bea Kaufman is in a pique. Empowered by her marriage (even if she "drove her husband crazy and was always picking at him," as the *Times* editor Arthur Gelb remembers) and a separately impressive career of her own—as head of the editorial department at Boni & Liveright in the 1920s (before Hirschfeld submitted his book on Russian theater there), East Coast story editor for Samuel Goldwyn (after Hirschfeld served in the art department there), a short-story writer in *The New Yorker*, and fiction editor at *Harper's Bazaar*—she holds great sway. To many single men, she is a beloved mentor and irresistible creature, and those at Bea's knees include Moss Hart, Harpo Marx, and Noel Coward. But beautiful she is not. And when Hirschfeld places her up front between Kaufman and Hart in a group drawing of that starlit opening night in 1939—staring out from saggy-baggy eyes—Bea sees red. And gripes to Arthur Hays Sulzberger at the *Times*.

"Mrs. Kaufman, who was a great friend of the publisher, Sulzberger, complained about a drawing I did of her, and I thought it was a flattering drawing of her," Hirschfeld recalls with a chuckle. "To this day, I keep looking at it, and I think it's a flattering drawing." Paula thinks it's a wonderful drawing, flattering or not. Whatever Sulzberger thinks, Al continues in the *Times*.

By summer's end, it's time for Snow White to show up. Alex King has moved on from his wife, Nettie, to a lovely young lass: Marjorie Belcher (the future Marge Champion). Her father is a well-known dance teacher in Los Angeles, and when Walt Disney started work on *Snow White*, he hired fourteen-year-old Marge as a model to twirl for the camera. Artists would then trace her movements with a rotoscope to animate the figure of Snow White. "Uncle Walt—as I was told to call him, because I was too young to call him Walt like everybody else did—Uncle Walt did not want people to know about my posing for actual 16-millimeter," she says seventy years later.

When *Snow White*'s a hit and Marge is eighteen, *Life* sends King to interview her in Los Angeles. His piece appears in April 1938. The following winter, Marge is in a variety show with the Three Stooges, which closes in Albany. Rather than go home to her husband, the Disney artist Art Babbitt, she comes to Manhattan and takes up with King.

After she celebrates her twentieth birthday at Hirschfeld's place in September, there soon comes a fake wedding. "Alex *pretended* that we had gotten married, and I had to keep my mouth shut." When the columnist Leonard Lyons and his wife throw a "wedding party" for them, she keeps still. "Sooner or later they found out it was *not* true, and Leonard never spoke to me again." (King is not yet divorced.)

At some point, Marge goes home to help Uncle Walt with *Pinocchio*. When it opens in 1940, Hirschfeld will critique it for the *Times*. Once again, Marge or no Marge, he hates certain looks: "the synthetic realism of the eyelashed, fingernailed, bookish fairy. She might look well on top of a cake by Oscar of the Waldorf but she is miscast in a major work like *Pinocchio*. Animated drawings do not have to imitate factual human, animal, geological, or architectural form. The camera can do that ably."

Disney and his oeuvre permeate the atmosphere, and now comes *Swingin' the Dream*, a jazz version of *A Midsummer Night's Dream* with sets designed "after cartoons by Walt Disney" and a score by the new team of Felix Mendelssohn and Jimmy Van Heusen. Few would deny that the creators are somewhat inspired by two recent black productions of Gilbert and Sullivan's *Mikado*—*The Swing Mikado*, produced by the Federal Theatre Project, and Mike Todd's *The Hot Mikado*, starring Bill "Bojangles" Robinson. The show features Butterfly McQueen, fresh from Tara, as Puck; Louis Armstrong playing Bottom, and trumpet; the Benny Goodman Sextet onstage in the corner; and dances by Agnes de Mille. No matter, this dream's misbegotten.

"It would have been better to throw Shakespeare out of the window," Brooks Atkinson writes. "'The Boys From Syracuse' did better by forgetting Shakespeare altogether."

Hirschfeld, who's done both black *Mikados*, does this one, too. For the *Playbill* cover, he does a *Swingin'* drawing of Goodman and Armstrong blowin' tunes for Shakespeare, who's jivin' on a cloud.

The producers refuse to pay for the program art (which is also used for ads and sheet music), and Hirschfeld isn't the only stiffee. The press agent Dick Maney recalls that "the show was already in hock and a troop of process servers circled the Center" when the producer Erik Charell proposes "to fill empty seats with chambermaids from the better hotels. Inflamed by the magic of *Swingin' the Dream*, these gals would return to their bases, corner the occupants of rooms in their patrol, and urge them to buy tickets." That doesn't quite work out.

When the show closes after thirteen performances, Hershkowitz the lawyer advises Hirschfeld to serve an injunction. As the story goes, the instruments are impounded—from kettledrums to Armstrong's trumpet—and brought up to his studio in the Osborne. The jazz critic Dan Morgenstern, a Hirschfeld friend, is skeptical. "It would have been a bit difficult," he says, "because most musicians don't leave their instruments around." Nonetheless, however he finagles it, Hirschfeld collects, receiving $323 as "payment of warrant and attachment" against the Midsummer Night's Dream Corp.

Every little bit counts.

16
HELLO, DOLLY

On February 14, 1940, Don Freeman opens his first one-man show at the Associated American Artists' Galleries, and Hirschfeld draws him for the catalog cover. The next day, a certain Beauford Delaney opens a one-man show at the Vendome Art Galleries, "perhaps the first time that a Negro painter has been asked to exhibit in that section," says the *New York Amsterdam News*. W. C. Handy shows up, posing with his Delaney portrait.

Delaney is Hirschfeld's protégé. In the mid-1920s, the artist was living in the basement of the Whitney Studio Galleries, working as a janitor and doorman, when Hirschfeld met him and became his guardian angel. In 1930, Delaney won first prize in an exhibition at the Whitney for his portrait of Billy Pierce, the choreographer who invented the "black bottom." In 1938, he was the only black artist in the Washington Square outdoor art show, and King included him in *Life*'s photographic essay, "Negroes: The U.S. Also Has a Minority Problem." Since then, he's been selling his work to Hirschfeld's friends.

Then there's Marge Belcher. A naïf beyond belief, she's beginning to dislodge herself from King. "He had certain bad habits," she remembers, "and I was having difficulty understanding him because he really was naughty. He had taken every dime out of my bank account and was taking money to back him in some kind of show from the cleaner on our block. He promised he was going to write a ballet for me and get me into Ballet Theatre." And so on. It's time to get out, but she doesn't know how. So she calls Hirschfeld.

"I was crying and carrying on and saying, 'I don't know what to do. What should I do?' And he turned around and said, 'Grow up!' It was like a slap in the face! But it was the best advice anybody ever told me. He just barked it out. It wasn't mean or anything. I stopped crying and realized that I didn't have to live like that. And it gave me the courage to move to the Paramount Hotel the next day with my cat and my violin."

Marge remains close to Al Hirschfeld for the rest of his life. "He was never fatherly, but he was—maybe it was older-brotherly, I don't know," she says, "because there was never any romance whatsoever, not even a nod from either one of us."

It doesn't take King long to recast his queen, and soon after Marge departs, he marries an Annis Grover. But the Hirschfeld circle stays tight, and King's ex-wife, Nettie, still gets private time with Al. With or without her King, she's a favorite, and their rapport remains constant.

Nineteen forty. Another year, another barn-and-tent tour, but it was an important one.

In July he's in Hershey, Pennsylvania, and sees a French farce called *Her Cardboard Lover*. The star is Dolly Haas, a piquant German redhead. The curtain rises on her cuddling a cute little pooch.

"I was smitten with her the minute I saw her," Hirschfeld says of Dolly. "He was very interested in my golden-haired cocker spaniel," corrects Dolly.

Next day, the run's concluded, they're all striking the set, and Hirschfeld does a drawing for the *Times*. The cast is lugging costumes and props, and Dolly's hauling a lamp. The picture runs on August 4, with Dolly smack in the center. She then goes to Hollywood, and Hirschfeld to Paula.

In the fall, however, he also goes to Hollywood and visits the Raphaelsons—the author-screenwriter Sam and his beautiful wife, Dorshka. At a dinner party one night, he asks if they know Dolly Haas. "Ask *this* fellow," says Sam, pointing to another guest. "He's her husband."

This fellow is John Brahm, a director. He and Dolly are separated, and Dolly has now gone on to New York.

"Hmmm," says Hirschfeld, his return ticket burning his pocket.

Born in Hamburg in 1910, Dorothea Clara Eleanore Haas was the second daughter of Margarethe Hansen and Charles Oswald Haas. Margarethe was German and a good pianist. Charles was British, with Danish forebears. He studied in Germany, fell in love, and somehow balanced his time between the family in Hamburg and a bookselling career with his father in London. Sadly, Dolly remembers him only as an invalid. Because he had tuberculosis, she was never allowed to get too close.

Dolly and her older sister, Margarete, attended a prestigious lyceum in Hamburg established by the progressive Dr. Jakob Löwenberg. At six, she studied ballet at the municipal theater and played the witch in *Hansel and Gretel*. At seven, she was a dancer in the children's ballet at the Hamburg Opera. At ten, she gave her first solo dance performance at the Hoch Conservatory in Frankfurt, accompanied by her mother at the piano. At ten, she broke a shin and there went the ballet career.

But she sang, and at sixteen was at Berlin's State Theater, auditioning for none other than Erik Charell—then considered a great producer of frothy musical comedies—and his production of *The Mikado*. He cast her as one of the playmates of Princess Yum-Yum, but she was a redhead. A black wig looked ridiculous, so her hair was powdered white. Soon she was appearing in political cabarets and even a Max Reinhardt revue, *How Do I Become Rich and Happy?* After closing a small gap between her front teeth in 1929, she was cast as a department store mannequin that comes to life in a movie called *One Hour of Happiness*, directed by William Dieterle.

Next, a farce directed by Anatole Litvak: *Dolly Gets Ahead*. As the shopgirl who becomes an overnight sensation, Dolly Haas "has eyes like wet plums and considerable ability for grotesque dancing," C. Hooper Trask oddly observed in *The New York Times*.

On to a bevy of pixieish roles. In *Scampolo*, *Things Are Getting Better Already*, *Girls Will Be Boys*, and others—often disguised as a man—she was invariably reviewed as "the impish little actress," "one of the most attractive of the gamin type of German screen actresses," "the attractive little actress who hardly can be beaten in gamine roles," and so on. When evil showed up at the premiere of *The Ugly Girl* in 1933—her Jewish costar, Max Hansen, was blitzed with rotten eggs and tomatoes—Dolly stood firmly by his side. And as writers and artists she knew started fleeing the homeland for London, New York, and Hollywood, Dolly stayed. Her popularity was enormous. Her photographs appeared everywhere from movie posters to cigarette cards.

But by 1934, she's had it. After being grilled by the Gestapo about friends and colleagues, Dolly jumps ship. In October 1935, she leaves for London and lands the leading role in a 1936 redo of *Broken Blossoms*, playing the waifish heroine made famous by Lillian Gish. D. W. Griffith goes over to direct her. A dialect coach helps her acquire a cockney accent. A stylist lightens her hair. But Griffith isn't on board. When he finds a French actress he prefers, he gets the heave-ho and is replaced by Hans Brahm, who's directed some films in the Weimar.

Once in England, Hans Brahm becomes John Brahm, and he and Dolly—who have known each other for years—make the melodrama.

Columbia's Harry Cohn is so impressed with it that he lures Brahm to Hollywood. Around the same time, the agent Myron Selznick, the fire-breathing brother of David, lures Dolly to Hollywood. When she arrives in 1936 and Selznick pitches her to Cohn, Cohn observes, "I wouldn't mind taking her on, but she's a cockney."

"When I came into his office at first I was stunned," Dolly remembers, "because I saw a bust of Mussolini above where he was sitting. I didn't ask any questions. Anybody who has a bust of Mussolini is already completely clear to me. Little did he know how I felt. He had great intelligence (besides making such an unbelievable fool of himself)."

Brahm signs with Cohn and gets a picture called *Counsel for Crime*. Dolly signs with Cohn and gets nothing. One vehicle considered—*Paris on Broadway*, a musical by Oscar Hammerstein II for which she learns acrobatic jumps—is shelved. For his brother's sake, David Selznick makes an attempt to hire her, but Cohn, to keep hold of Brahm, won't release her. In September 1937, she's announced for *Absent Without Leave*, to be directed by Brahm. That doesn't happen either. But the exiles remain a duo—and on September 21 they marry in Tijuana.

And the boss is in a stew. What to do with her? Bingo! He gets creative, and Dolly gets a new name. "Euphonics and a Webster's Dictionary editorial consultant were brought into play by Columbia Studios and a new star was born," exults *The Film Daily* on December 3. "She is Lilli Marlowe, the erstwhile Dorothy Haas. Name was selected by Dr. Ray Keeslar Immel, A.B., A.M., Ph.D., dean of the University of Southern California School of Speech and consulting editor of Webster's International Dictionary."

Immel has become indispensable to the industry since 1928, when he found a niche with the advent of talkies. Out went silents, in came horrible accents, terrible timbres, nasalities, lisps, and stammers. Armed with telegraphones (early audio recorders) to record every inflection, dictionists were hired to homogenize them. Maybe the screen's royalty would never speak the King's English, but they'd speak.

Dolly's name isn't just *selected* by this genius, it's *concocted*. "After due thought, Dr. Immel christened Miss Haas 'Lilli Marlowe' because he said this name was rich in liquid letters, which had a 'flowing rhythm,'" reports UPI's Hollywood correspondent. But, adds *The Boston Globe*, "Dolly is having a difficult time remembering her new name."

And she's more than ever displeased with Cohn when he revamps her tomboy image, dyes her red hair blond and orders an extravagant photo shoot: Lilli as seductress, in white fur and satin . . . Lilli as ingenue in a striped robe, curled up on the floor with a Scottie, records, and fan magazines . . . Lilli as screen goddess being dressed, coiffed, measured . . . Lilli next to Cohn, pen in hand, posed and poised to sign her contract . . . Lilli looking come-hither, demure, frightened, and proud.

But "Lilli" never takes off, and Dolly has now been at Columbia for a year and a half, at $1,200 a week, without making a movie. So she goes to Ernst Lubitsch and Myron Selznick (new partners) for $750 a week to do *The Shop Around the Corner*, a charming romance based on the Hungarian play *Parfumerie* and written by Sam Raphaelson.

Only Lubitsch doesn't want her. He doesn't like her screen test. She comes across as "agonizingly self-conscious," Raphaelson recalls ruefully. Lubitsch plays it safe. In October, Hedda Hopper announces that the lead will now go to Janet Gaynor. "Part changed to small town, homespun girl. Dolly doesn't think she's right for it." Nor, of course, is Janet Gaynor, since the part goes to Margaret Sullavan.

In June 1939, Dolly is finally announced for a Paul Muni picture, *We Are Not Alone*, and in August Jimmie Fidler has a scoop: Dolly and Brahm are living apart while she's working, but visit on weekends. Thing is, she's not working. Days into production, she's replaced by Jane Bryant.

"One of the most tragic stories in Hollywood is that of Dolly Haas. She is near a nervous breakdown," tsk-tsks Louella Parsons. "The unhappy Haas girl, who has had nothing but a series of disappointments since she came to America, is now down to 90 pounds, although she weighs only 103 normally." Louella sincerely wishes she could get a break. So does the gossip Helen Zigmond, writing that the excitement of finally getting her big chance, "together with the fact that the role called for extreme emotional display, was too much for her. This week, suffering from nervous strain, she had to step out of the part."

17
WAR AND PIECES

Al and Brooks Atkinon have become close friends. "They not only admired each other, but they really had a great fondness for each other," says Arthur Gelb, who's long cherished them both. "They had the same politics, they had the same judgments about . . . well, sometimes they argued about plays. But a lot of their judgments were alike. They loved to gossip about the theater. Al would bring Brooks some delicious gossip which Brooks would eat up, and during intermission everyone thought they were talking about serious things when they were usually looking over the women in the crowd, evaluating them."

Through the years, Hirschfeld draws him whenever he gets the chance, clenching his pipe, perfectly positioned on the page (dead center when possible, as in the group of 1940s theater critics refigured as his stalwart nine old men of the Supreme Court). Only Hirschfeld could transform a blue blood with no outstanding features but a brush mustache and rimless glasses into such a distinctive character, over and over again.

Dolly divorces Brahm and comes to New York, where she hooks up with an experimental company at the New School for Social Research run by Erwin Piscator, the noted German director and producer. The Studio Theatre is a vital force for refugees in the 1940s. In March 1941, she opens in *The Circle of Chalk*, an oft-revived play based on a Chinese fantasy about a mother forced to make a noble decision about her child. In the role of Hai-tang, Dolly is described by Atkinson in the *Times* as "an exquisitely beautiful actress with the limpid grace of a Chinese poem or print." In 1950, she'll reprise her part on Broadway, and Atkinson his, remarking that "*The Circle of Chalk* has by now become Miss Haas' play at least in this country because she acts it with so much limpidity and charm."

When Al sees *The Circle of Chalk*, it's not on a Thursday. Because Thursday nights belong to Joe Gould, another member of the Hirschfeld menagerie. Famously mad and presumably brilliant, he's been compiling his skeptically awaited *Oral History of Our Time* for close to twenty-five years. Hirschfeld describes him as a "Yankee bohemian, bearded, bald, toothless, a young man in an old body and dressed like a scarecrow. Joe is often mistaken for a bum. In reality he is a writer at work on a non-profitable book." While stealing other people's conversations and scratching them into notebooks, he gets sloshed in Village bars, imitates seagulls, begs for handouts, and is kept on a teetering pedestal by his many literary champions. In the Depression, he, like Bodenheim and other starving souls, recited their poems for a meal—his most highly regarded being the one with the lines "In summer I'm a nudist, in winter I'm a Buddhist."

Some claim to have read snippets of the Work, but Joseph Mitchell, obsessed with him, will eventually write two famous profiles in *The New Yorker*, questioning the book's existence. Ezra Pound, William Carlos Williams, and

E. E. Cummings remain loyal, despite not knowing if or where it is. Saroyan has worshipped him since reading an excerpt in *The Dial*. Even more than he wants to read the whole nine million words, he wants to meet Gould, this malodorous icon who scrambles around town being tolerated, touted, and fed.

Hirschfeld is one of the feeders.

Like others under Gould's spell, he contributes a dollar a week to the Joe Gould Fund. And every Thursday night, Gould shows up to fetch it.

Saroyan is at the Osborne on one of those Thursdays. "Bill just fell on the floor and *salaamed* and said, 'He's the greatest man that ever lived,' highfalutin praise," Hirschfeld recalls. Saroyan vows to get the epic published, which naturally involves reading it. And in Hirschfeld's telling, a long-festering mystery is finally solved.

"We got into a cab," Hirschfeld says, "went down to the Broadway Central Hotel, where Joe had a room—that he didn't live in, but for storing his manuscript. It was from the floor to the ceiling, the whole room. You'd just walk in between these papers—not publishable at all. But we picked up a few of the papers to read them, and it was complete nonsense, all kind of: 'Oh, yes?' 'Uh-huh.' 'Ooh.' 'You got a cigarette?' 'Hiya, Joe.' Handwritten, the whole thing. You could barely read it. Millions of pieces of paper."

As the story goes on, Saroyan hooks Bennett Cerf of Random House. But when they go downtown and tell Gould the good news, he takes off.

"The following Thursday, he didn't show up for his dollar," Hirschfeld continues. "He never showed up again. About six months went by, and I went down to the Village again, and there's Joe. And I said, 'Joe, what happened to you?' He said, 'I told you. Those bastards with all their big ideas. They don't want to publish literature.'"

Saroyan has cast the trumpet-playing Don Freeman in *The Beautiful People* as Harold Webster, the cornet-playing brother. All Freeman has to do is say three lines and toot a tune called "My Wonderful One." Hirschfeld—who later claims, "He wanted *me* to be in that thing"—urges Freeman to do it.

The night before the opening, Paula passes the cheese and crackers as Hirschfeld hosts a gathering at the Osborne. Atkinson is there—along with Saroyan, the Freemans, and Sergei Radamsky, the Russian tenor—to lift a stein and write a piece full of bubbly vignettes promoting play and playwright.

On opening day, Freeman panics. "You don't know what it's like!" he yells at Hirschfeld. "You just sit back in your barber chair and make caricatures. It's hell, I'm telling you. Living hell!" On opening night, Hirschfeld sends him a secondhand gas mask from an army-navy store. The reviews aren't much, and Atkinson admirably refrains from a rave, nonetheless calling it beguiling and tender. The play closes in the summer while Hirschfeld's tooling around the countryside.

Not only tooling around it, but actually buying a hunk in July 1941—twenty acres near Alex King's at Greenwood Lake. What happens to said property is lost to rural history because no further mention of it is ever made.

Saroyan is on the move, too. *Jim Dandy*, one of his odder creations, has become available for amateur productions, and in the fall at Princeton a young blonde named Carol Marcus is in the cast. Because this is a rare production of a rarer play, and the closest to Broadway it's likely to get, the New York critics are invited. Atkinson shows up with his date, Hirschfeld. After the show, they meet young Carol.

Her two best chums are Gloria Vanderbilt and Gene O'Neill's daughter, Oona. The three butterflies want to be actresses and grow up fast. Legend has it that one of the mothers (Agnes O'Neill? Rosheen Marcus? certainly not Gloria Morgan Vanderbilt) asks Al Hirschfeld, of all people, to take the girls to the Stork Club and introduce them to nightlife because they're so young. He does, buys them strawberry drinks, and reports back, "These girls are going to be fine, don't worry about them." Apparently so: within the year, Gloria's married to a Hollywood agent, Oona's in love with Charlie Chaplin, and Carol's dating Saroyan.

Everybody *but* Hirschfeld takes credit for introducing Carol to Saroyan—from Carol's pushy mother to Artie Shaw. Whoever does it, Carol is sixteen, Saroyan is thirty-three, and their romance is so tempestuous that years later when they're married, unmarried, or remarried, Hirschfeld himself is called in as referee. "He was not the marrying kind," Hirschfeld recalls. "He never understood Carol's great qualities. Never."

As for Paula, she's knocking 'em dead as the maid in *Junior Miss*, which Hirschfeld sees in Washington. The book, by Jerome Chodorov and Joseph Fields, is based on stories by none other than Sally Benson of *Meet Me in St. Louis*. The director is Moss Hart.

Offstage, she's been busy with her own creations: wire caricatures à la Calder. One of them, "Moss Heart," will be shown in *Dressing-Room Doodles*, a celebrity-studded exhibition to benefit the American Theatre Wing War Service.

Gordon Kahn, back in New York and now on staff at *The Mirror*, gives Hirschfeld a jangle. Pick up *The New Yorker*, he says, the November 22 issue. Hirschfeld does, having little interest in the magazine since being put on its blacklist. What Kahn wants him to see is a series of ads plugging "Chicago's favorite game," the Deadly Double. All the ads shout, "Uchtung Warning Alerte!" One, showing a group of merrymakers throwing dice at an underground party, recommends what to have on hand in your air-raid shelter, from candles to coffee to the Deadly Double. Others show a double-headed eagle with an *XX*, or a pair of dice bearing numbers including a 12 and a 7—significant numbers if, as the eagle-eyed Kahn believes, they are a cryptic message to Japanese agents about the timing of the immiment attack on Pearl Harbor. Kahn can't find the game in stores, nor the company that manufactures it. *The New Yorker* can't help, because the ads were paid for in cash.

Hirschfeld's hooked.

"Pearl Harbor comes," says Gordon's son Tony, "and Al is having dinner with my father and Walter Winchell. One of them mentions this game, and Winchell gets interested."

What follows: "Winchell went and talked to some of his sources at the FBI—it might have included Hoover, I don't know—and what they were able to determine was that this one of the ways in which the Japanese high command had alerted all its diplomats in America of the approximate time, date, and location of the attack on Pearl Harbor and that my father in a sense had stumbled upon a spy intrigue! And Al, of course, tells this with a great laugh and a great sense of showmanship and 'Isn't this is a kick!'"

On December 7, 1941, *Harlem as Seen by Hirschfeld*, an elaborate folio illustrating the Harlem Renaissance (inspired by Paul Colin's Paris folio, *Le tumulte noir*, of 1927), is published. It's a limited edition of a thousand copies with an introduction by Saroyan. But on this, the day of infamy, nobody notices.

Hirschfeld is five feet nine, 150 pounds, and thirty-eight years old when he registers with the draft board in February 1942. Drawing through the war-torn seasons—when even summer theater is so affected that gas rationing forces the Bucks County Playhouse into the ballroom of the Bellevue-Stratford Hotel in downtown Philadelphia—he is deferred in September, classified 1-H, too old to serve. Stationed at the Osborne, he nonetheless does his part.

While Saroyan is scrubbing latrines on some far-off base, he's sketching service men in canteens, camps, and the Brooklyn Naval Hospital. S. J. Perelman goes on a war bond tour for the Treasury Department, and Hirschfeld goes to Hollywood, demonstrating his habitual scorn in two assaults on the industry's indulgence. In August 1942, *On the Hollywood Front* is his take on wartime "sacrifice" for the Sunday *New York Times Magazine*. The following May, he'll recycle the goods in *Main Street, Hollywood* for *The American Mercury*. In both, he remarks on the first-aid stations that repair a broken fingernail or torn stocking.

When a team of theater friends produce a pageant called *We Will Never Die* at Madison Square Garden to protest the slaughter of European Jews, Hirschfeld is illustrating the program for *About Face*, "a soldier musical" with sketches and songs by Private Frank Loesser and others for the Army Service Forces, and his caricatures for *Thousands Cheer* and *See Here, Private Hargrove* are decorating the lobbies and marquees of Times Square. And when Theodor Geisel—even while creating a raunchy series of wartime Warner Bros. cartoons for sex-starved soldiers—is turning out anti-Nazi cartoons for *PM*, so is Al Hirschfeld.

PM, which hit the stands in 1940, is the adless and abundantly liberal afternoon paper created by Ralph Ingersoll, formerly of *Fortune*. Stocked with writers from *The New Yorker*, the *Trib*, and elsewhere, full of photographs by Weegee and Margaret Bourke-White and sports, food, wartime maps, and comic strips, it's also required reading for the best radio listings in New York. Hirschfeld's contributions in 1943 pitch war bonds and take aim at Nazis, senators, and other irritants of the moment.

But no one sells war bonds like Louis G. Schwartz. Of all the eateries on their beat, Hirschfeld and the boys are jolliest at the Sixth Avenue Deli. Sure, they go for the corned beef at Lindy's, the cherrystones at Lundy's, lobster at the Lobster. But this place has Louie the Waiter, a poet exalted for such slogans as "Schtickle for a Nickel," "No one is daring to criticize our herring," and, most famously, "Send a salami to your boy in the Army." Even more famously, the line is seized and promoted as its own concoction by Katz's Delicatessen down on Houston Street. But in fact, it has been cooked up by a young wordsmith in the Entertainment Section of the Armed Forces, based in Honolulu, who's writing shows for servicemen in the Central Pacific. He is lyricist Hal David, the future partner of composer Burt Bacharach (and the son of a Brooklyn deli owner), who pens "Send a salami to your boy in the army / It's the patriotic thing / That everyone should do . . ." for a song called "Shape Ahoy."

Louie has a third calling as well, and no one escapes his hustle. By mid-September 1943, Louie has sold $1.4 million in war bonds, aiming for $2 million before the end of the Third War Loan drive (for which Hirschfeld will draw an ad in the *New York Post*). Philip Hamburger writes a swell profile in *The New Yorker*, calling him "a short, round blob of a man," and in Freeman's *Newsstand*, Hirschfeld draws and writes an homage to the Hero of Sixth Avenue, "who speaks only in rhyme and dictates what you should order."

Whatever Louie's serving, he makes things verse. To wit: "OSCAR LEVANT of Information Please / Eats his Potato Pudding with greatest of ease," he offers in a handout, and "AL JOLSON hasn't come down a peg. / Give him Chicken—boiled—the leg," and "Then there's our own WALTER WINCHELL the Navy tar. / Eating a Sturgeon sandwich standing at the bar." And "AL HIRSHFIELD of the New York Times—a swell artist you bet. Devours our Cheese Blintzes (the Bronx Crepe Suzette)." Hirschfeld's caricature of Louie festooned in pins and medals while slinging a bowl of matzo-ball soup hangs on the deli wall.

Dolly, still involved with the Studio Theatre, opens in *War and Peace* in June 1942. This adaptation, by Erwin Piscator and three collaborators, is probably not a good idea. "The quartet would have been better off if it had confined itself to a rendition of *Sweet Adeline*," notes *The Billboard*.

When she does *Winter Soldiers* in November, Hirschfeld shows up backstage after the dress rehearsal. And when he invites her to a party at the Osborne, "I found him to be very engaging," she recalls, "and I was very impressed by his taste and very much taken." In fact, she's started cutting out and keeping his drawings.

Al's away in New Haven at *Away We Go!*, the first musical by Rodgers and Hammerstein. It's 1943, and the Theatre Guild producers are getting the bum's rush from backers—despite a ravishing score, choreography by Agnes de Mille, Alfred Drake as Curly the cowboy, and Howard da Silva as Jud Fry, the bad guy. Sniffing disaster, the vultures flock north. Cheryl Crawford and Kurt Weill think it's a flop. "No jokes, no legs, no chance," proclaims Mike Todd.

Lawrence Langner, a Welsh-born patent attorney better known as one of the founders of the Theatre Guild in 1919—which presents major plays and musical classics—invites Hirschfeld for coffee at the Taft, along with Todd and Billy Rose. "If it was *my* turkey, I'd close it here," snaps Todd. They look to Hirschfeld. "I shrank back," he later remembers. "You're asking *me*? *You're* the experts!" He likes the music, dances, costumes, but not the book, "but then I never have been able to take the book of a musical seriously—operas, operettas, and serious musicals are soporifics which hermetically seal my eyes. To me, the ideal musical forms are vaudeville, burlesque, and the satirical revue."

The show's press agent presses him to do it for the *Times*, but he says he's going to do his Sunday drawing of the *Ziegfeld Follies of 1943*, starring Milton Berle. *Okay, okay.* Because both shows will be trying out in Boston at the same time, he agrees to revisit *Away We Go!*—which has now been renamed *Oklahoma!*—and both pictures run in the *Times*, side by side. He hasn't changed his opinion, though. "The reason was not that *Oklahoma*! was so good," he recalls. "It was that the *Follies* was so bad."

A month later, he stirs even the heavens with a drawing of soldiers and sailors, tourists and vendors scrambling along Broadway on a Saturday night. Next to the popcorn stand in the center he puts a nun.

Holy smoke! "I will say for your information that Religious (NUNS) never appear on the streets alone after dark, even during the day they are always accompanied by a companion," writes an angry Lady of Charity. "We feel that you may not know that such an appearance is virtually impossible," scolds a Knight of Columbus. "It is universal that no Sister is permitted on the streets after sunset unless she is on some critical errand of mercy and under such circumstances she must always be accompanied by a member of her own community. It is difficult to imagine an errand of mercy which would have required the presence of the figure portrayed on Times Square at the time pictured."

"I answered the first batch of mail, pointing out that a lone nun is stationed outside the Capitol Theatre every night, including Saturdays," Hirschfeld recalls. "But the matter did not end there." After a contretemps with the *Times* editor Lester Markel, Hirschfeld seeks penance in a letter to the editor. "I meant no disrespect. In all humility I apologize to the U. S. Armed Forces, the French navy and marines, the pimps, shills, girls, blind man, lone nun, and all others in the drawing." The letter is not published.

Nonetheless, Markel is devoted to Hirschfeld. "I don't know what I'm looking at on Sunday," he grumbles around this time.

"You're doing work for the *Tribune*, the *Brooklyn Eagle*, the *Telegraph*, the *Telegram*, the *World*. We're beginning to look like all the other papers." He says, "We would like you to just work for us and not the others."

Fine with Hirschfeld. "Well, all you've gotta do is cross my palm with silver and I'm your fella," he replies. "I'd much prefer to work for *The Times*, no question about it." And with good reason. The *Times* is the only paper that pays him directly. With the others, it's the producers who pay, which means they make demands. "I didn't have full control," he explains of the system, "and I always felt corrupted by that in some way. I would much rather have the freedom to do whatever I wanted." Which he now gets, with a handshake. At forty, he is as free or engaged as he chooses to be—which allows him myriad assignments, time on the road, a silver palm, and nothing in writing. He has no contract with *The New York Times* and likes it this way.

18
THE WONDER CHILD

ALBERT HIRSCHFELD WEDS
Miss Dolly Haas, Broadway actress, was married
to Albert Hirschfeld, the artist and caricaturist,
last Saturday afternoon at Elkton, Md.
—*The New York Times*, May 11, 1943

That's wrong.

The tiny announcement, buried in the middle of page 16 between the Music Notes and an ad for Sol Hurok's Spanish Festival at the Metropolitan Opera House, is there because Hirschfeld has shared his happy news with the paper . . . with every intention of its happening.

But it hasn't.

He and Dolly set out for City Hall, all right, but there's a problem. "We were in the car with them," says composer Burton Lane's wife, Lynn. "And Al suddenly couldn't remember whether his divorce had gone through, and he got very nervous. Turned right back."

It hadn't.

Flo consents, the divorce is granted on May 21, and he's free. But the bells don't chime quite yet. It's September 9, when Dolly's in Baltimore, that Al drives down to marry her there.

They have and they hold, and they cherish the date. "Nine was our lucky number," Hirschfeld says.

"You'll never be rich," Dolly's mother has cautioned, "but you'll never be bored." And so they begin. The bride is thirty-three, the groom forty. Their honeymoon plans include Nantucket, but Hirschfeld resists. "I sit on a beach and within fifteen minutes everything in my body starts aching, itching," he explains. "I've got to get up, get inside, get dressed, and get away"—this from the erstwhile country squire. And so he asks his bride, "Would you mind if we went to Boston? I can't take the heat, it's making me nervous." They arrive just in time for a performance (and drawing) of *One Touch of Venus*, a new musical by Sid Perelman, Ogden Nash, and Kurt Weill. Directed by Elia Kazan, not known for musicals, this urbane offering concerns a statue that comes to life and falls in love with a barber. The marble love goddess in this version of the Pygmalion myth is played by young Mary Martin (who made her Broadway debut in Cole Porter's *Leave It to Me* in 1938, singing the song she'll sing forever, "My Heart Belongs to Daddy"). The art collector's wise-cracking assistant spouting Perelman pearls is played by Al's former lady love, Paula Laurence.

Paula has Hart and is known as "Moss's girl." Last week's Moss's girl was an actress named Edith Atwater. One night as Atwater and Hart came into a dinner party, Oscar Levant cracked, "Ah, here comes Moss Hart . . . and the future Miss Atwater." Now it's Paula's turn. Alexander Woollcott claims the line when he sees them going into the 21 Club and says, "There goes Moss Hart with the future Paula Laurence."

And what of Flo? Way up in Alaska—Alaska!—Hirschfeld later tells a reporter, "selling Helena Rubinstein cosmetics, makeup, whatever that is, up there. That was her territory."

But even this development has variations, none so far off as Alaska. "She ended up living in a trailer," says Frances Hershkowitz. "Portland [Hoffa] paid her living expenses till the end of her life. Al didn't give her anything. I remember Portie saying, 'I just sent some more money to Flo. She's living in a trailer park in California.'"

Or, she marries Irwin Frankel, an executive in the Glemby Company, which runs a chain of department-store beauty salons (where Al evidently picks up the cosmetics idea). "They had a cabana in Newport Beach, where all the yachts were out in the front, and then they had a house in the Hollywood Hills and knew a lot of famous people," says Michele Dabbeekeh, her granddaughter. "Irwin was the love of her life." Not Al? Not Al.

If Dolly isn't making much of a name for herself on stage and screen—and she isn't, what with her flimsy role in *Doctors Disagree*, a two-week flopperoo, for which Hirschfeld nonetheless makes her the focus of his Sunday drawing, and a bunch of movies in which she appears uncredited (from *The Bank Dick* to *Du Barry Was a Lady)*—she's not making a name for herself on the radio either. But that's intentional.

Anonymously serving the Office of War Information, she has a voice in two programs—and one language, German. One is *American Women Speak to German Women* with two other women, but *Music With Margarethe* is her own. Broadcast at 4:30 every morning, it's a satirical program of "propaganda, jokes, and stories against the Nazis," as she describes it, with scripts by writers for *Simplicissimus*, the satirical German weekly. "One day I would talk to the German women, and to men the next, telling them about the American way of life," she says. "Just as simple as that."

In June, she throws a surprise party for Al's forty-first birthday. She's found his address book and, bride-like, invited everybody in it. Although some people in it know or are about to know some people in it—such as Florence and Harold Rome (he being the composer-lyricist of the revue *Pins and Needles*), playwright Sidney Kingsley and wife Madge, Ruth and Gus Goetz (itching to write a play of their own), and the Hacketts (Frances Goodrich and Albert Hackett), revered for *The Thin Man*—other people in it aren't even speaking to other people in it.

Among the untheatrical guests are Eugene Lyons, the UPI reporter Hirschfeld and Flo met in Moscow on their honeymoon back in 1928, and Mrs. Lyons. As former Communists, the Lyonses stick out like red thumbs in this crowd and are virtually ignored. The studio sings with discord as rivals and regulars group and ungroup, and Dolly flutters around making effortful small talk. Meanwhile, Al does his social best, schmoozing and kibitzing and wishing the whole thing would go away. When Covarrubias shows up, he shows up alone since his wife, Rosa, is reputedly in the arms of Nelson Rockefeller.

There's always King (Alex) and Castle (Joan). Formerly the object of Saroyan's affections, Joan Castle is a stunner—an erstwhile understudy and good-time gal, sometimes married, sometimes not. And always noticed. "Joan Castle and Billy Rose are Adam-&-Eveing," Walter Winchell tattles in a column.

"She was *magnetic*, one of these people who locks in on your eyes," says one of her pals, "and she had a powerful effect on people. She had very good friends among the ladies as well as the men, and she dated a ton of men, and she knew all about men." She adores Al.

Gordon Kahn's here as well. In and out of Hollywood now, where his nickname is Genghis, he's been writing screenplays and doctoring dialogue for such vehicles as *Lights of Old Santa Fe* and *Song of Nevada* and regularly turning out pieces for *The Atlantic* on subjects dear to his heart such as the monocle. He's a natty chap, driving a Bugatti, riding in Central Park with English saddle and jodhpurs.

À la Perelman. "These guys had enthusiasm, had great talent, and were still Old European enough to say they want to look like an Austro-Hungarian belted earl or count and drive fancy cars," says Gordon's son Dr. James Kahn. "In their heart, they were common laborers, but their mind was up there, on being the royal family."

Especially Perelman, who loves all things British and speaks "in an extremely unusual way," says Woody Allen, admiringly. "Very highfalutin, very elegant." Not only do Woody and S.J. share a fondness for wordplay and tweed, they'll also share a page in *Hirschfeld's World*, published in 1981. Why? "We're in the same general ballpark, physically," Woody explains. "We're more alike than, you know, Perelman and Marlon Brando."

Briiing.

"How would you like to write a musical?" It's Sid Perelman on the horn. "What makes you think I could write a musical?" says Al. "A musical about the future," adds Sid.

And so is born a terrible idea.

Hirschfeld, who doesn't consider himself a writer—in spite of the peppy text he's written with Kahn for *Manhattan Oases* and the humorous captions and text blocks he's written accompanying his art—says, "Why not?"

They meet for coffee at the Lafayette Hotel in the Village on a summer's day in 1944 to start cranking out a farce about corporate America, space travel, and the relics in a time capsule from the 1939 World's Fair. The premise is based on their daffy assumption that Flushing Meadows will be entirely underwater by 2076, Hirschfeld later explains (with good reason, since the vast expanse was a wild wetland until Parks Commissioner Robert Moses filled it in, dried it up, and leveled it with tons of ashes). The opening scene features an actual opening, when the Westinghouse Time Capsule, planted for the World's Fair, is lifted from the muck. The real capsule—which weighed

800 pounds—contained products, samples, and swatches of the day (from a safety pin to a Lilly Daché hat), millions of words and pictures, sheet music and magazines on microfilm, and more. To these historical goods, Hirschfeld and Perelman add a bagel and a brassiere, among other items they expect will have 'em rolling in the aisles.

Eager to move beyond Prohibition, Depression, and war, the two dive feetfirst into the future. One can only imagine the chortles emanating from Perelman's study as they concoct this absurdity about a man who inherits the Futurosy Candy Corporation. Neither fella is much of a dramatist, not even Perelman. But humor they've got. To even his most devoted followers, Perelman is often considered funnier on the page than on the stage, and on this project it's Al's cockamamie take that gets them going. Their friends (and perhaps their collaborators, too) have no idea who's writing what with this thing, but it doesn't seem to matter.

In January 1945, Sam Zolotow is granted the scoop. "A keen observer of matters theatrical for some time, Al Hirschfeld, the well-known caricaturist, is plotting a musical comedy book with S. J. Perelman," he reports in the *Times*. "A rough outline is finished. No tunes, lyrics or producer yet."

Soon comes a lyricist—Ogden Nash, the poet who collaborated with Perelman on *One Touch of Venus*—and in April the three musketeers go to Hollywood to find themselves a leading man. No dice. Hirschfeld and Perelman stay with the Hacketts, and Perelman tries scrounging around for some movie assignments, but that doesn't work either. It's been quite a while since *Monkey Business*, *Horse Feathers*, and his other flicks of the 1930s.

For the music, they talk to Kurt Weill, who also worked on *Venus*. But he can't do it, says he has some Hollywood assignments. Talk to Harold Arlen, who says he's crazy about the script but is tied up for a year. Talk to Johnny Green, who says he's tied to a contract for two years. Talk to Harold Rome, who's involved with something else for at least a year. Talk to Vernon Duke, who wrote the music for Perelman's *Walk a Little Faster* in 1932 . . . such songs as "April in Paris," "Autumn in New York," "I Can't Get Started," "Taking a Chance on Love" . . . and classical music under his real name, Vladimir Dukelsky. Newly sprung from the Coast Guard, he's not only crazy about the script, he's available. They've got a composer.

In May, Zolotow announces the title: *45 Plus.* He reports that "Vernon Duke will devise the melodies" and "Boris Aronson the atmosphere" and the show will open in the fall. "No producer yet, but they're not worrying." What they're doing is courting Cheryl Crawford, who produced *One Touch of Venus* and is a known entity. Having been casting director of the Theatre Guild and a cofounder of the Group Theatre (producing Sidney Kingsley's *Men in White*, Clifford Odets's *Awake and Sing!*, and William Saroyan's *My Heart's in the Highlands*), she is, in this instance, the holy grail. But she won't commit.

Come summer, Nash is on Martha's Vineyard, Duke on Nantucket, Perelman in Bucks County, Hirschfeld in New York, and the work churns on. Duke gets a call from a conductor, referred by Cheryl Crawford. "Would that mean that she decided to do it?" he writes to Hirschfeld hopefully. Apparently so. In July, *45 Plus* makes the *Times*'s lineup for the fall season, with Crawford as producer. Leading-lady names are bandied about, from Bea Lillie to Gypsy Rose Lee ("She's a tall, marmoreal beauty with about as much acting ability as the Winged Victory of Samothrace," Perelman types to Hirschfeld). They hear that Jerome Robbins, on the town with *On the Town*, has heard the music and Crawford thinks he likes it, although Perelman isn't so sure *he* likes it. He wants revisions. To unruffle Sid's feathers, Hirschfeld sends him a salami from the Sixth Avenue Deli.

Aronson hasn't shown them any designs yet. "Don't you think things are now definite enough so he ought to go ahead and do a couple of models, or sketches, or whatever?" Perelman asks Hirschfeld. He's creating a spaceship and other settings using transparencies and opaques to give the illusion of endless space, "to imagine the future in theatrical terms, not to determine the shapes of things to come or to calculate the waves of the future," Boris writes in *Theatre Arts* magazine. His assistant, as on all his shows to come, is his wife, Lisa Jalowetz, an elegant Viennese designer who's recently assisted Jo Mielziner on *Carousel*. The newlywed Aronsons have taken Don Freeman's former flat on Columbus Circle.

To direct, Crawford wants Peggy Webster—the daughter of Dame May Whitty and inamorata of Eva Le Gallienne—who's lauded for her command of Shakespeare and Chekhov. Webster loves the script, the boys are told, but there's a problem: she has no idea how to direct a musical. They turn back to Crawford, who insists that Webster will triumph with the material, so they go along. For weeks. Finally (and frugally) they take Webster to lunch. So, they wonder, has she made a decision yet? Oh, yes, she says. She can't do it. She still has no idea how to direct a musical.

Back to Crawford, who again urges patience. But patience lasts just so long with these guys, and they've already been waiting for months. So they make their own decision: there's going to be no Peggy Webster, and no Cheryl Crawford either.

In August, they have a director: Curt Conway. In September, they have a new title: *Futurosy*. In October, they have a new producer. Crawford is out, and George Heller—an actor who played the xylophonist in *You Can't Take It with You* and "A Man" in *Waiting for Lefty*, among other roles—is in. He is neither a known entity nor a holy grail.

So ends the start of another caper in the life of Hirschfeld, featuring players of note and not, told and reprised to manifold friends and interviewers through the decades. As a fabulist, his stories, like his caricatures, are spun of whimsy, sass, and the perfect line.

As a wife, Dolly becomes a US citizen in August 1944, holding a red, white, and blue bouquet. And as a real hausfrau, she knows her place. On those malodorous evenings when Al and his cigar-infused cronies play poker and pinochle until 3:00 in the morning, she stays offstage—in the bathtub.

"She was a trained child because she was a performer, a German child that obeys orders," says one of her old compatriots, "and she was geared to behave herself—to stand in a corner, to not call attention to herself."

And then she is pregnant. Dolly is thirty-five; Al, forty-two. ("No spring chicken," Margie King Barab quips. "He was no spring chicken either.") After several miscarriages, this one takes, and Dolly's ordered to bed for months. She prefers the couch in the larger room so she can be close to Al at his board, and that's where she reposes in her pink and yellow Chinese silk bed jackets. "It was very confining, because she was a very active woman," says Marge Champion, "and we would all come and have fun, but she rarely left the couch." Al, who's able to ignore their laughter while he works, is unexpectedly considerate, although "he never really wanted children. He really didn't," Margie Barab confides.

On October 20, 1945, Dolly's in labor, and Al's in Philadelphia. Getting the call, he speeds back, arriving at Doctors Hospital . . . with time to spare. "During those hours in the waiting room," he recalls, "I nervously filled the remaining pages of my sketchbook with drawings of the dark-haired girl my mother had been praying for."

On Saturday night, their daughter is born, and all speculation ceases. "Congratulations, sir," the doctor proclaims, "you're the father of a red-headed girl!"

Nina.

Hirschfeld returns home to draw the Philadelphia show, *Are You with It?* for the *Times*.

"The musical had a circus background which I used in my drawing," he says. "On an imagined poster, hung on the sideshow tent, I facetiously drew a newborn infant reading from a large book. Lettered on the poster, as billing, I printed 'Nina the Wonder Child.'

"This little folly was, over the decades, to turn into a monster."

"Just think," muses a wag. "If he'd been doing *Hamlet*, the whole NINA thing may never have happened. Was he going to put Nina on *Hamlet*?"

Nina says she was named for Dolly's friends Nina Hansen (an actress) and Katrin Holland (a novelist more popularly known as Martha Albrand). Hirschfeld says, "It coincided with our unconscionable attraction for the number 9" (9/9 being their wedding date). Whatever: she's Nina Katrin Hirschfeld.

"We got your joyous news today," Oriana Atkinson writes from abroad. "Of course Al has ice bags on his head, & under his eyes & probably wishes he were dead," she warmly adds. "We are thinking of you & chuckling at the mad disorder which is probably making your apartment into a first-class insane asylum. Better get that country house built. If I'm any judge you're going to need it."

The columnist Leonard Lyons writes, too. "The proud father has no pictures of the baby, but whenever he's asked: 'What does Nina look like?' he draws a sketch of her," he reports. "Hirschfeld is resolved to introduce his daughter into all his work."

The drawing for *Are You with It?* appears in the *Times* on November 4 as part of a triptych—along with two other shows, *The Rugged Path* and *The Girl from Nantucket*. He then tries slipping his daughter's name into *State of the Union* the next Sunday. But when he prints "Congratulations, Nina" on a Western Union telegram in Ruth Hussey's lap, a *Times* editor changes it to "Congratulations, Poppa." Undeterred, he's at it again the following week. On November 18, in *The Day Before Spring*, "nina," written in cursive, appears in Patricia Marshall's blond hair.

On December 16, Hirschfeld's baby shows up in *Billion Dollar Baby*, her name under the collar on Mitzi Green's chest . . . and December 30 on Charles Fredericks's collar in *Show Boat*. In *The Magnificent Yankee* on January 20, 1946, he has Dorothy Gish stitching NINA into her needlepoint. He's having a fine time.

"Nina's saving grace was that Nina was a girl," suggests an insider. "If she had been a boy, I can't even imagine that he would have had any interest at all." But he has a lot of interest, and he can't keep his pen off her. He draws her at twelve days old in her mother's arms, and frames the sketch as a tray for Dolly's tea—which then splashes, leaving a stain. With his movie camera, he records her being cradled and bathed, bounced and swooped by her madcap parents and Milly the nurse.

Just a regular baby, clapping and cooing and playing peekaboo, while fame awaits.

19
SHOW ON THE ROAD

Dolly needs space. Nina has brought joy into their lives, but also apparatus. "It was a problem where to be with the child," Lisa Aronson remembers, "and I think they had to take a part of that studio and fix it up for her. And then Dolly's mother came to help out from Germany. But it was very tough to keep all this functioning, these different lives. Al had real life suddenly—the *ordinary* real life."

At this point, a country house might, once again, be the ticket. Everyone else has one—from bird-watching Brooks in the Catskills to the showbizzy bodies in Bucks. But Hirschfeld likes pictures, not the picturesque. Like Sartre, who "loathes the swarming life of insects and the pullulation of plants" . . . like William Shawn, who looks "surprised and vulnerable standing on grass and not on pavement" . . . like Gordon Kahn, who'd "rather have a salami hanging in the pantry than a liverwort on the garden wall," Hirschfeld is averse.

"I envy people who have a talent for loafing, always have had," he says. "I can't do it." Not even at Perelman's farm in Erwinna, a village in Bucks County. "Al was very uncomfortable in the country," says Abby Perelman, S.J.'s daughter. "He was a very urban person. Either it was too quiet, or the birds made too much noise." Nonetheless, Perelman has been *noodging* him to buy property nearby—despite his own well-chronicled crankiness about country life. "Outside of a spring lamb trotting into the slaughterhouse," he observes, "there is nothing in the animal kingdom as innocent and foredoomed as the new purchaser of a country place." Just what Hirschfeld needs.

That upstate purchase from years earlier is but a memory. Now he springs for a swath in Bloomsbury, New Jersey, ten miles from Perelman, with plans to build a house for ten thousand dollars. In November 1945, specifications are drawn up by Victor Elmaleh, a Moroccan-born architect, musician, squash champion, and husband of Sono Osato, "Miss Turnstiles" in *On the Town*.

But the price transcends their agreement, and Hirschfeld refuses to pay. "That was the deal: ten thousand dollars," he tells Elmaleh. The case lands in court, a settlement is reached, and Hirschfeld's off the hook. Which is just as well, since he has other fish to fry.

Such as his show. In December, it has a new title: *Sweet Bye and Bye*. Producer-wise, George Heller is out—something about "the booking jam" and finding "all the desirable musical houses tied up," according to Zolotow—and Shepard Traube is in. Fresh out of the Signal Corps, Traube is back where he produced *Angel Street*, which clicked big, and a few others which did not.

And soon a casting possibility appears on the horizon: Zero Mostel, who's been clowning around at Café Society and on the radio, is approached to play "a frenetic industrialist" in the show, Zolotow reports. Fred Kelly, Gene's brother, is lined up as choreographer. Even better, the fruit of Traube's *Angel Street* is angels, and Lyons reports in February that Nicholas Biddle and Tony Duke are among the show's "socialite investors." Josephine Hartford of the A&P fortune chips in, and a Whitney or two, but most of the backing comes from Ogden Nash's kith and kin in Baltimore.

Traube tells them they've got to think bigger than they've been thinking, and he wants to cast some real stars in the show.

So he takes off for Hollywood to find them. Hirschfeld and Perelman wait breathlessly. He's gone a week, three weeks, a month, and what's the news? No news. They hear that their producer is on another quest. Toting the script, touting the show he's doing back in New York, he's not out there looking for big names. He's out there looking for movie work.

What with the hubbub at home, Dolly gladly takes over for Mary Martin in *Lute Song*—directed by Paula's old friend John Houseman and flacked by Al's old friend Dick Maney. She'll play the final week on Broadway while Martin goes to Hollywood to (try to) be a movie star, then take the show on the road. *Lute Song* is another Chinese fantasy, another chance to enact love and sacrifice. This time, on a lavishly scenic stage, she plays a loyal wife caring for her husband's parents when he goes off to seek adventure. Yul Brynner—as a prince, not yet the King—is the husband.

Claudia Cassidy, esteemed critic on the *Chicago Tribune*, catches Dolly's first performance in New York before officially reviewing her later in Chicago. She's enchanted by this "actress of satiny skill" (and also by the wistful maid in waiting, played by the future first lady Nancy Davis).

Meanwhile, back at *Sweet Bye and Bye*, Shepard Traube is out, and Nat Karson is in. He's a known entity, at least to Hirschfeld, as designer of Paula's show *Horse Eats Hat*, art director of Radio City Music Hall, and, most recently, producer of *Nellie Bly*, a bomb musical. Whoever came up with Karson is a mystery, Hirschfeld claims disingenuously—having placed him prominently in his drawings for *A Southern Rhapsody* at the Music Hall in 1937 and *The Hot Mikado* in 1939. But poor Nat has had a rough time since his last show laid an egg, so the team agrees to give him a chance.

Karson wants Pat Kirkwood, a British actress, for the lead. She's about to open in MGM's *No Leave, No Love* with Van Johnson, so the timing's right. "She's *mahvelous*," Hirschfeld says. What's more, she's a hot ticket. Even the nearly infallible

George Kaufman tells them they've struck gold and wishes he could have snagged her for his new show.

For their leading man, Hirschfeld and Perelman want Gene Sheldon, a banjo-strumming comic. They're nuts about his commedia dell'arte vaudeville routine in which he sews his fingers together and gets them caught in a buttonhole. Al and Sid figure they've landed a big one, what a *bonanza*, with his lovable loony shtick.

One day in the third week of rehearsal, Pat Kirkwood doesn't show up. They call her hotel and her mother says Pat has a cold, but she'll be there tomorrow. The next day she doesn't show up again. Nothing serious. She'll be there tomorrow. With the New Haven opening on for October, the boys are twitchy. On the third day, they go to her hotel. Her mum is in the lobby.

"What's going on?" they ask. "Where's Pat?"

In an asylum.

Nat Karson goes back to the office, hires a car, and packs a pistol. Her savior. Mum and the boys hit the road to the asylum—or, as Hirschfeld likes to call it, "the laughing academy"—to find poor Pat wandering around, totally bonkers. She has no idea who they are (including Mum) or what they're doing there. When they corner her doctor to ask when she'll be able to get back to work, he implies never.

With little time before New Haven, they're able to snag Dolores Gray—a musical-comedy gal last seen in *Are You with It?* (the first NINA). They start rehearsing her and, within a week, she's picked up the lyrics, the lines, the moves, all the business, and she's *mahvelous*. While they're being bowled over by Dolores, they're ignoring Gene Sheldon, who, left to his own peculiar devices, is over in a corner, rehearsing his own moves, playing with his fingers, standing up and sitting down, and impressing them with his artistry.

Doing some business in another corner is a plastics expert hired by Karson—this being a show about the future—who's setting fire to plants and pieces of string.

"I realized that you're not in control of the medium," Hirschfeld will say years later. "I'm so used to being in complete control of what I do, but with writing a musical . . . it's a most difficult thing. Some chorus girl or waiter or carpenter might suggest something that we never thought of. It's a collaborative effort, you know, and I'm no good at it."

Baby Nina sends an opening-night telegram to Daddy from Chicago, where she and Dolly, Rebecca Hirschfeld, and the nursemaid Milly have trooped with *Lute Song*. And on October 10 in New Haven, the Hotel Taft is a-flurry with many more. The excitement extends all the way to Hartford, where the Touchdown Club is offering a "football special": for fifteen dollars, fans get a round-trip train ticket, a seat for the Yale-Columbia game, dinner, and an orchestra seat at the Shubert for the premiere of *Sweet Bye and Bye*. "Note: This trip is for MEN ONLY," the ad adds.

When the curtain rises, Walter O'Keefe—vaudevillian, radio host, and composer of "The Daring Young Man on the Flying Trapeze"—comes out, stares at the audience, and forgets everything. Then Gene Sheldon comes out, meets the girl, and proceeds with his routine—the fingers, the buttonhole, the whole shebang. All of it old, none of it new, and nothing to be done. The guy has worked up one routine, and that's what he's got.

When he comes off stage, the playwrights toss him then and there, before intermission. The stage manager goes out and tells the audience that Mr. Sheldon has had an attack of appendicitis, and they can get a refund at the box office. Meanwhile, an ambulance can be heard sirening out on College Street to rescue the guy, who's been knocked silly by Sid Perelman.

Next stop Philadelphia, with no leading man. They start auditioning. The delay costs them one of their two weeks at the Forrest, and they have to return the money (which doesn't sit at all well with Hirschfeld and Perelman, since the cast of a hundred is on full salary). Desperately they appeal to agents everywhere. Nobody's right for the role, whatever the role entails, until one shows up who might be. Why is he the answer? Because, says his agent, he's a fast learner: Erik Rhodes from *Gay Divorce* on Broadway, *The Gay Divorcee* on-screen.

The creators take adjoining rooms at the Warwick Hotel. Hirschfeld draws them in sequestered frenzy. There they sprawl, trying to fix their show—"and there was just no fixing to be done, as I understand it. The whole thing was a disaster," says Kay Duke Ingalls, Vernon's widow.

One morning Hirschfeld and Perelman are rewriting a scene when they overhear talk in the next room. Sid's listening at the door and pulls Al over to hear what he's hearing. It's Duke on the phone with a columnist in Philadelphia, telling the guy his music has been getting raves. And not only that, he's also been helping Hirschfeld and Perelman write the book.

Son of a bitch! says Sid to Al, who watches his partner turn an ugly shade of purple. Sid waits until Duke's off the phone, then takes a position near his side of the door. "Is this the *Daily Mirror*?" he yells. "Give me Walter Winchell!" The chuckling playwrights picture Duke in the other room now listening on *his* side.

Walter! he cries. It's Sid Perelman! I'm calling to tell you the critics down here love the book. He then adds that Al is even helping Vernon write the music . . . because Al plays piano.

Hirschfeld runs out of the room to get Nash, who arrives yawning in his bathrobe to find Sid thundering to the invisible Winchell. Now wide awake, Nash asks what's going on. Whatever they're doing, they'd better stop, because poor Vernon is beside himself. They explain the situation, convulsed with laughter, and Nash turns pale. Bad idea. Vernon has a heart condition, he tells them, and this could kill him.

Duke, who's having no fun at all, has nonetheless written some swell songs for the show—"Round About," "Just Like a Man," "Low and Lazy." But they have nothing whatever to do with the future. "You won't believe this, Al," he says one day. "I went to dinner last night and these people said, 'I understand you're doing a satirical musical about advertising in the future.' Can you imagine?"

"We looked at one another, baffled," Hirschfeld says, "because that *was* what it was about."

They're bleeding, so they hold a backers' audition at the Warwick. Rising to address his captive audience, Nat Karson tells them the show is doing wonderfully, they're hearing terrific things, great word of mouth, gonna be a winner . . . but they still have to raise more money to finish the run down here and get the show to Broadway. While he's yapping, he's nervously flicking a cigarette lighter, which captures Hirschfeld's attention.

When Karson winds down, two of the well-heeled lady backers signal each other and stroll from the room. After a while, they return with matching smiles. A nod to the creative team means they can deliver the money. With drinks all around and pats on backs, the future looks rosy indeed. Then one of the creators notices a glittering item lying on the table: a gold cigarette case—is it Karson's? can't be Karson's—embellished with red rubies, white diamonds, and blue sapphires. The team shares a look and a single thought. It could be worth a fortune.

"Hock it!"one of them mutters. And suddenly Nash, who's not only well acquainted with the rich but is married to them, puts up his hand. "Hold on, boys. Keep your shirts on." He says the lighter was put there intentionally to test them, the way one does with a new servant. They freeze. No hocking.

Before long, Curt Conway and Fred Kelly are out, and Perelman is directing. They move to the Erlanger, but rehearsals are held in the downstairs lounge of the Forrest, next to the men's room. When Hirschfeld arrives one day, he comes upon a terrifying scene. Perelman has young Tom Glazer, who's playing a stowaway on a spaceship, backed into a urinal. He's screaming, "You idiot! Don't you know how a robot acts?" There's a robot in the play?

Hirschfeld creeps out of the Forrest into the bright Philadelphia sunshine. That's when it really hits him. That's when he realizes they're in deep, deep . . . trouble.

By opening night, Rhodes, "the fast learner," hasn't learned the lyrics. And to no one's surprise, the show folds in Philadelphia. Too late to pull, a Gimbels ad runs to coincide with the opening, pushing a new contraption from RCA Victor. "Television now descends from the realm of the sweet bye and bye," it reads.

"Perelman and I were the culprits," says Hirschfeld. "We discovered it very late, too late to do anything about it"—although Lisa Aronson will eventually say, "Everything was wrong about it. Everything. Tell you the truth, I don't remember much about that show. I guess one doesn't *want* to remember."

Years later, when Hirschfeld is doing a drawing for an impending disaster, *Via Galactica*, he asks the producer what it's about. "The future," says George W. George, enthusiastically.

Hirschfeld nods.

20
TRAVELS WITH SIDNEY

They're enjoying a funereal cup of coffee at the Warwick, while the show is staggering to its death, when along comes Ted Patrick, editor of a new magazine called *Holiday*. "What are you going to do now?"

"I may join the Foreign Legion, or, on the other hand, I may take a hot bath," Perelman says. But Patrick has a better idea. "Why don't you take a trip for us?"

Or, as Hirschfeld puts it, "Sid said, 'Well, I don't know about Al, but I'm gonna get the hell out. I'm going fishing. I'm going down to Florida.' Patrick said, 'How would you like to do a piece for *Holiday* on fishing in Florida?' Sid said, 'Wonderful, fine. How about Al coming along and doing some drawings to go along with it?' So I said, 'No, count me out. I have to go to California.'" *Lute Song* will be opening in January, and he's promised to be there.

"So Patrick said, 'Well, why don't you fellas do a piece on Hollywood? You've both been there, you don't like it, and you could have a lot of fun.' Sid said, 'Nothing would please me more.'"

During lunch, Hirschfeld regales them with his experiences in Bali and Tahiti. He knows Sid would have a field day in Tahiti. Soon Ted suggests a trip around the world. And within a week, stepping out of the ashes of *Sweet Bye and Bye*, they've signed with *Holiday* for a series of articles and with Simon

& Schuster for a book. For Perelman, whose favorite book is *Ulysses*, this is a globe-trot come true. For Hirschfeld, it's an escape from domesticity. "We had to leave the country anyway after this stinker," he says with a chuckle, "so it worked out beautifully."

The Hirschfelds can be in Los Angeles at the same time. While Dolly's onstage and Nina's on somebody's lap, her husband will be on assignment. "There was Hirschfeld to be put on the train to Hollywood (and Hirschfeld to be taken off again, when it turned out to be the wrong train); there was Hirschfeld's thirteen-months-old baby to be shipped west to be present at our sailing, though the poor thing was so backward it could not even speak English; it was Hirschfeld this and Hirschfeld that until sometimes I thought I must go mad," Perelman reflects, at this point all in fun.

With the far-fetched idea of doing a series of shorts spoofing James A. FitzPatrick's popular *Traveltalks*—those Edenesque, news-avoiding Technicolor travelogues narrated by FitzPatrick ("The Voice of the Globe") for movie-chair travelers in the 1930s and 1940s—they use Hirschfeld's 16-millimeter camera on Hollywood's culinary culture (the Nu-Burger, Government Inspected Horsemeat, The Fetchitessen), religion ("1st Hebrew Christian Synagogue"), and medical science—from a sign reading MALE GLANDS 1 MONTH'S SUPPLY 90 TABLETS to Perelman getting his blood pressure checked on the street for fifteen cents.

On the eve of their February departure, Groucho Marx toasts them at Chasen's. "So I say to you two bold adventurers—stretch out your hands for the fruits of the world. Bring back tales of the African Veldt, of the snows of Kilimanjaro, of the Roumanian peasants. . . . Tell us more of the Dutch boy with his finger in the dike and, if possible, bring back a dike to each of us," and so forth.

Dolly and Nina move on to Chicago, and the boys sail off on the *Marine Flier*, a small cargo ship that Perelman describes as "little more than a cheesebox on a raft." Furthermore, he describes the appetite of Hirschfeld, who, "with the stolidity of the true peasant, outdid himself in gluttony. Bread by the bushel basket, whole beeves, firkins of butter, and hogsheads of jam vanished down his maw; his arrival at table spread consternation in the galley. He lived only for the ship's bell summoning us to meals."

While Dolly is acting a China doll, her husband is eyeing the real thing. "We sashayed up and down the Chinese coast for the next three weeks, going to Shanghai, back to Chinwangtao, and then back to Shanghai," Perelman writes. They see rickshaws and rowboats, wading bulls and rollicking monkeys. ("My father was very, very fond of animals," Perelman's daughter, Abby, recalls. "He was much better with animals than with children.") Hirschfeld shoots faces—people's faces, statues' faces, gargoyles' faces. And hands—at a loom, on a drum, painting a parasol, grooming a beard.

In Hong Kong, they meet some royals. Perelman sees the scene as bad comic opera, while Hirschfeld goes for more detail.

"This here blintz How Dai doesn't exactly look semi-divine," Al informs Ruth and Gus Goetz of Bao Dai, the deposed emperor of Annam (aka Vietnam). "He looks like a mens room attendant in a 52nd St. clip joint; or a pin boy in a Canarsie bowling alley." As for the eminences of Johor, "The Prince, a fat pansy with a falsetto voice," and his wife, "a wisp of a thing from Ripleys Museum," live in a palace guarded by barefoot sentries and a dozen dogs. Luncheon, "though not to be compared to the 6th Ave. delicatessen, was edible and neatly served by a crew of Zombies. After a few polite belches, and the flicking of loose rice from his back molars with an ivory tooth pick, the Prince took us to inspect his art collection. A more grotesque collection exists nowhere in the world."

They send their work to *Holiday*, and for Sid this means *work*. When Hirschfeld calls him a great disciplinarian, he's talking about his words, not his children. Tightly wound and neat as a pin, Sid won't erase or cross out a letter, a syllable, a phrase. Instead, he'll retype the whole page. Even worse, Al recalls, "He used to drive me crazy, because it was in '47 just after the War, and it was difficult to get these things back to the magazine. We'd have to go through the State Department to send them and sometimes there were special couriers and planes. And we would get to the base, and Sid would suddenly realize that he didn't remember whether he said 'the celestial empire' or 'the empire of China,' and he rips open the envelope and goes back to the hotel, types the whole thing all over again! I couldn't wait for him to get that thing out of his hands."

Singapore, Bangkok. "Everything is designed to make your jaws open involuntarily," he writes to Atkinson. "The temples are really breathtaking but similar to well designed scenery they are most dramatic when seen from a distance. On close inspection, the jeweled domes become old broken crockery inlaid in cement; the marble stairs are bricks covered with plaster and painted to resemble marble; the emerald buddha is made of broken green glass; the gold ones are stone painted with gold paint. The town was designed by Billy Rose rather than Cellini." But he loves it. "If they had no mosquitoes in Bangkok and all my friends lived here," he adds, "and I could be with Dolly 24 hours a day, I think I could live here for the rest of my life. That is, of course, if they had a Broadway."

Except when Perelman flies and Hirschfeld sails—"No! It's not a race," Hirschfeld writes to the Goetzes. "It's merely that Sid likes planes and I like boats"—they're very much together. "I can picture Al journeying with anyone and everyone, and I was surprised that Perelman was also a guy who was perfectly willing to get on a freighter or a cargo ship or something and go to places that I would never in a million years *go near*," says Woody Allen, cringing.

Dolly goes to Washington. Hirschfeld's *Lute Song* drawing runs in *The Washington Post*, and critic Richard Coe finds

Dolly "more ethereal, more delicate in the part" than Mary Martin ever was. Another article mentions that Nina and Yul Brynner Jr. are leading happy lives on the road, because their parents "are up on child psychology."

One of Nina's parents is actually up-country. Seeking solitude (or refuge from Perelman), Al takes off from Bangkok for Chieng Mai with an escort from the US Information Service. Perelman, too, welcomes the break. "Flying north at nine thousand feet," he writes in one of his *Holiday* articles, "it was possible to breathe again and pity Hirschfeld, who, with a lively concern for Hirschfeld, was creeping along the burning, barrren waste in a railway carriage."

Shopping in New Delhi, Perelman beholds "Hirschfeld haggling for a six-piece bedroom suite of carved ivory, priced at seven hundred thousand rupees, which had taken two men twenty-five years to complete. Why he wanted to possess all this dead tooth structure is beyond me, but he refused to yield to my entreaties and I ultimately had to hit him from behind with a knotted towel and drag him outside before his judgment returned." To illustrate his other needs, Hirschfeld draws "Noonday mirage, Old Delhi," a composite of longing—with a camel, the Taj, Cleo, her asp, and logos for Lindy's, 21 Club, and the Sixth Avenue Delicatessen.

In July, the boys are on the Nile, doing a piece that will offend, among others, the head of the Cultural Section of the Egyptian Education Bureau. In August, they're in France. Perelman goes to Nice, where he bumps into Somerset Maugham in the barbershop, and Hirschfeld's off to Paris. Another welcome break, it seems. Perelman's having great fun belittling Hirschfeld in the magazine, but behind the pages he's had it up to here.

"Hirschfeld went off to Paris two days after we arrived," he confides to his wife, Laura. "He said it was too hot to think here (I'm sure I don't know what thinking has to go into those hasty, distasteful drawings he's been turning out) and he said he was dying to get to Paris. This may have a wee something to do with a babe he's mentioned now and again who lives there—in any case, he departed and the air became breathable again. I shall have a matter of five weeks of his society until we sail, and I plan to spend as little as I can of it in his actual presence . . .

"I am as convinced as can be that he is not really compos mentis. I'll never be so glad to see the last of anybody. I don't believe that any woman could tolerate his smugness, his constant pettiness and insane desire to prove himself right about the most idiotic trivialities, and mark my words, it'll be only a matter of time with Dolly. His first wife and a number of girls couldn't take it, and I'm betting she won't. Of course he venerates her, he makes it plain that she is probably the most gifted woman in the world and is constantly cramming publicity clippings down my throat about her genius, and anybody would lap that up for a while, but I predict a degringolade."

Postwar Paris is bleak, especially in August, when everything's closed. Most dismaying is that the Select, where Hirschfeld began his affair with the city, is closed permanently. Prices are steep. Much of the Louvre haven't yet reopened. Montmartre is like Coney Island. "It's very, very tired," Perelman writes sadly to Laura, "and neither of us think it's because we're older. It's just gone, that's all."

They wrap it up in London, Perelman at the Athenaeum Court and Hirschfeld at the Savoy ("*Gott sei dank*," Perelman writes home a few days later; *thank God*). If Paris was bleak, London is Blitzed, but despite the rationed soap, houses pitted with shrapnel, and wreckage along Jermyn Street, the Brits, he informs Laura, "keep their chin up" and "are rebuilding to beat the band." Meanwhile, there are plays to see—courtesy of *The New York Times*. One of them is *Edward, My Son*, with Robert Morley, starting at seven o'clock. Perelman races to the theater. Hirschfeld doesn't show. He won't wear a watch, the desk forgets to wake him, and by the time he gets there, the tickets are gone.

They endure an uncomical comic at the Palladium, drive to Surrey with Joe Mankiewicz for lunch, bump into Erskine Caldwell at the Savoy, and visit their *Bye Bye* star Dolores Gray, currently the toast of the town in *Annie Get Your Gun*. They even make a stab at Ivor Novello's comedy *We Proudly Present*, which is not proudly enough presented for Perelman, who walks out after the first act. "H. got on his high horse about that," he grouches to Laura, "stating that he had never walked out on a show in his life (though he didn't like it any more than I did), but I won the contest . . . As you see, it's long since time that this lovely little duet got its divorce papers."

In September, they sail home on the *Queen Mary*. Arriving on September 9, his fourth wedding annniversary, Hirschfeld brings lace and perfumes for Dolly and a child's kimono for Nina. He and Perelman survive their odyssey and, back on familiar soil, will soon resume their deep rapport. When *Westward Ha!* is published a year later, it sells well enough to justify all the rigamarole. The subtitle is "Around the World in Eighty Clichés"—providing a Perelmanian foreglimpse of the Oscar-winning screenplay he'll cowrite a few years later for *Around the World in 80 Days*.

As for Hirschfeld, he's missed some important openings in the past nine months. And readers have noticed. Among his sacrifices: *Finian's Rainbow* (Don Freeman drew it), *Brigadoon* (a photograph), *Allegro* (Freeman), *A Streetcar Named Desire* (Freeman), and *High Button Shoes*, which gets a delayed Hirschfeld the next spring. Regarding *The Heiress*—a play written by his close friends the Goetzes—Hirschfeld unloads his suitcase, grabs his pen, and turns out a drawing to run in the *Times* on Sunday.

21
HOUSE AND HOME

Now that the family is back together, and back to back, it's time to get cracking on a move. In the fall of 1947, Al and Dolly go house hunting.

Some say they're directed to East Ninety-fifth Street by Jed Harris, the surly wunderkind who's just directed *The Heiress.* Others say it's Alfred Drake, the musical-comedy star, who recently moved to the block with his wife and two daughters. Whoever has lit the way, the Hirschfelds arrive on an exquisite block between Park and Lexington Avenues with private houses on both sides—all within the sound of the Third Avenue El and the scent of Jacob Ruppert's brewery.

This is Goat Hill. The south side of the street presents a row of twelve houses built for the middle class in 1887–1888. Designed by Charles Abbott French & Company, each has a different palette. "Details on the houses are rich in texture," notes the architectural preservationist Andrew S. Dolkart, "with most of them incorporating whimsical terra-cotta elements such as tile work and satyr heads."

But only one of the figures calls to Al Hirschfeld—smack in the center of the facade of No. 122. "Saw that gargoyle, that was it," he says of the figure with the flowing beard.

The house's first inhabitants were Jacob Rothschild, a carpet dealer, and Elias Einstein, a cloak-and-suiter who'd been a cotton broker in Georgia, and before that private secretary to General Howell Cobb of the Confederate army. (Cobb's the man who, when inspecting Andersonville in 1865, said he regretted any prisoners taken; they should all have been hanged instead.)

"I'm delighted that you will have a home of your own with plenty of room for the baby and Dolly," Alex King writes from the Federal Medical Center—a.k.a. the US Narcotic Farm—in Lexington, Kentucky, where he's currently detoxifying from the morphine he took for his kidney stones. "It seems almost too fantastic to be true."

Even while they negotiate and consider renovating what has become a rooming house, Dolly gets down to business. She's back on Broadway in December—this time as the mouse-like Sonia in *Crime and Punishment*. Hirschfeld's drawing on the Sunday before the opening shows her standing and looking down upon Lillian Gish, as the murderous John Gielgud skulks on the sidelines. Coincidentally, the drama is set in a crumbling lodging house.

Meanwhile, in another house, another drama unfolds. "Unfortunately, the necessary emotional fever for fighting a war cannot be turned off like a water faucet," E. L. Doctorow will later observe. "Enemies must continue to be found." And the House Un-American Activities Committee finds them.

In October 1947, HUAC opens hearings into Communist influence in Hollywood, and Gordon Kahn, now managing editor of the Screen Writers Guild publication, *The Screen Writer* (of which Dalton Trumbo is editor), is incensed and in hot water. He is not put on trial in Washington, but he's in the wings. And every day after the trial, he goes to a certain saloon with friends.

"One day he's going down the stairs," says his older son, Jim, "and who should be coming out of the men's room but John

Edgar Hoover—with makeup on. My dad never made a deal out of this. Hoover knew who he was, because he had seen him on the stand waiting his turn. My dad never broadcast this. He told some friends, but he never . . . he wasn't like that."

Kahn is not one of the Hollywood Ten, who go to jail for a year. He is No. 11. He's subpoenaed and denounced but not indicted, so he doesn't go to jail, but he does get blacklisted. When he's kicked out of Warner Bros., he starts writing at home. One of the things he writes is *Hollywood on Trial*, a book defending his colleagues. It sells about seventy-five thousand copies in the United States and does better abroad. "The Europeans had our number a long time before we did," says Jim. "And all the money he made from it he gave to the Committee to defend the Hollywood Ten."

In August 1950, Kahn dodges a subpoena and flees to Mexico. For the rest of his career, he'll write and doctor TV shows, short stories, articles, and movies (including *The African Queen* and *All Quiet on the Western Front*) as Hugh G. Foster, Norman Best, or uncredited. In May 1951, his wife and sons join him in Cuernavaca, and there they live until the fever has passed. When they move to Manchester, New Hampshire, in 1955, it's not a lot better, but there they stay.

Entering a new high school at thirteen, Jim is immediately "labeled as the son of a Communist," he sorely recalls. "They had to warn the teachers to stop bringing things up. This was in Manchester, New Hampshire, when William Loeb ran the *Union Leader*. Shortly after we got there, there was this headline in the paper—something like 'Local Red at 200 Prospect Street.'" With which Kahn is further tormented by Louis C. Wyman, the red-hunting state attorney general.

Through it all, Hirschfeld keeps the door open.

"Al was such a great beacon for me," Jim says. "He never questioned anything my dad did. He was never fearful of his reputation. He would call us up and say, 'Come on over for dinner when you're in New York. Just let me know.' A very loyal guy. He could have done what a lot of people did, and that is 'I don't know you anymore.' Al never had a finger pointed at him that I know of, but he had a great reputation, he could have fallen from much higher than Gordon fell. Never, it never came up. They would go out together, we would stay at his house, he would introduce Gordon to friends.

"I can remember how warm it was to sit around listening to these guys babble and sip their cocktails. And I can tell you, after all the shit that happened to my dad and how it seemed to be getting worse in New Hampshire, having Al to go to was like a refresher course in humanity. Gordon looked so much more healthy—he had a very bad heart, he was destroyed by this—but he just looked more robust, he was more engaged, more carefree."

In January 1948, the deed is done. Hirschfeld buys the brick-and-brownstone for twenty-seven thousand dollars from Ralph G. Albrecht, an international lawyer. As assistant prosecutor at the Nuremberg trials, this was the man credited for "weaving the skein of evidence around Goering, Albert Speer, Fritz Sauckel and Ernst Kaltenbrunner," said the *Times* in 1946.

The house has three stories and a basement—that is, the ground floor; there's no *cellar*, because of solid bedrock below—with an L-shaped stoop in front. Before long, Hirschfeld's huddling with a contractor; in May he signs a contract for $18,350 and the alterations begin. Out go the gas jets and coal bin, in come closets and showers. The seedy space is reconfigured from twenty-eight rooms to nine. The brownstone stoop is removed, the steps rearranged, and a new entrance created.

Alterations eventually rise to $22,944.57, and Hirschfeld balks. He coughs up $15,342, and that's it, claiming he was misled by the estimate, claiming dissatisfaction with the work. The contractor sues him for the rest, and after a year the case is settled.

In the midst of havoc, Hirschfeld goes off to summer stock—or to the "Citronella Circuit," as Dick Maney calls it in an article he writes (and Hirschfeld illustrates) for *The New York Times Magazine* in July. When he returns, he does *Where's Charley?* For its opening in October, Hirschfeld's elastic-limbed caricature of Ray Bolger decorates the *Playbill*, souvenir book, and sheet music. "Bolger once told me that he tried desperately to live up to my sinuous depictions of him," he recalls. "But all I did was translate the exaggerated character he'd made out of himself to the page through ink. Again, this is the kind of drawing I like to do. Bold characters leaping around, and occasionally off, the page. I was not handicapped, as he was, by gravity."

Some do look more like their Hirschfelds than themselves. Dick Cavett, fresh from Nebraska, is blissfully passing the Palace one day years later when he sees a man crossing Forty-sixth Street. "And I said to myself, 'Jimmy Savo.' And I suddenly thought, 'Why am I saying Jimmy Savo? I don't know who that is.'" But he does. He's half of Hirschfeld's cross-profiled caricature for *The Boys from Syracuse* in 1938. "I recognized a man from a drawing!" says Cavett.

"That's not me," says a crestfallen acquaintance when shown *his* caricature.

Says Hirschfeld, "It will be."

In September 1948, Dolly and Nina sail to London, where Dolly and Yul Brynner will reprise their roles in *Lute Song* (over the objections of the British Actors' Equity). The opening in October falls flat. "There's scarcely an atom of humor," says the *Daily Mail* man, adding that "as a musical entertainment it is a frugal piece." *The Daily Telegraph*, the *Daily Express*, and the London *Times* are no better. Although the producer had hopes of taking the show further, he packs it in, and soon the girls are back home in New York.

Later in the fall, they settle into their Ninety-fifth Street village—or theatrical ghetto, as one neighbor puts it. Soon after Hirschfeld skewers the "Fauna of Hollywood" for *Holiday*, he meets a femme fatale on his very own block. Marlene Dietrich has bought the house at No. 116 for her daughter and son-in-law. Maria Riva is an actress who will soon become Dolly's closest friend and confidante. Bill Riva is a scenic and lighting designer who will soon do Menotti's *The Telephone / The Medium* and Bernstein's *Trouble in Tahiti*.

Maria's father, Rudolf Sieber, is a movie man admired most, perhaps, for sticking by his gallivanting wife. It's he who found the place and Dietrich who grudgingly paid for it. "Over the years, my mother got so much good publicity out of this fabulously generous gift to her beloved daughter, I had no guilt about the house at all," Maria recalls.

Backyards are abloom with fauna and laundry, the gardens enriched by manure from the police horses stabled at the Squadron A Armory on Park. Refugee women come door to door selling lingerie. Horse-drawn wagons with milk and produce roll down the street, and the knife sharpener pushes his wheel up the sidewalk. Around the corner on Lex are the essential shops and telegram office of any orderly neighborhood. Two bakeries, Cushman and Hanscom, are at Lex and Ninety-sixth. But the whole neighborhood smells like a bakery. That's the yeast in Ruppert's beer.

The Hirschfelds' kitchen and dining room are on the ground floor, with a door to the garden. One floor up, the parlor floor is one large space front to back. "We wanted a gemütlich atmosphere, one that made good talk easy," Hirschfeld says, "so I split the space in two by installing a glass case as a room divider." The case holds Asian and African art, curios and masks traded for drawings, Balinese figures carved to Al's sketches. "There was every tchotchke he had ever found or put up," recalls a visitor. "There was not a wall that didn't have something double-hung, triple-hung on it, something on a desk or something like that."

Long sofas sit before the fireplace; end tables are drums. The walls display the Javanese shadow puppets that still delight him—and why? "It's line again," he says. A few paintings by friends, including Beauford Delaney's *Time of Your Life*, with Saroyan standing center stage. Al noodles at the upright, and jazz is his genre. A cabinet contains his cherished collection of 78s. "There was some of what you would expect—Armstrong and Ellington and stuff like that," remembers the critic Dan Morgenstern, "but he introduced me to Leo Watson and the Spirits of Rhythm, a wonderful group he had seen live. They were active on Fifty-second Street in the very early days of the street. He had some of their records, and I'd never heard them before. He went to the Onyx Club when they had this crazy fiddle player, Stuff Smith. The Three Deuces, the Famous Door. He was very hip."

Music tempers Hirschfeld's life, and it's key to his art. No one draws a more graceful line. No one's dancers—from shimmy to jeté to Fosse hip thrust—are more sensuous, with ribbon limbs, sinuous hands, and bodies arched like parentheses. No one's trumpeters toot more gaily, or skaters skim on more lyrical blades. The brooder, rogue, and spinster flow no less. "He let the line make the figure. Like jazz, it had a sense of *joy*," says the composer Charles Strouse. "The energy is syncopated," says Maury Yeston. "The line is rhythm."

"He made them fly and seem weightless," says the designer Tony Walton. "Just curlicues through space."

In his home space, framed Hirschfelds hang all about, and the rooms come in eye-grabbing colors. The foyer is a shade

Hirschfeld calls decayed plum, and the kitchen is yolk yellow. The powder room is papered in peppermint stripes, and the master bedroom in a leafy print à la the Beverly Hills Hotel, with a purple ceiling. "All the woodwork was a *ghastly* color of magenta—deep, like bad old-lady nail polish," remembers Judy Goetz Sanger, daughter of Ruth and Gus.

"I'm sure he got the paint cheap," says Artie Hershkowitz's daughter, Frances. "You can get paints on sale—odd colors. Everybody laughed at that, and it *was* funny. But because he was so delightful, it really didn't matter."

And up on the fourth floor, his crowning glory: the studio. Here at the front window overlooking the street, he installs the drawing board and barber chair.

His pal Abe Feder brings in the light—just as he's done for *Horse Eats Hat*, *Dr. Faustus*, *The Cradle Will Rock*, and *Angel Street* . . . for hotels, department stores, restaurants, gas stations, and beauty parlors. This great illuminator will, after Hirschfeld's, brighten the UN's General Assembly Building, the RCA Building, the altar at St. Patrick's Cathedral, and the penguin house at the Bronx Zoo.

The Hirschfelds paint the exterior in a color no one on the block has yet considered: pink.

"Dolly probably chose it. She loved acid colors," says Alfred Drake's daughter Samantha Popper of No. 132.

Nope. "Al chose every color in that house," says Judy Sanger.

"I would think *so*," says Maria Riva. "It's Al's kind of pixieness. We called it raspberry." Others call it "the bubblegum house" and grit their teeth.

Is Hirschfeld inspired by Monet at Giverny? By Utrillo's *La Maison Rose à Montmartre*? Probably he's just having a laugh saying, "Look at me!"

22
ON THE BLOCK

Nina enters kindergarten in 1950 at the Brearley School, an academy of privilege attended by the daughters of her parents' friends. She's terrified of being locked in the classroom, perhaps a form of separation anxiety, but she does make friends.

"She was like an angel," says Susan Harris, who meets her in kindergarten. "She was ungodly beautiful. This curly red hair, like a cherub, like Botticelli or somebody would paint." Many agree. "She was an absolutely adorable little girl, just adorable," says Alfred Drake's daughter Candy Wainwright. That summer, she travels with her parents to Europe, the start of a summer tradition aboard the *Nieuw Amsterdam*, the *Maasdam*, the *Mauretania*, the *Queens*.

Like Al, she has an affinity for the piano. Unlike Al, who can't read music but plays a mean stride, she begins proper lessons at seven with a teacher at Brearley. (Pianism runs in the family. Back in 1917, Al's cousin Malvina Ehrlich gave recitals to club ladies of the day. She was especially admired for performing Moszkowski's "Étincelles" in Washington and Poldini's "Étude japanoise" in Pittsburgh.)

Al buys a Steinway concert grand, which becomes not only a plaything for the family but a magnet for such party guests as the composer Karol Rathaus from the émigré-Hollywood days who scored Dolly's *Broken Blossoms*, as well as Hecky Rome, Harold Arlen, Jule Styne, and Dick Rodgers.

Rodgers shows up one afternoon, with Hammerstein. They're doing research for *The King and I*, and Hirschfeld is happy to help. Back in Bangkok, he happened to shoot footage of ceremonial performers styling their hair, being sewn into their costumes, dancing their intricate dance, and he's invited the songwriters to come see his movies. "They were very grateful and used some of the ideas in the elaborate costumes of the production," Hirschfeld remembers, without mentioning if the costume designer Irene Sharaff and the choreographer Jerome Robbins are there, too. In any case, *he* uses the research for drawing *The King and I* when it opens, and again and again for its revivals.

Meanwhile, he writes. He's illustrated books by others and shared the text with Gordon Kahn. But not until *Show Business Is No Business* does Hirschfeld put typewriter to paper for a book of his own.

Edified by decades of watching the stage from his fifth-row aisle seat, by a world of theater friends, and by his own cruel experience on *Sweet Bye and Bye*, he's highly qualified to define the perpetrators and pitfalls of the biz, from applause for the conductor ("You will not be alone in your ignorance of the conductor's fame. No one knows who he is") to the creators' reaction ("Restrain yourself from yelling 'Stop!' as the curtain goes up because you have at that precise moment thought of the perfect ending for the second act. It's too late"). It's a gleeful guide, and Atkinson's rave runs on the front page of the Drama section.

Nina's world is filled with celebrities. Her weekends are spent at their estates and compounds. Her parents' dining table is set for them. When she sits on Laurence Olivier's lap she has no idea who he is. When she sits on Charles Laughton's lap, she has no idea where she is.

At parties, she and Susan Harris hide under the dining table with pencils and pads, make-believe detectives taking notes. They squoosh under the coffee table when Al and Dolly return from the theater to eat cornflakes and watch the news. "It was such a liberal household, there was no bedtime for children," Susan recalls. "So we'd get under there and knock on the table, and Mrs. Hirschfeld would say, 'Do you hear knocking? Do you hear knocking?' and then we'd go, '*Ooohh!* We're taking notes on what you're saying!'"

It's no wonder Susan, unhappy at home, prefers to be here. "In some ways I had a dream childhood," she says, "because Nina and I were like sisters. I just wanted to be on Ninety-fifth Street. It was fun and laughter and hugs from Milly, and Milly was always baking cookies, and the house smelled good. That was where my childhood soul abided, and the love I got was from the Hirschfelds."

Nina's bedroom has flowered wallpaper, blue woodwork, and a blue linoleum floor—"quite hideous," says one playmate; "perfect for jacks," says another—a sheepskin rug next to the bed, dolls and toys piled on the window seat, although "Nina was not a doll person," says Liza Kronenberger Wanklyn, from No. 128. When Liza collects miniature animals, Nina decides to, too. Is it a passion? "No," says Liza. "I don't really remember a passion for Nina."

One toy is a stuffed white dog. "That's how I made friends as a child," Nina says now. "I tried to give that dog away. And then parents would call. 'I'm sorry, but little Roberta just can't accept that beautiful white dog that your daughter gave her.' And they'd have to return it." But soon she has a live one, a white Afghan from Dorothea Biddle, a minor actress and major socialite who, some whisper, shares a bit of puppy love with Al. "I was so happy," Nina says, "and that lasted about a week, because it was so cold and I didn't want to walk it."

She also has a green parakeet, the first in a series of fourteen—all of whom will be named Shelley. Somebody feeds them, but not Nina. "I don't think this was somebody who could nurture or take care of an animal," says Liza. One of the birds, maybe all of them, would "eat the lettuce out of your mouth," Susan recalls, and pose on the piano keys or nest in Hirschfeld's beard, to everyone's delight. "He would always tell us it lived in his beard," says Josh Rome, son of Harold. "He would hollow out his beard and let the parakeet sit in there."

But Nina's most colorful possession is her hair. "The most gorgeous shade of red you ever saw," says Samantha Drake Popper. "Not carrot red—rich red. Real red." Margie Barab says, "It wasn't just red hair, a sort of carroty red hair like Dolly's, but it was this unbelievable glorious auburn." Peter Stamm, at No. 120, remembers red hair in a pageboy with bangs. "She always had a tight little smile," he adds, "and was always properly dressed like a little adult in a coat with a little velvet collar, sort of like a little Eloise-type character, without the wild hair." Several neighbors compare young Nina to Eloise.

"I was just *enchanted* by her," says Tandy Cronyn, the actress daughter of Jessica Tandy and Hume Cronyn, who in third grade becomes Nina's other best friend at Brearley. "She was cute as a bug, and she was very sunny. We regularly had playdates. My parents were often out on tour, and I always had a full-time governess. Dolly was much more of a stay-at-home mom." When they pop in on Al in the studio, he's charmed by the interruption. "He had a ukelele," Tandy remembers, "and he could play it and sing ridiculous songs on it. And Nina, of course, picked it up from him, because I remember her taking the ukelele and imitating him. It was a *riot*!"

Not everyone is so enchanted.

Maria Riva, who met Nina at four, says, "She was already a strange child."

"She was this kind of wild thing that would come into a room and dart about, and she played the piano wildly, and that sort of thing," remembers her neighbor Gray Foy. "As a child she never had much personality for older people." But she knows how to get their attention. One night in the middle of a party, she comes downstairs naked as the guests focus on their salads.

"I felt she was threatening and spooky," says Judy Sanger, "and she said terrible things." As little girls, they teeter together on the Goetzes' diving board in Bucks County, play with Judy's dachshund, play in Judy's little playhouse. At seven, they share a room at Billy Rose's estate in Mount Kisco. And one day Nina quizzes Judy.

"Which would you rather have—your mother be burned alive or your father drowned? Which would you rather have—your father go to prison for his whole entire life or your mother be eaten by ants?" Judy pales at the memory. "As a child, I was frightened to be with her."

Around the same time, the Gish sisters invite Dolly and Nina to a screening of *Orphans of the Storm* at the Museum of Modern Art. When it's over, Nina looks up and asks, "Mommie, why can't the bad people be happy, too?"

Betty Comden lives across the street at No. 117 with her husband, Steven Kyle, their son, Alan, and their daughter, Susanna. This is where she and Adolph Green write their lyrics for *Wonderful Town*, *Bells Are Ringing*, and so on. The neighbors like to see Hirschfeld in his window. Some wave. Comden and Green watch. "I think they kind of regarded him as a cute neighbor," says the composer Larry Grossman. "I was in *awe*. If I lived across the street, I'd have a telescope."

Hirschfeld has a weekly poker game with Alfred Drake and Vincent Sardi from across the street. June Havoc throws garden parties. And Marlene Dietrich plays nursemaid with her grandsons. When she visits Ninety-fifth Street, which is often, she puts on a white uniform to push the pram to the park. Liza Kronenberger strokes her first fur when Marlene sashays up the block in her uniform and sable. Often she dines at the Hirschfelds', and often Al draws her.

The Riva boys and others add up to some thirty kids on the block, playing hide-and-seek, hopscotch, football, and stoopball. Maria calls her sons in for dinner by blowing a ship's whistle. Other mothers clang bells. The kids are inordinately interested in the Hinshaw house at No. 136, the "haunted house." Mrs. Hinshaw is the daughter of John Foster Dulles (Eisenhower's secretary of state), and some kind of minister. Nobody knows much about Mr. Hinshaw. "They were nuts," one of the kids recalls. "Their kitchen floor had holes through the middle of it. They were right down to dirt. The fire department had to come clear the place out one time, because Mr. Hinshaw had newspapers stacked to the ceiling." One of the daughters gives birth to a child in the house. One of the sons, "who knew how to build rockets and set them off," says another neighbor, "and occasionally started small fires," may be the one who throws a rock at the rabbi's window, at No. 119.

Their favorite meeting place is the doughnut-hole oasis between the backyards of Ninety-fourth and Ninety-fifth. A brick wall runs along the back of the gardens. On the other side of it is an abandoned greenhouse at the corner of Park and Ninety-fourth. This is "a huge rusty affair of crumbling brick, punctuated by rusting iron remnants from some ancient time," says Peter Stamm next door. It is, in fact, the last vestige of the mansion where Ganna Walska lived during and after her starring days at the Met. The glass is gone, the bottom's filled with water, and the kids are drawn like bees to honey. Even with a chain-link fence and steep wall, they wangle it.

Nina is not among them. Dolly tells a feature writer, "One of the enchantments of our neighborhood is the reassuring sight of the children playing happily together," but Peter Stamm says, "She was never let out to play with any of us. She was very withdrawn and protected, and just a delicate little flower."

Maria Riva's son Peter agrees. "There were older kids and younger kids, we all played together, because the block was *safe*. But Nina was never allowed to come out and play . . . or she didn't *want* to. Al and Dolly would come over to our house and be in the kitchen with Mom, and Nina—well, 'Where's Nina?' 'Oh, she's at home.' And it wasn't like she was ever *excluded* by any of us."

Nina remembers roller-skating and bike riding, and Susan Harris remembers chalk writing on the sidewalk, but mostly the two play indoors or on the patio. When they approach the back wall, it's for their own game. "We called it 'spooking,'" Susan says, "again with our little notepads. And particularly at twilight, when the lights come on, so you could stare into people's houses, and we'd imagine that maybe there was a robber in the house! We'd make up this absolute nonsense. It was meant to be scary. Or we'd see a bottle cap—just some stupid thing—or a jump rope. And we decided one of the kids had been strangled. We'd just make up this stuff about things we saw in people's yards. And then we'd just come home. Oh . . . *heaven*."

But Nina does share a wall with the boy next door. Peter Stamm recalls the two of them trying to making a hole between their bedrooms, hearing each other chiseling away on the other side. But a few inches in is as far as they get.

Nina remembers poking at it with another boy next door, the boy on the *other* side at No. 124—Chevy Chase.

"He was kind of the block leader," recalls Peter Riva.

"He used to come over in the morning, and Mom used to kick him out because we'd be laughing so hard we wouldn't eat breakfast," says Lisa Stamm. "It was very much open-door. Everybody came in and out."

On holidays, the block becomes a staging area for paraders. In winter, Peter Stamm earns a few bucks shoveling Hirschfeld's sidewalk. "He was a hard one to bargain with," he says. "He always had the raised eyebrow, making sure it was done properly." Peter also shovels for Mark Rothko, at No. 118. "My two toughest clients," he says.

They hold block parties and musicales conducted by Alfred Drake. At Christmas, Adelle Sardi, at No. 131, leads a chorus of carolers, and everyone visits the Rivas. "That Riva household was what I would call fantasy heaven," says Samantha Drake Popper. "They decorated their house for Christmas the way you've never seen a home decorated ever. Rockefeller Center was nothing. That was just *big*. Theirs was *extraordinary*. One year there were three Christmas trees in their drawing room, full of clear and yellow crystal ornaments and gold and silver, and one of the trees was very tall, and Bill Riva—not wanting to destroy the beauty of these special trees—went upstairs and cut a hole in the ceiling so the top of the tree could go up through it."

At the Hirschfelds' there's always a tree, and a mountain of presents for Nina—from friends and those who want to be friends. And for friends' children, Al and Dolly pile presents in the Cadillac and deliver them around town. Marc Aronson, son of Boris and Lisa, remembers them in the 1950s coming "from Nina." A son of the 1960s remembers Al at the door. "He looked totally like Santa Claus, and he would do the whole ho-ho-ho thing," he says. "How classic is that?"

But as a homeowner, Hirschfeld has no knack whatever. Consider the dishwashing machine.

It goes on the fritz and floods the kitchen. "Al's handsome beard stood out at right angles to his chin, and his fine brown eyes grew wide in horror," Oriana Atkinson remembers. The plumber comes and turns off the water, which turns off the neighbors' water. The repairman doesn't have the right part, so Al ignores the bill. Furiously, he composes a sign blaming the manufacturer, signs his name, and sends it to one of the papers, which won't run it, and finally, after months, a man from the home office comes and fixes it.

In fact, the process seems to require more strategy than Oriana recalls, and where she inserts a sign in the tale, other friends put a loudspeaker. It seems that the infuriated Hirschfeld goes up to his studio and knocks out a poster of himself nearly submerged by a tsunami of gloppy dishes. He then makes a recording of his disenchantment with the manufacturer, gets hold of a sound truck, and drives througgh the neighborhood blasting his diatribe to all who can hear. This naturally brings the cops, who arrest him not only for disturbing the peace but also for lacking the proper license to operate a sound truck. But damned if it doesn't work! Soon arrives a company man, who knows just what to do. He goes into the kitchen, fiddles around, and repairs the exhausted appliance. Sanity and sanitation are restored.

Love is in the air. In February 1953, Paula Laurence marries Charles Bowden, an actor, stage manager for the Lunts, and codirector of the Westport Country Playhouse. Dolly sighs with relief.

The next day, Alex King weds Margie, his third and most adoring bride. The witnesses are Victor Thall and his wife. Since his hobo days, the irascible Thall has done lithographs and paintings in the WPA's Federal Art Project, had a few shows of his work, and taught at the Art Students League. He, his wife, and two young daughters share a West End Avenue apartment with thirty-seven reptiles.

"He liked snakes," Margie says, recoiling. "And some of them got out and went into the walls."

The next couple gets hitched in Al's parlor. Edward Chodorov, the playwright-screenwriter, is a longtime friend with a longtime résumé. In 1953, his biggest success, *Oh, Men! Oh, Women!*, opens on Broadway . . . just as he gets named to the HUAC by Jerome Robbins. "The day after he testified," remembers Chodorov's daughter, Ginger Montel, "Robbins was back in rehearsal with *Wonderful Town*, sitting next to my Uncle Jerry whom he also named that day." But today's a day for kiss and no more tell.

It's June 1954, and Eddie, who's tickled fancies from coast to coast (the last one being a zaftig hat designer for Frederick's of Hollywood), is marrying a doll named Rosemary Pettit, fresh from a longtime thing with Charles Addams. "She was the first bride in white lace I ever saw," says Judy Goetz Sanger, who's there with her parents, along with Moss and Kitty Hart, the Hacketts, the Perelmans, the regulars.

"Going to the Hirschfelds' was like being invited to the palace," says Ginger. "I always knew that there would be people there who I wouldn't have an opportunity to see any other time, even if they were people like Moss Hart, who I'd known from the day I was born." Feeling self-conscious in her dress of dotted swiss—"I must have looked like some new flavor of ice cream," she says—she's flattered when Dolly beckons her over.

"I sat down and I thought, I can't have done anything wrong yet. I just got here. And she picked up from our last conversation, which had to have been months and months before, and I just looked at her. She was hostessing a wedding, really important smart nice people were in her house, and she drew me down on the couch and wanted to hear about something happening *back then*!

"She was so *fantastical*," Ginger says. "She was a real *creature*, partly of her own making, partly of Al's making, and partly what the world made of her."

Another creature of Al's making becomes a cause célèbre in the fall when he draws a reclining figure for *Reclining Figure*. Set in the art world, the new Broadway comedy by Harry Kurnitz calls for a fake Renoir nude, but the painting that's produced is no fun for publicity. So Dick Maney gets Hirschfeld to draw a nude, which he draws nude. The *Trib* agrees to run this sexy little wench, but the *Times* won't—unless Hirschfeld puts her in a bra. He does. Both ads run. "Broadway roared with laughter on viewing the conflicting treatments," Maney recalls. "In this crisis *The Times* reassessed its position, then rescinded the ban on the babe's breasts."

Not only is Hirschfeld illustrating John O'Hara's column in *Collier's* every month, he's also decorating columns in *Mademoiselle*, *Charm*, and *Seventeen* with entertainers and literati. His vibrant covers for *Collier's* and *The American Mercury* provide a Who's Who and What's What of the 1940s and 1950s—very different from the utopian covers of *The New Yorker* and *The Saturday Evening Post*. With punch in his pen and color in his pot, he shows Joseph McCarthy extinguishing the flame from the Statue of Liberty, John L. Lewis with coal dust spewing from his eyes, a swoony Liberace.

He's sure Liberace will hate his heart-shaped rendition, but not so. The piano man's man extends a glissando of praise, adding that Liberace would like to have it. Hirschfeld quotes a price. The man is appalled, claiming that no artist has asked for payment before. And so, Hirschfeld recounts, "I promised faithfully to dispatch, without further ado, the original painting to Mr. Liberace posthaste without payment of any kind, to hang in his living room . . . on one condition—that they send me Mr. Liberace to hang in mine."

With *TV Guide*, he's got a new row to hoe. The handy little guide to a dandy new medium, which first appears in April 1953, assigns Hirschfeld to do a caricature of Hal March in 1956. As host of the blockbuster quiz show *The $64,000 Question*, which debuted in 1955 and is broadcast to an enraptured viewing nation every Tuesday night, March has already appeared on the magazine's cover twice, in photographs. Now the art director turns the channel to Hirschfeld.

His September 1956 color drawing heralding an article presciently titled "Is the '$64,000 Question' Entirely on the Level?" (which time will soon prove it is not) presents March with silver dollars cascading from his eyes. It is the first of more than a hundred covers he'll produce, through half a century of television, of all the old familiar faces (including an acidic-green Alfred Hitchcock, imperious Jackie Gleason, clownish Arthur Godfrey, carrot-topped Lucille Ball) and the quartet of *Seinfeld* finale covers in 1998.

His last, produced in the somber days of December 2001, is a dignified American flag, with a cover line in addition to his signature: "May It Ever Wave by Al Hirschfeld."

23
WALL TO WALL

Broadway gets NINAs, but Nina takes no curtseys. "She's the most famous person nobody has ever met," says a family friend. "Who are you and what are you, except you're NINA?" Those four letters wound into the dresses and tresses of showbiz have nothing to do with the girl at home. "I think it creates a very difficult thing for a child to grow into," says Samantha Popper. "Before she's even become her own person, everybody who's ever heard the name Hirschfeld knows the name Nina. From a psychological point of view, this must have been a very tricky thing."

Does she blame Al? "She was angry," says a former schoolmate, Lynne Adams, "but I don't know that she knew she was angry at her father."

Maybe not, but another youngster in a similar circumstance certainly is. "I began to dislike him, and I found myself disliking him more and more the older I got," recalls Christopher Milne—aka Christopher Robin—of his father, A. A. And "it seemed to me, almost, that my father had got to where he was by climbing upon my infant shoulders, that he had filched from me my good name and had left me with nothing but the empty fame of being his son."

As a child, Nina has none of this insight, and her father seems to brush the issue aside. When asked what Nina thinks about being NINA, Hirschfeld replies, "I don't know. I've never asked her." But Dolly has. "I don't think she likes it."

While the world seeks NINA, Nina seeks herself. She has no interest whatever in art, but music comes easily. "The piano was my refuge as a child," she says. "I wasn't doing it for my father or my mother or my aunt. I just enjoyed it." She plays for two hours a day and has talent. "Nina loves her music and she has a long list of pieces which she plays with rare musical feeling," her piano teacher writes in a fourth-grade report. "Nina still needs to learn to concentrate and to practice more carefully so that she will make better progress in her reading ability and in developing her technique." Nonetheless, her fingers coasting through a Bach prelude or Beethoven sonatina give her pleasure and pride. The music, at least, is hers.

"Al *really* wanted Nina to be a big star like Dolly was in Germany," says Margie Barab. "She was the trophy child." Jim Kahn remembers "poor Nina being trotted out to perform and then back to her cage." While Harold Rome's daughter, Rachel, remembers being "hauled out to sing cute little French songs for company," and Jack Paar's daughter, Randy, recalls that "the thought of being in front of a million people didn't really bother me" after playing the piano on *Person To Person*, it does bother Nina.

"I was my parents' little toy, just the little girl who played the piano," she says now. "I do not believe I was ever an adult to my father."

And by keeping NINA in his work, he can keep her forever young. Which is just where she wants to be kept.

When *Peter Pan* opens in 1954, she and her friends see the show, but only Nina's father draws it in the *Times* (with NINA in the Lion's mane), and only Nina's parents know Mary Martin, who invites them backstage and sprinkles fairy dust on them. The girls are tickled; Nina's transfixed. In art class, she makes a green ceramic ashtray for Mary Martin inspired by the leaves on her costume. She sees *Peter Pan* as often as Dolly will take her. She wants to fly. She dreams of flying. "You just open the window and you *flyyyy*!" she lilts. And not just that.

One afternoon when she and Margie King are together, Margie asks the dear girl to get her a sanitary pad from the cabinet. "*Ucch!*" says Nina. "I'm *never* going to grow up."

Walls. In New York City, they're painted all over the town—Maxfield Parrish's Old King Cole on his throne (and breaking wind, to spite John Jacob Astor, who posed as the king and paid for the mural) over the bar at the St. Regis, Ludwig Bemelmans's whimsical Central Park in the bar at the Carlyle, Eugene Zaikine and Charles Vella's mischievous monkeys at the Monkey Bar in the Elysée, Howard Chandler Christy's nimble nudes at Café des Artistes, and all those caricatures by all those caricaturists in all those steak houses. So Al joins up.

In 1954, he creates a mural for the renovated Fifth Avenue Cinema at 66 Fifth Avenue. Like Covarrubias's starry assemblages for *Vanity Fair* and Ralph Barton's luminary-lit curtain for *Chauve-Souris* in 1922, the seventy-five players assembled here include the movie-household names he depicts so well.

"Al has done a mural for a new megalomaniac hotel in Miami called the Eden Roc," Sid Perelman pens to a pal about Hirschfeld's beachy assignment in 1955. "His reports on the spectacular vulgarity of the hotel make it tops in the field." Reports abound, and not just from Hirschfeld.

"The Eden Roc, designed on a Venetian theme which would set Venice back at least 500 years, features a statue of the Winged Victory of Samothrace with the prow of her ship pointing toward the parking lot filled with Cadillacs," Art Buchwald reports in *The Washington Post*.

This gaudy inn, designed by the architect Morris Lapidus as an encore to his even glitzier Fontainebleau, provides Hirschfeld the space for a five-panel, sixty-foot masterwork in the Villa d'Este Room, where he showcases fun- and sunseekers of stage and screen, Florida habitués such as Godfrey and Hemingway, and 1950s icons such as the Windsors, the Eisenhowers, even the cabaret impresario Julius Monk modeling an eye patch and a Hathaway shirt as the "Hathaway man."

By decade's end, he's drawn so many notables at Lindy's, the Stage Deli, Gogi's Larue, Nedick's, and the 21 Club in New York—for ads and magazine articles—that when the designer Norman Bel Geddes revives the Hotel Manhattan in 1958 and wants three murals for the Playbill restaurant, he too calls Hirschfeld. *Broadway First Nighters*—a crowded creation that includes New York's leading theater critics, columnists, and editors as well as assorted producers, designers, composers, and opening-night stalwarts from busybody Truman Capote to Mr. and Mrs. Al Hirschfeld themselves—is installed over the bar. *Great Ladies of the Theatre*—Tallulah Bankhead, Ethel Merman, Julie Harris, Shirley Booth, and others of the moment—decorates a wall of banquettes in the dining room. *The Marionettes*, in the foyer, shows three playwrights maneuvering their notable characters. These three murals, which are photo reproductions of his original drawings, the artist hand-paints himself.

Around this time, one of his celebriscapes even gets manufactured as black-and-white wallpaper so that anyone can have a Hirschfeld. But the paper's a flop and is rarely seen, except at the Frolic Room in Hollywood, where some smarty-pants on the premises puts it up and colorizes it with his own paintbox—and in Al Hirschfeld's living room. Here are goggle-eyed Joan Crawford and wild-haired Albert Einstein, scowling Buster Keaton and manic Danny Kaye, dashing Clark Gable and Picasso in the style of Picasso . . . and, of course, good friend Marlene Dietrich. "I noticed it simply because my mother was in it," says Maria Riva, "and I thought to myself, 'My God, can't I ever get *away* from her?'"

He also Hirschfelds his hearth. One day in the Village, he comes upon a chap peddling square tiles covered with Hirschfeld caricatures! Nothing *he* authorized, so he makes a deal: the guy gets permission to continue in business, Hirschfeld gets one of each tile. He ends up with forty-six of them and sticks them around the fireplace.

In 1958, he joins up with another World's Fair, the Brussels Exposition, when he's asked to exalt the American Theatre within the US pavilion designed by Edward Durell Stone. The man in charge of the American exhibit is Broadway's legendary angel, Howard S. Cullman of the tobacco-kingdom Cullmans—a backer of *Life With Father*, *South Pacific*, and other smashes. As US commissioner general, Cullman asks Broadway's legendary artist for a mural, and Hirschfeld provides the drawings from which a mural is made.

And when Vincent Sardi opens an East Side branch of the well-loved theater-district Sardi's in 1958, he also comes calling. It's interesting that Hirschfeld says yes, because he apparently said no at the West Side Sardi's after the death of the original caricaturist, Alex Gard. The story goes that Sardi wanted color and Al would do only black-and-white, but it's more likely he didn't want to take over the other guy's role. In any case, he's a loyal customer on Forty-fourth Street at opening-night parties, often dining with Dolly on pork chops and cannelloni.

Here, too, it's wallpaper. But it doesn't stick. "Well, we had the paper printed, and when we put it on the walls, it was clear that Al's work was never meant to be appreciated on such a scale," Vincent Sardi pussyfoots. "After all the expense and trouble, we painted over Hirschfeld's work." Before long, the whole restaurant is painted over.

As it turns out, the real Sardi's does have a Hirschfeld. Don Bevan, the artist (and cowriter of *Stalag 17*) who succeeded

Gard, drew a color caricature of Al in the early 1950s, with a cigarette. In a corner of the picture, Hirschfeld did a small pencil sketch of himself, signed it, and wrote, "Now I know how it feels."

One day Oscar Hammerstein's daughter is on Fifth Avenue when she sees Dolly walking a goat.

"I did," Alice Hammerstein Mathias insists. "It was a known thing at the time in the neighborhood, and nobody paid attention to it, you know?" Well, this *is* Goat Hill. But a *goat*?

"What *else* could it be?" snaps Alice. "I mean, it wasn't a *dog*. I don't know what else it could be. It wasn't a *lion*."

Was the creature on a leash?

"Yes, yes," she says. "She took it for a walk."

What really gets Dolly's goat is Nina.

"Think about Eloise, turn her into a redhead, and have her running up Ninety-fifth Street, tearing out the pages of her textbook," Samantha Popper says, recalling an autumn day. "And my mother stops her to say, 'What are you doing, Nina?' and she says, 'I'm not doing *any* of this nonsense homework.' She was just shredding it all over the place."

Another day, Nina wanders into the Drakes' house eating chocolate. "The house was being painted," Samantha recalls, "and she left her chocolate fingerprints all along our just-painted ivory walls from the ground floor up two flights to our bedrooms. So my mother called her Hershey—after the Hershey bar, but of course a play on the name Hirschfeld."

Hirschfeld does a drawing of her sitting on the floor under his drawing board and mischievously pouring black ink all over the papers and shattered jar beside her. He's on the phone, irate. Dolly's staring straight ahead, her face in her hands. An impish scenario, but not really.

"When I think of my mother, I just think of the darling, loving, kind, generous woman who loved me," Nina says. "What did I *learn* from her? What did she *teach* me about life? Zero. I was never punished for anything. I was never disciplined. The discipline I got at Brearley. My parents were loving, kind people who knew the difference between right and wrong, but they were not strict disciplinarians."

In June 1955, Dolly takes Nina to Israel. Her weepy role in *I Confess* hasn't ignited her career, so she's doing a concert tour with a male accompanist. When the redheads arrive at the home of friends in Haifa, they occupy the same room Al did when he was there in 1953. Nina even sleeps in the bed he occupied.

He'd been in Israel at the invitation of the American Jewish Committee—more for diversion than anything else, no doubt, because the girls were off to Alderney, visiting Dolly's sister. Margaret (originally Margarethe) is married to Peter Radice, clerk of the Court and States of Alderney. This is the smallest of the Channel Islands between England and France and a happy retreat for Nina, who can climb the rocks, explore the coves, and frolic with the goats. For Dolly, it's a form of paradise.

At the same time, Adlai Stevenson, the recently trounced presidential candidate, was in Tel Aviv on a peace-spreading tour and for some publicity-concocted reason asked Hirschfeld to fly with him—yes, *fly*—in a bucket-seated army plane to visit King Solomon's mines.

"I suppose there are historical sights duller than these mines," he wrote to Dolly and Nina of the mountainous site of these ancient mines near Eilat where copper may or may not have been grabbed in the time of King Solomon, "but in all of my travels I have never seen any." After lunch, the fellas got back in the plane and flew to Beersheba to view an exhibit by an untalented young artist. "I don't know about Stevenson," he griped, "but my ass is black & blue. And now I am through, but definitely through, with airplanes for the rest of my life."

Dolly's tour these two years later is even less amusing, apparently. "I'm sorry they are staying away from your recitals," Al writes to her, while telling their friends otherwise, and bucks her up by calling her attempt at least "a shot in the arm to your waning ego." Is Nina, nine, appearing with her onstage? he wonders. "You don't mention anything about her playing."

Meanwhile, he's playing at home. One night a friend from the Bali days composes a rijsttafel, the Indonesian spread consisting of many dishes, and Joan Castle brings saki. Deep in their cups, Joan and Dorothea Biddle, erstwhile actresses and constant Al fans, find a bone to pick. "They were yelling at each other like a couple of fish wives," Al writes to Dolly. "Joanie wanted to know where Dorothea got her phony accent and then proceeded to speak the rest of the night with a Brooklyn accent which hardly anyone could understand. She was really an exposed nerve."

On his birthday, he entertains Billy Rose and wife Joyce Mathews, the Kings, and three muses—Joan, Dorothea, and Daphne Hellman, an elegant jazz harpist who plays around town. With Fred Allen and Portland Hoffa, he sups at a joint called Lucky Pierre's, where "practically every dish is escorted in a flaming casserole like a burning oil well. Apart from this affectation the food is first rate. I had a veal and chicken combination with mushrooms and cherries and after I put the fire out of my beard I must say it was (the veal-chicken, not my beard) delicious."

His spread near Perelman's having come and gone, one summer he rents a house for the family in Pattenburg, a bucolic community in Hunterdon County, New Jersey. Another summer, they borrow their friend Katrin Holland's house in Bucks County. Many summers, they sail to Europe. Between times, Dolly does what she must to ease her daughter's boredom. With the Drakes, they take a picnic to Bear Mountain, where Nina pours milk all over the girls. With Ruth and Judy Goetz, they take a house at Martha's Vineyard for two weeks. Al, who will drive anywhere for any reason, delivers them in the Cadillac.

"By the time we got there, I think it was pouring," Judy says. "I remember my mother feeling, knowing, sensing, that Al drove too fast, which he probably did. And he dropped us off and got out of there so fast . . . I mean dropped *literally*! The two children fell out of the car, and the two women, and the suitcases, and it was kiss, kiss, 'Bye,' and off he went, and I guess made the next ferry back to New York. Now, a hundred years later, I realize that he probably had other plans.

"So it's getting dark, and the rooms are assigned, and Ruth starts to put dinner together. We all go to bed, and we hear howling, and Nina tells me that the house is haunted and there are ghosts. I'm sobbing with terror, and the howling is going on, and it's real howling. What is it? It turns out that the owners had forgotten their Siamese cat, who was in a cupboard under the eaves.

"The next morning, because Ruth and Dolly didn't have a car, they were going to use a taxi to go buy groceries. Lillian Hellman said, 'Well, there's a fella who drives for me,' so Ruth was looking for her wallet. The wallet's gone. No money for *two weeks*, with a child and crazy Dolly and crazy Nina and a rented house with poison ivy. Nothing, nothing, nothing. Lillian comes over with cash. Well, the wallet with all the money in it was found a day later, pressed down in the mud of the driveway. That's the speed with which Al Hirschfeld left the scene of the crime."

At Billy Rose's place in Mount Kisco, Nina teaches Al to swim. "The few times I saw him dunking himself in water he was about as buoyant as an anvil," Alex King recalls. "And then, under the aegis of his young daughter, Nina, he suddenly became glibly amphibious."

Al wasn't much of a swimmer, "and he really wasn't much of a bather either," Margie Barab says with a laugh. "I think it was Dolly who got him to bathe more often."

As for Alex, it's Al who helps *him* get clean.

Hooked on morphine since the mid-1940s, he's been in and out of the Narcotic Farm in Kentucky, the thousand-acre prison-hospital that's treated William S. Burroughs and Nelson Algren's Man with the Golden Arm. When King is sprung, Hirschfeld's usually there to pick him up. Now, in the mid-1950s, he gets to save him again, this time from Bellevue after an ulcer-and-drug event. It's a cold winter's night, King is in a hospital gown, Hirschfeld gives him the coat off his back—"like *La Boheme*," says Margie—grabs a wheelchair, and whisks him away. "Like the good shepherd," says Florence Rome.

But King makes Nina queasy. "Alexander King was a drug addict, and he used to shoot up heroin in the living room," she recalls with disgust. "He was told that he can't come over anymore."

"He shot up anywhere," Marge Champion says, "because he always said that he had migraine headaches and that he had to give himself a shot, and we all bought it."

"In a café in New York he once shot up in his thigh, through his pants leg," adds Margie, his wife.

"He was just awful," says Frances Hershkowitz. "He wouldn't take his hands off of you. Alex liked the young girls."

But he's not banned by the Hirschfelds. When you're Al's friend, you're Al's friend.

24
FACING FACTS

It's the 1940s and 1950s, and rich pickin's on Broadway. And those at the *Times* with the power—the critic Atkinson, his assistant critic Arthur Gelb (covering off-Broadway and the nightclub circuit), the drama editor Lewis Funke (who also writes the Sunday column "News of the Rialto"), and Seymour Peck, editor of the Sunday Drama section—know which to pick for Hirschfeld's picture. "It was always obvious," says Gelb, "because it was either a star that made it, or sometimes the playwright. If you had a new Arthur Miller play, let's say, you're going to *choose* it. And we knew something about the play because there were always out-of-town tryouts."

In February 1956, Hirschfeld is at one—another musical he thinks won't work. This one's called *My Fair Lady*, although its creators don't like the title much. The composer Fritz Loewe prefers *Fanfaroon* (because it sounds like *Brigadoon*). Some prefer *My Fair Liza* or *Come to the Ball*; others simply call it "the *Pygmalion* musical." Even with Moss Hart directing, everybody's anxious. The leading man, Rex Harrison, wants to turn and run. The sets often won't turn at all.

Hirschfeld was skeptical when Hart first mentioned it. "I remember sitting up with him til about three o'clock in the morning trying to talk him out of doing *My Fair Lady*," he recalls. "I said to him that *Pygmalion* is a complete work of art. And it had just been made into a movie starring Wendy Hiller"—for which Hirschfeld did a caricature of Shaw wearing sandwich boards. "I said, 'How're you going to improve that by having somebody sing a song or do a little dance?' And he said, 'Well, you're probably right, but I have a point of view about it.'"

By the time he sees the show in Philadelphia, it's loverly. "The minute that curtain opened, you realized you were in the presence of a great musical," he says. "Not only did I like it better than *Pygmalion*, but I realized that if you believed in something you could do a musical about it, even if it was about a cigar store." (Perhaps not the *future.*)

The original *Playbill* cover bears a photograph, but the window card, cast album, souvenir program, and ensuing *Playbills* have a Hirschfeld. This is the iconic one, with marionetteer G. B. Shaw working the strings of Henry Higgins, who's working the strings of Eliza Doolittle, whose scarf flies two names in its fringe: NINA and HIRSCHFELD. This is one of Hirschfeld's best-known works, his best variation on one of his best themes.

He used it in his 1922 ad for Selznick's *What Fools Men Are*, for Bil and Cora Baird in the *Ziegfeld Follies of 1943*, for the evil Dr. Goebbels in 1946, for Shaw in the 1948 poster of *Man and Superman*, and for Fred Allen and his radio characters in 1954, and he will keep it in the repertoire. It keeps working.

The Kronenbergers live three doors away, and the fathers are confreres. In addition to being a prolific essayist and historian, Louis Kronenberger is *Time*'s longtime drama critic and editor of the *Best Plays* series—an annual compendium with illustrations, for years and years, by Hirschfeld. On occasion they take their girls to the theater together, but true friendship blooms on the block.

Like Susan Harris, Liza Kronenberger prefers the Hirschfeld life. "My father was always working, my mother was not the type of mother that made brownies or wanted to have kids in the house, so I found the Hirschfeld house really nice," she says. After school, she stops in every day. If Nina isn't home yet, she's allowed to go up and say hello to Al. He and Dolly welcome her as another sister to Nina. In the summer of 1957, the girls visit Liza's grandparents in Canada.

Meanwhile, Al goes to Connecticut to draw Alfred Drake at the Shakespeare Festival. He's appearing in *The Merchant of Venice* with Katharine Hepburn.

So is Dick Cavett, an apprentice.

"During a rehearsal one day, I went out—the house was empty, of course—and I saw a guy standing about eight rows back with a sketch pad," he remembers. "And I knew what Hirschfeld looked like because somebody had given me a copy of *Show Business Is No Business*. Jesus! That's Hirschfeld! And I'm seeing him drawing! The thing about it was he'd stand there—not in the center, for whatever reason, about halfway over on the side—and he would just stand and look, motionless, and then it seemed like a *long* time, and then he would make a line. And then he would stand motionless some more. It was almost as if it were an automaton—just no body movement, no nothing, just intense concentration—and draw another detail. How do you *do* that?

"What Hirschfeld could have gotten a big caricature of was Hepburn's first entrance as she floated down from upstage on an island of scenery and got out, '*Nerissa*, my little body is weary of this great—' *Bang!* A woman fires off a flashbulb right in her face! And she stopped. And held up her right hand and said, 'We'll pause now while one *self-ish* woman gets all the *goddamned* pictures she wants.' A wonderful moment. Better than anything in the play. It would have made a great big Hirschfeld."

When Al gets back to town, Gordon Kahn is at the house. So when Al goes upstairs to draw his *Merchant of Venice*, he hides the names of Gordon's sons in the picture. He puts JIM on an actor's boot, TONY among the fringe of his sleeve.

It's not the first such violation. While his friends—Covarrubias, Freeman, King—illustrate books for children, Hirschfeld does not. His way to a child's heart is through the name. MAGGIE shows up in the *Collier's* portrait of her father, John Held Jr. In 1957, Hirschfeld celebrates Samantha Drake's twelfth birthday in his drawing for *Eugenia*, when SAMMY shows up in Tallulah Bankhead's lace. "What happened to Nina and who is Sammy?" an angry reader writes.

For *The World of Suzie Wong*, he sneaks BREARLEY into the signage in Chinatown (and later gives the drawing to Susan Harris for a wedding present). SUSAN shows up on a Roman helmet in *Caligula*.

In 1954, he celebrates Liza Kronenberger in *Mademoiselle Colombe*, an Anouilh play her father, Louis Kronenberger, has translated for Broadway. LIZA can be detected in the feathers of Edna Best's fancy hat. And again he hears from readers. "Flowers and telegrams arrived, congratulating my wife and me on the new arrival!" he remembers.

Regarding his own playmates, the *Times* gang shows up together in his illustration for a 1957 Sunday magazine piece about off-Broadway. There in the intermission crowd are Sam Zolotow, Arthur and Barbara Gelb, Louis Calta, Lew Funke, Dolly in an unlikely mink stole smoking a cigarette, Atkinson in the doorway, Hirschfeld looking aghast, and others . . . while the shop fronts proclaim THE A. GELB CO., English tailors; L. FUNKE & SON, poulterers; L. CALTA, shoe repair; and ZOLOTOW, new manager of Rattner's.

"Where do I buy a bed?"

"Nina, why do you need a bed? You have a bed," says Ginger Chodorov on the phone.

"I have to move. I have to leave here. So where do you buy a bed?"

"Well, first you get an apartment. Are you ready to take a lease on an apartment?"

Nina is twelve, Ginger in college.

"Do your parents know about this?" she asks.

"No. But where do you buy a bed?"

"Well, you go to Macy's or Bloomingdale's, and you pick out what you like, and you find out how much it costs. But it has to be *sent* somewhere. You have to have an apartment to which the men can deliver the bed."

"Oh," says Nina. "I didn't think of that. Thank you."

To this day, Ginger can't figure the call. "I had never had a private conversation with Nina in my whole life," she says. "I had only seen her in the living room for the twenty minutes that she made her appearance on whatever the occasion was.

"She must have been having some hissy fit. I don't think Al was ever a huge disciplinarian, but I think that Dolly, with all the gentle firmness in her body—and I have only the most wonderful things to say about Dolly—probably had said, 'Go to your room' or 'If you're not happy here, we have to find another solution.' Probably meaning boarding school, not exactly going to Macy's and buying a bed. I never mentioned it to Dolly, because it would only hurt her. I certainly wouldn't mention it to Al. And the next time I was there and saw Nina, it was done. She never called me again."

Frances Hershkowitz, three years older than Nina, takes her to Lindy's for lunch, "because she never went anywhere," she says. "Dolly and Al were so close and so together that Nina was like a lost little girl. There wasn't room. It was really sad. And the clothes she wore! I mean, she was in tatters all the time. But so was Dolly. I mean, she must have gone to the thrift shop around the corner and picked these things off the racks. She put it together very bohemian, but still you could see it wasn't new clothes."

Like many girls in girls' schools, Nina develops a crush on one of her teachers. She writes love letters and takes a subway to Queens to knock on her door. But she's unnerved by the headmistress, who dances the jig and wears a black cape—just as she is by Al's masks. ("They scared *me*," says Susan, and so did "the Balinese puppety things going up the steps. When that staircase was dark, it looked like they could float down and start dancing or something.")

As the girls get older and Milly is no longer required to babysit when the parents go out, their greatest pleasure is watching *The Honeymooners*. While Hirschfeld is seeing *The Most Happy Fella* at the Imperial, Nina and Susan are running around the living room, taking turns being Art Carney.

And taking a turn with art.

One of Hirschfeld's treasures is a wire horse given to him by Alexander Calder. "I was this horsey person. That was my thing," says Susan of her teenage passion. "I decided I didn't like it exactly the way it was.

"I altered the Calder."

The Hirschfelds will later donate this piece to the Whitney Museum. "I think it should be called Calder-slash-Harris," Susan says today. "They don't realize that my artistic input is on that Calder horse at the Whitney! Isn't that *hilarious*?"

Alexander King has written a memoir. Perelman shows the manuscript to an editor at Simon & Schuster, and bingo! *Mine Enemy Grows Older* is published in November 1958 . . . during a New York newspaper strike. With no usable reviews, S&S is buried in unsalable books.

But Hirschfeld knows Jack Paar, so King goes on the *Tonight* show. "It gets to be about eleven thirty, Alex is still not on," Hirschfeld remembers. "We're sitting here—this is our last chance to save this guy—and about a quarter to twelve he gets on. Jack introduces him and he says, 'Look, Jack, it's very nice, that introduction, but I don't recognize myself. I'm a cantankerous old man, and I'm very nervous. Before I came on this goddamn program, I stopped in a coffee shop downstairs and I got myself a cup of coffee to quiet my nerves. And there's a fellow sitting next to me, ordered a steak. He says, 'You know how Americans like their steak, like an exploded hysterectomy?'

"And I said to Dolly, 'That's *it*. I'm finished with Alex. I'm not running a clinic here. I'm never going to talk to him again. I'm not gonna let him in the house.' Then he went on to talk about how he stopped in the men's room and discovered he was peeing blood. And I thought, Jesus Christ." King rambles on about his wives, drug addiction, the Catholic church. Nothing's off-limits.

"Well, before the program was over, he had received telegrams, people were phoning in, saying, 'This is the first adult conversation we've heard on this medium. Get him back!' So Jack said, 'Would you like to come back next week?' and Alex said, 'Never. Jesus. This is the stupidest goddamn thing I've ever done in my life.' Then he says, 'If it sells books, I'll be back. Otherwise, the hell with it.' And off he goes."

The book takes off, too, and by April 12, 1959, it's number one on the *Times* bestseller list. Hirschfeld draws a caricature to go with the ensuing publicity, but Alex doesn't like it. For a guy with such a mouth, it's closed tight. "He didn't have any teeth," Margie explains. "He'd been on drugs and his teeth just fell out."

King isn't the only one disappointed by his Hirschfeld, and Hirschfeld himself concedes that on occasion "an exposed nerve may be aggravated by an offending caricature."

Consider Julie Andrews, said to have the most Hirschfelds ever (thanks to a promotional campaign for *Star!*, the 1968 flop for which he drew ever so many on-set sketches). But whenever he drew her, "he always made my chin quite pronounced—even slack-jawed," Andrews recalls, so Tony Walton, her devoted ex-husband, "tactfully suggested to Hirschfeld that he modify the likeness a bit and the dear man did!" Colleen Dewhurst doesn't like her Hirschfeld jaw either, but neither should fuss, considering the dueling chins he's given Kirk Douglas and Faye Dunaway in *The Arrangement* and Bernadette Peters in everything.

As for Carol Burnett's, when an oral surgeon extends it by three millimeters, she's *thrilled*. "I could feel the rain on my chin without having to look up," she says happily. "But Mr. Hirschfeld was upset with me because I'd ruined it for *him*. He said I'd had too much plastic surgery and he wasn't happy that I'd changed my chin. I was sorry he felt that way." Hirschfeld says, "She didn't look like herself. She used to have a clown's face, a real comic face. Maybe she did it for medical purposes, I don't know. Whatever, it's disastrous." When she sees him at Betty Comden's Christmas party, she apologizes.

Then there's Joel Grey. "When you're drawn by someone, it's very often not the way you see yourself," he says tactfully of his *Cabaret* caricature, "but if you believe in the artist, then you accept that." William Ivey Long is more to the point. Regarding Grey in *Chicago*, "He made him look like a monkey," the costume designer says.

Alas, David Merrick isn't sore at all. In a rare exhibition of wrath, Hirschfeld portrays the devilish producer as a sneaky, bearded Santa Claus (looking in fact like Hirschfeld). Not only does Merrick love it, but he buys it to use as his Christmas card. "He was absolutely over the moon about it and reveled in its success," affirms a henchman.

"I like all the ones he did of me. I think they're wonderful!" exudes Liza Minnelli, although rumor has it she doesn't really.

And when her father, Vincente, gets drawn in 1983, "I don't think he liked the way Hirschfeld made him look, but he *loved* Hirschfeld!"

Sarah Jessica Parker, who's been Hirschfelded from *Annie* to *Sex and the City*, is rumored not to like them all. Matthew Broderick says that in the *Brighton Beach Memoirs* picture, "I have sort of demonic eyes—these black dead circles—and evil-looking eyebrows. I wouldn't have thought that's how it would look." So are their Hirschfelds stowed in the attic, as one snitch suggests? "We don't put them up because it would seem too crazy if we had walls and walls of pictures of ourselves," Broderick says. They're not up in the attic at all; they're out in his mother's studio.

When the writer Sidney Zion buys Broadway Joe's restaurant in the early 1980s, he commissions Hirschfelds of Mencken, Liebling, Hecht, MacArthur, Lardner, Fowler, Runyon, and Winchell for the steak-house walls. He also orders one of himself, which he doesn't put up. "He appeared drunk in it," says his son Adam, "so of course he didn't like that aspect of it, although it was probably deadly accurate. The other thing was that he's drinking a beer in a highball glass, with a foamy head on it, and that was a mischaracterization that cut to the core! Sid was gonna drink a Scotch on the rocks in a stem glass, and that was the way it was ever going to be. So he sent it back, or whatever. Didn't want it."

Jules Feiffer doesn't either. "He hurt my feelings because I didn't think I looked like that," he says of his 1982 caricature in the *Times*, "besides which I'd had a beard for three years and he didn't seem to have noticed. Having seen it in later years, it's much better than I first thought it was, but I still don't love it."

"The real caricature part of all the drawings are my eyebrows," says Nathan Lane, with his famously querulous frown. "They seem to have a life of their own. They look like two birds meeting to have a conversation on my forehead."

"I know I've got poppy eyes, and I know I've got glasses on my head," says Hal Prince, "but every time I look at it, I think I look more like Sean O'Casey than I look like myself."

Tommy Tune: "I look like Lily Tomlin."

Lily Tomlin: "I look like Cher."

Allen Funt looks terrible. When Hirschfeld includes the *Candid Camera* man in a CBS promotional campaign, Funt explodes. "It made me look like a vain ass. A Ubangi," he tells *Newsweek*. "I felt I had caught him perfectly," contends Hirschfeld, "but I seem to have hit a nerve." Persuaded by the network boys to revise it, he adds, "So I made a Ziegfeld beauty out of him." Warfare is averted when "It's better," Funt concedes. ("I had nothing whatever to do with the way Mr. Funt looked," Hirschfeld will later remark. "That was God's work.")

"People do not like their Hirschfelds? Well, that's *their* problem," bellows Geoffrey Holder. "They're neurotic. That means they do not like *themselves*."

"What's not to like if you're drawn by Al?" says Jonathan Schwartz. "What do you want? Picasso?"

Thanks to his ongoing shtick with Paar, King gets his own television program on WNTA in New York. Primitively produced and wanly lit, *Alex in Wonderland* has a "talk" format, with King doing most of it. Wrapped in bow tie and cigarette smoke, the raconteur sits at a table with Margie, his young wife, who sings songs and plays drums. Guests come on and off. In March 1959, when *Lute Song* opens yet again, in a revival at City Center, a costumed Dolly comes on to warble, "If you need me, I will be nearby," to a guy who isn't Yul.

Nina's in *Lute Song*, too, for the last five performances. "She had this little Oriental wig and makeup, and she just was dancing along, following a float in some kind of parade. I thought it all magical," says Tandy Cronyn, loyally out front.

And on April Fool's Day—wearing a taffeta dress, bangs, and a serious face—she's on King's show. King points out the NINAs in a Hirschfeld drawing on his easel, then says, "I was outside in the hall when she was born." Finally, he allows her to play. But Mozart is a piece of cake. The real challenge is sitting at the table, poised and attentive, as King goes off on Hollywood, Popsicles, Sherpas, and stomach cancer.

At Brearley, she was an angel in the fifth-grade production of *The Green Pastures*. In *Alice in Wonderland*, the cook. In assembly, she did a vaudeville routine. Now she's at Billy Rose's house on Ninety-third, costarring with Vicky Berle, the daughter of Milton and Joyce Mathews, in *Li'l Abner*. "Nina and she were playing all the parts," says Judy Sanger, "and Vicky made Billy and my mother and Al sit in director's chairs and watch. Al didn't give a shit and wished he were somewhere else. I don't know where Dolly was. It was Billy, Ruth, and Al. And those three people sat there the whole afternoon."

As a teenager, Nina has long lashes, a small waist, and a chest Susan Harris calls "spectacular. A voluptuous figure you could die for. She was short, but Elizabeth Taylor was short, too." She also develops "a wonderful sort of mezzo-alto voice," says Tandy, "and I thought for sure, 'Yeah, you'll be a musical-comedy star.' She was completely unpretentious and unself-concious. Because she was this adorable little redhead and funny and charming and happy, she was very popular."

In the summer, when she goes with Liza to Arcadie, a girls' camp in Nova Scotia, Susan is on a girls' tour in Europe. One afternoon in Florence, as she wanders the Piazza della Signoria . . . Al Hirschfeld! While Dolly's in the Uffizi, he's at a café with an espresso. She asks why he isn't in the museum, too. "Look what's out *here*," he says, his arm sweeping the crowd. "There's too much to see out *here*."

25
A HEAVENLY HOST

Al's look.

Like "a remarkable combination of Walt Whitman, Lawrence of Arabia, and Moe, my favorite waiter at Lindy's," is how Perelman sees him.

Whatever can be said of a beard—that it's plumage or disguise, cultivated to herald an artiste or hide a weak chin—may all apply to Hirschfeld in some measure. Rusty red, reddish brown, blackish brown, graying brown, or snowy white, it's as emblematic as any eyeball or bulge of a Channing or Mostel. When John Steinbeck invites him to judge a beard contest in Sag Harbor, he accepts with delight. When Leonard Lyons reports that "his bearded influence is so dominant that the block has become the only Amish-looking community in Manhattan," he mentions Drake, Riva, Viveca Lindfors's husband, George Tabori, and June Havoc's husband, Bill Spier. When Hirschfeld trims his whiskers, he does it himself. (Not in the barber chair.)

He's strong in presence, and shorter than people expect. The legs that look bowed are actually the product of a bone condition called Paget's disease, but they lend him a Chaplinesque charm. Indefatigable, he scampers up the three flights to his studio—"like a little goat," says one friend; "like a gazelle," says another—and hobbles up with crutches when he breaks his left ankle in 1968. His dark brown eyes are usually described as "piercing," but Alex King calls them "soft-boiled" because they are kind.

Nimble or noble, the voice doesn't match. It's hearty and deep, flavored by St. Louis, slathered with slang. "He has that midwestern way of talking, and yet he looks like an Italian nuclear scientist from maybe lower Slobodia," says Walter Matthau in his own droll drawl. "You just wouldn't believe how *American* he sounded," says Faith Stewart-Gordon. "It sort of startled you, because you were looking at this *patriarch*."

A patriarch with panache, and dressed to the nines. "Quite a Beau Brummell," says the writer Bel Kaufman. "He liked interesting clothes." Silk shirts, black turtlenecks, a theater cape and silk faille slippers, a tux or plaid jacket, always a pocket square, and, most capriciously, a Clarney shirt from Turnbull & Asser with built-in ascot instead of a tie. He will not wear a tie. He does not own a tie. "Ties are useless, serve no purpose that I can see," he mutters. As host, he wears velvet slippers and a smoking jacket—even if he quit smoking years ago.

And regarding the nines, they inform his day. As he often remarks, nine is his lucky number. "If I have a choice of days on which to make a date, I'll make it on the ninth," he says. "When I wake up in the morning, I lie in bed until 9, even if I'm not tired."

At work, he wears what works. It's most often a blue cotton jumpsuit, the same worn by French garage mechanics. Lightweight, roomy, and washable: for a man who erases and spatters, it suits him.

He slumbers in nightshirts from the shop of Alexander Shields and the hand of Ruth Goetz, whose knack with a needle intrigues him. Hands do. If his pianists' hands are unrealistically arched—"not exactly the way one would play," says cabaret prince Steve Ross—that's okay. They look swell on Rubinstein, Horowitz, and Ellington. If they come without knuckles or nails, that's okay too, although Perelman kvetches that he draws the same hands on everyone.

And his own? "Absolutely *glorious* to look at, masculine hands, large hands," says the writer Patricia Bosworth. "They had so much character and expression," says the artist Joel Spector, who paints Hirschfeld's portrait for the Players Club Hall of Fame and puts his hands front and center because they're "just as important as his face."

Many artists have painted and drawn Hirschfeld. But no one does Hirschfeld like Hirschfeld. Just as he himself pops up, Zelig-like, in locations real or romanticized—from Gertrude Stein's salon to the Hotsy Totsy Club—his character pops up in his drawings, sometimes with Dolly, sometimes with Dolly and Nina, but usually alone. Whether he's jitterbuggin' at the Stage Door Canteen or sneaking into the Caprice, buried in the audience, the crowd, or some godforsaken bazaar, he casts himself as a wild-eyed extra with bushy brow, merry or sly as befits the shenanigan.

His self-portraits are the best record, because they track him unflinchingly through the seasons. He's not afraid of aging. He just draws it as he is.

He works seven days a week from 10:00 to 5:00 and takes breaks on a very strict schedule. Otherwise, he says, "where does the money come from?" But for all his cracks about getting back to the grindstone, it's the best place to be. "I draw because I like it," he says. "It's not work for me. Work is something you *don't* like to do." At noon he has lunch downstairs with Dolly. It's invariably Campbell's tomato soup with Ritz crackers—but don't tell Andy Warhol, for whom Hirschfeld has no appetite at all. He says that Warhol "has his finger in the public rectum." When it's time to get back to work, he also says, "Up to the mines."

In years past, when he put the pen down late in the afternoon to descend to his other black-and-white pleasures, he'd unwind at the Steinway—flexing the fingers, stretching the hands—then watch old shoot-'em-ups on Channel 9. Now, instead of Autry, he has Dolly. Up she comes at 4:00 on the dot, bringing tea for two and Pepperidge Farm cookies (four).

If they aren't going to the theater, they're dining at the homes of friends—where "C'mon, Dolly. There's not a dime to be made here" is one of his favorite exit lines—or, most often, having friends in. The powwows that began in the 1930s—with Mom's food, the card games and cigars—have evolved into dinner parties two or three times a week. Al needs people in all the time, they agree. The parties are large or intimate, the guests old and new. One night when it's just Alex and Margie King, the doorbell rings, there's a gust of German chatter—"Liebchen!"—and suddenly there's Marlene. "My childhood idol," says Margie with a sigh, "this sophisticated, elegant woman, in her nurse's uniform!"

"I could not believe the absolute *glamour*," says Jules Feiffer, who meets the Hirschfelds through the Kings. "Here is this guy who knew everybody in the world, was feted by everybody in the world, was loved by everybody in the world, and half of those people in the world he had to his house for dinner." As he breaks bread with Marlene and chitchats across the dinner table with Kenneth Tynan about Papa Hemingway, he thinks, *This is not happening. I am making this up*. Paris and Bali! Chicago and Chinwangtao! The Thailandese white moth that flew into Al's eye requiring beer poultices and a remedial trip to a leper colony! Alex getting locked in a zoo! "Ach, the stories they would tell—or make up and tell," says Lisa Aronson with a laugh.

Festivities begin upstairs in the library. Al serves his Pimm's Cup and his very own pâté:

HIRSCHFELD'S PÂTÉ

Fry 1 pound chicken livers with onions
Blend in mixer, adding a package of Philadelphia Cream Cheese, ¼ pound of butter, a couple of shots of brandy
Salt and pepper to taste
Pour on top: consommé mixed with red wine or sherry
Put in icebox. Forms jelly.

Standing at the bar, sipping a bourbon or Scotch, he likes talking one-on-one. When he sits in his easy chair, "we're all trying to sit near him," remembers Bel Kaufman, who did that with her grandfather, Sholem Aleichem.

Dolly tells stories with flourish. "She was always on the stage," says Gray Foy, "with everything she did. Not that it was offensive, but I just feel that in her mind she was always in a play." She dolls up in flamboyant yellows, oranges, and scarlets, in capes and shawls, mohairs and silk. "She had an Isadora Duncan quality—theatrical," says Maria Riva. "She didn't clothe herself, she draped herself." Her makeup is almost Kabuki-white, her hair increasingly tangerine.

"She enjoyed being in the limelight," Margie Barab says, "and these German friends who knew her as a big star listened attentively. But Al would sometimes say, 'Get to the point, Dolly. Get to the point.'"

Perelman, of course, always gets to the point. "I am forced to admit that the cumulative weight of Dolly's personality now affects me like a fishbone in the throat," he snipes. "To all of Al's very considerable merits as a human being, I think we must add the fact that he has the patience of Job, because in his situation, I should have long ago slipped a shiv between her ribs."

At 7:00, Milly clangs the cowbell for dinner and the company descends. The place cards are in place. "You knew where you had to sit," says Lisa Aronson. "It was not a choice." Here are

Eddie and Rosemary Chodorov, currently lodging upstairs since their return from England, after fleeing blacklisted Hollywood. "Those times were so intricately woven with people who *knew* or *named* or *didn't* name," says Eddie's daughter, Ginger, "but I would swear on my life that Dolly said, 'No politics at the table.'" One of the namers is Elia Kazan, a pariah to some, but never to Al.

Here's the lawyer Artie Hershkowitz with Jackie Susann, his second-biggest client (his biggest client having been Jackie Gleason). And Gloria Vanderbilt with Sidney Lumet. "Sidney adored her," whispers a frequent guest, "and he was paying for everything. Carol Marcus said they got together because Gloria believed he was going to make her a star, and Sidney believed she was going to make him not Jewish."

Dolly sits at the north end, Al with his back to the garden. He spins the old yarns, which everyone knows and never minds hearing again—many involving minor embarrassments of one kind or another, always hilarious—but otherwise he doesn't lead the conversation. "Generally, he was the finger pointer and other people would do the talking," says Feiffer. "He might say, 'Tell that story about blah-blah.' But if somebody asked him to tell something, he'd tell it but get rid of it fast. He didn't really want to be hearing himself talk. He liked really to let other people shine."

"It was people entertaining each other," says Lisa, "but it was essentially *entertaining Al.* He was not interested in nature, but he loved people, and he loved talking and making little fun of other people, and he participated in everything, including serving the meal. Oh, it was a whole ceremony." When the guests are seated, Al's at the sideboard carving, spooning, arranging the plates.

His favorite dish is *nasi goreng*, a fiery Balinese concoction. Here on Ninety-fifth Street, it involves chicken or lamb, rice, celery, onions, eggs, and Tabasco sauce, and it varies through the years, according to who's cooking. He's also fond of Cornish hens. Or baked salmon with sautéed mushrooms, served with a curious blend of frozen creamed spinach and mayonnaise (which he calls "green salad"), although Dolly considers trout more elegant for Gloria Vanderbilt. In summer, he grills steaks in the garden. Ginger remembers them as four inches thick, served black and blue. "He didn't ask anybody what they wanted because it was only one way anyway," she says.

Carol Channing brings her own fare, in stacking enamel-ware pots. "It annoyed people terribly," she admits. "I took what I knew I wasn't allergic to: plain beef and plain vegetables, and a small amount of the water I drank. I didn't know what I was allergic to, so I had to stick to that." Otherwise? "My voice. It got cloudy."

"Uh-huh," murmurs Maria Riva. "She thought that that kept her alive."

During dinner, Al doodles. "Even if he didn't have a pencil," says Randy Paar, "he'd draw with his finger, doing caricatures on the tablecloth." The man *has* to draw.

"Let's dirty up another room!" he cries, leading them up to postprandial brandy. But first comes business, according to Frances Hershkowitz. "You were expected to tip the help," she recalls hearing. "I just found it unbelievable!'"

Sometimes he pulls out the home movies—Hacketts on the Vineyard, Nina on a donkey in Mexico or paddle boating with Dolly on a European lake, smiling and waving in Croatia and Corfu. "A tad *National Geographic*, a tad," says a friend. Marc Connelly sings a song from the Franco-Prussian War, and Dolly sings "Sweet Georgia Brown," tooting an invisible trombone. "She could be a clown performing or a clown verbally," says Maria Riva, "but she was a clown." The dinners are topped by New Year's Eve. There are other starry shindigs in this orbit—Carl Van Vechten's, Sol Hurok's, and Lee Strasberg's—including many of the same guests. But this one's the biggest draw. "One had to go from Strasberg's place on the West Side," says Lisa Aronson, "but you wanted to wind up in the *best* place, and that was Al Hirschfeld's. The others were just . . . you come in, meet people, say hello, and blah-blah. Al's was the one where you wanted to *stay*." Dolly bakes her famous pumpernickel and Al tends bar, tasting every drink until he has to be toted upstairs at 3:00 in the morning.

All of Broadway brings Broadway. "All of everybody brought everybody," says Liza Kronenberger Wanklyn. "When *West Side Story* opened, I fell madly in love with Larry Kert, and Al invited him to New Year's Eve for me!" Artie Shaw makes a play for any girl he can grab, among them Susan Harris. Lumet plays one of Al's drums so vigorously he ruptures it. The playwright Harvey Breit drinks so steadily he walks through the garden door.

One year, Joan Castle, with sequins on her eyelids and bells on her toes, lifts her skirt to reveal a substantial petticoat. Al draws a caricature of himself on it, reclining, with an arrow piercing a heart (and between the layers, some say, may be more than a flouncy flirtation). Years later, when she's run out of husbands, cash, and the hats she's selling for Mr. John, Joan will try to sell the piece at auction, but nobody bids.

"My father's happiest times were at Al's New Year's parties," Tony Kahn recalls, but on the last day of 1962, as Gordon is preparing to drive down to New York, he has a heart attack and dies. The FBI, with its relentless persecution and surveillance even after the blacklist, has finally taken its toll.

In 1963, the parties stop after Kennedy is killed, and the gossip Radie Harris reports that "this year the Strasbergs are forgoing their traditional festivities, as are caricaturist Al Hirschfeld and his actress wife, Dolly Haas, who usually draw the same mob of celebrities, meeting themselves coming and going between the two parties. The same reason for canceling both these seasonal affairs was given by the Strasbergs and the Hirschfelds: 'Since show business has lost its greatest friend in the White House, and since the untimely death of Molly Kazan, we don't feel in a celebrating mood. Neither do our friends.'"

The forebears in Albany (Photograph by the author)

DAILY NEWS
NEW YORK'S PICTURE NEWSPAPER
HOME EDITION
Vol. 6. No. 111 — 28 Pages — New York, Saturday, November 1, 1924 — 2 Cents

RUM RUNNERS SHANGHAI CREW

Flo hits the front page in 1924 (Courtesy of the General Research Division, The New York Public Library, Astor, Lenox and Tilden Foundations)

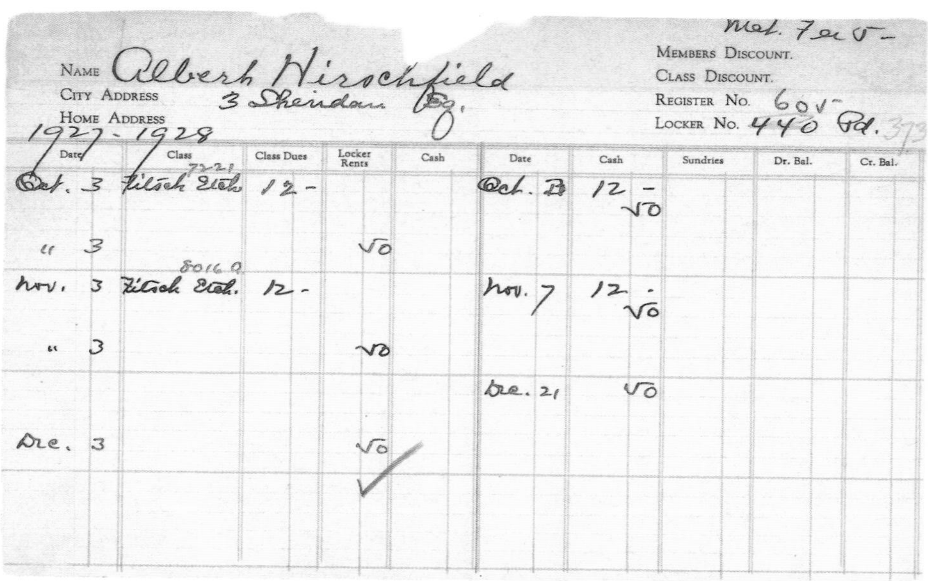

Mat. 7 & 5 –
MEMBERS DISCOUNT.
CLASS DISCOUNT.
REGISTER NO. 605
LOCKER NO. 440 Pd.

NAME Albert Hirschfield
CITY ADDRESS 3 Sheridan Sq.
HOME ADDRESS
1927 - 1928

Date	Class	Class Dues	Locker Rents	Cash	Date	Cash	Sundries	Dr. Bal.	Cr. Bal.
Oct. 3	7221 Fitsch Etch	12 –			Oct. 3	12 – √0			
" 3			√0						
Nov. 3	8016 Fitsch Etch.	12 –			Nov. 7	12 – √0			
" 3			√0						
					Dec. 21	√0			
Dec. 3			√0 ✓						

Receipt for night classes at the Art Students League (Archives of the Art Students League of New York)

THIS IS A MARRIAGE LICENSE, AND NOT A MARRIAGE CERTIFICATE. The Marriage Certificate on reverse side should be filled out and filed promptly by the Clergyman or Magistrate as required by law, with the Town or City Clerk who issued the License. See that your marriage is thus recorded.

PLACE OF REGISTRY
STATE OF NEW YORK
County of New York
City of New York

NEW YORK STATE DEPARTMENT OF HEALTH
Division of Vital Statistics

MARRIAGE LICENSE Registered No.............

Know all Men by this Certificate, that any person authorized by law to perform marriage ceremonies within the State of New York to whom this may come, he, not knowing any lawful impediment thereto, is hereby authorized and empowered to solemnize the rites of matrimony between Albert Hirschfeld of U.S.A. in the county of New York and State of New York and Florence R. Conrad of U.S.A. in the county of New York and State of New York and to certify the same to be said parties or either of them under his hand and seal in his ministerial or official capacity and thereupon he is required to return his certificate in the form hereto annexed. The statements endorsed hereon or annexed hereto, by me subscribed, contain a full and true abstract of all the facts concerning such parties disclosed by their affidavits or verified statements presented to me upon the application for this license.

In Testimony Whereof I have hereunto set my hand and affixed the seal of said City at the Municipal Building this 13 day of July nineteen hundred and twenty Eight

SEAL

W. J. [illegible]
City Clerk.

The following is a full and true abstract of all the facts disclosed by the above-named applicants in their verified statements presented to me upon their applications for the above license:

FROM THE GROOM:		FROM THE BRIDE:	
Full name	Albert Hirschfeld	Full name	Florence Ruth Conrad
Color	White	Color	White
Place of residence	598 W 177 St	Place of residence	598 W 177 St
Age	25	Age	26
Occupation	Artist	Occupation	Writer
Place of birth	St. Louis Mo	Place of birth	U.S.A.
Name of father	Isaac	Name of father	Charles T. Hobby
Country of birth	U.S.A.	Country of birth	U.S.A.
Maiden name of mother	Rebecca Rothberg	Maiden name of mother	Sarah E. Brophy
Country of birth	Russia	Country of birth	U.S.A.
Number of marriage	First	Number of marriage	Second
I have not to my knowledge been infected with any venereal disease, or if I have been so infected within five years I have had a laboratory test within that period which shows that I am now free from infection from any such disease.		I have not to my knowledge been infected with any venereal disease, or if I have been so infected within five years I have had a laboratory test within that period which shows that I am now free from infection from any such disease.	
Former wife or wives living or dead		Former husband or husbands living or dead	Living
Is applicant a divorced person		Is applicant a divorced person	Yes
If so, when and where and against whom divorce or divorces were granted		If so, when and where and against whom divorce or divorces were granted	July 11/18 [illegible]
I declare that no legal impediment exists as to my right to enter into the marriage state.		I declare that no legal impediment exists as to my right to enter into the marriage state.	Florence [illegible]

Al and Flo tie the knot in July, 1928 (Municipal Archives, City of New York)

Ruygrok 70244-2000-2-'32

BALI-HOTEL

DEN PASAR .... 193.......

Brothers Chaplin —

Our landlord has a pig that he'd like to roast and we have a hundred and fifty pound turtle that has lived long enough now. Can you join us to-morrow night in consuming them? We shall eat to the tunes of a Balinese orchestra and fifty or so natives inhaling rice.

If this appeals to you tell the messenger in your best Malay "Yah"! If not agreeable — "Tidak".

Al and Flo Hirschfeld

Invitation to a feast and a most enchanted evening (Chaplin Archives, Roy Export Co. Ltd. Scan courtesy Cineteca di Bologna)

Dolly Haas in *Girls Will Be Boys*, a British comedy of 1934 (Photofest)

Dave's Blue Room, a favorite hangout (Author's collection)

The Osborne on West 57th Street, a happy home for Hirschfeld (Art & Picture Collection, The New York Public Library, Astor, Lenox and Tilden Foundations)

Hirschfeld by Don Freeman, around 1940 (Courtesy of Roy Freeman)

His gal also drawn by his pal (Courtesy of Roy Freeman)

Catching a run-through of *The Moon Is Down* at the Martin Beck (later to be renamed the Al Hirschfeld) (Photofest)

On the road with *Sweet Bye and Bye* (left to right: S. J. Perelman, Ogden Nash, Vernon Duke, Hirschfeld) (Courtesy of Abby Perelman)

Al and Sid charm new friends in Bangkok (Courtesy of Abby Perelman)

Two on the isle: Al and Dolly visiting the Hacketts on Martha's Vineyard (Courtesy of Liza Kronenberger Wanklyn)

Nina at a frisky fifteen (Courtesy of Liza Kronenberger Wanklyn)

Schuyler Chapin, New York's former Commissioner of Cultural Affairs, gets sketched (Photograph by Ted Chapin)

The caricaturist caricatured for Sardi's. "Now I know how it feels," he scribbles (Courtesy of Sardi's)

Al and Louise, newlyweds (*New York Daily News* Archive/Getty Images)

Passion in black and white: his keys and his characters (Photo by Michael Tighe/Donaldson Collection/Getty Images)

Where the art is: the studio on East 95th (Photograph by Sandra L. Levine)

One man's gargoyle (Photograph by Sandra L. Levine)

But they do the following year, and in 1964 Louise and Leo Kerz—new friends, introduced by the Chodorovs—join the fun, too. Leo, an émigré from the Weimar Republic, has designed sets for the Jooss Ballet, *The Deputy*, and the movies (from Paddy Chayefsky to *This Is Cinerama*) and has taught costume and makeup design at Piscator's Dramatic Workshop at the New School. And in 1961, he brought Ionesco's absurdist *Rhinoceros* to Broadway. When the *Times* didn't ask Hirschfeld to draw Zero Mostel and Eli Wallach in it, Leo did.

Louise, a beautiful young model/actress, showed up to audition. "You don't have to read for me, but you have the part," Leo told her, promptly hiring her as Anne Jackson's understudy and his secretary. It's said that Ionesco himself was so smitten he put the moves on her at a banquet, whereupon Leo threw an ashtray and bonked him in the head.

Artistic, musical, and an émigré from Nazi Germany, Kerz is also "a kind of fiery guy," says the set designer David Hays. "*Very* difficult," says Eli Wallach, whose contract demanded that Kerz not speak to him during *Rhinoceros*'s run. "I really didn't like him," says the press agent Harvey Sabinson, who resigned from the production midstream.

"When I first met him, I couldn't stand him," says Ginger Montel. "He seemed mean and grouchy and judgmental. And one night, I ended up sitting next to him, and I suddenly fell in love with him. I just *got* it, got what he was about." Dolly's elated that he saw her in cabaret back in Berlin.

Louise is a rookie, but she knows how to play her part. "I sat there and listened, and I participated a little," she says. "I knew what was happening in the arts and in the theater and in culture in New York in general, but I didn't have the experience that they did, and how could I? I was basically the youngest, and I was very impressionable. I was all ears." Among those whose feet she sits at are Philip Hamburger, the *New Yorker* writer who calls her "the kid," and S. J. Perelman, whose mustache twinkles whenever she looks his way.

26
GAME OF THE NAME

Early movie studios such as Biograph and Pathé concealed their trademarks in ads and on scenery to protect their product. Bach and Shostakovich wove their names into musical cryptograms. Hirschfeld has NINA.

To his chagrin, the *Times*'s publisher, Arthur Hays Sulzberger, discovers there may be several NINAs in a picture and wants to lessen the stress for readers (as well as himself). "Yours for only one-NINA-per-Hirschfeld-cartoon," he suggests to Al. But a subscriber has a better idea. Would it be possible, she wonders, to insert the number of NINAs in the corner somewhere? It would make her Sundays much more relaxed. And so it comes to pass: a number following his signature to denote the number of NINAs in the drawing. Not that it's always accurate. In *Tenderloin*, for instance, he indicates one NINA where there are five. There are times he himself can't even find them all and has to ask Dolly, Nina, or Milly to check.

Everybody benefits from NINA but Nina.

In November, the Federal Aviation Agency inquires if it would be possible to use the drawings to test perceptual ability. "It occurred to us that the total time required to find 'Nina' in each of several Hirschfeld illustrations would be a pretty good measure of several perceptual abilities thought to decline with age and/or cerebral damage," the chief of the Behavioral Sciences Section writes. "Since our research will include a longitudinal study—a retest of a sample of pilots each five years for as long as we or they or the project lives—we must have several different but equivalent sets of stimulus plates."

In 1976, Dr. Calvin Nodine, a researcher at Temple University, receives a sixty-thousand-dollar grant from the Department of Defense to use NINAs "to model the effects of camouflage on target search and detection." The findings from Project Nina, presumably used to instruct pilots, prove that "you can stare at a Nina and yet not see it!" This further inspires him to study the search behavior of radiologists in identifying the locations of missed tumors. He writes articles based on his research for the *Bulletin of thes Psychonomic Society* and the Radiological Society magazine, and in 1992, using Hirschfeld's *As You Like It* in the *Times*, conducts a study at the University of Pennsylvania searching for NINAs hidden in chickens and cuffs.

Even beyond NINA, Al is a boon to science. A psychologist at the University of Illinois asks to use his overlapping George Kaufman/Edna Ferber drawing to aid visual perception. And a researcher at Harvard's Center for Cognitive Studies wants the overlapping Dromio twins from *The Boys From Syracuse*—the one Cavett likes—for the same reason.

Hunting her name has become an obsession—or, as Hirschfeld says, "a national insanity." And when, rarely, he doesn't bring NINA into the picture—if, perchance, he considers the drawing too complicated and thinks it unfair to commit his readers to looking for a needle in a haystack, as he puts it—the insanity swells even more.

The neighbors love being in on the game. "As kids, we were *fascinated* by that," says Peter Riva. "So was Mark Rothko. Rothko thought that was just the coolest thing."

Feiffer doesn't. "I thought it demeaned the work, from the level of the art that it truly was, to have this gimmicky stuff in it," he says. "You saw this lovely drawing of Mary Martin or Carol Channing or Zero or Liza Minnelli . . . he had this stable of people he loved to come back and do even better work on, just getting the essence of them. And to muck it up with a secret NINA in the corner there took away from the seriousness, brilliance, and artfulness. It cheapened the aesthetic."

Is Hirschfeld concerned?

"I don't know that Al gave a shit," Feiffer says with a laugh. "My guess is that if he cared about it, he would have found a way of stopping. I think there was some level in Al that went back to the early newspaperman, and that's what he was. He was a newspaperman of the '20s and '30s, where they scoffed when people took them seriously. They scoffed at the notion of being artists. There's something very cynical in newspaper guys, and deep down in Al there was a touch of cynicism about the game he was in."

It's popular even among those who set it in type. "The engraving department at the *Times* has a kind of pool on this," Hirschfeld tells Geoffrey Hellman in *The New Yorker*, and "the first to spot 'Nina' is the winner." Years later, Guy Flatley, an assistant to *Times* editor Sy Peck on the Sunday Drama section, is in the cacophonous composing room overseeing his Debbie Reynolds interview with its Hirschfeld for the incoming *Irene*. "I saw the typesetters looking at the proof, and I thought they were reading my piece and I was kind of flattered," he says, "but they were actually trying to find the NINAs."

Who has the most NINAs? Carol Channing brags that she's Hirschfeld's favorite, but Whoopi Goldberg holds the record with forty. (Aaron Copland's sixty don't count because they're in a drawing commissioned for his sixtieth birthday, and Punch Sulzberger's fifty-five don't count for the same reason.) Whoopi simply charms him, it seems clear.

She's rehearsing her first Broadway show at the Lyceum in 1984, when she looks out at the empty house and notices "Santa Claus sittin' there. He was just kinda *there*. Just this smile, and doin' what he was doin', and I didn't think anything of it. I didn't know who it was." When he leaves, she asks the director, Mike Nichols, who he was. "I thought you knew," he says.

"That's Al Hirschfeld." And she thinks, *Oh my God! Oh wait, wait. Where'd he go?* Home to draw the picture, hiding forty NINAs in five of her characters. The most ever? She nods. "Ever. Ever."

In a wink-wink homage, Don Freeman hides a NINA in one of his own children's books, *Norman the Doorman*. Tony Walton takes it further. For *All That Jazz,* the movie version of Bob Fosse's career, he draws a caricature for the wall, signs it "Waltfeld" and hides an EMMA, his daughter's name. And what of Roz Chast, frazzle-lined cartoonist for *The New Yorker*, whose daughter's name is Nina? Would she do it? "That's Hirschfeldland," she replies, "and I wouldn't want to invade, or even pitch my tent in the backyard!"

It's a name to conjure with, and he conjures. Using various typestyles—block letters, cursive, stand-alone, or run-in—he works NINA into wimples and wrinkles, bathrobes and bracelets, pantaloons and boas, ashtrays and mirrors, an Arthur Miller script and a Sondheim score, the cliffs of *Camelot* and the knife handles at the Algonquin Round Table, the tail of Eastwood's horse and the ash of Gershwin's cigar, Courtenay's bookshelf and Rutherford's rump. And in *Ivanov*, he tucks his daughter's name into Paula Laurence's skirt.

He even fools with his own.

In Baghdad and Bali, Tiflis and Tehran, when watercolors were his medium, he signed his name in cursive, the style he learned in grade school. Then came HIRSCHFELD in elongated letters, standing upright in the lower right corner, until he started pushing it around. It's been seen in all corners, often slanted or squeezed. It's been slid under David Frost's foot, translated into Greek and Japanese, swapped for the name of Steinway on Liberace's grand.

For a name so familiar on the page, it's often misspelled, mistyped, and mispronounced. "Dear Mr. Hershfield," writes the general manager of Christie's in 1965, inviting him to auction his "collection." The eminent Victor Hammer, his very own dealer, addresses him as Herschfeld. Richard Halliday, the producer husband of Mary Martin, thanks Harry Hirshfeld for his drawing of *Peter Pan* in the *Times*.

The chairman of the Literary Awards Committee at the National Arts Club, inviting him to a dinner for Perelman, addresses the letter to Mr. Albert Hischfeld. Lotte Lenya writes to dearest Dolly (her replacement in *The Threepenny Opera* off-Broadway), hoping that "you and Alfred are well."

Then there's the mix-up stirred by Groucho Marx. When asked who should decorate the cover of his 1963 book, *Memoirs of a Mangy Lover*, Groucho says "Hirschfeld." So his editor calls Leo Hershfield, an illustrator and courtroom artist (who is not the same as Leo Hirschfeld, who invented the Tootsie Roll). "Are you sure you got the right guy?" asks Leo Hershfield. "Yep," the editor assures him. So the book, with cover by Leo Hershfield, hits the shelf.

May 1960. Down comes the curtain on the theatrical career of Brooks Atkinson, because he's reached the unacceptable-to-the-*Times* age of sixty-five. As Hirschfeld recalls it, "He's sitting in his office one day and a boy comes in with a notice saying, 'Don't forget you're retiring in July' or something. Brooks put his hat on, wrote a note saying 'Not in July. Today,' and never set foot in his office again. He was furious. At the height of his powers."

After much politicking as to his successor—with Atkinson pushing for Arthur Gelb but the brass blowing for Howard Taubman—the deal is done. Many are taken aback by this plum going to the music critic. Even those at other papers. "Somehow I never thought I would be left here at the Tribune without the comfort and consolation of your presence on the Times," Walter Kerr telegraphs to Atkinson. "I feel pretty bleak this morning.

And the theatre should feel bleaker." In fact, Atkinson keeps on typing through June. Then he retreats to the Catskills and starts a twice-weekly column called "Critic at Large," absorbed in bucolia. John Mason Brown calls him "Manhattan's Thoreau," O. O. McIntyre "a plow boy with a movie villain mustache," and Hirschfeld—well, Hirschfeld. In a birthday tribute, he remarks on the small furniture factory Atkinson maintains at his farm and says, "If it weren't for this gala tonight, Atkinson would probably be hammering out a spittoon at this very moment . . . occasionally staring through the binoculars riveted to his eyes to observe a double-breasted seersucker perched on a bird bath outside the tool shed window."

The theater community renames a theater in his honor. In 1960, the Mansfield on West Forty-seventh Street becomes the Brooks Atkinson. Hirschfeld is asked if he thinks this will embarrass the man. "Certainly not!" he replies. "He'll be tremendously flattered . . . who wouldn't be, f'god's sake."

27
BEHIND THE SCENES

In 1960, Al and company are off to Brazil. He's been invited by the US Information Agency with an exhibition celebrating the American theater at the Copacabana Palace in Rio. And to participate in lectures and seminars, too.

On the SS *Brasil*: "It is, without a doubt, the most beautiful ship that I have ever sailed on," Nina writes buoyantly to Liza. While Al plays King Neptune at the costume party, she plays shuffleboard, swings at a barn dance, and swims in the teenagers' pool. Such fun! Nina likes boys!

After the Rio opening in July, Al takes off on his own. "I made the trip up to Brasilia via Belo Horizonte by droshky, tram, bicycle, ox-cart, jeep and taxi . . . returning here nine days and two hundred flea bites later," he writes to Atkinson. He finds Brasilia commercial but Rio "a delightful city with white sand beaches, wide boulevards set against Disney mountains. Tall buildings, short men and bearded women," and adds that at a party he was asked, "What happened between Tennessee and Gadge? Was it a lovers' quarrel?"

And when they visit the Bienal in São Paulo, Hirschfeld finds nothing in the museum at all. But Nina likes a few things, so they go back the next day. "We got to the second floor," he says, "and she picked out a painting, a white painting, white on white, had an aluminum frame on three sides. It was about eight feet high and about three feet wide. And I'm looking at this thing very carefully, and trying to figure out what she sees in that. There were a couple of little scribbles, and what looked like pencil marks. I thought, 'Well, maybe it's the texture that I'm not tuned into' . . . and as I'm studying this very seriously, trying to latch on to it, and be with it, the thing swings open, and it's a *door*. A fellow comes out with a mop and a pail!" They laugh.

But not for long.

After her sophomore year, Nina is asked to leave Brearley after a disastrous run of failed academia and disruptive behavior. Dolly keeps the lid on as Al keeps drawing. Nina transfers to Professional Children's School, whose students are engaged in various professions or whose parents are. She starts at PCS, "and then it happened—whatever happened," says a neighbor. "Either she took LSD or something and had a bad trip, or it was hormonal." She's fifteen. "She was getting into wrong company sometimes, and everybody at that time was experimenting with whatever they experimented with," adds Marge Champion.

"Something kind of went awry during adolescence," remembers Tandy Cronyn. "It was when she had to face being an adult that we suddenly became aware. She had to move into an adult world and didn't know how to cope with it, and suddenly you had an angry and unhappy person where before there'd been this carefree, magical kid. There may have been something wrong with her thyroid. I'm sure it was something like that that put her out of kilter. They didn't talk about it. I think a lot of it got swept under the rug. They did the best they could. And I'm not sure there was anything to be done."

"All of a sudden she started making life very hard for them," Margie Barab agrees, "with terrible knock-down-drag-outs."

"Dolly did not discuss it," says Maria Riva. "She endured it. A good German. I think this was Dolly's great tragedy, because Dolly could pinpoint people within seconds, and she knew, she knew. And couldn't do anything about it. She had to choose the husband over the child."

"I think it has a lot to do with being somebody who's famous and yet not being anybody, and not feeling like anybody," says Samantha Popper. "I mean, who *are* you? You're the most famous name in caricature drawings, you're a famous kid from *The New York Times*, and who are you? I wonder what Al could or couldn't give her in terms of whatever attention or additional love she felt she needed. I think it does relate to a father-daughter thing." (It doesn't help when *The American Theatre as Seen by Hirschfeld* is published, and the *Times* slugs its review "Nina's Father's Book.")

"He was such a strong figure in her life, and all she wanted to do was for him to be proud of her, and he *wasn't*," says Judith Rosenblum Halevi. So she looks elsewhere. She dates boys she knows and boys she doesn't. Bel Kaufman remembers Nina coming home during a dinner party "with a young man who was a driver of a car that she was in—a very uncouth, ill-dressed, uneasy young man. And everybody pretended, you know, 'How do you do?'"

Alas, poor Al. "He couldn't stand any of them," says Susan Harris. "All Nina's boyfriends—they were in the shower, they were picked up on cruise ships—and wherever they came from, he called them all 'Ginsberg.' He couldn't remember their names. They were all just 'Ginsberg.' I remember Tandy's father, Mr. Cronyn, used to call all her boyfriends 'Meatballs.' Didn't matter who they were. 'You going out with Meatball?' With Hirschfeld, it was 'Ginsberg.'"

Work is his solace, the studio his refuge. Here, he's above and beyond. But sometimes he's further beyond. On the road, out of town, other voices, other rooms.

If he dallies during tryouts, Dolly looks away. "I would have thought there would have been one in every New Haven tryout.

I would have thought," says Maria Riva. But "Dolly was a European as far as his girlfriends were concerned. That goes with having an affair and really not getting too emotionally involved except for a weekend, or knowing that Dolly loved him and that sufficed and made an excuse for any behavior, because she allowed it—so nobody questioned anything, you know." No names, no scandal, and maybe nothing at all. But maybe something.

He goes on location, too. Turning out a lot of campaign art for United Artists in the 1950s and 1960s, he sketches *Elmer Gantry*, *The Apartment*, *The Young Savages*, *West Side Story*, *Two for the Seesaw*, and *The Manchurian Candidate* on set and polishes the drawings on the barber chair.

Wherever he's sitting, Hirschfeld uses photographs for reference. Some are his own Polaroids, some come from the library, most come from the press agents. Using a few elements or stealing the scene, flipping positions and remodeling classic profiles, he takes off from the shot and creates.

Through the years, thousands of production photos will get stashed in a metal cabinet, on the back wall shelves, in file drawers, amounting to a final drift thirteen feet long. Most people envision Hirschfeld sitting out front at rehearsal and doing a complete drawing of what he sees onstage. But that's not the way he works. His theater and movie drawings are based on the publicity shots, from which he then takes flight, always making them Hirschfelds.

Every illustrator uses photographs for reference. "It's in a long tradition as a tool. To some people, it's an end result. To others, you steal what you need," says William Ivey Long. While the caricaturists Edward Sorel and David Levine rely on antique sources for Austen, Brahms, and Voltaire, they need photographs, too. As does Richard Baratz, Sardi's current caricaturist.

Martha Swope, best of the theatrical photographers, has a unique collaboration with Hirschfeld. They're covering the same performances at the same rehearsals, but seeing different things. As a former ballet dancer light on her feet, she's shooting from all over the house. He's sitting still, sketching. "A swift line here, a swift line there, and he's got 'em," she knows from peeking over his shoulder. Press agents scan her contact sheets and send out the stills, but Swope likes to take the photos up to Hirschfeld herself.

So do press agents like Frank Goodman and Harvey Sabinson, old friends, men of the theater. It's a golden time when they can share a smoke and a schmooze. "To get an Al Hirschfeld picture for a press agent, that was a coup," says Sabinson. "That meant your show was the important show opening that week.

"Some years later," he goes on, "I was visiting my urologist, and the urologist said to me, 'Do you know Al Hirschfeld?' and I said, 'Yeah, I know Al Hirschfeld.' He said, 'Well, I'm a great collector of Al Hirschfeld art. Do you think you could get me an introduction to him? I'd like him to sign some of these pictures.' So I called Al up and I said, 'Al, you've got to do me a favor.' 'What do I have to do?' I said, 'You've got to give an audience to my urologist, because keep one thing in mind: he's given to poking his finger up my rear end, and I don't want him to get too sharp." Hirschfeld sees the guy; all is well.

Sometimes the photographs are taken so early—before the pirouettes are frozen, the bustiers finished, the leading lady replaced—that Al, working weeks in advance, can get caught. Readers may not notice, but theater folk do. "I think he must have come to New Haven on *A Funny Thing Happened on the Way to the Forum*," says the musical's designer, Tony Walton, "because there are a couple of elements in his caricature that didn't remain in the show by the time it got to Broadway." Which is why he puts the name of the town next to his signature. "Don't blame me," it says. "This is how it looked in Philadelphia."

He checks out swatches and sketches, too. Ann Hould-Ward, costume designer for *Sunday in the Park with George* and *Beauty and the Beast*, among other productions, sends hers up before he sees the show. Touching, feeling, tell him how the fabric will swing or drape. It's research, and it matters.

After designer Carrie Robbins sends up her sketches for Frank Langella's *Cyrano*, the phone rings.

Hirschfeld: "I want you to send me the *real* costume sketches."

"Those *are* the sketches."

"They can't be."

"But they *are*." Robbins, who's designed for *Grease*, *Agnes of God*, and other shows, is a superb draftsman. Her mandate for this one is to keep it spare.

"But where's the *panache*? Where are the feathers? Where are the hats?"

"I'm so sorry, Mr. Hirschfeld. The panache is in the language, and I'm sure it will be there in the performance."

"But what can I draw?"

"He was right," she says now. "He was looking for the *sweep*."

All actors come with a face, a coif, a costume. But it's their fluster and grace that come from Hirschfeld. What he doesn't see out front he finds in the dressing room, on cassettes, on video. He wants tics, manners, moues. His sketchbooks teem with imposing wigs, complicated carpets, bedposts, and military medals—with scrawled descriptions of "loose flesh," "pixie fey," "small ass," "fried eggs" for eyes, "spaghetti" or "Brillo" for hair. In the dark of a run-through, he scribbles with pencil stubs on scraps in his pocket. "The lines don't join, but I can read it," he explains of his sneaky shorthand.

It's all in the details.

John McMartin is playing Caesar at the Public. "I had a bit of a gut," he says, "and I thought, 'They won't see that in a toga.' So the paper comes out, and the characters are all standing around looking at this corpse, which is me in the toga, and the *telltale line* that showed the gut. He *found* that."

"He brings out the sort of limp rag in me," says Jeremy Irons. "And God help you if you have a *carbuncle* on your nose."

The features he gives them—plucking from his arsenal of noses, galaxy of eyeballs (or stars, spirals, notes, and clefs), forest of hairdos, brows, and lashes—mark them forever. And if they come with their own accessories, that's a bonus. "It's something to hang on to, an outstanding feature," says Woody Allen of his glasses, "like a cleft palate or something."

But not everything works.

"Wish I could think of a better way to handle it," Al says one day, scratching away at Itzhak Perlman. "He always has a handkerchief under his chin, and it's so confusing with the handkerchief and this bow tie, it's driving me nuts. They want him with his eyes *open*, but when I open the eyes he looks like a *comedian*. If I had the eyes open, I don't know that that looks like him. It might, I don't know. He's more concentrated when he's got his eyes closed. Well, that's as good as I can do with it. To hell with it."

On another day, composer Mitch Leigh's wife is distraught when she sees the Hirschfeld she's just paid six thousand dollars for. In his birthday present, Mitch isn't dreaming the impossible dream, but his eyes are closed. For another thousand dollars, Hirschfeld opens them.

Upon seeing his drawing for *The Royal Family* in 1975, Eva Le Gallienne, the star, and Anne Kaufman, the playwright's daughter, react with alarm. He's included a pooch in Le Gallienne's arms, but not the rabbit's foot dangling from her mirror—which Anne gave her. "Bring me the rabbit's foot and the drawing, and I'll put it in," he tells her. And into a frame goes the renovated drawing, if only to be seen by the royal family.

It's 1962. Hirschfeld wants a raise. After he's submitted his expenses for a day in Philadelphia—$20.35—the *Times* accounting department has deducted fifty cents for "meal disallowance." Such pettiness displeases him, so he writes to Lester Markel—enclosing a list of his expenses (taxes, telephone, Nina's piano lessons, Mom in a nursing home, and so on) and reminding him that his annual income from the *Times* averages $3,500. Like so many at the paper, he has a love-hate relationship with the mercurial Sunday editor. "I don't recognize who that is," or "the nipples are showing," Markel customarily nags, but he remains true to Hirschfeld, even asking him to illustrate articles he himself writes for the magazine. When the raise goes through, Hirschfeld jumps from $150 a picture to $175.

Nina wants out. She lands a summer apprenticeship at the Centre Theatre in Ontario, and off she goes. When Dolly writes her of Al's bout with gout and Big Al's death, she gets no response, but she keeps at it, offering overwrought sympathy for Nina's long hours. That's how it is. In letters, Dolly and Al are soft, lest they antagonize her. Even Dolly's sister walks on eggshells, writing to commend the girl on selling lemonade. In midsummer, Dolly visits her. Al doesn't.

She returns to PCS, but her time there is . . . not there. It seems that Nina has been playing hooky again, the head writes to Dolly, advising that Nina consider whether there's any point in returning. There isn't. And then comes another summer.

While Nina's painting flats at the Barter Theatre in Virginia, Liza Kronenberger is tending William Styron's children on the Vineyard. Rooted in responsibility, she is serious about a career.

Yearning to be done with Dalton and on to the future, she applies to Parsons to study fashion design and asks Al to help with the application. He helps her create a collage—influenced by Ryder's moonscapes and Munch's *Scream* that reflect her own distress—and architectural drawings. With happy results. "I couldn't have gotten into Parsons without him," she says. As a graduation present, he draws her in a white dress and attaches a miniature rolled-up diploma containing a fifty-dollar bill. In return, she entrusts him with her girlhood bulletin board—covered with pictures of Audrey Hepburn and paintings by Ingres, Whistler, and Sargent—for safekeeping while she's gone. He hangs it in the studio.

Liza, Susan Harris, Randy Paar, Judy Goetz—these are the daughters manqué. Close to Nina or not, they adore Hirschfeld, no strings attached. "Kids liked him because he didn't treat them as less than the adults," says Randy. "He respected them and asked their opinion or if they liked some play, and that was great for a kid. While my dad would go into a room and try to control it, Al would listen." When Rachel Rome is studying calligraphy, he talks with her about borders, space, and color.

When Judy Goetz is a tot and her parents go to London with *The Heiress*, he sends them a drawing of her. When she writes a play, he's a booster. When Dolly can't go to an opening night, she can. "One of the joys of my life was that I was not related to him," Judy says now, "because I think that being a wife or a child or a family was not good news with Al. He was busy. His mind was elsewhere. Our relationship was about laughing and about people. I always wanted to amuse him." And that she does. Charming and fanciful, she gives him happiness. At her beautiful country wedding in 1991, he gives her away. And so fond is he of Susan Harris that he will later pay her tuition at graduate school.

The fledglings flock to him. "Gordon never said, 'Call me Dad or Father.' I think he had a lot of trouble being a father," says Jim Kahn. "My father was a very, very closed person," says

Adam Perelman, Sid's under-embraced son. "My relationship to Al was much better, because he was more open. He was not an uncle, but he was close, somebody I valued very much. I liked him, and I didn't like many people. He was always there for me, regardless of what my problems were with my family." When Adam's in trouble, his father is stonily unsympathetic. Not Al.

Later, when Adam opens the Nevermore in the Village, Al illustrates the menu and lends more than a hand. "He was like a second father to my brother, really," says sister Abby Perelman. "Al was a very huggable person. I was looking for surrogates, and he was there for me as well as Adam. We both loved him."

Carol Channing's son, Chan Lowe, is at Williams when he shows Hirschfeld the thirty-page comic book he's doing as an independent project. Hirschfeld critiques it and follows his artistic career. "Obviously he held my mother in tremendous esteem, but I have a feeling that our relationship was a separate one, and for that I appreciated what he was doing.

"He had a great effect on my technique," says Lowe, the renowned political cartoonist, "because I use that kind of line gesture, and I crosshatch a lot too. Like him, I feel that there's a great deal of information to be imparted by the line. He was the one who really lit the fire under me about that."

When Carol Brahm—the daughter of John Brahm and his post-Dolly wife, Anna—seeks Al's advice regarding a career, he has that too. "If you really want to succeed in New York City," he tells her, "open a delicatessen. People always need to eat."

In 1964, Nina moves on to Quintano's School for Young Professionals. Established in 1951, this is known as the place "where you sent your talented kid if he or she was, or wanted to be, in showbiz; it was also where you sent your wayward brat if he or she had been thrown out of another school," according to *Spin* magazine. While Nina will later drop the names of famous classmates, she hangs out at Downey's on Eighth Avenue with the actor Michael Dunn, who is a dwarf.

That summer she flies abroad to study at the École des Beaux-Arts at Fontainebleau. Before classes start, some of the American students take a trip to Belgium and Holland, which is how Nina connects with Judy Rosenblum, a singer, whose father is a violinist. They meet at the airport and instantly bond. "After the initial 'You're *Nina*'—where the animated face sort of froze for one or two seconds—we became really good friends," Judy says. "She had a *wonderful* sense of humor back then, and the two of us were giggling all summer."

Dolly's letters are scattered with questions and sunny motherisms about enjoying the work and discovering ways of expressing herself. Al's letters solicit any information at all. "We realize, of course, that writing is a chore but we also realize that interest, affection or love is not a one way affair," he pleads. "Reciprocity is an essential even between child and parent."

As the summer of 1964 suffers rioting in New York, Nina and Judy are wining and dining in local bistros with architecture students. As Mayor Wagner cuts his European vacation short to restore law and order, Nina and Judy are weekending in Paris. They're doing too much, and doing too little, and the school calls Hirschfeld to report that they're the only students who stay out after hours in defiance of the rules at their pension, the hotel d'Albe.

In response, Al coats his disappointment with a paternal boost. "The important, essential quality to survive and grow as an artist is complete dedication," he writes. "There is nothing wrong in having fun nor is there anything wrong in being a creative artist . . . balance, my dahlink, balance is the mysterious tricky ingredient in any recipe for a well rounded career."

Once again wary of alienating her, he leavens his advice by signing off with the spiral-eyed self-portrait.

For Nina, the summer is a turning point. "She'd thought she played the piano really well," says Judy. "And when she got there, they were not pleased with her piano playing, and she was not chosen to play in any concerts or anything. Not that she really cared, but it was the first time she had an inkling . . . if she was even *considering* becoming a concert pianist. I was studying voice, and I certainly didn't want to go into opera or anything like that, but my dad had gone to Fontainebleau and I went mainly to study French and learn French music and the repertoire. So I wasn't crushed. I never had any illusions. I think she had more illusions, musically, than I had. Because she was Al's daughter, she had played on television and things like that.

"My dad heard her play. He said, 'She plays like a typewriter.'"

The Hirschfelds tell friends that Nina is studying with Nadia Boulanger, the venerated pianist-composer-conductor—as have Aaron Copland, Virgil Thompson, and Quincy Jones—but she isn't. She attends Boulanger's lectures, but her twice-weekly piano lessons are with Jean Casadesus, the son of the pianists Robert and Gaby Casadesus.

"He had a car crash," is what Nina remembers of Jean. "He went off a cliff." She believes his 1972 death on an icy road in Ontario was a suicide. "I think he was really tired of trying to measure up to his parents," she says. "I don't think Jean Casadesus could accept having any failure in his life. I mean, he had to be perfect in everything. And he just decided, 'Hey, I don't want to live like this anymore,' and so he went over a cliff." That same summer, one of her closest friends dies of an overdose in Tangiers. She becomes fixed on fatal accidents and suicides.

She and Judy plan to audition in November for RADA, the Royal Academy of Dramatic Art. So after Fontainebleau, Nina goes to London, where Al wants her to learn the city and prepare with a coach. She studies acting, voice, French, dance, and jazz. She sees family friends and a lot of theater, then visits Joan Castle in her castle. Joanie's now married to William Sitwell of the Sitwells and presiding over Barmoor, the family's Gothic mansion in Northumberland that's become a bed-and-breakfast.

When Judy's due in London, Nina and Dolly—who's arrived to help set the girls up—are supposed to meet her at Victoria Station, but Dolly does and Nina doesn't. "I always thought that was very odd," Judy says. Dolly gets them settled at the English-Speaking Union, where she's a member, and then finds them a bedsit near Notting Hill. Judy makes spaghetti dinners. Nina makes dates. "She always had boyfriends," Judy says, "and was not very careful."

When they finally audition for RADA, Judy gets in and Nina doesn't. "It was a little sad," Judy says, "especially because Dolly had lunch with John Gielgud, and they put in a lot of pull for Nina to get in. Nina said, 'Oh, I don't care.'"

28
HOW MANY NINAS?

In January 1964, *Hello, Dolly!* opens at the St. James—and hello, Carol Channing! She has *adored* Hirschfeld for *years*, ever since he included her in a group of supporting players whose numbers stopped the show back in 1948. Then came her delectable Lorelei Lee in *Gentlemen Prefer Blondes*, with Hirschfeld decorating the sheet music and the souvenir book.

"She's captivating," Hirschfeld says. "She comes onstage, looks at the audience, and the audience applauds. Why, I don't know. There's a glow. It's just mysterious." She's a force and a friend, and he draws her over and over. "He gets what I'm *thinking*," she says in that voice of hers. "Others just draw the features. I look at what he's drawn and think, *Oh my God, that's what I was hoping to look like!* On-screen I look like George Channing's daughter, like Aunt Alice, like the whole Channing family. But with Al, I look like the character I'm trying to be." If it's Lorelei Lee, Hirschfeld gives her eyes like doorknobs and a mouth full of lips. As Dolly Levi in bouffant and feathers, her eyes are buttons, her smile a boulevard.

"I remember meeting her at Al's house and thinking that I was looking at a live drawing by Hirschfeld," says Randy Paar. "He *got* her," says Chan Lowe. "She was *invented* for him!" says Tommy Tune.

Channing couldn't be cheerier. "Dolly told me, 'You are his very most favorite beyond anyone,'" she declares. "I wasn't *one* of them. I was the *most* favorite." She's so attached to her Hirschfelds that she takes them with her on the road, hanging them in hotel rooms. "They're my lifeline," she says.

And so attached is she to the actual Hirschfelds that one night when *Hello, Dolly!* is still in the works, she snips a strand of Dolly Haas's red hair from her head and has her wig made to match.

The musical is such a smash that the title song is grabbed for stumping. At the 1964 Democratic National Convention in Atlantic City, Carol Channing steps up to the podium and belts, "Hel-*lo*, Lyndon! Well, hel-*lo*, Lyndon!" and in he sweeps.

Through the years, Hirschfeld depicts the presidents of all parties—FDR and JFK, Eisenhower and Nixon, Truman, Reagan, and the founding fellas in *1776*—but it's LBJ's party that inspires one of his favorite tales.

In January 1965, Hirschfeld draws the rehearsal for the star-studded inaugural gala being produced and directed by the composer Richard Adler. On March 9, 1965, he's invited to the White House to present this gift from the theater world and arrives at the Oval Office with Dolly and Nina.

"The door was opened by a standing President who seemed genuinely pleased to meet the family," Al remembers. "The day was an historic one. At the moment of our arrival, Dr. Martin Luther King was heading a march of civil rights demonstrators into the armed camp of white supremacists in Selma, Alabama. A telephone bell rang as we entered the room; the President excused himself with a pointed gesture to a divan." He recounts how Johnson presses a button and the voice of Dr. King fills the room, allowing the Hirschfelds to overhear a conversation between the two men on speakerphone—LBJ at his desk, King on the bridge. The allotted fifteen-minute visit stretches into an hour, Hirschfeld says, and he leaves the capital radiant with regard.

Back in New York, he tells the story at dinner. "Last Tues. he and Dolly and Nina drove to Washington to present his picture to the President," Margie King reports to her family back in Nebraska. "Johnson couldn't have been more cordial and gracious to them. He saw them privately despite his crammed schedule and the crisis in Selma. They were there when he spoke with Martin Luther King."

Not exactly.

The president's daily diary does not, in fact, show a phone call to or from Martin Luther King on March 9, nor do the White House operators' logs—although they meet in person on March 5 and speak by phone on March 14. "During Hirschfeld's visit, perhaps the President talked about King's visit earlier that week," suggests the head archivist at the LBJ Presidential Library.

In fact, the entire visit—which includes Dick Adler—runs from 12:07 to 12:31 p.m. and includes a stop in the Cabinet Room, where the president gives them copies of the State of the Union message and the inaugural address. And at 12:39, Johnson's off with McGeorge Bundy and Henry Cabot Lodge for a lap around the grounds.

After delivering *Ship of Fools* to the *Times* in 1965—the first movie he draws for the paper—Hirschfeld sails to Europe, abiding by Atkinson's belief that "flying wastes a glorious ocean." Dolly joins him there for a grand tour. In Greece, they encounter mosques and mosquitoes, and Hirschfeld scrambles over rocks to the Acropolis. They tour the Greek isles with Roger Furse and his wife, now living a life of wild splendor on Corfu (next door to Emlyn Williams), and visit Sergei

Radamsky on Elba, where he's running a music school. From the patio, Hirschfeld is struck by the blue of the sea, the silence of the island. He captures it all with his movie camera.

Stateside, Nina gets another shot. When Al's good friend Sidney Lumet is casting *The Group*, the director includes her as one of the college girls, but she ends up invisible in the crowd or on the cutting-room floor. Nonetheless, she claims to be in it, just as she says, "Almost got *Exodus*. I was up for the lead in that." She then takes a speed-writing course in the fall.

Then City Center presents a brief revival of *Where's Charley?* in May 1966. "I was an actress!" she exults. "That's what I wanted to be, and that's what I *trained* to be." Even in the chorus, she makes an impression.

"Jessica Tandy lent Nina a long blond wig because she was meant to look like a little girl with a little bow and long blond hair," says Susan Harris, who's out front. "Nina had to come onstage with a penny-farthing bicycle. It had wheels. And the wig got caught in a wheel!" Nina remembers an even more painful snafu. "My father came to the opening," she recalls bitterly, "and he said, 'You look bored.'" Whatever he says, he's in a jam. Annoyed by her diffidence, deflated by her failures, he's both booster and buffer.

She studies briefly at the brand-new American Musical and Dramatic Academy, founded by Philip Burton, adoptive father of Richard. She takes a summer course at Emerson College in psychology. And when she decides to apply for the fall, Al entreats two prominent friends to write reference letters. One is Harold Taylor, the former president of Sarah Lawrence, who's a political, influential, and popular figure in the Hirschfeld circle. The other is Philip Burton.

She applies elsewhere as well, from Florida to Minnesota, letting Al do the paperwork while she's in Boston. He spends a lot of time fielding applications, checks, test schedules, and rejections. Withal, his letters remain loving, no matter how great the aggravation; each is a tapestry of rebuke and apology. Dolly, tiptoeing on even softer slippers, adds more than her two cents when Nina can't live within her budget. "I realized what a tough time you are going to face in this crazy society of ours, where you have to account for such a thing as money," she cajoles, "and don't go around borrowing, I find it downright degrading." With which she encloses a check.

Nina is accepted at Emerson, where she follows her course as indifferent student and unreliable correspondent. Dolly pursues her nonetheless, even sending one of those self-addressed check-the-answers cards—"I am Well, Sick, Married, Broke, Bored"—that other mothers send their nine-year-olds at camp. It is not returned.

Nonetheless, Hirschfeld depicts her as the darling of the day. Never has she looked so fetching as in the full-page caricature *Gentlemen's Quarterly* runs in November 1966. Hiding two ALs and two DOLLYs in her bouncy hair, polka-dot dress, and checkered thigh, Hirschfeld calls the drawing *Nina's Revenge.*

Would this were all.

In February 1967, Nina inherits five thousand dollars from Billy Rose, who died a year before. But Emerson is not so charitable. In the same month, she's placed on academic probation . . . and five library books are overdue. "I, for one, am not at all troubled by this mid-term warning," Hirschfeld writes. "We love you and trust you and hope your new semester will help you achieve the person you secretly want yourself to be." He signs it "Your silly father."

Onward. In April 1968, Dolly writes an upbeat letter to downbeat Delaney. Since financing the artist's move to Paris in 1953, the Hirschfelds have visited him often, sent money and clients, helped pay the bills after a suicide attempt in 1961. Now, soon after Martin Luther King's assassination, Dolly tries to hearten him, adding that Nina's having a tough time, too. "We are delighted she decided to go to a lovely country place with a group of young men and women who need the country and activity in the open air to find orientation and purpose," she writes.

It seems that the place in the country is a treatment center, not a resort, although Susan Harris, who drives up for weekend visits, calls it a "gorgeous" place, where "everyone had their own rooms that were decorated like a nice New England B&B." It is nothing like a vacation.

29
A PIECE OF WORK

Enter Margo Feiden.

Through the years, Al's work has been seen in many venues. Back in 1938, he appeared in a group show at the Delphic Studios with other caricaturists such as William Auerbach-Levy, Irma Selz, his pal Don Freeman, and Alex Gard of Sardi's. In 1939, he had a solo at the Charles Morgan Gallery and had his lawyer noodge his subjects—from Norma Terris to Edward G. Robinson—not to miss it. In 1960, he was in a group with Piscator, Brecht, Gropius, and Leo Kerz and in a solo show at the John Heller. And even beyond the sidewalks of New York—from FDR's home at Hyde Park to the Washington Federal Savings and Loan in Miami Beach, from the Staten Island Museum to the House of Humour and Satire in Bulgaria.

In 1966, he opens at the Hammer Gallery with a glittery vernissage. This is the eminent domain of Armand Hammer, his benevolent host back in Moscow, and his younger brother, Victor. In a concise review in the *Times*, the art critic John Canaday writes of his colleague, "Let's just say that he is the Ukiyo-e master of the 20th century, the Sharaku of Broadway, and let it go at that. After all, that's starting at the top." Atkinson offers a more personal review. "I thought the exhibition was—and is—triumphant," he writes to Al. "There was so much excitement. You chose a good gallery, I think . . . Their exhibition radiates enthusiasm for you."

But apparently not enough. He has a fine forum, but not a champion to whom he matters above all others.

That's when Margo shows up.

She is the one who will sell and promote—if not always serve and protect—Al Hirschfeld. If Mom, schlepping the family hither and yon, was Mother Courage, this one's Mama Rose.

Born to an electrical contractor and a mother she says was the second woman in America to earn a stockbroker's license, Feiden wants *firsts*.

In the summer of 1959, she and her parents spend a weekend at Bill Hahn's Hotel, a family resort in Connecticut. One of the acts is Kuda Bux. Margo is a fourteen-year-old from Flatbush. Kuda Bux is a mystic from Kashmir.

Known as "The Man with X-Ray Eyes," he covers his eyes with fresh dough and then asks members of the audience to come up and swathe his head in cloth. In real life, Kuda Bux has lousy eyesight and will eventually develop glaucoma, but onstage, under wraps, he can see and read anything. Margo sees possibilities.

After the performance, she finds him. "When I'm old enough, I'm going to produce your shows and I'm going to be your agent," she says. He gives her his phone number.

At sixteen, while still at James Madison High School, Margo mounts a production of *Peter Pan*, the Comden and Green musical (Nina's favorite). Unlike Nina, who doesn't want to grow up, Margo does. Eventually, she'll wangle an entry into the *Guinness Book of World Records* as "Youngest Broadway Producer."

"I was listening to a late-night radio show called *The Happiness Exchange*. This girl comes on who's in high school, and she wants to put on a production of *Peter Pan*." Bruce Stark, a young theater hopeful, can't sleep, so he's listening to the host, Big Joe, raise money for the woebegone. Suddenly there's Margo, with a pitch. Impressed, Stark calls in to offer his help and becomes her stage manager. *Peter Pan* flies for ten performances in April 1961—with a cast of teenagers from the High School of Performing Arts. As for "Broadway," well, Wurlitzer Hall is somewhat off the Main Stem.

Calling herself Margo Eden, she writes a play called *Out, Brief Candle* (and its theme song). Next, she calls Kuda Bux.

"I'm old enough," she tells him. And soon she's booking him for weekend gigs in murky venues. She remembers, "We were standing room only, and this went on and on and on and on and on for years."

One day in the late 1960s, she gets a call from a photographer who wants to shoot him. Diane Arbus.

Arbus's taste would surely run to Kuda Bux, so they meet. Margo and Diane click, she recalls—pronouncing it "Dy-ann" instead of "Dee-ann," which the photographer prefers and those who know her know to use. She's about twenty-four; Arbus, forty-six. Feiden has a private pilot's license—yes, she really does—and Arbus has "flight phobia," she says, although Arbus has been shooting and flying all over the world for years. "She had no hesitation with me at all," Feiden claims. "She loved it. She would always ask me to take her. Any photos you see that she took from an airplane, I was always the pilot."

So who's seen them?

Not Elisabeth Sussman, curator of photography at the Whitney Museum. "Granted, I saw a lot of Arbus contacts over the years," she says, "but it would have stood out as being very strange and totally atypical. I don't think I would forget anything like that."

"Wow!" says Jeff Rosenheim, curator in charge of the Metropolitan Museum's department of photographs, who put on the major Arbus show at the Met Breuer in 2016. "I can't *imagine* that. But anything is possible."

Continuing Feiden's account: She's on her way to meet Arbus for a flying date one day in 1969 when she passes an empty shop in the Village. She rushes to Arbus's studio a few blocks east and calls the landlord. "I dragged her with me," she says. "Had the lease forty-five minutes later."

In the former Schnauzers Only Inc. at 51 East Tenth Street, Margo Feiden becomes an art dealer, but without art. Fortunately, Diane Arbus is at her side. "When we come back from the airport," Arbus graciously tells her, "you'll come to my studio, we'll go through things, take whatever you like." And by midnight, Feiden says, as the bells of Grace Church are chiming, she has hung her walls. "Dy-*ann* Arbus was the first artist I ever showed," Margo says.

Winter comes, and the Hirschfelds' card shows his drawing of a stone lion at the New York Public Library wearing a wreath and ribbon. The message within reads, "Our love and dearest Christmas wishes from your devoted trio," written in Dolly's wide-ranging script, with a drawing of the family: Al looking wilder-eyed than usual and Dolly with her hair in a tight knot, sandwiching a sullen Nina.

For such an observer, Hirschfeld is remarkably naïve about mental distress. When Millicent Osborn, the wife of the playwright Paul Osborn, mentions her anxiety pills at dinner one night, Hirschfeld is flabbergasted. "What are you talking about?" She says, "Al, I'm taking pills for anxiety," and he laughs. "What do you *mean*?"

In a social setting, he opposes therapy for Nina ("Just growing pains," he says) and psychiatrists ("head candlers" he calls them). Some friends consider him oblivious to her plight; others that he's an unemotional slab of marble. But in private, Nina is seeing doctors, one place or another—when she isn't playing hooky there, too.

In 1969, she lands on an indie film called *Make a Face*, written and directed by Karen Sperling (who also plays the multi-personality lead, named Nina). As Harry Warner's granddaughter, Sperling has movies in her genes. And she has Nicolas Surovy, a handsome young actor who's the son of the opera star Risë Stevens, in her life. Nic and Nina Hirschfeld know each other, and through some connection she's hired as an assistant to an assistant for the eight-week shoot in Sperling's apartment at the Dakota. But she's not on set for long. In a letter from Europe at the time, Dolly commiserates with her losing this "job that most certainly was that of an errand boy." So Nina takes a typing course at the Claire Lux Secretarial School.

In retrospect, Nina laughs extravagantly about her inconstant employment. "Each week it was a new job," says Samantha Popper. "I don't know whether she got fired or she quit." Among her occupations: receptionist at an exercise studio on Fifty-seventh Street (until she's fired for confusing the appointment schedule but ends up dating the gym master), assistant at a children's theater, assistant to Jean Dalrymple at ANTA, assistant to actor Robert Ryan, various spots at CBS, Tams-Witmark, and Young & Rubicam—all procured through her parents and their friends.

She takes classes at the Mannes College of Music and in the summer of 1970 flies to the Alliance Française in Paris for more French, soon shifting to the Sorbonne for poetry and philosophy. Although she has convinced her parents she needs time on her own, she spends little of it alone. Most of it's convivial, but one night she goes home with a stranger who locks the door and won't let her leave—she says. Her New York friends know nothing of this event, nor of her touring France with that rock-and-roll band.

Back home, she enrolls at Finch College, an East Side enclave from which Susan Harris has graduated. There she develops an interest in costume design.

Nina was "a tortured soul, I think," says Isaiah Sheffer, who teaches a drama course there. "She seemed very distraught. She was not unconnected to the other girls in the class, but she wasn't light and silly, as many of them were. She was a serious type."

Margo Feiden spots Raphael Soyer at a gallery in 1969 and approaches him. "I said, 'I'm very pleased to meet you. I'm an art dealer.' And he said to me, 'You are the most beautiful art dealer in New York City.' And that wasn't hard to be, because at that time art dealing was strictly a man's profession. My only competition was Bella Fishko, who owned the Forum Gallery that represented Soyer's paintings, and I assure you she was not in the running for the most beautiful art dealer in New York City."

Margo wants to sell Soyer's etchings, and they meet at the Bank Street Atelier, a printing studio in the Village owned by a fellow named George Goodstadt. He's invited Hirschfeld, Soyer, Calder, and a few other artists to come do their lithographs with him.

Goodstadt is a colorful figure. In addition to a background in art, he has a background in background. James Rosenquist has described him as "the artist who was designing the patches for the space program."

According to Feiden, he was at the CIA making forged documents.

"What he did for the government he would never talk about," his wife, Alexandra, allows. "He has lots of fun letters that I have in a box from really weird places, and he would go to very strange places at strange times. For instance, he was in Egypt right around the time where Carter, Begin, and Sadat were doing the peace thing—and Sadat was shot. He was *there*.

And then he was in Bulgaria for some strange reason where someone was shot with a poisoned umbrella tip. And he was in China even before Nixon came in there. So he was definitely working in strange ways—interesting, strange ways."

For Hirschfeld, such intrigue is catnip. When Goodstadt suggests printing editions of Hirschfeld celebrities, it's a deal. He starts selling them at Bloomingdale's. After Margo meets Goodstadt, she starts selling them, too. Those prints are the first Hirschfelds she sells.

30
WHEELING, DEALING

Hirschfeld walks into Feiden's gallery for the first time around 1970. He's there to see the work of her WPA artists, especially Soyer. "He didn't say a word for an hour and forty-five minutes. I knew who *he* was; he didn't know who *I* was," she says. "And he came to a bookcase, and on that bookcase there was a photograph of me—a photograph taken by the very famous Joel-Peter Witkin. And when Hirschfeld saw the photograph, it dawned on him that I might be Margo Feiden. He turned toward me and he said, 'Is that you? And what are you doing dressed that way, standing in front of an airplane?' I was dressed like Amelia Earhart, and the photograph was in front of an old Piper, so it looked like it had been taken in the '30s. I got up from my chair. 'Yes, it is I, and I'm dressed that way standing in front of an airplane because that's my hobby. I fly airplanes.' And there was a pause. And he sort of shook his head and said, 'Any woman who can fly an airplane can sell my art.'"

This from a guy who won't fly.

Feiden zeroes in. When she mentions that she's also a camel rider, that does it, because he himself mounted a camel back on the Sahara. She has the gumption; he has the goods. It's a match ready to be struck.

She pitches and woos him from Hammer. "I know that Victor loved him and would have lost him very, very reluctantly," says Hammer's stepdaughter, Nancy Wicker. "I think he was lured away rather than chose to go with her, because I know Hammer did very well with him." But apparently not well enough.

"She's such a self-promoter, she sold herself to him," says Susan Harris. "He wasn't Mr. Businessman. That wasn't his forte. He was a divine person who was a divine artist. It wasn't like he was advertising for people and interviewing people. No. It was just a serendipity kind of thing."

With a Flatbush take-charge kind of thing that reminds him of Paula.

Babe of the Stutz has shifted into Hirschfeld of the Cadillac. Convertible or hardtop, black or navy blue, he trades it in every other year. In Europe, it's a Simca or Renault. And in Britain, it's the other side of the road. Behind any wheel, he's fearless, to every passenger's dismay.

"It was miserable when you went driving with him," says Lisa Aronson.

"When he drove, you wished you were dead," agrees Lynn Lane.

"He drove like a cowboy!" says Marge Champion.

"Like a madman," says Maria Riva. "Many of us checked our wills before we went out with him. But we went, oh yes, not to disappoint him. Like with children, you never tell them the truth about themselves. You just adjust, you know."

He drives to the theater in Washington and Boston. He drives through the summer circuit. He drives to Fort Lauderdale for dinner, then turns around and drives home—with Dolly in the back seat because she won't sit next to him.

When they stop at a gas station one day, he gets out and she's asleep. He gets in again and takes off. Thirty miles later, the highway patrol pulls him over. "You left your wife behind," says the cop. "No, she's in the back seat." Which she's not. So he drives back and retrieves her.

"Left her at the gas station," says Frances Hershkowitz with a grin. "He loved that story."

And he loves knowing the shortcuts to avoid tolls. Peter Stamm from next door still uses "Al's secret ways into the city."

One day he picks up Chan Lowe for lunch. Dolly's in the back seat, so Chan gets in front. "Al's caroming around, all over the place, and he realizes he's overshot where the restaurant is, so he just starts barreling backwards to the intersection. I'm terrified. He's going really fast. For some crazy reason, nobody came down the street going the other way, and we were able to back into Third Avenue and go the way we were supposed to go." The press agent Adrian Bryan-Brown remembers waiting for the Hirschfelds at the 21 Club when the block is jammed. "And then we look, and driving down the street, going the wrong way, is Al!"

"He was not quite Mr. Magoo, but people got out of his way," says Rachel Rome. She, like Marge Champion, sits in the back with Dolly.

For Vicky Traube, the daughter of producer Shepard Traube, driving to dinner with Hirschfeld "was terrifying. It was like Mr. Toad's Wild Ride," she says. "I just remember thinking, 'I'm going to die.'"

Chauffeuring Randy Paar and her husband home through Central Park one night after the theater, he sails through a red light and hits something and keeps on going. "Must have been a pothole," he says. "No," says Dolly, "it was another car."

As for parking, there's not a Hirschfeldian in the pack who doesn't marvel at his karma.

"He would drive to a Broadway opening," remembers the newsman Jerry Tallmer, "and he would park it any goddamn place in the world around Times Square that he felt like, and I don't think he ever got a ticket."

Press agents are impressed when the Hirschfelds arrive early on opening nights.

These are the nights they sit in the Cadillac noshing out of brown paper bags.

Taking over the adjoining shop, Feiden renames her establishment the Margo Feiden Galleries. Some of the enhancement might accommodate her work as a paper restorer, but it also impresses Hirschfeld, and he agrees to let her mount a fifty-year retrospective.

For the exhibition, to open in 1973, she'll need more of Hirschfeld's work. "And then," she says, "a whole van of his art came down." She describes the three thousand or more drawings as "wondrous things," comparing the trove to King Tut. "There were these perfect drawings that were unsold," she says. "They'd been there for decades."

She goes to the house and rummages through the studio, coming up with treasures long buried, never seen, never shown. Then she gets to work.

"Hirschfeld was the hardest thing to sell in those days. People would say, 'But he's an illustrator. But he's an illustrator. But he's an illustrator. I can cut it out of the paper. Why do I need an original?' I heard that I don't know how many times. Dozens and dozens and dozens and dozens. Thousands." But to Feiden, Hirschfeld is not just an illustrator; he's an *artist*.

Not to her other artists he ain't. "The WPA crowd," as she calls it—which includes Soyer, Chaim Gross, Alexander Dobkin, and Leonard Baskin—are angry that she's hanging Hirschfeld, she says. "I don't know whether they were jealous because he had such popular recognition, or what. I have to believe that it's because he wasn't part of their clique. What I've learned about art is that it's so cliquish. That's probably the most surprising thing I've learned as an art dealer." She claims that Hirschfeld has always wanted to be in "that club—the club of the grand masters of American art"—but they won't let him in. The irony is "that's why he *came* to me, because I had those other guys. I mean that's basically what I opened my gallery with."

More to the point, his work is *commercial*. "He was a populist," she says, explaining their disdain. "Illustration was an orphan, not taken seriously, because they felt the artist did not create it out of his *inner turmoil*." No matter. He's creating like crazy, and if it's on assignment, so be it. "Great art has always thrived only with great patrons," she adds. "The Sistine Chapel was commissioned by the pope."

Until now, Al has, on occasion, even sold his drawings himself, at pretty humble prices. "I will happily ship to you, prepaid, the drawing of Orson Welles in return for $350.00 to be added to my dwindling money collection," he'd reply to a request. Now that all changes.

The show opens at the gallery on March 16, 1973, and Hirschfeld is celebrated in an article but no review. The *Times* won't cover him because it doesn't want to pat itself on the back, explains Feiden (forgetting that the *Times* reviewed him at the Heller in 1958 and at the Hammer in 1966), and other papers won't cover him because they don't want to give the *Times* a plug. So she invites the TV critics to review him.

But there's another force at work. The *Times* is now trying to ease him out. His caricatures have been appearing less frequently than every other Sunday, and his front-page position is fading fast.

When Max Frankel becomes the paper's Sunday editor in 1973, he orders a redo of the Sunday department, most visibly in Arts and Leisure. This is "not only the largest and most widely read of all arts journals," as the outraged music critic Alan Rich points out in *New York* magazine, "it is also the most powerful." Nonetheless, the longtime Sunday drama editor Sy Peck is dispatched to the magazine and replaced by the former travel editor Bill Honan.

"If *The New York Times* wants to run a dumb entertainment section, it has exactly the right man to do it," snarls Nat Hentoff in *The Village Voice*. With crumbs tossed to Hirschfeld, whose drawings have graced Arts and Leisure—née section 2, or the Drama section—since 1928, he is virtually unfindable as he's moved inside, when used at all, with photographs replacing him on the front page.

How fortuitous, then, that on February 14, 1974, Hirschfeld signs a contract with the Feiden gallery, starting at ten thousand dollars for the first year. As his exclusive representative now, selling his work and controlling the reproduction rights, she swells their coffers. "She gave him a new financial security," says *Daily News* critic Howard Kissel.

Meanwhile, *Times* readers are puzzled by his irregularity, and so is he. "There hasn't been anything going on in the theater, particularly, so there's been very little for me to do," he tells a friend. But something's going on. After all these years, the boys upstairs have concluded that his art is more promotional than editorial, geared more to flackery than delight. . . and insight. They consider him "archaic," says the art director Steven Heller. They seem to have forgotten how important his drawings are to Broadway and its audience, and what a bellwether he is.

"I thought, *What goddamn nonsense!* Tradition for tradition's sake. I like tradition," says Hal Prince, who produced *Fiddler on the Roof* and knows from tradition. "*The Times* has to resume amorous relations sooner or later," Atkinson consoles Al from the woods.

No one will say whose decision it is, but everyone has a guess. Some home in on Honan, but others think not. "Dumb as a stick," says a copy editor, "and he doesn't have the backbone." "He would *never* have had the guts to dump Al," says Arthur Gelb, who knows everything but isn't saying who would.

Others point to Lou Silverstein, the corporate art director. "He certainly didn't fight it, and he may have agreed, because Lou was revamping everything, and the Sunday sections were key to what he was doing," says Heller. And what does Max Frankel say? "I was not a party to any of those discussions. It may be that Al himself resented no longer being atop the section and pulled away from *The Times*." Unlikely.

Whoever's to blame, "it was getting a little dark for Al, and he needed all his friends, all his acquaintances, to get behind him," says Louise Kerz. So they write letters, collect signatures, petition the *Times*. Among the supporters are Milton Goldman, the theatrical agent, and Arnold Weissberger, the theatrical lawyer, titans in their fields. Frankel replies to Weissberger that Hirschfeld "does not wish to 'illustrate' mere articles—he prefers shows of Broadway and particularly new shows," and he says, "We have a deal with Al Herschfeld [*sic*] for a certain number of drawings a year and we're going to try to use them to the best possible effect." The deal is for twenty-three drawings, but it's just a deal. As an independent contractor, Hirschfeld still has no contract with the *Times*.

Feiden to the rescue. "The *Times* stopped commissioning him," she says, "so I did two things. Just like a political campaign. I called everybody that had ever purchased anything from us. 'How are you enjoying your Hirschfeld?' 'Oh, it's wonderful.' And I would say, 'You noticed that Hirschfeld isn't in the *Times*?' and they'd say, 'Yes. What happened?' I'd say, 'Well, we don't know exactly what happened, but if you would write a letter to the *Times* . . .' I called hundreds of people to get them to write to the *Times*.

"And I did something else. I developed a very strong private-commission campaign so that he would keep working, because it was killing him. It was *killing him*. I was afraid it would kill him, literally." She calls actors and collectors, informing them that Hirschfeld is available for private commissions.

"I built that business," she says, "because *The New York Times* dropped him."

Said subjects arrive at his studio dressed as they want to be immortalized. He points them to the chair, engages them in brief conversation. Sometimes he doesn't bother meeting them at all, when photographs will do. Sometimes he includes a favorite prop. "He knew a lyric of mine," says Sheldon Harnick. "and it was personal to me about trying to break down walls to communicate with people." In his drawing, Harnick is shown holding a pencil with "breaking down walls" on the pad before him. (NINA's there, too, in his armpit.)

Hirschfeld draws crooners for CD covers, writers for dust covers, and accountants and Realtors who don't know theater but do know that having a Hirschfeld is a trophy on their wall. He draws Stanley Marcus for his ninetieth birthday, Rosie O'Donnell for something or other, the agent Sam Cohn as *Annie*.

He draws Frank Loesser (who wrote Al's favorite musical, *Guys and Dolls*) at the request of his widow—after the fact. "He had not drawn Frank during his lifetime," says Jo Sullivan Loesser, "so I said, 'You've got to do Frank!' I gave him loads and loads of pictures and ideas, and he said, 'and I'll think of what I remember,' and that's what he drew." So Frank's at the piano, a cigarette in his teeth, hanging with the many Hirschfelds of Loesser shows in her country house.

James Earl Jones's hallways and stairways are similarly decked, and when he wants a picture of his young son, Flynn, it's Hirschfeld. "I engaged him like you would hire any artist to do a sitting of a family member," he says in that voice of his. He provides a photograph and is delighted with the result. "Hirschfeld gave him Beowulf eyes, through which you can see eternity," he adds majestically.

When a drawing is done, it must be *presented*. Feiden calls: you may pick it up at the gallery. She craves the *Ah!* moment.

When Hirschfeld does his first drawing for *The New Yorker* in 1993 (Ross's long-ago ban now long ago), it's a self-portrait to go with a ninetieth-birthday tribute by Mel Gussow. Chris Curry, the magazine's illustration editor, is summoned. When she arrives, Feiden keeps her waiting. An entrance is essential. The watercolor, on an easel, is unveiled. "Even though I could feel the controlling presence of her," Curry says, "it made my eyes water because it was *really, really beautiful*. It's like she kind of expected that, but I didn't. So I was, Okay. It's worth the wait. It's worth the trip."

With less *Times* on his hands, he's at Sardi's one night in January 1975 when he sees his friend Harold Rome across the crowded room. Rome is dining with *Newsweek*'s Japanese bureau chief, Bernard Krisher, and Hirschfeld joins them. In the blink of an eye, Krisher asks America's theatrical illustrator if he'd consider illustrating the theater of Japan. "Sure," says Al, "if I don't have to give any speeches or go to any cocktail parties."

Promptly, the Japan Foundation issues an invitation for April. Hirschfeld has always cited Hokosai, Utamaro, Sharaku, and other Japanese woodcut artists as his greatest influences (although Margo Feiden disagrees and is convinced that his line is inspired by the artists of ancient Egypt.) Now, he'll gladly go to Japan and have *his* way with Kabuki and Noh—applying his hand to the designs and postures, the masks and makeup, the dance and nuance. Some of his Broadway drawings are shown at the Okura Shukokan Museum in Tokyo, but he's there to fill his sketchbook with new images.

Back at George Goodstadt's Bank Street Atelier, Al creates a suite of twelve Kabuki dancers in ink and watercolor, demonstrating a delicate balance of detailed patterning, sweeping motion, and dignity. He signs his name in Japanese figures, and NINA is nowhere in sight.

Goodstadt publishes them, and Feiden fumes. "I never got what I was supposed to get," she says. "I got a few of them but not the edition." A very confusing business. Ironically, the work is cherished today, but not so then. "Kabuki was exquisite," says an arty friend, "but George couldn't *give* it away. He used to offer it with his regular Hirschfeld stuff. He did a mailing every year, and he would include that."

And then, redemption! The *Times*'s executive editor, Abe Rosenthal, takes over Sunday. Frankel is dispatched to the editorial page, and Gelb regains his grasp on Culture. The first thing he does is reinstate Hirschfeld.

On February 29, 1976, a caricature of Ruth Gordon and Lynn Redgrave in *Mrs. Warren's Profession* appears on page 1 of Arts and Leisure. "Once Hirschfeld came back, it was an interesting response within the art department," says Heller, "because there were some people who thought, 'Yeah, Hirschfeld represents the old,' without looking at how timeless his line was . . . and how many people really copied it." He's once again a mainstay, once again embraced.

The work is delivered by messenger (no more does Hirschfeld bring it down himself) and made safe. Linda Brewer, one of the Sunday art directors, remembers a flat file with a lock as the repository. "The drawing could never be left unattended," she says.

Next, it's photostated. This, too, is an artistic process, deftly performed by one Nestor Delgado. "Hirschfeld had a lot of very fine lines in his drawing, and Nestor had to expose this thing just right so that all those fine lines showed up," explains Eric Seidman, a photo-cropping clerk at the time. The operation involves acids, washes, and timing. "The photostat machine and Nestor were one. He loved his work, and he prided himself on doing a good job."

The photostat is what the art director plays with, or "manipulates" (never does one touch the original art). If more space is needed for copy, it's adjusted a teensy-weensy bit—with Hirschfeld's permission.

When the original is returned, the envelope stays . . . and becomes a collector's item. Large or larger, it's manila, and Hirschfeld always decorates it—often with a self-portrait, always with the pointing finger sweeping from addresser to addressee, and the directive "Do not fold, bend, stomp on, or dunk in hot chicken fat."

"I have two or three of them," says Steve Heller.

"I've got a lot of them," says Adrian Bryan-Brown. "They're the only Hirschfelds I have."

On April 30, 1976, the *Times* introduces its new Weekend section on Friday. It's chock-full of culture, with a compendium called "Broadway." Once upon a time, such briefs appeared in Zolotow's column or in Lew Funke's Sunday "News of the Rialto," but now they appear here. Hirschfeld, back on the beat, is chosen to illustrate one of the items every week. His first Friday drawing highlights a revival of *The Heiress*, by the Goetzes.

His weekends are getting more profitable. Friday brings in more bucks; whereas he's been making $400 for a Sunday picture, this adds $275. Press agents send him photo after photo. But oops! One week he receives the wrong one and draws the wrong actor. Caught just in time, a photograph replaces the caricature, and the theater world is aquiver—Where's Hirschfeld? Is he out again?—not to mention the actor who misses getting a Hirschfeld.

Friday or Sunday, Feiden's hustling. "She'd call the second it'd run to find out if the producers wanted to buy it or not,' says Bryan-Brown, "and if it was a big show, she'd say, 'I've got a lot of people interested. Before I sell it, do your producers want it?'"

Although her relationships with many subjects, clients, and art directors is a miasma of delay and deflection—request background material or pictures and the response can take weeks, ask a question she'd rather not answer and she changes the subject so deftly you don't know it's been changed—Feiden's relationship with Hirschfeld is cordial and rewarding.

But often when she puts him in the light, she slides in next to him. And not everyone wants her there. "Hirschfeld could do no wrong," says a magazine art director of the day, "but one of the horrors about dealing with him was that I had to deal with Margo. She was very protective of him, but she's a one-woman self-promoter. She's a ruthless self-promoter, in my opinion—to Hirschfeld's detriment, actually, because she generated so much bad feeling. But clearly he didn't want to deal with anyone, so he let her do it. I'm sure he understood what the price was, and he was willing to pay it.

"Invariably I wound up with Margo and wanted to kill myself rather than speak to her. I found her so unpleasant and so unbearable that on the days when I had to call, I would steel myself in the morning to make that phone call, because I never knew how beastly she was going to be. And to me, even though his work is great, it says a great deal about a person if you allow a viper to represent you."

Wherever his work is seen—even deep in the background—Margo wants credit. Lynn Redgrave and her husband, John Clark, show their apartment in a decorating magazine, and two Hirschfelds on the dining-room wall catch Feiden's eye. Scolding the two, she claims that the gallery should receive credit just as the draperies do. Clark strikes back, informing her that "in the picture you see my shirt. It is an 'Arrow.' I paid for it. It did not receive a credit. Neither did my Jockey shorts."

31
LONE STAR

"Will the real Nina Hirschfeld please stand up?" On her twenty-fifth birthday in 1970, Nina appears on the popular TV game show *To Tell the Truth*. It's a game of who's who. Three people try to fool the judges as to which is someone famous. The one who *is* is the only one to tell the truth.

Because panelist Kitty Carlisle is a family friend and has known Nina forever, she swaps places with the moderator, Garry Moore. Because Bennett Cerf hasn't seen Nina since she was four, he stays put. Peggy Cass and Bill Cullen don't know her at all. The two impostors are good, but Nina, acting almost too intentionally tentative—and looking a lot more Hirschfeldian than the glossy brunette and the braided blonde—is voted the real Nina Hirschfeld.

So who *is* the real Nina Hirschfeld?

She packs her bag and sets off to find out. In 1972, she gets a summer job at the Dallas Theater Center painting sets and playing animal parts in a *Mother Goose* production. And along comes love! They meet walking dogs in the park next to the apartment complex where they live. Nina has a mutt named Natasha she hasn't trained or bought a leash for. Mike Russell has two schnauzers. Bearded and bespectacled, he's an engineer at Texas Instruments and, as it turns out, a hang-about at the Dallas Theater Center. He paints, he ushers, he shoots candids of the actors. He also plays the piano and writes music.

He has a red Volkswagen. She has red hair. "She was drop-dead gorgeous," he remembers. "A short, voluptuous lady. And very outgoing." When she writes home about him, misspelling his name, she tells her parents how grateful she is to have met him, adding that "you need to drive a car here otherwise you are dead," and she doesn't drive.

Mike and Nina have known each other for five months when their engagement is announced in the *Times* and *Variety.* Dolly registers them at Tiffany and performs other loving tasks, while Al enters the gifts and givers in an album. Nina lends a hand, and Mike is "just kinda hangin' on for the ride," as he puts it. The wedding takes place at the Unitarian Church of All Souls on Lexington Avenue on December 27. Nina, radiant in a white satin gown, is attended by Tandy Cronyn and other friends.

Just before showtime, Hirschfeld's zipper gets stuck. Dolly finds a sewing kit and the ceremony manages to take off on schedule, conducted by a rabbi and a minister. "We did some of the Jewish traditions—the goblet and the canopy and breaking the glass afterwards. I had to learn this stuff, you know," says Mike, a Methodist.

The reception is at home, although an upstairs pipe burst earlier in the day. Daphne Hellman plays the harp, and the photographer Peter Basch records the event as celebrities troop through to celebrate. Mike and his Austin parents are overwhelmed by the wall-to-wall, sequin-to-sequin guests. "I knew some of them from movies," says Mike.

After honeymooning at Elia Kazan's house in Montauk, the newlyweds return to Dallas, where Nina takes music courses at Southern Methodist University. In July 1973, they move to Austin, where Mike attends graduate school at the University of Texas and Nina takes more music courses. They live on the cash they received as wedding gifts and Dolly's supplementary fifteen dollars a week for food. All is seemingly swell. Except Nina hates Texas.

Hirschfeld might have given her away, but soon she's back.

Diligently, he's been sending Mike the *Times* want ads. "I'll get you a job in a day," he promises, and he does—at Warner Bros., which is computerizing its publishing interests. The couple comes to New York, and Al pays their rent on East Eighty-eighth Street. They come for dinner twice a week, and he gets them theater tickets. He engages Mike and seeks his opinion. After a year, Mike moves to Wall Street, working for a subsidiary of the stock exchange called the Depository Trust.

Nina is more than slightly pregnant before she realizes—or acknowledges—it. In August 1975, she gives birth to Matthew.

"Was your grandson born with red hair and a white beard?" Atkinson writes. "I should think that would be the least he could do for the family." Nina breastfeeds him, as she will for the next five years, friends say (which is nothing compared with the eight years Mom devoted to Al, according to Margo Feiden). She takes him to Carl Schurz Park on the East River. "There I was, Mrs. Russell, and boy, I tell you, my self-esteem went way up," she says. "I was the happiest woman in the world being married to that guy. And in love with him. It was a new life. I had a baby, and everything was great. And the past—I really didn't think about my parents very much. I concentrated on my family."

But Mike can't adjust to New York, and after two rough years they return to Austin, where she makes no friends and doesn't cook or clean and Dolly calls twice a day.

Mike tries giving her driving lessons, but they don't take.

Meanwhile, Hirschfeld catches a ride upstate when John Berg, the art director for Columbia Records, offers an offbeat assignment. On a ninety-eight-acre spread near Armonk sits the

Cenacle, a former convent built around 1900 and once owned by Billy Rose, of all people. Now it's a retreat for Aerosmith, and they want Hirschfeld, of all people, to draw the lines for their new album called *Draw the Line*.

"We had a huge kitchen, a dining room, a place for the crew to sleep and work, and our massive Studio A along with smaller rooms," Steven Tyler recalls. "It was an incredibly creepy place. . . a lot of big dark living rooms and a lot of long hallways—a cavernous, grim place, especially at night. And then there were the little tiny rooms where the nuns had slept."

Hirschfeld isn't checking the rooms. He's checking the fellas. "It was very important to him, to actually *know* these people," says Berg, who's designed some five thousand covers but never seen a match like this. "They wanted Hirschfeld. It was their idea. It would not have been my idea. It's a really loud rock-and-roll band, and that kind of a cover was not really indicated by the music they made. But they were being creative, and more power to them. I certainly agreed with them, because I loved Al Hirschfeld."

He sketches, he chats. "They were feeding off of him, and he was feeding off of them, and it was backing-and-forthing," says Berg. The result of this encounter is a long-haired portrait of the five, and they're delighted. "He really nailed us," Tyler says. "We look like freakish botanical specimens pinned under glass." Adds Berg, "The drawing does not *look* like them—except it looks *exactly* like them. What that kind of magic is, I don't know. He gets the essence of it, without getting the particulars."

Does he get their music? "No," says Berg. "As far as I know, he was strictly a Broadway-tunes guy. But a gig is a gig."

Somebody breaks into Betty Comden's house, and the neighbors are on alert. Dolly walks up Ninety-fifth Street, and a group of girls mug her. "What are you *doing*?" she explodes. "I'm an older woman, you're mugging me? Don't you have *jobs*?" No jobs. "Then come with me. *I'll* give you a job." Propelling them home, she orders them to clear the backyard, then gives them five dollars.

More darkness follows when a blackout attacks New York on July 13, 1977. Neighbors light candles and sit on their stoops with wine and cookies, listening to looters north of Ninety-sixth Street. The Hirschfelds, out on the town, inch home and pick up hitchers on Park Avenue. The next day, order is restored. "Just now I hear a terrific cheer from the street and shouts and screams from Daddy," Dolly writes to Nina. "The lights are back, screams of relief. It feels a little like New Year's."

In October, Al and Dolly are in France, where they visit with Liza Kronenberger Wanklyn, her husband, and their daughter. They tour the modern art museum at the new Centre Pompidou, and while Hirschfeld is taken with the Matisses, Braques, Picassos, and Bonnards, "the whole effect is like Steeplechase at Coney Island," he writes to Nina.

In Bruges, he admires the Michelangelo in the cathedral and the Dutch masters ("I don't mean the cigars") at the Memling. Thence to London, where his new book, *The Entertainers*, comes out. Paid a paltry poundage, he gets, at least, a hilarious prelude by Perelman. "Gay as a grig yet solemn as an owl; keen as mustard but dull as a hoe; faster than light and slower than a poke. . ." Sid jests. They dine with Joan Castle, no longer of the castle; she's in the midst of an angry divorce.

Turns out she's not the only one.

"There wasn't another woman. I thought we were getting along fine," says Nina. But no.

"He stayed as long as he could. He just couldn't take it any-more," Dolly confides to a friend.

In retaliation for something, everything, Nina chops off her hair. "I liked being a redhead," she says, "but the day I got divorced, I became a blonde. It was 'I don't want to be that redheaded little girl ever again. I'm not that person anymore.'"

The blonde and her son come back to Ninety-fifth Street. "What was I going to do?" she says. "I didn't have any money, I had no job, and I had a two-and-a-half-year-old." Having failed at marriage, Nina blames Al. "He never said, 'Gee, I'm sorry your marriage didn't work out.' It was just sort of like, 'Ohhhhh, you're *home* again?'"

The more Nina depends on her parents, trapped in her own trap, the more childish she feels. They argue about money, responsibility, boundaries.

Hirschfeld designates Dolly the fixer and slams the studio door, focusing on work. They enlist real estate agent Herbert Sanders to find Nina and Matthew an apartment, but after three months Nina breaks the lease. They're back. While she and Matthew reside upstairs, the usual merriment goes on below.

One night Gloria Vanderbilt brings a young writer who's recently interviewed her in *Women's Wear Daily*—Ben Brantley, a stripling obsessed with the theater. "I was so much younger than anyone there I might have been an embryo," he says now, as theater critic of the *Times*. But that night he's hobnobbing with Lillian Gish, the Kerrs, the Osborns. "I asked Millicent Osborn if she'd been involved in theater," he says. "I think she said something like, 'Well, in 1928 they called me the Ingenue of the Year.' And it was like *ahahahah!* You could just see this long, long vista of decades going back, which to me is heaven. And Al—I'd mention Mae West, and he'd go, 'Oh, I was at her first Broadway opening.' Or John Held. Things we think of as cultural references were living people for him. That was the great thrill with Al Hirschfeld, that continuity. And he was so relaxed about it. It wasn't like he was bringing out a little plum or jewel to show you. This was just his *life*."

Another at table is the beautiful Louise Kerz, with long wavy hair and gray-green eyes. Since Leo Kerz's death in 1976, leaving her with two young sons and no income, the Hirschfelds have virtually adopted her. Often they turn up at the same soirees, including those of Joseph Machlis, an eminent musicologist who's an old lefty friend of Al's and was one of Louise's mentors at Queens College. Machlis hosts legendary musicales, but most spirited is his annual "Alger Hiss's 80th Birthday" party, where Louise's beau Harold Taylor gives the toast every year. "She was very much around," says the journalist Victor Navasky, a regular at these things.

Howard Dietz introduces her to William Paley at CBS. Paley directs her to Alexander Cohen, who's compiling a fifty-year celebration called *CBS: On the Air*. And before long, Louise is a researcher, extrapolating highlights from news and documentaries. She loves it, because she once wanted to be a history teacher, and presto, she's got a career.

And a camera. She's shooting the players in this glamorous world, and keeping a journal, and stepping lively. "The curvaceous Mrs. Kerz rang up a few minutes ago, tanned and restless from a week in New England," Perelman (a widower since 1970) writes to a friend. "Says she has an adorable new green sweater that stopped traffic on West 42nd Street this noon."

But soon the fun is over. The gang is thinning out. In October 1979 (shortly after the death of Hirschfeld's troubled protégé, Beauford Delaney, at St. Anne's Hospital for the Insane in Paris), Sid Perelman dies of a heart attack alone in his apartment at the Gramercy Park Hotel. He leaves his Royal portable, toaster broiler, and two hundred books written mostly by him (and appraised at thirty-five dollars). He's cremated on his son Adam's birthday, and his ashes are buried near his daughter Abby's upstate home.

There's no funeral, but friends sit shivah at the Hirschfelds'. A few months later, the Manhattan Theatre Club throws a "Salute to S. J. Perelman." The invitation is decorated with Hirschfeld's come-hither drawing of the reclining Perelman, drawn for the Book Review in 1970 (akin to the reclining nude in *Reclining Figure* and the reclining Hirschfeld on Joan Castle's petticoat). Friends reading and reminiscing include Hirschfeld, Marc Connelly, Phil Hamburger, and Ruth Goetz.

Four-year-old Matthew is developing a taste for caviar (while still being breastfed).

Nina prefers pizza. Her days revolve around Matthew—walking him to school, taking him to museums and toy stores. Her nights are spent at home.

"I didn't go to one theater," she says, "didn't take advantage of anything the city had to offer." When she does dine with the grownups, "I always felt that everybody was uncomfortable with Nina, and Nina was uncomfortable with them," says Jules Feiffer. "Matthew would be hiding under a table, and she'd be trying to relate to all these older people, and it would be quite hard for them," adds Louise. So most often, Nina takes meals in her room. To spite whom? And still she blames Al.

"My father should have said, 'Nina, let's change the room around. Listen, you can't share a room with your son. Let's work on this—let's get this thing organized.' But there was no organization. It was like I was still twelve, playing the piano, and he was with my mother going to the theater. I wish I had been able to talk to him more about Matthew. But I figured, 'Daddy's busy. He's up there doodling all day so that I can eat, so that my son can go to school. And I can't bother him.'"

Her savior—everybody's savior—is Herb Sanders, the real estate guy, with whom she and Matthew spend weekends in his bachelor flat near Sutton Place. Nina's in love again.

32
OUT OF LINE

At an Algonquin party in 1981, Paula Laurence comes table-hopping. No longer a vixen, she's still got *something*. In fact, says Margo Feiden, Paula has been a constant in Hirschfeld's life—and a thorn in Dolly's side—all these years.

"They slept together all the time during his marriage to Dolly," she claims. "Everybody knew about it, and they all took Dolly's side. It's not a question that he didn't lie to her. It's a question that he didn't give a damn. He did what he wanted when he wanted to. He was constantly unfaithful to Dolly. I'm not betraying any confidences here, because his seeing other women was well known. I mean, he went *out* with them. He spoke about them as though he was a polygamist."

Although Maria Riva contends that Dolly has long abided Al's peccadilloes in her courageous German way, Feiden says not so with Paula. "Dolly gave him an ultimatum," she says. "She threatened to throw him out of the house, so he gave her up. I think he did. I *think* he did."

In 1982, the White House calls, and Hirschfeld agrees to join sixty other artists in decorating wooden eggs in honor of the annual Easter Egg Roll. Not to be confused with the eight thousand hard-boiled eggs hidden in the bushes, these will be exhibited in children's museums throughout the land. Buckminster Fuller contributes a geodesic egg, sculptor George Segal sends a painted egg with Reagan's face replacing Washington's on the dollar bill ("a sort of nest egg," suggests *The Washington Post*), and, because the cast of *Annie* will be performing on the South Lawn, Hirschfeld draws Annie with NINA "on the back, if eggs have a back," writes the reporter. Due to the previous year's assassination attempt on Reagan, security is intense. All guests, even toddlers, pass through metal detectors as Secret Service agents disguised as cartoon characters watch the crowd.

While Hirschfeld is preoccupied with Clark Gable, Marcel Marceau, and Marilyn Monroe for George Goodstadt's lithos, with John Chancellor and Gilda Radner for NBC, and with sporty vignettes for *Outdoor Life*, Dolly takes off for Germany. She's being honored in a special program called "Six German Actors in Exile" at the Berlin Film Festival in 1983. And with Al so busy, Louise Kerz—whose parents were German and Austrian, whose husband was German, who speaks German—volunteers to be her traveling companion. Louise is touched by Dolly's confident posture, stride, and smile. And no wonder. Dolly is appearing before an audience again—her own audience—and basking in the long-absent warmth of that glory.

But when Dolly returns home, it's to Al's world. "I feel that, in a sense, Dolly's life has been wasted," observes the writer and wit Leo Lerman. "She had so much to give and our theater did not permit her to give it." But she has a role. Maria Riva, who knows her best of all, says that "she gave him the kind of security and life that was necessary for him to be able to sit in his barber chair and draw lines."

Mike Russell has been flying back and forth, visiting his son in New York, occasionally taking him back to Texas. Mike and Matthew, now ten, want more of each other, and Hirschfeld wants less. Despite her pleasure in being a grandmother, Dolly does what Dolly knows is best. "Your son needs his father," she tells Nina over and over again. But Nina drags her feet.

And lashes out. "You have no idea the way they argue," says Teresa Gonzales, the Peruvian housekeeper who has replaced Milly. "If she was there for five hours, she could fight her father for four and a half." Five minutes before Hirschfeld takes his noon lunch break, five minutes before his four o'clock tea break—and oddly abiding by this schedule—Nina runs upstairs to have at him when the clock strikes.

"You could be on the first floor and listening to her screaming to her father. About money, always about money. And calling him all the words I will never repeat. Many times I am standing right there in front of him with his cup of soup, and she started screaming, and Mrs. Dolly staring into her plate. It was terrible the way she treated the father." Hirschfeld sticks to his pens. His output during Nina's infiltration is typically, defiantly, prolific.

He's noticeably relieved when Nina hits the road. Herb Sanders won't commit to more than weekends and the occasional excursion to Paris or Disney World, so back she goes to Texas.

With which Susan Dryfoos, a member of the *New York Times* dynasty, shows up. As director of the *New York Times* History Project, she's been conducting oral and filmed interviews with *Times* folk, and when Dolly sees some she just *knows*. "You are the one!" she tells Dryfoos. "You must make the film on Al!"

For the next ten years, Dryfoos will tape and tail Al, interview his friends and join him at the theater, become part of his life and another daughter manqué. The result is the Oscar-nominated documentary *The Line King*. Al calls it the Dead Sea Scrolls.

It's 1986, and the revels resume. "We could hear the piano, and it was like being on an ocean liner in the '30s," says the Hirschfelds' next-door neighbor Shari Thompson, her ear to the wall. When she moved in a while ago, Dolly welcomed her with a jar of chutney. It's been in the pantry ever since.

"My dear, I'm having a party," Dolly calls one night to say, "and we've run out of chutney. Do you happen to have any?" Shari runs over and hands it to Al at the door. "Not so fast!" he says, pulling her in for a drink. "And there I was in my pajamas!" she says. And who else was there? "Probably the world. I was too naïve to know."

While the company's chic, the house is shabby. "It was falling apart. I mean, absolutely falling apart," remarks Frances Hershkowitz.

"It was dim," says Gray Foy. "Neither one of them cared about housekeeping."

"Just dismal," adds Sidney's wife, Piedy Lumet.

When a pipe leaks, Al turns to Dolly. When the TV fizzles, he calls Maria Riva's son Paul. One day, he does what no one should do: responds to a flyer in the mailbox. Making a date with Dynasty General Contractors, he welcomes a rep to the house and gives him a down payment of eight hundred dollars for repairs. Never to be seen again. "He was completely helpless," says Maria Riva. "He was a child."

In January 1987, Lynn Surry is walking briskly from Balducci's when she passes the Feiden gallery. She's always loved Hirschfeld's work, and carrying her groceries, she comes in to look, she says, although Margo remembers her asking about a part-time job. She likes Lynn on the spot. "I need somebody right away," she says. "It's for Al Hirschfeld."

They've never met. Lynn has never been to the gallery before. She has no arts background. Her degree is in political science; she's been a property manager and has done "some event planning," she says. "Right," says Feiden. "She ran Renta Yenta."

An interesting career move, says Lynn's husband of the gallery job, and she figures why not. Feiden has some part-time college kids, a bookkeeper, and no computer. She's mainly at home writing a book. *The Calorie Factor* will be published in 1989, after much research and weight loss, and "you're not likely to find a calorie/carbohydrate counter as hefty in both physical size and comprehensiveness as this," says the review in *Library Journal*.

Surry digs right in. One of her projects involves raising the prices of Hirschfeld's work. "You could buy a print for $150, and you could buy an original for $1,500," she says, "so we went through every single one, and we repriced every single thing.

"It was very expensive to reproduce these lithographs and etchings," she says. "We only did one or two editions a year. When we got a little more money in, we were able to do probably six or eight editions a year. But considering the amount of work Mr. Hirschfeld did, it wasn't very many. And that made these lithographs and etchings quite valuable. If they were in an edition of a hundred, the first ones might be $500. Then they went up, as there were fewer, to $750, then $1,000." The big-cast Broadway shows go for $15,000 to $25,000. The single-character Friday drawings are obviously less.

"I realized that most aspiring actors and actresses wanted to be Hirschfelded. Now many of them are very famous, but in those days they weren't, and they weren't making much money. I set up a plan where they would pay weekly, monthly, until it was paid off, and then they'd have their drawing. That just made me so thrilled, because if you got Hirschfelded, if you appeared in *The New York Times*, you were on your way. It was like a stamp of approval."

Before the installment plan, some have been following their own plan.

Charles Busch is doing *Vampire Lesbians of Sodom* in 1985 when Enid Nemy interviews him for the Friday column in the *Times*, and he awaits his Hirschfeld. "I looked and I thought, 'Well, it *sort* of looks like me,'" he says, "and then I realized it was Lily Tomlin. So they bumped me a week, okay. The next week it came out, and it was *gorgeous*.

"I don't know whether the Feiden gallery called me or whatever, so I went over with the idea of purchasing it, obviously. I was so excited; it was such a new thing for me. So I went in and she was very grand, Margo Feiden. They brought the picture out on this easel covered with a velvet cover, and they lifted the cover and I saw it in person and I was kind of startled because I'd never really seen a Hirschfeld up close. He had taken it from a photo, and even though I was in drag, I was so thin that I never wore any falsies, but since he actually hadn't seen the play, he had first drawn these really big knockers on it, and then he had changed his mind for whatever reason and he took Wite-Out and whited it over and you could see where these big boobs had been.

"So I was kind of like, 'Oh, gee.' I guess I said something like, 'Oh, you can see where the knockers were,' and Margo Feiden got very snippy and said, 'Well,' with great hauteur, 'it's called a pentimento. You can see where the earlier sketch was, which proves it's an original.' So, you know. *Oh, really*. I think it was about five thousand dollars at the time, which was a lot of money, but she was no nasty and patronizing to me that I said, 'I'll think about it, dear.' So I left. I didn't buy it. And a friend of mine made a wonderful stat of it, and I had that framed."

"They were bootlegged all the time," says Adrian Bryan-Brown. "People used to scan them from the *Times*."

Even Hal Prince. "Opening nights, I would take the Hirschfeld—just copy it and frame it and give it to everybody in the company," he says. "And Margo heard about that, and she raised holy hell and she said, 'Why didn't you get our permission? That costs money.' And I thought, 'I'm sorry.' It was a good opening-night present. Stick it in a picture frame and let them have that. And she bitched like crazy. But I went right on doing it." Did he pay her? "No!"

That may be, but with Margo at the helm there are always untapped markets, undrawn customers. And on a sunny day in the late 1980s, one steps in.

Julius Cohen has come to buy a Zero Mostel, and Margo's attention is grabbed. Now divorced from Stanley Goldmark—a congenial fellow who was in charge of matting and framing at the gallery (Feiden's first ex-husband, the father of her two children, being long gone)—she falls almost immediately in love. Julius is a jeweler, and what better for the daughter of Jewel Feiden?

"He was teeny, as big as a minute. She could have put him in her pocket," recalls one of the clients at his Madison Avenue firm. "He looked like Sam Jaffe."

Others think he looks like Al Hirschfeld.

"When I was with Julius—and this happened all the time—people thought he was Hirschfeld," Margo mentions. "We went to Michael's Pub one night to hear Mel Tormé. Very romantic, and Julius and I were holding hands and necking off in the corner. And at the end, Gil Wiest, the owner, came over to us, after Mel Tormé was done and the lights were back up and checks had been given out, and he said, 'Miss Feiden, Mr. Hirschfeld, it's been so nice to have you for this evening.' And I said, 'Julius, we're going to end up in the gossip columns! That I'm out with Albert Hirschfeld necking.' And Dolly was still alive! I mean, can you imagine this? It happened all the time."

When Julius is in the gallery, people ask for his autograph. At a party, a playwright kneels and grabs his ankles, gasping, "I've always wanted to meet you!" Margo savors the confusion.

She moves the gallery to University Place in 1988 and is just hanging the first wall when in comes Joseph Solman, one of the artists she's been showing. What he sees is Hirschfeld, only Hirschfeld, and assumes the whole place is Hirschfeld.

He pulls his work and calls Will Barnet.

Barnet, still painting at 101, says of Hirschfeld, "I know that he achieved a lot with his cartoons." He has stayed with Feiden for years, but now he also pulls out, and it is not pleasant. "Certain things of mine that she should have returned, she never did," he says. "She was very difficult. At the beginning, she seemed to be right, but in the end she seemed to be wrong."

Feathers get ruffled, egos get bruised, calls are stalled, checks drag through the mail. But through it all, Hirschfeld is loyal and true. If she can fly a plane, she can sell his art.

But does she fly the artist? "Oh, no!" says Stan Goldmark, with a laugh. "If he wouldn't fly in a big 747, I doubt whether he'd go in a little Piper Cub."

Whereas there's a brass band for Al's eighty-eighth birthday party, Margo toots her own horn. Much of her promotional material—the full-page gallery ads, announcements, invitations, and press releases—features her portrait by Hirschfeld in which she's sitting in a director's chair before her hearth, with tiny portraits of Al and Dolly on the wall behind her. There's also his drawing of her on a camel. And the one in her Amelia Earhart getup, posed with her plane.

But the panache is past. "She was Elaine Kaufman in size," says Joel Kaye remembering more of the up than the up-and-down of Feiden's weight, "and she wore funny clothes, to hide things. And funny hats." She's roundly remembered for making her entrance at the National Portrait Gallery in Washington, where Hirschfeld is to be interviewed. It's a small event, invitation only, with a strict start time because it's being filmed. Feiden shows up late and takes her seat in the front row, wearing a tall, striped Cat-in-the-Hat hat.

She and Julius buy a home on East Ninth Street, which she bills as "A Stanford White Townhouse," although it was built in 1845, some years before White was born.

There's a "ballroom" and the "tree house" room, which she says inspired the view from Jimmy Stewart's apartment in *Rear Window*. (The courtyard inspiring Hitchcock's set design is blocks away, between Tenth Street and Christopher. Feiden's rear window overlooks the yards of neighboring town houses.)

She looks to move up in other ways as well. On a winter's day in 1989, trucks are parked on University Place to move her operation to Julius's office building on Madison Avenue near Sixty-second. Rather than mention it to Hirschfeld, she plans to surprise him when the move is made. The furniture is stacked on the sidewalk, the art is wrapped, and into the empty gallery walks Hirschfeld with Alistair Cooke, the British journalist best known in the States as the elegant host of *Omnibus*, a cultural series on 1950s television, and *Masterpiece Theatre*. They've come to view the work before Cooke writes the introduction to a new book of Hirschfeld's drawings. It's not one of their best moments.

But they do continue, uptown and down. Feiden says she's at Al's home so often "they didn't even notice me. I was sort of invisible. I was like a wall. And they knew I'd never talk about them. I hate gossip." No matter that friends say they never see her there, that she's not part of the evening circle. Feiden insists she's treated like a member of the family, "as though I lived there, as though I were another daughter."

Al's niece, Belle Herzon, a real member of the family, is now on the scene. For years a hotshot interior decorator in Los Angeles, Big Al's daughter now lives in New York. Long divorced, Belle lives on the East Side and paints watercolors. She dines frequently with Al and Dolly, and because of her tough intelligence, they consider her a powerful trustee for Nina and make her coexecutor with George Goodstadt of their wills.

She meets him in a hot tub . . . and he's a dishwasher. "I went from the crème de la crème to the crap de la crap," Nina says of husband number two. Danny West scours fry racks and tongs at Burger King.

Why would Nina, in her forties, go for a lunk in his twenties who's said to have been arrested for loitering and has what's been described by Herbert Sanders as having "a wild look, like somebody who could kill you"? Nina sees something, though. "I found him attractive, 'cause I had *no* self-esteem," she explains. When Matthew meets Danny, he thinks he's the TV repair guy.

They come to New York, and Al is "beside himself," says Judy Rosenblum Halevi. "My father wouldn't even *talk* to me, because he was totally—*totally*—wrong for me," Nina admits, "even though my mother was very *happy*. She said, 'Somebody loves my daughter. Isn't that wonderful? He doesn't have a great *job*, but isn't that nice?'"

"He was fat, lazy," Teresa confides. "He went to Bloomingdale's with Nina one day, tried on jackets, walked out in one, and was arrested. Nina said, 'He made a mistake.' Dolly fixed it, probably didn't tell Al. After that, they stayed in a nearby hotel." Margo Feiden also remembers the visit. "I think Danny was eager to marry her because of Hirschfeld. But they were not married when I went around New York with them," she says. "He kept saying that they were, and it got Nina very agitated because they weren't. He'd say, 'I'm his son-in-law. I'm her husband. Why aren't I in this photograph?' And she kept saying to me, 'He's not my husband.'"

But that's soon remedied. They are wed at Great Hills Baptist Church in Austin, Danny being Baptist, Nina being seven months pregnant.

Hirschfeld refuses to attend, but Dolly does her duty. So does Judy, as matron of honor. "It was part gym, part church," she says of the setting, "and the fellow who married them had cowboy boots on. Nina rented a dress. I can't even remember the service. It was a little bizarre."

"It was a beautiful dress," adds Susan Harris, "a very unusual dress. All draped, like an upside-down letter C, just billowing and billowing."

After the ceremony, somebody hosts a reception miles away. "So we go to this nice modest house filled with people," says Judy. "Dolly's there, and she's saying, 'Isn't this *wonderful*? Isn't this the most *charming* thing you've ever *seen*?' She has her gloves on, looking very European. 'Oh, look at that! Oh, look at that piece of art!' They didn't drink, so they had 7UP and ice cream and then cake. That's what they were serving."

Margaret West is born in July 1989 and named for Dolly's sister. Despite Nina's ambivalence about being pregnant with this child, she now considers motherhood her calling and churchgoing a close second. She gets baptized at Great Hills and harangues Hirschfeld that he should convert to Christianity because if he doesn't he's going to die and go to hell.

Love-wise, Danny's the one. He brings her flowers. He says he loves her and wouldn't leave her even if she were in a wheelchair—"little things that women love to hear," she points out—although at times, by her account, he may have come close to putting her in one.

Usually, she says, his punches just make holes in the wall. "I was *scared*, because he'd say, 'Be glad that wasn't your *face*.' Had I not called the police and let him know, 'Hey, I don't want to be treated that way,' who knows what would have happened?" she says. She reports him to Family Violence Protection but doesn't press charges.

Matthew remembers none of the violence—"maybe because I was in my own room and I blocked it out," he says. In fact, he thinks of Danny more as a brother than as a stepfather. They play video games together. He thinks Danny's cool.

They split when Danny takes up with a friend of Nina's. Margaret is two and a half, the age Matthew was when she split from Mike.

33
CHANGING *TIMES*

The Friday column has been renovated. New writer, new format . . . no Hirschfeld. The art is a photograph of Marilyn Monroe.

Nobody's told Hirschfeld. And nobody does until he finds a letter in the mailbox—*written on the same day*: October 26, 1990—from the new culture editor. "Forgive me, please, for not being in touch with you before now," writes Paul Goldberger, blaming the "foul-up in communications" on being out of town and relaying a decision made by the brass. "We have decided to make a change in format for the Friday theater column, effective with today's issue. . . . This will mean, therefore, that we will not be using your drawings in this Friday space from now on."

The column has been renamed "On Stage, and Off." The writer, Alex Witchel, a former theater gossip on *7 Days*, is new at the *Times* and the girlfriend of the current theater critic Frank Rich.

So who's axed Hirschfeld?

Hirschfeld asks Gelb, who says he had nothing to do with it and doesn't know who did. "I thought it was the stupidest thing that could possibly have been done," he recalls, "and whoever did it did an incredibly ridiculous thing. That drawing every week was a delight." Having recently retired, Gelb has gone from news to the Times Foundation when the ax swings. "They waited for me to leave, and then they did it, because they knew I would never allow it under any circumstances. *No way* could this have happened when I was there. No way."

Who's "they"?

Some point to Witchel, suggesting that she doesn't want to share the spotlight, that behind the scenes she and Rich may have jockeyed Hirschfeld out.

No. Frank Rich says Hirschfeld was dropped "to everyone's horror, including Alex's. She was *furious*."

Al is in the dark. When a die-hard fan sends a note, mentioning that he's written to the *Times* to protest, Hirschfeld promptly replies. "Have they personally acknowledged your letter?" he asks. "If so—would be very grateful if you would inform me of their arbitrary decision to replace drawings with photographs."

But whatever the reason, Al's trust in the paper is unshakable. On November 28, 1990, he receives an envelope by messenger. "Please sign the enclosed contract and return to me," requests an editor there. The one-year contract, dated November 7, 1990, states that Hirschfeld will provide twenty-two drawings during the year for Arts and Leisure (Sunday) or Culture (Friday), for thirty thousand dollars. He is eighty-seven, and this is his first contract with *The New York Times*.

The messenger waits while he signs it. "What did the contract say?" Feiden demands when he tells her later. "I have no idea. I didn't read it." She's on fire. "What do you *mean* you didn't read it?" He's calm. "Well, the *Times* isn't out to get me," he says. "I'm sure it's fine."

Inventive as always, Feiden turns her gallery into a post office in 1991, when the US Postal Service issues a book of twenty-nine-cent stamps called "Hirschfeld's Comedians." It's a set of five—Laurel and Hardy, Abbott and Costello, Bergen and McCarthy, Benny, and Brice—and the first caricature art in the history of U.S. stamps.

As they're ready to roll, Postmaster General Anthony Frank says, "Where are the NINAs?" The advisory committee reminds him that they've told Hirschfeld no NINAs, because stamps can't carry "secret marks" such as signatures. "What's a Hirschfeld without a NINA?" he says. "It's *not* his signature. It's something he hides in there."

It's not easy this late in the game, but Hirschfeld squeezes NINA into all but Laurel and Hardy, and—whoops!—leaves out the *I* in the NINA he's placed on Jack Benny's bow tie. For twenty-five drawings, he gets seventy-five thousand dollars, or three thousand dollars apiece.

The stamps are unveiled in July at the Video Software Dealers' convention in Las Vegas and at the Hollywood Post Office in August. The public is tickled, but not philatelists who prefer the historic and engraved.

When the committee chooses a second set from Hirschfeld's original twenty-five, they can't include Gloria Swanson (whose rights people reject the Hirschfeld and suggest they use Gloria's self-portrait instead) or Mary Pickford (whose people feel Mary deserves a *real* painting). But there are ten gems, and "Silent Screen Stars" will come out in 1994.

Meanwhile, back at the ranch, Hirschfeld is falling out of the saddle. His barber chair is unraveling beneath him. It's bound with twine, its springs have sprung. Naturally, Surry worries.

"Mr. Hirschfeld, you're going to get hurt!" she cries. "Would you like a new one?"

"Sure," says Al. "Where's it coming from?"

"I have it." Luckily, Lynn's husband had been the real estate agent for the Chrysler Building, and during renovations in the 1970s a treasure was revealed: the Terminal barbershop in the arcade beneath the lobby. It had been hermetically sealed, with three barber chairs intact. Rather than scrapping them, Bruce Surry had put them in a friend's basement.

So now, in 1992, Lynn retrieves one. She has the tonsorial artifact trucked in and hauled up. Hirschfeld's happy. Feiden's furious.

"We had a very, very nasty blowup," Lynn says, "because she said I had no right to be giving Hirschfeld—who belonged to *her*—presents." Hastily, Feiden calls Alex Witchel, informing her that Hirschfeld is donating his old barber chair to the Smithsonian and that she has replaced it with one from the Chrysler Building. The item runs in the Friday (Al-less) theater column.

As it turns out, the broken Koken is far beyond saving, much less commemorating. Parts of it are trashed, the leftovers kept by Feiden.

Hirschfeld hops off for Hollywood. His flexible regard for Disney is one thing, but now Disney's regarding him. It seems that Eric Goldberg, an animator creating the Genie for *Aladdin*, realizes he's been spirited by Hirschfeld. The more Goldberg draws, boiling his lines down to the essence, the more Hirschfeldesque his character becomes. He longs to meet the master! And the Genie grants his wish. When the feature is screened at the Ziegfeld in New York, Goldberg is designated the Hirschfelds' escort.

Hirschfeld likes the movie, telling Goldberg, "It looks like it was all done by one hand"—a great compliment because some five hundred people worked on it—and after the movie's release in 1992, Disney Studios invites Hirschfeld out to conduct classes for animators.

"It was like God was coming to town," says Goldberg. "We'd just spent two years trying to get his style onto the screen, and now here he is!" One day, Goldberg takes Al and Dolly to Disneyland. Small World! Fantasmic! Haunted Mansion! They have a *mahvelous* time, even when Dolly loses her straw hat to the murky waters sloshing through Pirates of the Caribbean.

They call it "The Hirschfeld Bake-Off."

As the *Times* turns to color, the authorities turn to their crystal ball. Hirschfeld is ninety, and they're thinking about an heir—an artist who could appear concurrently for a while in Arts and Leisure, and then, quietly, succeed him.

They call in portfolios. "It was very hush-hush and very sensitive and very awkward, because they weren't telling *him* this," says John Kascht, one of the caricaturists enlisted by the art director, Steven Heller. "I think the whole thing was very uncomfortable for them. I frankly thought it was a terrible idea. It's not as if Hirschfeld would leave this gaping hole. There wasn't a great need for theater caricature. There hadn't been since 1940! He *was* the position, and it wasn't a position that needed to be filled. His black-and-white style had become so much the signature of the paper for seventy years, there were concerns that he really wasn't a good fit for a color Arts and Leisure section." No one seems to realize that he's been doing color for years.

They assign a caricature of David Letterman. "So we were auditioning for this position, even though there *was* no position," says Kascht, who wins. "It was humbling to be considered as his maybe successor, but very awkward for me because I didn't think it was a great idea. I was very aware that these are shoes that can't be filled. I love Hirschfeld and always did.

I knew nothing about theater, but the wit and expressiveness and sheer beauty in his work—that I understood. I devoured every curlicue and dot.

"I think the subject of 'What are we going to do post-Hirschfeld?' would have been very natural to come up in planning meetings. And the catalyst was the paper going into color. It makes sense; it's totally legitimate. But I think Hirschfeld should have somehow been involved in the conversation."

He isn't.

Kascht's color caricature of Letterman nearly fills the front of Arts and Leisure on April 10, 1994. Hirschfeld's *Beauty and the Beast*, his first color drawing for the section, runs a week later. The picture is more beast than beauty, and no one is less surprised than Hirschfeld. He's been reluctant to do it because newsprint absorbs the ink and doesn't print color vividly.

It was "just *awful*," says Linda Brewer, the then art director, who has another reason. "He basically took one of his black-and-white ink drawings—not one of his better ones—and just kind of washed some weird colors over it. And we all looked at it and we said, '*Uh*.'"

"It looked a little muddy to me," adds Barbara Richer, another art director at the time. "What I love about Hirschfeld is pure, pure line, and it just seemed muddy." The colors aren't accurate either. Belle's dress should be yellow, not orange, as the show's costume designer points out. "At ninety, he may not have been a great colorist anymore," suggests Kascht. "I think these were all legitimate concerns and questions."

But Al's got more personal concerns. By summer, Dolly is dying of ovarian cancer, and he can't face it. Everyone knows she's the love of his life, the glue, the pillar—but in health, not sickness. Dolly, who understands this better than anyone, moves into Nina's room. When that's no longer feasible, she leaves for Mount Sinai. "Remember," says Lynn Surry, "he worked in his home. He would never ever leave that. So why would anyone question that the hospital might have been a better place for both of them?"

But Al doesn't visit. "If he witnessed a kind of leave-taking and a kind of mourning as a boy, it would have influenced his reaction to Dolly," says Maria Riva, referring to his brother Milton. "You have to have tremendous courage to watch somebody you love die, and I don't think Al had that form of courage." And with Teresa running the houshold, life continues on Ninety-fifth Street, with friends in for dinner and taking him out. "Al was a force of life. He had to *live*," says Liza Kronenberger Wanklyn. "I don't mean *survive*, I mean *live*."

Unable to accept her mother's condition, Nina remains in Texas. Friends beg her to come home. No need, Nina tells them. "The doctor says she's getting better"—which Dolly has probably asked him to. When Nina calls, Dolly can't speak with her. "She was just too sick," says Margie Barab. Louise Kerz offers to go get her. "No, darling," Dolly says. "It just wouldn't work."

With unimaginable grace, she bids her friends farewell. "She told us who we were, really," says Margie. "She motioned for us to come close," says Bel Kaufman, "and told us what she expected we would be doing in our life, what she wanted us to do, what she hoped we would do. And then she said, 'You may go now.' My husband said to me, 'You know what she did? She blessed us.'"

When Maria Riva arrives, she dismisses the nurse and takes Dolly in her arms. "I spoke to her in German—when one is dying, one reverts to one's childhood language—and I said, 'Let go, my darling, I'm here.' And she recognized me, and I said, 'Nobody is going to touch you, nobody is going to do anything to you, you can die in peace.'" And so, on September 16, she does.

"I think I got a phone call. I guess my dad must have called me," Nina says. "I honestly don't remember."

But she knows what she has to do. Leaning on Matthew and her ex-husband Mike, she flies to New York for her mother's memorial service at Frank E. Campbell's. It's a starry crowd. Speakers include Jean Kerr, Betty Comden, the producer Robert Whitehead, the literary agent Robby Lantz, and the theater critic Brendan Gill. Bobby Short sings "Honeysuckle Rose" and "The Most Beautiful Girl in the World."

Gloria Vanderbilt isn't among the friends at the house, and Al is hurt. "She never showed up, never called or anything," recalls Aaron Shikler, the portrait painter who is Gloria's current swain. "That's the way she is. I remember Hirschfeld's line. He said, '*That's* strange.'" And especially so, because Al has drawn her time and again in her various theatrical attempts and because Dolly arose in the middle of one night to be with her when her son Carter killed himself. "Gloria had great respect for Dolly and adored Al," says Maria, "as long as she can adore anybody."

Margo Feiden is very much there. "No tear was shed by anyone in the room—by anyone but me," she declares. Judy Sanger and her husband, Dr. Sirgay Sanger, longtime favorites, clearly remember Feiden's behavior. "Bizarre and rude," says Sirgay. "Al was sitting in his chair, and she threw herself at his knees, and looking up said, 'Oh, this is so terrible, Dolly not being here,' crying and beseeching him to comfort her. I said, 'You'll have to leave the house. This man is too old. You can't do this to him.' And I actually took her out and put her in a cab."

Hirschfeld is overcome by helplessness. "Who's going to take care of me now?" he asks his friends. Nina's no help. She's ensconsed at a hotel, because Al won't have her at home. She comes for meals, but not to stay. "She knew that was the rule," says Teresa.

Dolly's wish was to have her ashes buried on Alderney near her sister, Margaret, who died in 1987 (leaving five hundred pounds and her mink stole to Nina). So when Maria Riva offers to take them there on her way back to Europe, "everybody jumped at it, particularly Al," she says. "He wanted her to have what she wanted, but he also wanted it finished, out of the way. I was willing to take that burden from him, and he accepted it, with great affection and great gratitude."

Liza Kronenberger Wanklyn, who idolized Dolly and for whom Alderney was so meaningful one summer when she accompanied Nina and Dolly there, joins her. Maria enlists a minister, and Dolly is buried in the upper graveyard behind St. Anne's Church.

But why is Dolly not buried closer to Hirschfeld, her beloved *Engel*, who is unlikely to show up on Alderney? "I think," says Maria," it was her last need for escape."

34
SING OUT, LOUISE!

Now it's Nina and Al, one in Texas and one who intends to keep her there. "That's the attic," says Margo Feiden. "Austin is the attic." Divorced from Danny, supported by Al, she's virtually helpless. She won't drive (her father's passion) and will no longer fly (her father's phobia) and doesn't lock doors, even in public restrooms, lest she be trapped.

She taxis everywhere, from Saks to supermarket, letting the meter run. She doesn't know how to pay for her utilities and asks a cabbie's help.

"I said, 'Well, the gas and electric you can pay at the grocery store, the H-E-B,' so I took her there," says one of her regulars. "She was just fascinated that you have to pay these bills every month."

She considers the drivers her friends. "Better than any psychiatrist," she says with a laugh. "I got it off my chest, and it didn't seem to bother them too much. They still picked me up." Then she tries to pick them up. But when she invites them in for coffee, most decline.

She's raising her children in a singular style, keeping them close, breastfeeding Margaret until the age of five, as she did Matthew. "I was left alone with the babysitter or with the piano, because my father *had* to go to the theater," she says sourly, "so I raised my kids the exact oppposite. I was home all the time." As are they.

She takes them to school and picks them up in a cab, waiting not out front but outside their classrooms. They don't play sports or instruments, or with other kids. She doesn't take them to the Children's Museum or the Austin Zoo, to Round Rock or Barton Springs, to the LBJ Library or Lady Bird Lake. She takes them home, to watch television and eat spaghetti. She laughingly refers to herself as "the spaghetti lady."

And out of the kitchen, she's found love again. With her father-in-law.

Her father isn't alone either.

"They came out of the woodwork," says Maria Riva. Bel Kaufman calls them "the ladies with casseroles." Lynn Lane calls them "a posse," says they came with pot roast and chicken soup. Margie Barab calls them "the widder ladies," says they set their caps for him because not only was he dear and kind and smart and wonderful but he also had opening-night tickets. "*Well*," she says. "The *claws* came out."

At ninety-one, Hirschfeld is ripe for the plucking, and the ladies (many of them enriched by ten-thousand-dollar bequests from Dolly) are ready to pluck. Joanie Castle is leader of the pack, Rosemary Chodorov (widow of Eddie) and Florence Rome (widow of Harold) evince interest, Louise Kerz is vivacious, and there's always Belle, the needy niece.

But there are nights when he's undone. At Chez Josephine, where he and Dolly dined for years under a nude painting of Josephine Baker in the *Folies Bergère*, Jean-Claude Baker is startled by his appearance. "Suddenly he was *old*," the charming host recalls. "He had never been *old* with Dolly." He sits waiting at table 15, and his friends don't arrive. It's the wrong night.

Time after time, it's a night too soon or too late. "A lost soul, a lost man," Jean-Claude says. "I would give him his soup, he would go back in the car, and that's it. Dolly was taking care of everything. He's that kind of man who needs a woman. The woman is like the private secretary of the *life* of those men, and he was one of those men."

By January, though his dance card is full, he's kissing Louise goodnight at the door. In March, he includes her in his *Times* drawing of *Inherit the Wind*. In April, she invites him to her son Jonathan's wedding. They dance, and they could have danced all night. "She must be all attention with him probably," Teresa says later, "because that's when they fall in love with each other! She had Al Hirschfeld all night by herself."

Her rise to leading lady seems sudden to some, inevitable to others. But Louise wins the prize. She tells a friend that she has "decided to devote herself to Al. Period." She's solicitous and sexy. Protective but fun. She picks him up in her red Toyota, zipping through traffic like a flash, and Flash is aflutter. "You drive like a New York taxi driver!" he cheers, and she knows he's falling in love with her. "I never really intended for that to happen," she says. "It just happened."

Now when they stroll into Chez Josephine, "I look at them with shock!" says Jean-Claude Baker. "I welcome them of course, like the great host I *am*, but with a certain smile: What's going on here? So they sit down, they have supper, and suddenly he says, 'Jean-Claude, I must tell you something. Louise and I are together.' So that's a wonderful wonderful *new life* for Al."

Even Paula Laurence is glad. "He hadn't been alone for decades, and the threads began to come unraveled. He stopped taking care of himself and didn't look well-groomed and was kind of a mess," says Paula's friend Stephen Pascal. "And then Louise came in and he suddenly was dapper again and behaving much younger. She was very happy that Louise had hooked up with him. There was no jealousy."

But the Furies do still fly. Belle, who considers herself Dolly's successor, is so upset she won't come to the house. Joan keeps calling Teresa to ask where Al is. Margo is predictably proprietary and cuddles close to Belle and Joan. "It seemed that they were like the three spirits that . . . I don't want to get Shakespearean here, but . . ." says Louise with a laugh.

Belle tells Margo that Louise has been flirting with Al for years. "She described to me in detail sitting at the table—and she always sat next to Al on his right—with Louise on his left rubbing his leg with her foot. *I* never saw that," Margo makes clear, "but I believe it from a first-person witness. Belle was as right as rain." On the other hand, on another day, she says she doubts there was any hanky-panky during Dolly's life. "I would have picked up on that," she says.

In August, they're holding hands at the theater, then at home. Joan glowers; Louise glows. They travel and visit friends. She introduces him to McDonald's, and he introduces her to more stars than there are in heaven.

Soon they're in Boston catching *Moon Over Buffalo*, and Al wants to see Feiden's new gallery next to the Colonial Theatre. Opened in March 1995, it's being run by a nameless friend and client of hers, "a real entrepreneur in the theater, who thought he could make a go of it." Apparently, he can't. So she closes it. Without telling Hirschfeld. Who arrives with Louise, to find it gone. Another Margo surprise!

In the fall, when he invites Louise to move in, she keeps her own apartment just in case. "He made a decision about me, and I made a decision about him, so it was like a rehearsal," she says. "And it worked." Taking over Nina's room, she splashes blue paint over the pink, hangs new drapes, adds a desk and bookcase. And when she returns to Ninety-fifth Street every evening from her research duties on TV specials, now including the Tonys, Hirschfeld's at the piano. His legs may not run up and down the stairs anymore, but his fingers still stride that keyboard.

Their first dinner party. Al and Louise blow kisses across the table, and Arthur Gelb is charmed. "There was no question about how much in love they were," he says. "Later I said, 'Louise, it was just entrancing the way you behaved during dinner.' And she said, 'Al is wonderful'—and she looked at me with sort of a wicked little smile—'and I mean in *every* way.' The implication was . . . there was only one implication," he says, laughing.

She brings new blood to the table as well—Woody Allen and Soon-Yi, Andy and Marge Rooney, Grace Mirabella and Bill Cahan, Arthur and Alexandra Schlesinger, Leila Hadley and Henry Luce III, Rocco and Debby Landesman, David Levine, Ed Sorel. "I was the only person I had never heard of," says Sorel.

She also includes Frank Rich and Alex Witchel. No longer the *Times* drama critic, Rich is now a columnist on the Op-Ed page, and Witchel is writing features and books. But they're still a catch.

She brings up marriage. "Never thought of it," he responds. But when he takes her to Europe in July 1996, she considers it a prenuptial honeymoon. Hirschfeld hates to speak in public and grunts one-word answers to the most evocative of questioners, but speaking on the *QE2* pays for the voyage. Louise writes a lecture for him, which he delivers with brio.

Chugging by train and schlepping their luggage—Hirschfeld at ninety-three with a rolling suitcase!—they visit the Sangers at their château in Perpignan. It's late when they get there, with no one to meet them. "Oh, darling!" cries Judy on her crackling French phone. "We're expecting you tomorrow night!" But she shows them a wonderful time, offering cold lobster, medieval tapestries, and songs beneath the stars. Thence to Italy—from Venice with Regina Resnik to Tuscany with the Kazans.

The day after her sixtieth birthday in September, Louise writes a marriage proposal and hands it to Hirschfeld. He reads it, gazes into her eyes. "When do you want to do this?"

October 23, 1996, in the rabbi's study at Temple Emanu-El. For the first time in his thrice-married life, Hirschfeld wears a wedding ring—size 9, his lucky number. Oddly, Louise's lucky number is three, and he's thirty-three years older than she. The bride wears a sapphire-blue dress and removes her shoes so as not to appear taller than the groom. The witnesses are Susan Dryfoos (*The Line King* having opened a month earlier) and her husband, Daniel Selznick, son of David. Guests include Jean Kerr (whose Walter died two weeks earlier), Louise's two sons, and not Al's daughter, who says she can't make it. There's no Nina in this picture. "The fact that she married my father still blows my mind," she says. "I just thought they were friends. I didn't know that they were *more* than friends."

After the ceremony, the Selznicks give a small dinner at their home, and in January, Margo throws a bash at hers, where Hirschfeld's *Man and Superman* poster hangs prominently near the white marble fireplace.

Belle refuses to come, but more than a hundred luminaries light Margo's "ballroom," which is decorated with miniature villages set on café tables, indicating by shop names and street signs where the guests will sit (Newman & Green Flower Shop, Kazan Corner, Lane Lane). There is music by two harpists and a cake topped with a Hirschfeld self-portrait. The critic Howard Kissel remembers seeing a gigantic bowl of salad while waiting for the main course, but, he says, "that *was* the main course." And then the entrée makes her entrance. "Suddenly, down the staircase comes our hostess," he says, "in what I can only remember as one of the most garish dresses I've ever seen."

Louise wears golden pajamas by Bill Blass.

But not at first.

Born in 1936 at the New York Infirmary (formerly the New York Infirmary for Indigent Women and Children), Louise was tucked in a drawer because there was no money for a crib. She and her mother, Catharine Sohn, an unmarried German émigré, lived at 345 East Nineteenth Street in Manhattan. Her father, Louis Tittmann, had a wife and three children in Queens.

Louis, originally Aloysius, was from Austria. In February 1917, he'd been married and in June claimed exemption from military service because he was supporting his "mother, wife, and expected child." He worked as a machinist at the E. W. Bliss torpedo works in Brooklyn.

Just before Louise's fifth birthday, her brother Alois was born, and soon the family moved to a tenement near the Seneca Avenue El in Ridgewood, on the Brooklyn-Queens border. Catharine, known as Kathe, worked the lunch counter at Woolworth's and did piecework in a sweatshop in Queens, where Louise recoiled from the lint in the air and the dreadful chorus of sewing machines. Louis, wherever he laid his head at night, played drums in the rathskellers of Yorkville.

Louise's escape was in summer, when she and her brother stayed with Kathe's parents on Long Island. Louise mowed the lawn and trimmed the hedges. She wasn't allowed to ride her grandmother's bicycle, but she'd sit on it and pretend she was pedaling down the highway to beautiful places. At ten, she'd snatch coins from the money jar and ride the El to the end of the line and back again. It was a lonely loop, a ride to nowhere for a girl who longed to be elsewhere.

Compelled to wear braids until fourteen, she'd hide them under the hats her mother crocheted. But she couldn't hide the clothes her mother sewed for her (always too large, with room to grow) or the bed she shared with her brother.

She sang along to the radio and dreamed of becoming a journalist like Edward R. Murrow. At Bushwick High School, Louise Sohn was engaging and active on committees, mastheads, the student council, Arista—in charge, an organizer—and when she graduated in 1954 was chosen Happy-Go-Lucky. At Queens College, she became Louise Tittmann, a glamorous blonde.

Her plans to study political science went sideways when she saw her first Broadway play, *Anastasia*, with Viveca Lindfors and Eugenia Leontovich. "I didn't know what was going on," she recalls. "It was just magic. I thought I was in heaven." (What she also didn't know was that Dolly Haas was about to take the show on the road.) When the campus charmer Martin Charnin came along, directing a play that she auditioned for, she won his heart as well as the part. And when she was crowned Rose Queen of Queens College, the judge of the beauty contest was Huntington Hartford, who had a modeling agency.

Louise Sohn Tittmann became Louise Manning—just as her half brother Howard Tittmann had become Howie Mann, the handsome drummer in Elliot Lawrence's band, and was clearly eclipsing their father's musical career.

As a Hartford model, she was soon doing commercials for Richard Hudnut shampoo, Maxwell House coffee, Johnson wax, Beech-Nut gum, Helene Curtis, and Colgate. Dressed as a milkmaid, she led a Foremost Dairies cow up the steps of the New York Stock Exchange. For Consolidated Electrodynamics, she demonstrated a radiation-leak detector. And for her parents, now married, she bought a house in Levittown.

Kathe was elated. Louis wanted more. Louise considered herself the goose laying the golden eggs, and was pressured by her father to turn over whatever she earned. Kathe was now making couturier copies and ribbon handbags for private clients. "I used her a lot, and I was very fond of her," says Enid Nemy, then on the women's page at the *Times*. "She really could do anything."

As a pre-Christmas treat for the entertainment-starved troops in 1956, Louise flew to Greenland with Ella Logan of *Finian's Rainbow*, Billy Reed of the Little Club, Burt Bacharach of the music, Adolph Green of *Bells Are Ringing*, and other Hartford girls on one of Drew Pearson's do-good tours. In their Ceil

Chapman gowns and Pelser furs, the models did their best to thaw the GIs in their Arctic isolation.

She was Colleen Queen in the 1958 St. Patrick's Day Parade and waved from a float in the Steuben Day Parade. After an acting class at Lonny Chapman's Theatre Studio, she and other acolytes joined him at the Cecilwood Theatre in Fishkill. In the same summer Barbra Streisand was there in *Separate Tables* and Dustin Hoffman in *Blue Denim*, Louise was in *Make a Million* and *You Can't Go Home Again.* Nor did she want to.

The next summer, she was at the Allentown Tent. She couldn't read music, but she sang well enough for the chorus in a slew of musicals. Although she quivered with stage fright, the agent Stark Hesseltine at MCA took her on and sent her out. "I got some small parts, but they were all cut," she says of her movie career, forgetting *Girl of the Night*, a forgotten Anne Francis vehicle.

"Letters, we get letters," Perry Como's Letters Girls harmonized on his TV show in the late 1950s, and one of them was Louise. Around the time Al Hirschfeld was drawing a *TV Guide* cover of Como, Louise was enjoying an occasional on-air moment with him, costumed as a Fräulein or perched on a swing. Eager to expand her options, she persuaded the writer-composer Buz Kohan to give her singing lessons. Meanwhile, she stood in for Judy Holliday on the movie of *Bells Are Ringing.*

When MCA sends her to read for Leo Kerz's *Rhinoceros*, she doesn't get the part, but she gets him.

And now she's got Hirschfeld.

35
POINTING FINGERS

"Boy, he sure knew how to pick wives!" cheers Carol Channing.

"He was so happy to have her. She was lively and fun. And she didn't monologize. She didn't butter him. She wasn't intrusive. She was so appreciative of him," says Piedy Lumet.

"She was amazing to Al," adds Judy Halevi, "and for that God bless her."

Lynn Surry knows that "he adored her. He was like a little kid in love. When he didn't have anything to draw, he drew her." Not only is she upbeat and take-charge, but she's interested in his world, his work, his everything. And she restores him.

"Please, please, please—more than restore," insists Jean-Claude Baker. "She gave him back years. I like Louise. She's a woman of great elegance. She's exactly what Al needed at that moment in his life. He would have died six months later from Dolly. He was happy. So he was *picobello*—he was beautiful from head to toe, he was clean, he was manicured, he was pedicured, he was dressed with beautiful clothes, he smelled good. She gave him the gift of life."

The dinner parties resume, and Louise rustles up chicken Provençale and Hungarian goulash. "The food improved immensely when she came in," says Tony Walton's wife, Gen. One night, Betsy Cronkite asks Frances Kazan where she lives.

"I'm right on the next block," replies the blond Brit.

"*Eww*," says Betsy, "you must live near that dreadful Elia Kazan."

"Why, yes," says Frances. "I'm his wife."

When they have no more compelling plans, Al and Louise watch television. But never alone. For years, there has been a cat on the premises—one vagabond after another who'd wander in from the garden, stick around, and be named Felix no matter its gender—and now there is Tom. When the Kazans donate two kittens and Louise wants to call them Stella and Stanley, Al calls it pretentious and names them Blacky and Tiger. Tiger struts the drawing board, placing a paw on the players before him. But it's Tom who joins them for *Jeopardy!*, wrapping himself around Hirschfeld's neck and snuggling in his beard.

In 1998, a retrospective of Hirschfeld's work opens at the Katonah Museum of Art in Westchester. It's been a long time a-borning and has grown tentacles along the way. When Lisa Aronson first suggested it to the museum in 1996, it seemed a fine idea. Hirschfeld agreed with pleasure and suggested a young fellow named David Leopold to curate it.

Leopold was his archivist. He'd arrived through the mail. In 1989, Leopold was twenty-three, ambitious, living in Pennsylvania, and thinking about a show of theatrical illustration. While cataloguing the work of his great-uncle-in-law, an artist named Ben Solowey, he wrote a letter to Hirschfeld, in care of the Feiden gallery. He sought Hirschfeld's opinion of Solowey's work, had questions, solicited memories—because both artists had drawn Broadway for the *Times* and the *Trib* in the 1930s and 1940s—and enclosed a self-addressed stamped envelope for the reply. Encouraged by Hirschfeld's warm response (signing it, as he often did, "fraternally yours"), Leopold went to the gallery to do some research, and there he ingratiated himself with the staff.

At the time, he says, "Margo had an English professor who was the archivist, but he was really just essentially keeping an inventory. It wasn't a real archive in any stretch of the imagination." When the archivist had to leave for family reasons, Lynn Surry wanted Leopold to replace him and convinced Margo, who hired him, even though "the minute I met him: this guy is no good," she remembers feeling.

It was supposed to be a part-time gig. But before long, Leopold had expanded his territory, shuttling between Margo's gallery and Hirschfeld's studio—creating a database, organizing, documenting, photocopying, chuckling at the old stories, taking notes, and taping the maestro as he reminisced. He and Surry would often visit together and stay for lunch. Soon he was helping choose the drawings for Hirschfeld's next coffee-table book, carving himself a niche, making himself increasingly indispensable.

By 1997, he's become so invaluable that Hirschfeld wants him to curate the Katonah show. But the museum doesn't, because he works for the gallery, and that's a conflict. This causes "an *incredible* amount of tension and jealousy," says Louise. "I guess Margo felt her power was eroded." Leopold reminds everyone he's just a freelancer anyway, so he quits (or is fired). Digging into Hirschfeld's oeuvre, he starts soliciting works for the show from major museums, private holdings, and the Mel Seiden collection at Harvard. But when he makes advances to the gallery's clients, and Jack Lemmon's business manager mentions it to Margo, he's gone too far. Considering this at the very least a conflict of interest, and feeling betrayed by Hirschfeld as well, she tries to block the Katonah exhibition.

"Al thought that David would be very good as a curator of his retrospective," says Louise. "He also liked David, he wanted to give him a chance, and there was room for everybody. But instead it was an acrimonious, unfortunate explosion. He felt this lunge of power that Margo was exercising over him and he was not happy with it, and it really got to a boiling point."

Hirschfeld invites them to the house to resolve the matter, and Margo doesn't appear. Leopold calls her on the phone, and she won't speak to him. Finally, Hirschfeld does bring them together. "I wasn't present," says Louise, "but I heard the screaming and yelling. When Al came up, he was white."

But the show goes on, and so does Leopold. He curates an exhibit of Hirschfeld's summer-theater drawings at the Norman Rockwell Museum in Stockbridge, Massachusetts, then takes Katonah on the road.

Hirschfeld has caricatured virtually every famous Black performer since the 1930s—Sammy Davis, Eubie Blake, Ella Fitzgerald, Lena Horne, William Warfield, Ethel Waters, Marian Anderson, André Watts, Duke Ellington, Count Basie, Sidney Poitier, Morgan Freeman, Richard Pryor, Wynton Marsalis, the casts of *Porgy and Bess*, *St. Louis Woman*, *The Green Pastures*, *Cabin in the Sky*, *Carmen Jones*, *Hallelujah!* And Louis Armstrong time after time after time.

Until *Time*.

In 1998, he is commissioned to draw five icons for the cover of *Time* magazine's issue on artists and entertainers of the century, one of five special issues leading up to the year 2000. The editors choose Lucille Ball, Steven Spielberg, Chaplin, Picasso, and Armstrong for the cover. Armstrong is on the list because the managing editor, Walter Isaacson, pushed for him.

"When we got the painting in, we were thrilled because it was fantastic," says *Time*'s art director, Arthur Hochstein. "Whenever you work with an artist who's older, there's always a little bit of nervousness about whether that person still *has* it. But he still had everything—all the energy and the vitality and the draftsmanship. Everything was still there." But before an issue is published, the cover is passed around for feedback, and not just from the editors. "They'd call in the guy changing the lightbulb," says Hochstein. "It was a very odd and often torturous process."

But the editors have the final say, and they're about to say it when senior writer Christopher John Farley, an African American man, pipes up. "You can't do that," he pronounces. Can't do *what*? "Louis Armstrong. He looks like a black Sambo. And you can't do that." Another in the room says Armstrong looks like "a real lawn-ornament-type thing."

Satchmo as Sambo has never crossed Hirschfeld's mind, much less his board. He's drawn him for years, and in fact his drawing here—all mouth and teeth—is nearly identical to the one he did in 1990 that no one complained about. "If you do a *Ne-gro* with Negroid features, you're going to have broader noses and thicker lips than if you're doing Caucasian features," says James Earl Jones, who has often been Hirschfelded, to his pleasure. "How could you not?"

But *Time*, still suffering the fallout from its darkened O. J. Simpson cover in 1994, is jittery. "The level of sensitivity was so high that once that genie was out of the bottle, the toothpaste was out of the tube—whatever cliché you want to use—you couldn't put it back in," says Hochstein. "So nobody said, 'Oh, come on, get off it,' because you might be branded as a *bigot*."

"As I recall it, it wasn't that *they* were offended, but they said, 'People are going to give you shit about this.' So it wasn't *their* PC; it was their *fear* of PC," says Daniel Okrent, the writer (and proprietor of Hirschfeld's original drawing of Zabar's that many would like to sink their teeth into).

Hochstein goes back to Hirschfeld for a fix, who tells him no. "This portrait is based on African art, and it's a caricature," Al says. "With any caricature, whether the person is white, black, green, or chartreuse—the features are accentuated." He also tells Hochstein that many subjects have been unhappy with his depictions of them, and he hasn't ever let it bother him. But it bothers *Time*, and Hochstein asks for alterations. Hirschfeld refuses. "I've never changed a piece in my life," he tells Hochstein, "and I'm not going to start now."

"Al didn't do cosmetic surgery," says Dan Morgenstern. "No real Armstrong fan would have found that objectionable. But there are always stupid people. And unfortunately some of them have influence."

Which puts the managing editor, Walter Isaacson, in a pickle. He can't run the picture, but he wants to run a Hirschfeld. The solution: commission a new piece—without Armstrong. This suits Hirschfeld fine. "He wasn't bringing his political or social judgment to it," says Hochstein, "he was bringing his artistic integrity to it. 'This was a job, I *did* it, and if you give me another job, I'll *do* it.'" For another full fee.

The new drawing shows a slightly altered Ball, Spielberg, Picasso-in-the-style-of-Picasso, and a brand-new Bob Dylan. Armstrong is gone—and so, to everyone's dismay, is Chaplin. The hand that giveth . . .

But Louis the Alligator stays in the *picture*. Named for Armstrong, this Louis is one of the syncopated characters in "Rhapsody in Blue," a segment of Disney's *Fantasia 2000*. The animators, Eric and Susan Goldberg, have long been obsessed with creating an animated ode to Hirschfeld and Gershwin, and this is it.

Hirschfeld has not only approved this feature within a feature involving characters in 1930s New York, but also joined in the process. Some at Disney wonder why Goldberg needs him. But he does.

A week before Hirschfeld's ninety-sixth birthday, he sees the story reel and model sheets, then adds his touch. Placing tracing paper on each model sheet, he makes his "improvements" to each character—skinnying the legs of the ballet teacher, crosshatching the rivet driver's beard, and so on—which Goldberg then draws onto *his* pages. Otherwise, he says, "the cost would have been prohibitive for Disney—or Disney thought it would have been prohibitive." Hirschfeld is paid as artistic consultant.

His caricatures become characters of "Rhapsody." The drummer comes right out of his *Harlem*, the nanny is based on his Edna Ferber at the Round Table, and Jobless Joe on his vaudevillian Teddy Hart. The producers get into the picture, as do the animators. The layout artists work their names into the backgrounds, à la NINA. "Eric Loves Susan" is scrawled on a fence. And everyone streaming out of the "Hotel Goldberg," from Brooks Atkinson to Al and Dolly Hirschfeld, is a caricature, too.

Matthew is twenty-three and on his own in Texas. But at nine, Margaret's still at home. Currently indulging herself in a relationship with Roy Russell, Mike's father—a widower and former Air Force pilot twenty-one years older than she who doesn't want to live with her, marry her, or be responsible for Margaret—Nina has time for other men as well.

In the summer, mother and daughter return to New York, and the reunion predictably devolves into chaos. And in 1999, there are other storm clouds gathering over the house of Hirschfeld as well.

For months, Louise and Leopold have been discreetly conferring with Ellen Harrington, the director of exhibitions at the Academy of Motion Picture Arts and Sciences in Los Angeles, about a show of Hirschfeld's film work. In September, Hirschfeld writes to Feiden that a show called *Hirschfeld's Hollywood*—which he carefully calls "an outgrowth of the retrospective mounted in Katonah"—will open at the academy the following April, to be curated by David Leopold. He encloses a list of the sixty works he wants to borrow from the gallery.

When she refuses to cooperate, he calls for a peace conference, inviting her and Leopold to the house. "A disaster," says Louise. "Horrible," says Leopold, "because Al got very angry. It was a frustrated angry." The house rings with vitriol. When Margo huffs out, she tells Hirschfeld that if he tries to claim his artwork, he'll spend the rest of his life in court.

"He was very, very, very offended, because she called him a crazy old man. She really humiliated and belittled him," says an insider. "I'd never heard him take offense. He just kind of walked through everything, like a spoon through soft ice cream. But when she lashed out at him and called him names, it was horrifying to him."

In October, Robby Lantz, Hirschfeld's literary agent, writes a letter, informing Feiden that a book will follow the exhibit and arrangements need be made to obtain the artwork for it. In November, he writes again, asking how much notice she'll need to get the material together.

But the material is not coming.

Katonah, and now *Hollywood*? Feiden goes at the Academy with so many demands that it decides to drop the show.

Maybe they should just drop Leopold. The Academy asks him to step aside. Louise asks him to step aside. Sure, he says, but he won't turn over all the treasures he's uncovered on his own time and his own dime.

Now it gets legal. In January 2000, Hirschfeld's lawyer writes to Feiden. He seeks to resolve the museum matter and other matters as well, especially regarding just whose decision it should be to determine where and when Hirschfeld's work is to be shown. If a formal clarification of their arrangement isn't made within a month, Hirschfeld will terminate all arrangements with her.

When nothing emerges from her, a lawsuit emerges from him. Katonah "was the event—the immediate thing—that triggered the lawsuit," says David B. Wolf, Al's copyright attorney, "but there were lots of other issues, too." The papers start flying in May. Hirschfeld is grilled for two hours in Feiden's lawyer's office. "That's when his age really showed," Louise remembers.

He says, she says. Hirschfeld says Feiden said "she did not work for him, he worked for her." Feiden says Hirschfeld said "he was my 'boss' and 'I had to do what he wanted me to do.'" And so forth. She accuses Leopold of stealing a fee to write material for a CD-ROM of Hirschfeld's work, grabbing tickets intended for Hirschfeld, and other schemes. But mostly she accuses him of lying about ever so many things, which seems to her the greatest crime. Thrusting and parrying like crazy, the warring gatekeepers seem to have forgotten just whose domain this is.

The *Times* gets wind of this. On May 17, a story runs on the front page of the Arts section, providing morsels from the affidavits: Hirschfeld has dismissed Feiden, seeks the return of his work and over five million dollars in damages, and so on. When Leopold is asked about Feiden's accusations, he cracks, "She has also called me a thief, a murderer, and said I'd done everything except kidnap the Lindbergh baby." But it's the headline that causes more grief: "Al Hirschfeld Sues Gallery, Asserting It Cheated Him." Now everybody's upset.

"The word 'cheated' was not used in the court papers," says David Wolf. "That wasn't the focus really of our lawsuit. But it was a catchy headline."

Louise calls it misleading. "Al had no financial problems with her," she says. Surely not, if she has indeed made him "a multimillionaire," as Margo claims, "giving him about a million dollars a year, every year." A correction runs two days later without clarifying much. "Yes," mutters Margo, "but they shouted an accusation and whispered a withdrawal."

Hirschfeld has won a special Tony, the Drama League's Special Award, and the Brooks Atkinson Award for lifetime achievement in the theater. He's been named a Living Landmark by the New York Landmarks Conservancy and a Living Legend at the Library of Congress. But with Nina, it's a no-win situation. This summer, when she comes a-calling, she brings a hard-drinking new lover. Hirschfeld keeps clear of the fumes.

Back in Texas, and unable to disentangle her mother from this guy, Margaret, ten, tells a school counselor that the guy's home with a bottle all day. In comes Child Protective Services, out goes the lover, and Margaret is removed from Nina's home and placed in a group foster home. Hirschfeld hires a lawyer to return her to Nina, but the girl later tells a family friend, "The only time I was mad at my granddad was that he paid the lawyer to get me back into the house." She says, "I would have been better out of the house."

Meanwhile, Al's niece Belle Herzon is definitely out of the house. Presumably due to her scorn for Louise, she's bumped as coexecutor of Hirschfeld's will and replaced by Louise.

Because the case against Margo won't go to trial until September, Al and Louise sail to Europe in July. The price is just another lecture or two, and Louise has proved to be an able ghostwriter.

Hirschfeld's in and out of a wheelchair and often uses a cane ("my broomstick"). For a while now, he's been in intermittent pain from his legs and back, and Louise pushes the chair. Even so, there's not a moment unscheduled. So many pilgrimages, so many personages. At the Adlon in Berlin, they run into Hal and Judy Prince! Just back from a trip to St. Petersburg with Sondheim!

"We said big hellos and 'Let's have dinner,'" Prince says. "And he remembered *everything*. Over a whole long lifetime, he remembered every name. He never did hesitate or say, 'Louise, what's that name?' Everything crystal clear. He had all his marbles, and it was stunning.

"And then at the end of dinner, which was probably 9:15 or something, Judy and I said, 'Well, this has just been the most fun. We're going to go upstairs now and talk about it and go to sleep.' And Al said, '*We're* going to theater.' And I said, 'What the hell are you talking about?' He said, 'We have tickets for the 10:30 show' somewhere on the Ku'damm or whatever, and they were off to theater. And she was going to push him, and they were going to see a show. They had gone to theater every single night after dinner, and they knew everything to see."

In Dresden, Prague, and Budapest too—speeding along the autobahn, maneuvering over cobblestones and ancient steps—they see Ta Fantastika Theatre's *Alice in Wonderland* and the Forman brothers' barge theater on the Moldau. They meander along the Danube, dine to gypsy violins. In Paris, he shows her his first seedy hotel and installs her at the Lutetia. In London, Ben Brantley takes them to lunch. And so on, *ad exhaustium*. It's an itinerary almost too breathless to ponder, much less carry out at the age of ninety-seven. Al's not going gently.

Upon his return, the *Times* runs a huge color drawing of the actors he sketched in Europe (inside, on page 7), and the lawsuit ends with a settlement. The *Times* reports on a new contract, giving Feiden the rights to sell and license the drawings, while Hirschfeld controls the exhibition of his work in museums. She says the new contract is "very much the same" as the old one. He says the new contract is "dramatically different." Nonetheless, he publicly commends her integrity and devotion.

Feiden makes clear that she was never accused of cheating Hirschfeld. "I'm the one that handles the money *still*," she says years later. "Now how could it be that they were suing me for cheating him and they go back and say, 'But that's okay. You handle the money, you just keep handling it'?"

36
END OF THE LINE

On September 11, 2001, Louise is leaving the gym when she looks south and sees a very dark cloud. She runs home, where Hirschfeld is at breakfast, races to the TV, screams when she sees the North Tower on fire. Together they watch the building implode. "It's a religious war all over again," Hirschfeld murmurs, dropping his head.

Louise goes down to the firehouse on Eighty-fifth Street to hang his gouache of Irving Berlin, with flag waving, on the wall. Hirschfeld goes up and does his *Times* drawing. Strindberg's *Dance of Death*.

Perfectly timed to lift metropolitan spirits, *Hirschfeld's New York*, a colorful paean to New York and its players, opens in October at the Museum of the City of New York, even while *Hirschfeld's Hollywood*—now given the green light—gears up on the other coast. Estelle and Carl Reiner welcome them west with a dinner party. For dessert, they seat Hirschfeld in Reiner's easy chair, and the guests—including Mel Brooks, Anne Bancroft, and Larry Gelbart—draw caricatures of *him*. "He wasn't hard to make," Reiner says, "with that wonderful beard and white hair and those eyes." Hirschfeld judges; Bancroft wins.

Back in New York, Louise has a lunch date with Arthur Gelb—still at the *Times*, as director of the College Scholarship Program—because she's been thinking about a Hirschfeld centennial for 2003. Not only is Gelb game, but he has an idea. How about naming a Broadway theater for Al? Louise suggests calling Rocco Landesman, who runs the Jujamcyn Theaters empire and might have a spare house lying around.

Before long, plans are made, the deal is done, and Louise and Gelb interrupt Hirschfeld at his drawing board. They tell him the Martin Beck will be renamed the Al Hirschfeld. What an honor! He's delighted. But embarrassed—even when reminded that he'll be in the marquee'd company of Brooks Atkinson and Walter Kerr.

In March, the Hirschfelds attend Liza Minnelli's splashy wedding to David Gest, where they mingle with old Hollywood, including a barefoot Elizabeth Taylor, and with Michael Jackson—"complete with newly bleached chalk-white skin," Louise recalls.

In August, Hirschfeld is commissioned to do a color drawing of *Hairspray*, but not by the *Times*. When the producers learn that the paper hasn't ordered it, they do.

One day when he's dressing Harvey Fierstein on the drawing board, a relic of another past trundles up the stairs. It's a Munchkin. Meinhardt Raabe, eighty-six, from *The Wizard of Oz*, is here for a sitting. He's accompanied by one Daniel Kinske, a Hirschfeld fan, who's helping the little man write his autobiography. Not only do these two plan to include some of Hirschfeld's 1939 promotional movie work in the book, but they've also snagged him to draw the cover. As the Munchkin struggles into his Munchkin suit, Al sketches. The drawing on the book jacket will show Judy Garland holding a bouquet of flowers and Raabe, as the Munchkin coroner, holding a death certificate.

In December, he draws Tommy Tune in his new white-tie revue, multiplying his lengthy legs (as he has done for Danny Kaye, Marcel Marceau, and many dancing others). This is his last picture for *The New York Times*.

He signs an edition of lithographs, Chaplin with a cane and rose, toddling away, called *The End*.

He toils on the sketch for a new commission, Kinske and the Marx Brothers, and for some reason this one's an ordeal. On Friday afternoon, he endures Nina's weekly call. But on Friday evening, a call from Washington perks him up. He has been chosen to receive the National Medal of Arts. "If you live long enough," he tells the chairman of the NEA (throwing out a line he's been using for decades), "everything happens."

The next night he's in bed with a fever. On Sunday, he's fidgety. Louise gives him a massage, and Tom the cat nuzzles close.

In the afternoon, Louise sees him drawing in the air. "What are you doing?" she asks. "Practicing my perspective," he replies. In the evening, he makes an airy gesture with his left hand, as if brushing his hair.

And soon before dawn, Al Hirschfeld stops.

Stops drawing, stops breathing.

Stops.

"I usually do things in nines," he has said. He's ninety-nine.

When Sirgay Sanger arrives to sign the death certificate, Hirschfeld is on his back, his hands folded. "Tranquil," Sanger says.

The Kinske sketch never becomes a drawing, and he's denied his place in the pantheon. Louise is reluctant to discuss it. "I thought it was an outrageous request," she will allow, "and it made Al very, very sad and angry. And it was *then* that he actually got sick, while doing that drawing."

Margo blames his despair on the estrangement from his niece, the Nina-Margaret predicament, and primarily the lawsuit. "Do you know how this *killed* him?" she says now. "He died a broken man.

"It hurts me so."

The private memorial service at Frank E. Campbell's is standing room only, with a background score of Hirschfeld's favorite music—Broadway to jazz to "Honeysuckle Rose"—compiled by Louise. Many pay tribute, and Bel Kaufman reads one of her poems.

As a man of the present, Hirschfeld never discusssed death and made no reservations. But he once mentioned cremation, so Louise picks up her cue. He makes his final exit in a beige suit and Clarney shirt. In his pocket, a ticket stub from the Martin Beck Theatre.

His ashes are interred at Kensico Cemetery, as starry a garden as ever was planted. "I just knew I wanted a place in Westchester, near the Hudson River, because he knew the Hudson as a child," Louise says. "So I went to Valhalla and I said, 'Well, Valhalla is a very good name to begin with, for this.' And then there was this absolutely beautiful cemetery over many acres." Never reluctant to drop the names of the names they've dropped, the Kensico staff provides tours and a visitor's map. When Louise learned that here lie Flo Ziegfeld, Tommy Dorsey, Marc Connelly, Paddy Chayefsky, and even her favorite composer, she knew this was it. "They took me to Rachmaninoff's grave site," she says, "and it was large—it contained the wife and the child—it's beautifully arranged, and I said, 'I want the same thing for Al Hirschfeld.'"

Dolly's on Alderney. Flo, who bit the dust in 1985 (after moving in on her forsaken daughter in Illinois and then being dispatched to an old actors' home) is in California. But Louise will be here. This grand swath, landscaped by her niece, affords accommodations for twelve—including her sons, unlikely his daughter. No matter. Colonel Ruppert and Lou Gehrig are in the neighborhood.

The self-portrait Hirschfeld drew on his ninety-eighth birthday has been etched on his gravestone. It shows him at his drawing board, uniquely pensive. "There's something otherworldly about it, and so different from everything else he'd ever done," Louise says. "I had never seen anything on his face that was so spiritual. It was like . . . The End." Shakespeare supplies the final line, on the stone beneath the portrait: "But thy eternal summer shall not fade."

Given the subjects of this peaceable kingdom, it's likely that Hirschfeld knew—and drew—most of them. And Ziegfeld? Did Al and Florenz have any kind of relationship?

Louise smiles. "They do now."

37
EVER AFTER

On June 23, 2003—two days after Hirschfeld's one hundredth birthday—Louise and Arthur Gelb cut the red ribbon, releasing the veil and lighting the lights of the Al Hirschfeld Theatre. Never mind that Martin Beck's granddaughter has had to be persuaded to go along with the name change and that a few actors report sightings of Martin Beck's unhappy ghost flitting about with a scowl. *100 Years of Al Hirschfeld* is the party of parties.

Barbara Cook sings "A Wonderful Guy" and Brian Stokes Mitchell sings "Look at That Face." Prince and Channing, Whoopi and Marge, Arthur Miller and Kitty Carlisle perform their words, but Feiffer puts it best: "Al's drawing had become not a comment on the show, but the show itself—live theater made out of newsprint." Nathan Lane and Matthew Broderick deliver "Something Seems Tingle-Ingleing" from *High Jinks*, the first Broadway show on Hirschfeld's calendar. Victor Garber croons a song called "Nina," and the real Nina—in long red hair, black gown, pink coat, and red sandals—dances with him. But it is Hirschfeld's drawings that dance, truly dance, across the screen.

Nina is heavy, in body and soul. She dresses in shapeless florals, junk jewelry, and a tiara. Her Austin condo is decorated with bright-painted walls, artificial flowers, and sticky dishes. She has a spinet she rarely plays and a Hirschfeld of herself with the children, with a crack in the glass. When she chose this place to be close to Roy, they were close. But in 2009, he leaves her, too, ascending from Alzheimer's to a stroke to the great beyond. She attends grieving classes, then looks to the greatest father figure of them all.

Returning to Great Hills Baptist, where she married West (and where two ministers have been convicted of child sex abuse), she gets religion. Ignoring her brief appearance at Central Synagogue's Sunday school as a girl, she now attends prayer meetings and church suppers. She offers to help in the church library. She calls the Bible the best book ever, and at a birthday party full of church ladies her favorite gift is a glittery bag with a crucifix of fake diamonds on it. Margaret lives with a fellow named Aaron and they have two children. They all depend on trust funds provided by Hirschfeld, Nina's being the most substantial.

Matthew and his wife, Karen, who married in 2001, are in real estate. He manages apartment complexes; she's an insurance agent representing commercial properties. And while they and their sons make their home in an Austin suburb called Cedar Park, his great-grandparents Isaac and Rebecca Hirschfeld make theirs in a New Jersey cemetery also called Cedar Park.

Nina acquires dogs she sometimes forgets to feed and babysits for the grandchildren she overfeeds. Transported by taxi, she spends hours wandering the Arboretum, the Domain, and other malls, lunching and munching and crunching on cookies, cough drops, and ice cubes. She swims in the pool at a big hotel. She shows up at the clubs down on Sixth Street, dancing alone but buying the drinks. She puts ads in the paper to meet men and meets them.

"I miss acting," she says in a Baby Jane voice, with the illusions of a lifetime. Over and over again.

In the fall of 2009, the television producer Jac Venza introduces Louise to Lewis Cullman, an Our Crowd-er, elegant widower, and philanthropist who long ago left the family tobacco business for science and finance, becoming known as the father of the leveraged buyout.

Lewis never knew Hirschfeld, but his uncle Howard did. Not only was Howard Cullman Broadway's top angel for years, but he was also commissioner general of the Brussels Exposition in 1958, for which Hirschfeld did that theatrical mural, and was included in Hirschfeld's *Broadway First Nighters* mural in the Hotel Manhattan.

Things take off, and Venza clucks with approval. By spring, they're a twosome. In December, they're the Cullmans. "I knew we had a lot of things in common, like theater and the arts, and I was impressed with his personal philanthropy," Louise tells the *Times*. The bride is seventy-four, the groom ninety-one. "When Al died, I figured her next husband would be the Prince of Monaco or something," says her friend David Hays. "She's an adventuress, but a lovely one, and why not?"

Once settled in Cullman's Park Avenue penthouse with a terraced suite of her own—decorated with Hirschfeld caricatures and watercolors and photographs of herself with him—Louise has no further need of the house on Ninety-fifth Street. Mixing now with a classier crowd, seeing her own picture on many a Bill Cunningham Sunday page, in early 2011 she puts the house on the market. Within three weeks, it's sold for $5.31 million to a couple buying it as an investment. The friends are aggrieved. Some say it should be a museum, some that it should have gone to Nina.

On a Wednesday, the house is stripped. Louise and Teresa lay out the mementos on the dining-room table for friends to choose from. Marge Champion takes a tin tray, Frances Kazan a jar of exotic coins, David Hays one of Hirschfeld's Japanese brushes. Sirgay Sanger and Jules Feiffer choose books, and by the time Margie Barab arrives, all she can scrape up is a dictionary of symbols. Tony Walton selects a tile with an owl on it and two mugs with Hirschfeld caricatures. Margo Feiden is sent a blue goblet. Nina gets the dinner dishes, and Susan Harris's son gets the table.

Hirschfeld's collection of 78s is offered to the Library of Congress but declined.

His Steinway is included in the sale of the house.

In the pre-auction days at Doyle, potential bidders finger the books written and inscribed by his friends, trinkets from his travels, shadow puppets and tribal drums from his history. Even Hirschfeld, pragmatic and unsentimental, would be dismayed to see so much of his life up for grabs.

On June 22, 2011, some of the loyal show up to buy things they can't bear to see taken by strangers. They watch a bridgescape by Charles Marks, his art teacher in St. Louis, go for a hundred dollars and a streetscape by Beauford Delaney for thirty thousand dollars. But it's the things that made Hirschfeld *Hirschfeld* that they mourn most.

For three years, the new owners of 122 East Ninety-fifth Street renovate the house. A dumpster remains out front for the duration, demoralizing the neighbors, demeaning the block. The owners never move in and in 2015 put it up for sale, asking $9.2 million. It's a sterile space they present, bare of Broadway (except for the mural in the living room, now framed to perhaps imply something more original than wallpaper), devoid of glamour, denied its legacy.

And at the top, the studio's bare. No barber chair, no drawing board, no blue-cushioned captain's chair. No mountains and mounds of materials. Gone. Nothing is left to suggest what was here.

Except all the pictures.

NOTES

AT THE TOP

1 *"I spend most"*: "Architectural Digest Visits: Al Hirschfeld," *Architectural Digest*, January 1983.

2 *"It goes up and down"*: "Architectural Digest Visits: Al Hirschfeld."

2 *"Al simply looked"*: Ted Chapin, interview with the author, December 17, 2012.

3 *"I thought he was"*: Sheldon Harnick, interview with the author, May 25, 2012.

3 *"Is there anything"*: Maury Yeston, interview with the author, December 6, 2012.

1. MEET HIM IN ST. LOUIS

8 *"I come from a very poor background"*: Al Hirschfeld, interview with Art Spiegelman, "Theater Talk," November 12, 2001, theatertalk.org, https://theatertalk.org/an-afternoon-with-al-hirschfeld-and-art-spiegelman/.

9 *"She had her own religion"*: Al Hirschfeld, interviewed by Rachel Chodorov, oral history memoir, October 1974, William E. Wiener Oral History Library of the American Jewish Committee, New York Public Library.

10 *Clark Public School*: "This is not Clark Elementary," says Louis F. Kruger of the St. Louis Public Schools system. Adele Heagney, reference librarian at the St. Louis Public

Library, and Jason Stratman, assistant reference librarian at the Missouri History Museum, concur.

10 *"It never occurred to me"*: Al Hirschfeld, interview by Studs Terkel, Studs Terkel Radio Archive, courtesy Chicago History Museum and WFMT Radio Network, November 14, 1997, https://studsterkel.wfmt.com/programs/interviewing-painter-and-illustrator-al-hirschfeld.

10 *"They make high-class oil"*: *Pen and Sunlight Sketches of Saint Louis* (Chicago: Phoenix, 1898), 267.

11 *In 1912, the Hirschfelds hit New York*: Although Hirschfeld puts his arrival in New York at anywhere from 1913 to 1915, records from Clark Elementary show that he was withdrawn in October 1912, and Milton's death certificate of October 1918 states that the family has been in New York for six years. In many interviews, Hirschfeld mentions Fort George Amusement Park, in full swing when the family arrived. It burned to the ground in June 1913.

2. MANHATTAN TRANSFER

13 *"It begins with a laugh"*: " 'High Jinks' Brings Good Cheer to Lyric," *New York Times*, December 11, 1913.

14 *"all the kids"*: Hirschfeld, oral history memoir, October 1974.

14 *"a village in itself"*: Dorshka Raphaelson, *Morning Song* (New York: Random House, 1948), 23.

15 *"I was the most naïve boy"*: Hirschfeld, oral history memoir, October 1974.

16 *"I am as sound"*: Milton Hirschfeld to Rebecca Hirschfeld, May 3, 1918, Al Hirschfeld Foundation.

16 *"I've got some job!"*: Milton Hirschfeld to Rebecca Hirschfeld, May 7, 1918, Al Hirschfeld Foundation.

16 *"I am still feeling fine"*: Milton Hirschfeld to Rebecca Hirschfeld, May 10, 1918, Al Hirschfeld Foundation.

3. POSTER BOY

18 *"Samuel Goldfish and the Selwyns"*: George S. Kaufman, "Broadway and Elsewhere," *New-York Tribune*, December 3, 1916.

19 *"neither warm nor tactile"*: Jonathan Schwartz, interview with the author, November 25, 2014.

20 *"You know for you I would die"*: "Scandinavia" was written by Ray Perkins, published by Stark & Cowan, and made a hit by Eddie Cantor in 1921.

20 *"guess right"*: David Thomson, *Showman* (New York: Alfred A. Knopf, 1992), 44.

21 *"I hadn't the least idea"*: Emily Grant Hutchings, "Art and Artists," *St. Louis Globe-Democrat*, January 23, 1927.

21 *"A skidding truck"*: Hutchings, "Art and Artists."

21 *"a Stutz as low"*: F. Scott Fitzgerald, *The Crack-Up, with Other Uncollected Pieces*. Edited by Edmund Wilson (New York: New Directions, 1956).

22 *"There were two"*: Maxwell Bodenheim, *My Life and Loves in Greenwich Village* (New York: Bridgehead Books, 1954), 157.

24 *"you had to be there"*: Al Hirschfeld, interviewed by Ronald L. Davis, oral history memoir, March 17, 1987, Ronald Davis Oral History Collection on the Performing Arts, DeGolyer Library, Southern Methodist University.

4. FLO

25 *"squares of broken"*: Bruce Kellner, *Carl Van Vechten and the Irreverent Decades* (Norman: University of Oklahoma Press, 1968), 17.

25 *"Carl was giving us parties"*: Alice B. Toklas, *What Is Remembered* (New York: Holt, Rinehart and Winston, 1963), 146.

26 *"Miguel influenced me"*: Adriana Williams, *Covarrubias* (Austin: University of Texas Press, 1994), 36.

28 *"We haven't changed a thing"*: "Stage Marines Soften 'Damns'; 'Vanities' Balks," *New York Herald Tribune*, September 26, 1924.

28 *"Chorus Girl in Taxi"*: *New York Evening Journal*, November 1, 1924.

28 *"Show Girl Silent"*: *World*, November 1, 1924.

28 *"Why did pretty Florence"*: *Daily Mirror*, November 1, 1924.

29 *"Please do not ask"*: "Beauty Swallows Poison," *Daily Mirror*, November 1, 1924.

29 *"I had driven a block"*: "Beauty Swallows Poison."

29 *"She was 'Suicide Sadie'"*: Ellen Stern, "Lunch at the Algonquin with Marc Connelly, 60 Years Later," *Daily News*, September 13, 1980.

29 *"the cry of a baffled soul"*: "Death Ends Dream of Love," *New York Evening Graphic*, November 17, 1924.

29 *"stomach pumps and antidotes"*: "Florence Allen Won't Tell Why She Tried Suicide," *Variety*, November 5, 1924.

29 *"Perhaps some day"*: "'Vanities' Chorus Girl Drinks Poison in Taxi," *New York Herald Tribune*, November 1, 1924.

29 *"Why would such a beautiful woman"*: Margie King Barab, interview with the author, November 10, 2011.

31 *"An empty bottle"*: Al Hirschfeld to Flo Allyn, January 23, 1925, Al Hirschfeld Foundation.

32 *"doing a lot"*: Hirschfeld to Allyn, March 30, 1925, Al Hirschfeld Foundation.

5. AN AMERICAN IN PARIS

34 *"So I arrived there"*: Hirschfeld, oral history memoir, October 1974.

35 *"Oh, Al"*: Allyn to Hirschfeld, October 12, 1925, Al Hirschfeld Foundation.

35 *"I shall not be content"*: Hirschfeld to Rebecca and Isaac Hirschfeld, October 12, 1925, Al Hirschfeld Foundation.

36 *"Howard is as much"*: Hirschfeld to Allyn, October 17, 1925, Al Hirschfeld Foundation.

36 *"Women, at least a hundred of them"*: Hirschfeld to Allyn, October 17, 1925.

36 *"a long, narrow thoroughfare"*: "Paris Attic Home of Lafayette Descendant," *Boston Daily Globe*, December 4, 1927. In 1945, the street was renamed Rue Raymond Losserand, after a hero of the Resistance executed by the Nazis in 1942.

37 *"I was shopping"*: Hirschfeld to Allyn, October 17, 1925, Al Hirschfeld Foundation.

37 *"God knows what"*: Hirschfeld to Allyn, October 25, 1925, Al Hirschfeld Foundation.

38 *"am getting to like"*: Hirschfeld to Allyn, October 17, 1925, Al Hirschfeld Foundation.

38 *"Very well written"*: Hirschfeld to Allyn, October 17, 1925.

38 *"Am glad you have not"*: Hirschfeld to Allyn, October 25, 1925, Al Hirschfeld Foundation.

38 *"there were no teachers"*: Alexander Calder, *Calder: An Autobiography with Pictures* (New York: Pantheon Books, 1966), 78.

39 *"Each one had"*: Hirschfeld, interview with Steven Heller, August 12, 1988. Steven Heller Collection, Milton Glaser Design Study Center and Archives/School of Visual Arts, Visual Arts Foundation.

39 *"I don't care"*: Hirschfeld, interview with Terkel, November 14, 1997.

39 *"There was an ambition"*: Hirschfeld, interview with Heller, August 12, 1988.

40 *"Not one of my favorite fellows"*: Hirschfeld, interview with Heller, August 12, 1988.

40 *"very funny"*: Hirschfeld to Allyn, October 25, 1925, Al Hirschfeld Foundation.

40 *"Never felt better"*: Hirschfeld to Rebecca Hirschfeld, October 25, 1925, Al Hirschfeld Foundation.

41 *"More than ten million"*: Genet [Janet Flanner], *New Yorker*, October 10, 1925.

41 *"They put on"*: Hirschfeld to Allyn, November 3, 1925, Al Hirschfeld Foundation.

41 *"Please keep away"*: Hirschfeld to Allyn, November 11, 1925, Al Hirschfeld Foundation.

42 *"I noticed people"*: Thomas Quinn Curtiss, "Al Hirschfeld: The World's Theater at the Stroke of a Pen," *International Herald Tribune*, August 26, 1985.

42 *"No one pays any attention"*: Hirschfeld to Rebecca Hirschfeld, "Friday the 13th" [n.d.], 1925, Al Hirschfeld Foundation.

42 *"He only wrote poetry"*: Hirschfeld, interview with Heller, August 12, 1988.

42 *"It's all on cockeyed"*: Hirschfeld to Allyn, November 11, 1925, Al Hirschfeld Foundation.

43 *"It is very warm"*: Hirschfeld to Allyn, November 17, 1925, Al Hirschfeld Foundation.

43 *"the Times Square"*: Hirschfeld to Allyn, November 21, 1925, Al Hirschfeld Foundation.

43 *"Felt something tickling my spine"*: Hirschfeld to Allyn, November 21, 1925.

44 *"Too bad that Al Hirschfeld's canvas"*: Arthur Moss, "Over the River," *New York Herald Tribune*, Paris edition, November 1925, Al Hirschfeld Foundation.

45 *"Paris . . . is paradise"*: Hirschfeld to Allyn, November 28, 1925, Al Hirschfeld Foundation.

45 *"It was a great place"*: Hirschfeld, oral history memoir, March 17, 1987.

45 *"you knew you would"*: Neil Grauer, interview with the author, June 3, 2013.

45 *"Haven't you enough"*: Hirschfeld to Allyn, December 4, 1925, Al Hirschfeld Foundation.

45 *"Paris in the winter"*: Irwin Shaw and Ronald Searle, *Paris! Paris!* (New York: Harcourt Brace Jovanovich, 1977), 92.

45 *"I decided that I've got to get someplace"*: Hirschfeld, oral history memoir, October 1974.

46 *"Imagine the thrill"*: Hirschfeld to Allyn, December 9, 1925, Al Hirschfeld Foundation.

46 *"Am on the verge"*: Hirschfeld to Allyn, December 22, 1925, Al Hirschfeld Foundation.

46 *"Am sorry to ask"*: Hirschfeld to Allyn, December 27, 1925, Al Hirschfeld Foundation.

47 *"There is no excuse"*: Hirschfeld to Allyn, December 22, 1925, Al Hirschfeld Foundation.

47 *"her chocolate arabesques"*: F. Scott Fitzgerald, *Babylon Revisited and Other Stories,* edited by Matthew J. Bruccoli (New York: Scribner, 2003), 214.

48 *"Inside Zelli's"*: Ernest Hemingway, *The Sun Also Rises* (New York: Charles Scribner's Sons, 1926), 62.

48 *"proudest and most"*: Hirschfeld to Allyn, December 27, 1925, Al Hirschfeld Foundation.

6. LINES IN THE SAND

49 *"Millions of Arabs"*: Hirschfeld to Allyn, January 15, 1926, Al Hirschfeld Foundation.

50 *"I'm very lonesome"*: Hirschfeld to Allyn, January 18, 1926, Al Hirschfeld Foundation.

50 *"The street scenes"*: "'Al' Fezzes Up Fez," *Brass Tacks* [n.d.], Al Hirschfeld Foundation.

50 *"While walking back"*: Hirschfeld to Allyn, January 18, 1926, Al Hirschfeld Foundation.

50 *"Are you going to the hospital"*: Hirschfeld to Allyn, January 18, 1926.

51 *"knows all the Pashas"*: Hirschfeld to Allyn, January 18, 1926.

51 *"I suppose by this"*: Hirschfeld to Allyn, January 27, 1926, Al Hirschfeld Foundation.

51 *"Insufficient Sweetie"*: "Insufficient Sweetie," a hit of 1924 with music by Isham Jones and lyrics by Gilbert Wells, includes such sentiments as "Insufficient sweetie, you haven't got the kind of love for me . . . Insufficient sweetie, you're just as insufficient as can be . . . The man I love must be a real world-beater, with a kiss that kicks like a Colt repeater."

51 *"superbly arranged"*: Hirschfeld to Allyn, February 12, 1926, Al Hirschfeld Foundation.

51 *"They sure looked"*: Hirschfeld to Allyn, February 14, 1926, Al Hirschfeld Foundation.

52 *"Bits of marble"*: Hirschfeld to Allyn, February 14, 1926.

52 *"Judging from"*: Hirschfeld to Allyn, February 19, 1926, Al Hirschfeld Foundation.

53 *"Glad to hear you are getting picture work"*: Hirschfeld to Allyn, February 19, 1926.

53 *Matisse arrives home*: Gary Herwood and Robert Stevens. "A Life in Art: Victor Thall" [unpublished].

53 *"better than New York"*: Hirschfeld to Allyn, March 21, 1926, Al Hirschfeld Foundation.

53 *"Al Hirschfeld, returning beaverless"*: Arthur Moss, "Over the River," *New York Herald Tribune*, Paris edition, [May] 1926, Al Hirschfeld Foundation.

54 *"All I remember is getting very drunk"*: Hirschfeld, oral history memoir, October 1974.

7. HIS INFINITE VARIETY

55 *"Later to come upon"*: Gordon Kahn, "The Broadway Diary of Samuel Eppis," *Zit's Weekly*, May 25, 1926.

55 *"only light-skinned Negroes"*: Bricktop, with James Haskins. *Bricktop* (New York: Welcome Rain, 2000), 75.

56 *"a scene of blazing color"*: Claude McKay, *Home to Harlem* (Boston: Northeastern University Press, 1987), 320.

56 *"a terrible wood burn"*: Al Hirschfeld, interview with the author, March 26, 1987.

57 *Here he deals with a fireplace*: Al Hirschfeld, "Counter-revolution in the Village," *New York Times Magazine*, April 23, 1944.

58 *"a very literate guy"*: Hirschfeld, interview with Terkel, November 14, 1997.

59 *"Some of the strongest"*: Hutchings, "Art and Artists."

59 *"That was considered a successful show"*: Hirschfeld, oral history memoir, October 1974.

59 *"It would please me very much"*: Hirschfeld to the St. Louis Museum of Fine Arts, December 16, 1926, Director Correspondence 1926, 18:1927, Albert Hirschfeld, *Tunis*, Saint Louis Art Museum Archives.

60 *"The watercolor was not too bad"*: Al Hirschfeld, *World of Hirschfeld* (New York: Harry N. Abrams, 1970), 16.

60 *"giving them"*: Rosemary Traxler to Hirschfeld, May 2, 1927.

60 *"The endorsements were received"*: Traxler to Hirschfeld, June 10, 1927.

60 *"I was a great"*: David Leopold, *Hirschfeld's Hollywood* (New York: Harry N. Abrams, in association with the Academy of Motion Picture Arts and Sciences, 2001), 14.

60 *"that's all Johnny"*: Hirschfeld, interview with Heller, August 12, 1988.

61 *"I used to work in my shorts"*: Hirschfeld, interview with Michael Kantor, "The Broadway Project," December 18, 1996.

61 *"It was not a state law"*: Hirschfeld, interview with Kantor, February 11, 2002.

62 *"somehow seemed to catch"*: David Leopold, interviews with the author, November 28, 2012, and

September 16, 2013. Calder experts are not aware of a life-size sculpture of Helen Wills. "I can find no evidence for a 'life size' wire sculpture depicting Helen Wills," writes Barbara Zabel, professor emeritus of art history at Connecticut College, in an email to the author. The two known Helen Mills sculptures, at the Calder Foundation in New York, are smaller. The piece from 1927 measures 13¼ × 17 × 8 inches; that from 1928, 20¾ × 29 × 8½ inches.

62 *"The editor was not an easy man"*: Don Freeman, *Come One, Come All!* (New York: Rinehart, 1949), 140.

63 *"But it was too late"*: Freeman, *Come One, Come All!*, 167.

8. BABE IN THE WOODS

65 *"Because the papers"*: Hirschfeld, interview with Heller, August 12, 1988.

66 *"Hirschfeld was a very"*: Martin Gottfried, interview with the author, June 10, 2013.

66 *"implies a critique"*: Al Hirschfeld, *Hirschfeld: Art and Recollections from Eight Decades* (New York: Charles Scribner's Sons, 1991), xvii.

67 *"Dear Mom"*: Allyn to Rebecca Hirschfeld, July 22, 1928, Al Hirschfeld Foundation.

67 *"We went up"*: Allyn to Rebecca Hirschfeld, July 25, 1928, Al Hirschfeld Foundation.

68 *"I believed then"*: Hirschfeld, interview with Terkel, November 14, 1997.

68 *"at night we study"*: Allyn to Rebecca Hirschfeld, August 3, 1928, Al Hirschfeld Foundation.

68 *"Meat in one place"*: Allyn to Rebecca Hirschfeld, July 30, 1928, Al Hirschfeld Foundation.

69 *"Immense big things"*: Allyn to Rebecca Hirschfeld, August 19, 1928, Al Hirschfeld Foundation.

69 *"dirt is Broadway slang"*: Allyn to Rebecca Hirschfeld, August 25, 1928, Al Hirschfeld Foundation.

69 *"The motors started"*: Allyn to Mac and Cecile Macmullen, October 15, 1928, Al Hirschfeld Foundation.

70 *"We knew we were"*: Allyn to Rebecca Hirschfeld, September 6, 1928, Al Hirschfeld Foundation.

70 *"the character of"*: Eugene Lyons, *Assignment in Utopia* (New York: Harcourt, Brace, 1937), 70.

71 *"we buy buns"*: Allyn to Rebecca Hirschfeld, [n.d.] 1928, Al Hirschfeld Foundation.

71 *"Food is good"*: Allyn to Rebecca Hirschfeld, September 6, 1928, Al Hirschfeld Foundation.

9. TO RUSSIA WITH LOVE

74 *"always looks like"*: Allyn to Rebecca Hirschfeld, [n.d.] 1928, Al Hirschfeld Foundation.

74 *"That was a transitory"*: Hirschfeld, oral history memoir, March 17, 1987.

75 *"I think we're going to freeze to death"*: Allyn to Rebecca Hirschfeld, September 27, 1928, Al Hirschfeld Foundation.

75 *"The Blue Blouse was organized"*: Albert Hirschfeld, "Moscow's Blue Blouse Revue," *New York Herald Tribune*, October 21, 1928.

76 *"stands for acting first"*: Albert Hirschfeld, "The Kamerny of Moscow," *New York Herald Tribune*, November 4, 1928.

76 *"We've worked"*: Allyn to Rebecca Hirschfeld, [n.d.] 1928, Al Hirschfeld Foundation.

76 *"Flo has been"*: Hirschfeld to Harry Rothberg, October 22, 1928, Al Hirschfeld Foundation.

76 *"Moscow is about to have"*: Florence Hirschfeld, "Russia Builds a Film Rival of Hollywood," *New York Herald Tribune*, November 18, 1928.

77 *"Flo has proved"*: Hirschfeld to Rothberg, October 22, 1928, Al Hirschfeld Foundation.

77 *"these trick stoves"*: Hirschfeld to Mac Macmullen, October 15, 1928, Al Hirschfeld Foundation.

78 *"Mom, your son"*: Allyn to Rebecca Hirschfeld, October 7, 1928, Al Hirschfeld Foundation.

78 *"When I leave here"*: Hirschfeld to Rebecca and Isaac Hirschfeld, October 15, 1928, Al Hirschfeld Foundation.

78 *"Babe wants"*: Allyn to Rebecca Hirschfeld, October 11, 1928, Al Hirschfeld Foundation.

78 *"We bought"*: Allyn to Rebecca Hirschfeld, October 27, 1928, Al Hirschfeld Foundation.

78 *"Imagine it, Mom"*: Allyn to Rebecca Hirschfeld, October 27, 1928.

79 *"the prettiest bit of Russia"*: Allyn to Rebecca Hirschfeld, October 27, 1928.

80 *"Tell Pop"*: Allyn to Rebecca Hirschfeld, October 27, 1928.

80 *"with oodles of red"*: Allyn to Rebecca Hirschfeld, November 7, 1928, Al Hirschfeld Foundation.

80 *"piles of queer pottery"*: Allyn to Rebecca Hirschfeld, November 21, 1928, Al Hirschfeld Foundation.

81 *"Don't think many women"*: Allyn to Rebecca Hirschfeld, November 14, 1928, Al Hirschfeld Foundation.

81 *"a party of men"*: "Women's Movies Burns in Persia; Men Suspected," *Chicago Daily Tribune*, November 2, 1928.

81 *"Lot of fun"*: Hirschfeld to Mac and Cecile Macmullen, November 21, 1928, Al Hirschfeld Foundation.

81 *"So they showed me a photograph"*: Hirschfeld, oral history memoir, October 1974.

82 *"It's nothing short of a miracle"*: Allyn to Rebecca and Isaac Hirschfeld, November 28, 1928, Al Hirschfeld Foundation.

82 *"The color is not"*: Hirschfeld to Mac and Cecile Macmullen, November 21, 1928.

82 *"The place is a fairyland"*: Allyn to Rebecca and Isaac Hirschfeld, November 28, 1928.

82 *"He is so happy"*: Allyn to Rebecca and Isaac Hirschfeld, November 28, 1928.

83 *"Don't we make a great team?"*: Allyn to Rebecca Hirschfeld, December 28, 1928, Al Hirschfeld Foundation.

10. THE *TIMES* OF HIS LIFE

84 *"Hirschfeld, a young American artist"*: B. J. Kospoth, "A Painter and the Orient," *Chicago Sunday Tribune*, Paris edition, January 13, 1929.

84 *"a remarkable study"*: Georges Bal, "Paris Art Notes," *New York Herald Tribune*, Paris edition, January 12, 1929.

85 *"I went to Teheran"*: "Artist, Home, Tells of Near East Jaunt," *New York Times*, January 24, 1929.

85 *"a Persian beggar's outfit"*: "Explorer Returns with Curios from Bagdad," *New York Evening Journal*, January 30, 1929.

86 *"The secretary said"*: Hirschfeld, interview with Terkel, November 14, 1997; Hirschfeld, interview with Heller, August 12, 1988.

86 *"I was a young man then"*: Hirschfeld, interview with Terkel, November 14, 1997.

86 *"I had a red beard"*: Hirschfeld, interview with Heller, August 12, 1988.

87 *"who seems to be some kind"*: Hirschfeld, interview with Terkel, November 14, 1997.

87 *"You fellows know each other"*: Hirschfeld, interview with Heller, August 12, 1988.

88 *"You're the most mysterious"*: Hirschfeld, interview with Terkel, November 14, 1997.

88 *"I got fed up with the Village"*: Christopher Gray, "Building That Was 'the Uptown Headquarters of Art,'" *New York Times*, August 9, 1998.

88 *"She absolutely adored"*: Michele Dabbeekeh, interview with the author, March 28, 2013.

89 *"the big hangout"*: Milton Berle, with Haskel Frankel, *Milton Berle* (New York: Delacorte Press, 1974), 150.

89 *"could tout it as"*: Tony Kahn, "Biographical Note on Gordon Kahn," in Al Hirschfeld, *The Speakeasies of 1932* (New York: Glenn Young Books, 2006), 93.

90 *"I sewed that myself"*: John Beaufort, "Hirschfeld Show: 'Smiling at Something Beautiful,'" *Christian Science Monitor*, March 22, 1973.

90 *"a cantankerous sour-puss"*: Al Hirschfeld, "Fred Allen: A Grim Success Story," *New York Times Magazine*, July 2, 1944.

90 *"stout waterfront fighters"*: "Hotsy Totsy Killer Suspect Seized at Wire," *New York Herald Tribune*, August 25, 1929.

90 *"staggering and tumbling"*: "Bullets Kill 2 in Night Club Gangster Fight," *New York Herald Tribune*, July 14, 1929.

91 *"Beards for young men"*: *Variety*, October 23, 1929.

91 *"when one Albert Hershfield"*: *Variety*, November 6, 1929.

91 *"Is it not a fact that you"*: Hirschfeld, *World of Hirschfeld*, 33.

92 *"The Jury say"*: *Albert Hershfield v. Variety, Inc.*, sealed verdict, New York Supreme Court, November 12, 1932.

11. BALI HIGH

93 *"Francis Musgrave"*: Juana Neal Levy, "Society," *Los Angeles Times*, April 28, 1930.

94 *"Sometimes, when I'm"*: Kahn to Hirschfeld, January 12 [1931], Al Hirschfeld Foundation. Permission of Jim and Tony Kahn.

94 *"reading matter"*: Merton S. Yewdale to Hirschfeld, July 27, 1931, Al Hirschfeld Foundation.

94 *"Let nobody dare say"*: Hirschfeld, dedication of *Speakeasies of 1932.*
95 *"I got my listing"*: Hirschfeld, oral history memoir, October 1974.
95 *"I remember going to"*: Hirschfeld, interview with Kantor, February 11, 2002.
95 *"It was a silly time"*: Hirschfeld, oral history memoir, March 17, 1987.
95 *"arrival of the 'S. S. Monowai' "*: Hirschfeld, *World of Hirschfeld*, 17.
95 *"pimply-faced natives"*: Hirschfeld, oral history memoir, October 1974; Hirschfeld, oral history memoir, March 17, 1987.
96 *"Miguel had written to me"*: Hirschfeld, *World of Hirschfeld*, 17.
96 *"The food was great"*: Al Hirschfeld, "Recalling Miguel Covarrubias" in Beverly J. Cox and Denna Jones Anderson, *Miguel Covarrubias Caricatures* (Washington, DC: Smithsonian Institution Press, 1985), 19.
97 *"although the artist is regarded"*: Miguel Covarrubias, *Island of Bali* (Singapore: Periplus, 1973), 137.
98 *"The Balinese sun"*: Hirschfeld, *Hirschfeld: Art and Recollections*, xxii.
98 *"I met him ten years ago"*: Al Hirschfeld, "A Man with Both Feet in the Clouds," *New York Times Magazine*, July 26, 1942.
98 *"before the day was over"*: Hirschfeld, *World of Hirschfeld*, 19.
98 *"Our landlord has a pig"*: Al and Flo Hirschfeld to the Brothers Chaplin [n.d.], Chaplin Archives, Roy Export Co. Ltd.
98 *"dark and sultry"*: Charles Chaplin, *My Autobiography* (New York: Simon & Schuster, 1964), 369.
99 *"I told the compound"*: Hirschfeld, oral history memoir, March 17, 1987.

99 *"To the Balinese"*: Covarrubias, *Island of Bali*, 4.
99 *"That was the experiment"*: Hirschfeld, *World of Hirschfeld*, 19.
99 *"have a difficult time"*: Hirschfeld, interview with Terkel, November 14, 1997.
99 *"The ship went off without him"*: Hirschfeld, oral history memoir, October 1974.

12. THE GIRLFRIEND

101 *"We would pose"*: Hirschfeld, interview with Heller, August 12, 1988.
101 *"We are not Republicans"*: *Americana*, November 1932.
102 *"They were given a page"*: Hirschfeld, interview with Heller, August 12, 1988.
102 *"King, who did a piece"*: Helen Lawrenson, *Stranger at the Party* (New York: Random House, 1975), 88.
102 *"I think Al was more involved"*: Margie King Barab, interview with the author, November 10, 2011.
103 *"They felt that we were taking circulation"*: Hirschfeld, interview with Heller, August 12, 1988.
103 *"Dick Maney said"*: Hirschfeld, interview with Heller, August 12, 1988.
104 *"I also had"*: Hirschfeld, oral history memoir, October 1974.
104 *"I guess it would be my grandmother"*: Michele Dabbeekeh, interview with the author, March 28, 2013.
104 *"He was a very intense guy"*: Frances Hershkowitz, interview with the author, March 20, 2013.
104 *"I do know that Flo"*: Margie King Barab, interview with the author, November 10, 2011.
104 *"He was going"*: Susan Harris, interview with the author, November 21, 2011.
104 *"You seemed so"*: David Leopold, lecture, Society of Illustrators, April 1, 2012.

105 *"And why did you break up?"*: David Leopold, interview with the author, October 19, 2011.

105 *"a Federal Forestry Camp"*: Thall to Al and Flo Hirschfeld, "New Years Day" [n.d.].

105 *"I had malnutrition"*: Thall, oral history interview conducted by Betty Hoag, June 8, 1965, for the New Deal and the Arts Project, Archives of American Art, Smithsonian Institution.

107 *"quite a very special beauty"*: Jean-Claude Baker, interview with the author, February 12, 2013.

108 *"a life saver's physique"*: Al Hirschfeld, "The Real McCoy Is in the Army Now," *PM*, July 18, 1943.

108 *"He was wildly gay"*: Barab, interview with the author, August 7, 2013.

108 *"she sort of moved in on him"*: Margie King Barab, interview with the author, May 2, 2012.

109 *"I have very little truck"*: Hirschfeld, oral history memoir, March 17, 1989.

13. AND READ ALL OVER

111 *"There was always a rumor"*: Michael Sommers, interview with the author, March 14, 2013.

111 *"Paula was intimidating"*: Joel Kaye, interview with the author, April 23, 2012.

111 *"She had* too much *personality"*: Gray Foy, interview with the author, April 23, 2012.

111 *"I was so enthusiastic"*: Hirschfeld, oral history memoir, March 17, 1987.

112 *"And this is when people"*: Hirschfeld, oral history memoir, March 17, 1987.

112 *"The sleepy"*: Paula Laurence to Hirschfeld, September 1, 1936, Al Hirschfeld Foundation.

112 *"12E is just"*: Laurence to Hirschfeld, September 10, 1936, Al Hirschfeld Foundation.

113 *"He does all the proletariat artists"*: Laurence to Hirschfeld, October 20, 1936, Al Hirschfeld Foundation.

113 *"seem more Russian"*: Hirschfeld to Rebecca Hirschfeld, September 8, 1936, Al Hirschfeld Foundation.

114 *"Russian dramas are not"*: Brooks Atkinson, "Drama in Moscow Fails to Impress," *New York Times*, September 13, 1936.

114 *"the much overrated"*: Al Hirschfeld, "Dramatic Russia," *Stage*, May 1937.

114 *"It all deteriorated"*: Hirschfeld, interview with Heller, August 12, 1988.

114 *"the goddamnest bunch"*: Hirschfeld to Rebecca Hirschfeld, September 8, 1936, Al Hirschfeld Foundation.

115 *"discursive bundle of humors"*: Brooks Atkinson, "The Moscow Art," *New York Times*, September 27, 1936.

115 *"Darling"*: Laurence to Hirschfeld, October 6, 1936, Al Hirschfeld Foundation.

115 *"original lithography"*: "Prospectus, London County Council School of Photo-engraving and Lithography for the Session 1935–36," University of the Arts London, Archives and Special Collections Centre.

115 *"Dear More-so-than-ever"*: Laurence to Hirschfeld, September 30, 1936, Al Hirschfeld Foundation.

116 *"I am filled"*: Laurence to Hirschfeld, October 17, 1936, Al Hirschfeld Foundation.

116 *"Now start the"*: Laurence to Hirschfeld, October 20, 1936, Al Hirschfeld Foundation.

116 *"I'm glad my"*: Laurence to Hirschfeld, November 9, 1936, Al Hirschfeld Foundation.

117 *"I know you"*: Laurence to Hirschfeld, October 20, 1936, Al Hirschfeld Foundation.

117 *"The smaller hotels"*: Hirschfeld to Rebecca Hirschfeld, [n.d.], 1936, Al Hirschfeld Foundation.

117 *"Howard's a surprisingly nice guy"*: Laurence to Hirschfeld, October 6, 1936, Al Hirschfeld Foundation.

118 *"It's de-licious"*: Laurence to Hirschfeld, November 16, 1936, Al Hirschfeld Foundation.

118 *"I float out on the stage"*: Laurence to Hirschfeld, November 16, 1936.

118 *"Are your eyes"*: Laurence to Hirschfeld, November 21, 1936, Al Hirschfeld Foundation.

118 *"I'm glad you got"*: Hirschfeld to Rebecca Hirschfeld, November [n.d.] 1936, Al Hirschfeld Foundation.

118 *"foaming at the mouth"*: Laurence to Hirschfeld, December 1, 1936, Al Hirschfeld Foundation.

118 *"and there's something wrong"*: Laurence to Hirschfeld, December 6, 1936, Al Hirschfeld Foundation.

14. FIDDLING ON THE ROOF

120 *"on or about the 17th day"*: Action for Absolute Divorce, Florence R. Hirschfeld, Plaintiff, against Albert Hirschfeld, Defendant, March 18, 1937.

120 *"caught by Professor"*: "About Babes in Arms," *Brooklyn Daily Eagle*, May 9,1937.

120 *"The people in these prints"*: George Grosz, introduction to *10 Lithographs by Hirschfeld*, 1937.

121 *"We tried ballrooms"*: John Houseman, *Run-Through* (New York: Simon & Schuster, 1972), 262.

123 *"It was like a ship"*: Faith Stewart-Gordon, interview with the author, October 18, 2011.

123 *"Pop didn't have a lot"*: Aram Saroyan, interview with the author, June 27, 2012.

123 *"Every time I've had Sunday supper"*: William Saroyan, "Al Hirschfeld's Greatest Lines," in Al Hirschfeld, *Hirschfeld's Harlem* (New York: Glenn Young Books, 2004), 9.

123 *"gloomy as Beethoven"*: Brooks Atkinson, *Tuesdays and Fridays* (New York: Random House, 1963), 39.

124 *"Hirschfeld wants to do"*: S. J. Perelman, *Westward Ha!* (Simon & Schuster, 1948), 10.

124 *"Mr. Hirschfeld's doodles"*: "Speaking of Pictures . . . These Are Photo-Doodles," *Life*, August 2, 1937.

125 *"transmute one autocrat"*: "Speaking of Pictures . . . These Are Photo-Doodles."

125 *"This was the death blow"*: Hirschfeld, interview with Heller, August 12, 1988.

125 *"Al, congratulations!"*: David Leopold, interview with the author, October 19, 2011.

126 *"a classic"*: Frank Nugent, "The Music Hall Presents Walt Disney's Delightful Fantasy, 'Snow White and the Seven Dwarfs,'" *New York Times*, January 14, 1938.

126 *"these inspired gnomes"*: Al Hirschfeld, "An Artist Contests Mr. Disney," *New York Times*, January 30, 1938.

15. PARTY LINES

127 *"They were playing cops and robbers"*: Hirschfeld, oral history memoir, March 17, 1987.

128 *"The worker, for instance"*: Hirschfeld, interview with Heller, August 12, 1988.

129 *"with swastikas etched"*: Hirschfeld, *World of Hirschfeld*, 14.

129 *"What happened?"*: Hirschfeld, interview with Heller, August 12, 1988; Hirschfeld oral history memoir, March 17, 1987.

129 *"I just interpret"*: Hirschfeld, interview with Heller, August 12, 1988.

130 *"drove her husband crazy"*: Arthur Gelb, interview with the author, August 8, 2012.

131 *"Mrs. Kaufman"*: Hirschfeld, oral history memoir, October 1974.

131 *"Uncle Walt"*: Marge Champion, interview with the author, November 14, 2011.

132 *"Alex* pretended": Champion, interview with the author, November 14, 2011.

132 *"the synthetic realism"*: Al Hirschfeld, "Disney Versus Art," *New York Times*, March 17, 1940.

133 *"It would have been better"*: Brooks Atkinson, "Swinging Shakespeare's 'Dream' with Benny Goodman, Louis Armstrong, and Maxine Sullivan," *New York Times*, November 30, 1939.

133 *"the show was already in hock"*: Richard Maney, *Fanfare* (New York: Harper & Brothers, 1957), 17.

133 *"It would have been"*: Dan Morgenstern, interview with the author, January 20, 2015.

16. HELLO, DOLLY

134 *"perhaps the first time"*: "Young Artist Gives One-Man Exhibition," *New York Amsterdam News*, February 15, 1940.

134 *"He had certain"*: Champion, interview with the author, November 14, 2011.

135 *"I was smitten"*: Geoffrey Hellman, "Caricaturist," Talk of the Town, *The New Yorker*, December 6, 1958.

135 *"He was very interested"*: Dolly Haas, oral history, October 6, 1986, interview by Ronald L. Davis, Davis Oral History Collection on the Performing Arts.

136 *"Ask* this *fellow"*: Hellman, "Caricaturist."

137 *"has eyes like wet plums"*: C. Hooper Trask, "Audible Films Inspire German Producers," *New York Times*, November 23, 1930.

138 *"I wouldn't mind taking her on"*: Dolly Haas, interview with Gero Gandert, September 1982. Courtesy of Gero Gandert.

138 *"When I came"*: Haas, oral history, October 6, 1986.

138 *"Euphonics and a Webster's"*: "Renamed by Expert," *Film Daily*, December 3, 1937.

139 *"After due thought"*: "All Is Not Food That Flickers on the Screen," *Washington Post*, December 8, 1937.

139 *"Dolly is having a difficult time"*: "Movie Facts and Fancies," *Boston Globe*, December 12, 1937.

139 *"agonizingly self-conscious"*: Scott Eyman, *Ernst Lubitsch: Laughter in Paradise* (Baltimore: Johns Hopkins University Press, 2000), 264.

139 *"Part changed to small town"*: "Hedda Hopper's Hollywood," *Los Angeles Times*, October 4, 1938.

140 *"One of the most tragic"*: "Louella O. Parsons," *Washington Post*, August 19, 1939.

140 *"together with the fact"*: Helen Zigmond, "Hollywood Chatter," *Jewish Advocate*, August 25, 1939.

17. WAR AND PIECES

141 *"They not only admired"*: Gelb, interview with the author, August 8, 2012.

142 *"an exquisitely beautiful actress"*: Brooks Atkinson, "Drama of Celestials," *New York Times*, March 27, 1941.

142 "The Circle of Chalk *has"*: Brooks Atkinson, "Dolly Haas Appears in 'The Circle of Chalk'," *New York Times*, December 2, 1950.

142 *"Yankee bohemian"*: Hirschfeld, "Counter-revolution in the Village."

143 *"Bill just fell on the floor"*: Lawrence Lee and Barry Gifford, *Saroyan* (New York: Harper & Row, 1984), 217.

143 *"We got into a cab"*: Lee and Gifford, *Saroyan*, 218.

144 *"He wanted* me": Lee and Gifford, *Saroyan*, 47.

144 *"You don't know what it's like!"*: Freeman, *Come One, Come All!*, 212.

145 *"These girls are going to be fine"*: Louise Kerz Hirschfeld and David Leopold, lecture, Sheldon Arts Galleries, St. Louis, September 8, 2012.

145 *"He was not the marrying kind"*: Lee and Gifford, *Saroyan*, 133.

146 *"Pearl Harbor comes"*: Tony Kahn, interview with the author, April 9, 2013.

148 *"No one is daring"*: Al Hirschfeld, "Hero of Sixth Avenue," *Don Freeman's Newsstand*, Spring 1943. Courtesy of Roy Freeman.

148 *"Send a salami"*: Eunice David, *Hal David: His Magic Moments* (Pittsburgh: Dorrance Publishing Co., 2016), 6.

148 *"a short, round blob"*: Philip Hamburger, "The Bard in the Delicatessen," *The New Yorker*, March 18, 1944.

148 *"who speaks only in rhyme"*: Hirschfeld, "Hero of Sixth Avenue."

148 *"OSCAR LEVANT of"*: Louis G. Schwartz, "Everyday but Monday" (unpublished poems), Philip Hamburger Papers, Manuscripts and Archives Division, New York Public Library, Astor, Lenox, and Tilden Foundations.

149 *"The quartet would"*: "Studio Theater 'War & Peace,' " *Billboard*, June 6, 1942.

149 *"I found him to be"*: Dolly Haas, oral history, March 17, 1987, interview by Ronald L. Davis, Davis Oral History Collection on the Performing Arts.

149 *"No jokes"*: Sheldon Patinkin, *"No Legs, No Jokes, No Chance"* (Chicago: Northwestern University Press, 2008), 18.

149 *"If it was* my *turkey"*: Hirschfeld, *World of Hirschfeld*, 42.

149 *"I shrank back"*: Stephan Chodorov, interview with the author, October 30, 2013.

150 *"The reason was not that* Oklahoma!*"*: Hirschfeld, *World of Hirschfeld*, 44.

150 *"I answered the first batch"*: Hirschfeld, *World of Hirschfeld*, 33.

150 *"I meant no disrespect"*: Hirschfeld, *World of Hirschfeld*, 35.

150 *"I don't know"*: Hirschfeld, interview with Heller, August 12, 1988.

151 *"I didn't have full control"*: Hirschfeld, interview with Heller, August 12, 1988.

18. THE WONDER CHILD

152 *"We were in the car"*: Lynn Lane, interview with the author, October 6, 2011.

153 *"Nine was our"*: Al Hirschfeld, interview with the author, April 30, 1987.

153 *"You'll never be rich"*: Margo Feiden, interview with the author, July 21, 2015.

153 *"I sit on a beach"*: Hirschfeld, oral history memoir, March 17, 1987.

153 *"Would you mind"*: Alex Witchel, "At Home With: Al Hirschfeld; Anarchy Behind a Santa Beard," *New York Times*, December 14, 1995.

153 *"Ah, here comes Moss Hart"*: Oscar Levant, *The Unimportance of Being Oscar* (New York: G. P. Putnam's Sons, 1968), 104.

153 *"There goes Moss Hart"*: Steven Bach, *Dazzler: The Life and Times of Moss Hart* (New York: Alfred A. Knopf, 2001), 245.

153 *"selling Helena Rubinstein"*: Witchel, "At Home With: Al Hirschfeld."

153 *"She ended up living"*: Frances Hershkowitz, interview with the author, March 20, 2013.

154 *"They had a cabana"*: Dabbeekeh, interview with the author, March 28, 2013.

154 *"propaganda, jokes"*: Haas, interview with Gandert, September 1982.

154 *"One day I would talk"*: John L. Scott, "Anti-Axis Sally Plays Role Here," *Los Angeles Times*, January 12, 1947.

154 *"Just as simple as that"*: *The Exiles*, documentary produced and directed by Richard Kaplan, PBS broadcast, September 24, 1989.

155 *"Joan Castle and"*: Walter Winchell, *Daily Mirror*, January 13, 1954.

155 *"She was* magnetic*"*: Gregory Todd, interview with the author, April 16, 2012.

155 *"These guys had"*: James Kahn, interview with the author, March 18, 2013.

156 *"in an extremely unusual"*: Woody Allen, interview with the author, January 18, 2013.

156 *"How would you like to write"*: Hirschfeld, interview with Kantor, "The Broadway Project," December 18, 1996.

157 *"A keen observer"*: Sam Zolotow, "'Rebecca' Arrives on Stage Tonight," *New York Times*, January 18, 1945.

158 *"Vernon Duke will"*: Sam Zolotow, "Orr-Denham Play Arriving Tonight," *New York Times*, May 29, 1945.

158 *"Would that mean"*: Vernon Duke to Hirschfeld, June 12, 1945, Al Hirschfeld Foundation.

158 *"She's a tall"*: S. J. Perelman to Hirschfeld, June 19, 1945.

158 *"Don't you think things"*: S. J. Perelman to Hirschfeld, June 19, 1945.

159 *"to imagine the future"*: Boris Aronson, "Designing Sweet Bye and Bye," *Theatre Arts*, October 1946.

160 *"She was a trained child"*: Maria Riva, interview with the author, October 10, 2011.

160 *"No spring chicken"*: Barab, interview with the author, July 12, 2012.

160 *"It was very confining"*: Champion, interview with the author, November 14, 2011.

160 *"During those hours"*: Hirschfeld, *World of Hirschfeld*, 36; Hirschfeld, *Hirschfeld: Art and Recollections*, xxvii.

161 *"Just think"*: Feiden, interview with the author, July 21, 2011.

161 *"It coincided with"*: Hirschfeld, interview with the author, April 30, 1987.

161 *"We got your joyous news"*: Oriana Atkinson to "Dolly and Al (and Nina)," October 24, 1945, Al Hirschfeld Foundation.

161 *"The proud father"*: "Leonard Lyons," *Washington Post*, November 17, 1945.

162 *"Nina's saving grace"*: Feiden, interview with the author, July 21, 2011.

19. SHOW ON THE ROAD

163 *"It was a problem"*: Lisa Aronson, interview with the author, November 11, 2011.

163 *"loathes the swarming life"*: Simone de Beauvoir, "Jean Paul Sartre: Strictly Personal," *Harper's Bazaar*, January 1946.

163 *"surprised and vulnerable"*: Allen Shawn, *Wish I Could Be There: Notes from a Phobic Life* (New York: Viking, 2007), 31.

163 *"rather have a salami"*: Gordon Kahn, "Green Thumb in Your Eye," *The Atlantic*, December 1947.

163 *"I envy people"*: Hirschfeld, oral history memoir, March 17, 1987.

163 *"Al was very"*: Abby Perelman, interview with the author, November 11, 2012.

163 *"Outside of a spring lamb"*: S. J. Perelman, *Acres and Pains* (Short Hills, NJ: Burford Books, 1995), 13.

164 *"That was the deal"*: David Leopold, interview with the author, October 19, 2011.

164 *"the booking jam"*: Sam Zolotow, "'Brighten Corner' Will Open Tonight," *New York Times*, December 12, 1945.

164 *"a frenetic industrialist"*: Sam Zolotow, "'Therese' to End Run Next Monday," *New York Times*, December 24, 1945.

164 *"socialite investors"*: Leonard Lyons, "Times Square Tattle," *Washington Post*, February 8, 1946.

165 *"actress of satiny"*: Claudia Cassidy, "On the Aisle," *Chicago Tribune*, June 9, 1946.

168 *"and there was just"*: Kay Duke Ingalls, interview with the author, March 3, 2012.

169 *"You won't believe"*: Hirschfeld, oral history memoir, March 17, 1987.

170 *"Everything was wrong"*: Lisa Aronson, interview with the author, November 11, 2011.

20. TRAVELS WITH SIDNEY

171 *"What are you going to do now?"*: Perelman, *Westward Ha!*, 11.

171 *"Sid said, 'Well, I don't know'"*: Hirschfeld, interview with Heller, August 12, 1988.

172 *"We had to leave the country"*: Hirschfeld, interview with Heller, August 12, 1988.

172 *"There was Hirschfeld"*: Perelman, *Westward Ha!*, 14.

172 *"So I say"*: Groucho Marx toast, typewritten page [n.d.], Al Hirschfeld Foundation.

173 *"little more than a cheesebox"*: Perelman, *Westward Ha!*, 36.

173 *"with the stolidity"*: Perelman, *Westward Ha!*, 37.

173 *"We sashayed up and down"*: S. J. Perelman to Gus Lobrano, May 2, 1947. Permission of Abby Perelman.

173 *"My father was"*: Abby Perelman, interview with the author, November 11, 2012.

173 *"This here blintz"*: Hirschfeld to Ruth and Gus Goetz, April 12, 1947, *T-MSS 1999-003, box 6, folder 22, Ruth and Augustus Goetz Papers, Billy Rose Theatre Division, New York Public Library for the Performing Arts.

174 *"He used to drive me crazy"*: "Perelman's Revenge," BBC, January 12, 1979.

174 *"Everything is designed"*: Hirschfeld to Atkinson, April 21, 1947, *T-MSS 1968-001, box 4, folder 10, Brooks Atkinson Papers, Billy Rose Theatre Division, New York Public Library for the Performing Arts.

174 *"No! It's not a race"*: Hirschfeld to Ruth and Gus Goetz, April 12, 1947.

174 *"I can picture Al"*: Allen, interview with the author, January 18, 2013.

175 *"more ethereal"*: Richard Coe, "'Lute Song' Drenches National Stage in Rare and Colorful Beauty," *Washington Post*, May 28, 1947.

175 *"Flying north"*: Perelman, *Westward Ha!*, 100.

175 *"Hirschfeld haggling"*: Perelman, *Westward Ha!*, 103.

175 *"Hirschfeld went off"*: S. J. Perelman to Laura Perelman, August 7, 1947, Henry W. and Albert A. Berg Collection of English and American Literature, New York Public Library, Astor, Lenox, and Tilden Foundations.

176 *"It's very"*: S. J. Perelman to Laura Perelman, August 15, 1947, Berg Collection.

176 "Gott sei dank": S. J. Perelman to Laura Perelman, August 21, 1947, Berg Collection.

177 *"H. got on his high horse"*: S. J. Perelman to Laura Perelman, August 21, 1947.

21. HOUSE AND HOME

178 *"Details on the houses"*: Andrew Dolkart, lecture to the Goat Hill Neighborhood Association, *Goat Hill Neighborhood Association History Book* (New York: Goat Hill Neighborhood Association, 2010), 43.

178 *"Saw that gargoyle"*: Hirschfeld, interview with the author, April 10, 1987.

179 *"I'm delighted that"*: Alex King to Hirschfeld [n.d.], Al Hirschfeld Papers 1931–1983. Archives of American Art, Smithsonian Institution.

179 *"Unfortunately, the necessary"*: E. L. Doctorow, *The Book of Daniel* (New York: Random House, 1999), 23.

179 *"One day he's going"*: James Kahn, interview with the author, March 18, 2013.

181 *"weaving the skein"*: Raymond Daniell, "U.S., Britain End 6 Germans' Cases," *New York Times*, January 9, 1946.

182 *"Bolger once told me"*: Hirschfeld, *Hirschfeld on Line* (New York: Applause, 1999), 87.

182 *"And I said to myself"*: Dick Cavett, interview with the author, April 30, 2013.

182 *"That's not me"*: Lynn Surry, interview with the author, May 29, 2013.

182 *"There's scarcely"*: "Lute Song in London," *New York Times*, October 12, 1948.

183 *"Over the years, my mother"*: Maria Riva, *Marlene Dietrich* (New York: Knopf, 1993), 600.

183 *"We wanted a gemütlich"*: Avis Berman, "Architectural Digest Visits: Al Hirschfeld," *Architectural Digest*, January 1983.

184 *"There was every"*: Clare Bell, interview with the author, December 17, 2012.

184 *"It's line again"*: Hirschfeld, oral history memoir, March 17, 1987.

184 *"There was some"*: Morgenstern, interview with the author, January 20, 2015.

184 *"He let the line"*: Charles Strouse, interview with the author, February 27, 2012.

184 *"The energy is syncopated"*: Yeston, interview with the author, December 6, 2012.

184 *"He made them fly"*: Tony Walton, interview with the author, April 5, 2012.

185 *"All the woodwork"*: Judy Goetz Sanger, interview with the author, February 22, 2012.

185 *"I'm sure he got the paint"*: Hershkowitz, interview with the author, March 20, 2013.

185 *"Dolly probably"*: Samantha Drake Popper, interview with the author, July 10, 2012.

185 *"Al chose every color"*: Judy Goetz Sanger, interview with the author, February 22, 2012.

185 *"I would think* so": Maria Riva, interview with the author, October 10, 2011.

22. ON THE BLOCK

186 *"She was like an angel"*: Harris, interview with the author, November 21, 2011.

186 *"She was an absolutely"*: Candy Wainwright, interview with the author, March 16, 2012.

187 *"They were very grateful"*: Hirschfeld, *Hirschfeld on Line*, 115.

187 *"You will not be alone"*: Hirschfeld, *Show Business Is No Business*, 84.

187 *"Restrain yourself"*: Hirschfeld, *Show Business Is No Business*, 79.

188 *"It was such a liberal"*: Harris, interview with the author, November 21, 2011.

188 *"Nina was not a doll person"*: Liza Kronenberger Wanklyn, interview with the author, March 15, 2012.

188 *"That's how I made"*: Nina Hirschfeld, interview with the author, June 28, 2011.

189 *"He would always tell us"*: Josh Rome, interview with the author, November 29, 2012.

189 *"The most gorgeous shade"*: Popper, interview with the author, April 9, 2012.

189 *"It wasn't just red hair"*: Barab, interview with the author, November 10, 2011.

189 *"She always had"*: Peter Stamm, interview with the author, April 2, 2012.

189 *"I was just* enchanted*"*: Tandy Cronyn, interview with the author, January 22, 2013.

189 *"She was already a strange"*: Riva, interview with the author, October 10, 2011.

189 *"She was this kind of wild"*: Foy, interview with the author, April 23, 2012.

190 *"I felt she was threatening"*: Judy Goetz Sanger, interview with the author, February 22, 2012.

190 *"Mommie, why can't the bad"*: Haas to Lillian Gish, November 29, 1972, *T-MSS 1996-011, box 19, folder

5, Lillian Gish Papers, Billy Rose Theatre Division, New York Public Library for the Performing Arts.

190 *"I think they kind of"*: Larry Grossman, interview with the author, April 2, 2012.

191 *"a huge rusty affair"*: Stamm, interview with the author, April 2, 2012.

191 *"One of the enchantments"*: Phyllis Ehrlich, "Good Neighbor Policy Brings Upper East Side Families Together," *New York Times*, October 23, 1959.

192 *"There were older"*: Peter Riva, interview with the author, September 29, 2011.

192 *"He used to come over"*: Stamm, interview with the author, April 10, 2012.

193 *"from Nina"*: Marc Aronson, interview with the author, March 12, 2012.

193 *"He looked totally"*: Jonathan Kerz, interview with the author, January 24, 2013.

193 *"Al's handsome beard"*: Oriana Atkinson, *Manhattan and Me* (Indianapolis: Bobbs-Merrill, 1954), 131.

194 *"He liked snakes"*: Barab, interview with the author, January 8, 2015.

194 *"The day after he testified"*: Ginger Montel, email message to the author, May 1, 2014.

195 *"She was the first bride"*: Judy Goetz Sanger, interview with the author, February 22, 2012.

196 *"Broadway roared"*: Maney, *Fanfare*, caption in photo insert.

196 *"I promised faithfully"*: Hirschfeld, *World of Hirschfeld*, 46.

23. WALL TO WALL

198 *"I think it creates"*: Popper, interview with the author, April 9, 2012.

198 *"She was angry"*: Lynne Adams, interview with the author, October 6, 2011.

198 *"I began to dislike him"*: Milne, *Enchanted Places* (New York: E. P. Dutton, 1974), 97.

198 *"it seemed to me, almost"*: Milne, *Enchanted Places*, 165.

199 *"I don't know"*: Elizabeth Venant, "Hirschfeld's Who's Who—Still the Best Line on Broadway," *Los Angeles Times*, August 19, 1984.

199 *"The piano was"*: Nina Hirschfeld, interview with the author, June 27, 2011.

199 *"Al* really *wanted Nina"*: Barab, interview with the author, November 10, 2011.

199 *"poor Nina being trotted"*: James Kahn, interview with the author, March 18, 2013.

199 *"hauled out to sing"*: Rachel Rome, interview with the author, May 22, 2013.

199 *"the thought of being in front"*: Randy Paar, interview with the author, March 18, 2012.

199 *"I was my parents' "*: Nina Hirschfeld, interview with the author, June 27, 2011.

200 *"You just open the window"*: Nina Hirschfeld, interview with the author, June 27, 2011.

200 "Ucch!": Barab, interview with the author, November 10, 2011.

200 *"Al has done a mural"*: Perelman to Leila Hadley, February 22, 1956. Permission of Abby Perelman.

200 *"The Eden Roc"*: Art Buchwald, "They've Built a Hotel They Can't Pronounce," *Washington Post*, March 18, 1956.

201 *"I noticed it simply because"*: Maria Riva, interview with the author, October 10, 2011.

202 *"Well, we had the paper"*: Vincent Sardi Jr. and Thomas Edward West, *Off the Wall at Sardi's* (New York: Applause Books, 1991), 104.

203 *"I did"*: Alice Hammerstein Mathias, interview with the author, October 11, 2013.

203 *"Think about Eloise"*: Popper, interview with the author, April 9, 2012.

204 *"When I think of"*: Nina Hirschfeld, interview with the author, June 28, 2011.

205 *"I suppose there are"*: Hirschfeld to Dolly and Nina Hirschfeld, June 11, 1953, Al Hirschfeld Foundation.

205 *"I'm sorry"*: Hirschfeld to Dolly, June [n.d.] 1955, Al Hirschfeld Foundation.

205 *"They were yelling"*: Hirschfeld to Dolly, June [n.d.] 1955.

205 *"practically every dish"*: Hirschfeld to Dolly, June [n.d.] 1955.

206 *"By the time we got there"*: Judy Goetz Sanger, interview with the author, February 22, 2012.

207 *"The few times I saw him"*: Alexander King, *Mine Enemy Grows Older* (New York: Simon & Schuster, 1958), 174.

207 *"and he really wasn't"*: Barab, interview with the author, January 8, 2015.

207 *"like* La Bohème*"*: Barab, interview with the author, November 10, 2011.

207 *"Alexander King was"*: Nina Hirschfeld, interview with the author, June 28, 2011.

207 *"He shot up"*: Champion, interview with the author, November 14, 2011.

207 *"In a café in New York"*: Barab, interview with the author, December 8, 2011.

207 *"He was just awful"*: Hershkowitz interview with the author, March 20, 2013.

24. FACING FACTS

208 *"It was always obvious"*: Gelb, interview with the author, August 8, 2012.

208 *"I remember sitting"*: Hirschfeld, interview with Michael Kantor, "The Broadway Project," January 12, 1997.

210 *"My father was always"*: Wanklyn, interview with the author, March 15, 2012.

210 *"During a rehearsal"*: Cavett, interview with the author, April 30, 2013.

211 *"Flowers and telegrams"*: Hirschfeld, *Hirschfeld: Art and Recollections*, xxviii.

212 *"Where do I buy a bed?"*: Ginger Montel, interview with the author, April 3, 2012.

212 *"because she never"*: Hershkowitz, interview with the author, March 20, 2013.

213 *"They scared* me*"*: Harris, interview with the author, November 21, 2011.

214 *"It gets to be about eleven thirty"*: Hirschfeld, interview with Heller, August 12, 1988.

214 *"He didn't have any teeth"*: Barab, interview with the author, January 8, 2015.

214 *"an exposed nerve"*: Hirschfeld, *World of Hirschfeld*, 44.

215 *"he always made my chin"*: Al Hirschfeld, *Hirschfeld's British Aisles* (New York: Glenn Young Books, 2006), 225.

215 *"I could feel the rain"*: Carol Burnett, interview with the author, December 6, 2012.

215 *"She didn't look like herself"*: Witchel, "At Home With: Al Hirschfeld."

215 *"When you're drawn by someone"*: Grey, interview with the author, June 13, 2012.

215 *"He made him look"*: William Ivey Long, interview with the author, February 10, 2015.

215 *"He was absolutely"*: Samuel ("Biff") Liff, email to the author, March 12, 2013.

215 *"I like all the ones"*: Liza Minnelli, interview with the author, July 10, 2012.

216 *"I have sort of demonic eyes"*: Matthew Broderick, interview with the author, July 8, 2013.

216 *"He appeared drunk"*: Adam Zion, interview with the author, October 11, 2012.

216 *"He hurt my feelings"*: Jules Feiffer, interview with the author, March 5, 2012.

216 *"The real caricature"*: Nathan Lane, interview with the author, June 27, 2013.

217 *"I know I've got poppy eyes"*: Hal Prince, interview with the author, August 7, 2012.

217 *"I look like Lily Tomlin"*: Tommy Tune, interview with the author, October 1, 2012.

217 *"I look like Cher"*: Lily Tomlin, in phone message to the author, April 24, 2014.

217 *"It made me look like"*: "Candid Caricature," *Newsweek*, October 14, 1963.

217 *"I had nothing whatever"*: Hirschfeld, *World of Hirschfeld*, 45.

217 *"People do not like"*: Geoffrey Holder, interview with the author, August 11, 2014.

217 *"What's not to like"*: Schwartz, interview with the author, November 25, 2014.

217 *"She had this little"*: Cronyn, interview with the author, January 22, 2013.

218 *"I was outside in the hall"*: *Alex in Wonderland*, April 1, 1959, WNTA.

218 *"Nina and she were playing"*: Judy Goetz Sanger, interview with the author, March 5, 2012.

218 *"spectacular"*: Harris, interview with the author, November 21, 2011.

218 *"wonderful sort of"*: Cronyn, interview with the author, January 22, 2013.

218 *"Look what's out* here": Harris, interview with the author, November 21, 2011.

25. A HEAVENLY HOST

219 *"a remarkable combination"*: Perelman, *Westward Ha!*, 12.

219 *"his bearded"*: Leonard Lyons, "The Beavers of Broadway," *Playboy*, July 1958.

220 *"soft-boiled"*: Barab, interview with the author, November 10, 2011.

220 *"He has that midwestern way"*: Walter Matthau, interview with the author, April 1987.

220 *"You just wouldn't"*: Stewart-Gordon, interview with the author, October 18, 2011.

220 *"Quite a Beau Brummell"*: Bel Kaufman, interview with the author, October 26, 2011.

220 *"Ties are useless"*: Hirschfeld, interview with the author, April 30, 1987.

220 *"If I have a choice of days"*: Phyllis Ellen Funke, "Hirschfeld: Drawn from Life," *Los Angeles Times*, July 26, 1981.

220 *"not exactly the way one"*: Steve Ross, interview with the author, June 30, 2014.

221 *"Absolutely* glorious": Patricia Bosworth, interview with the author, July 24, 2012.

221 *"They had so much"*: Joel Spector, interview with the author, February 16, 2012.

221 *"where does the money come from?"*: Teresa Gonzales, interview with the author, December 19, 2014.

221 *"I draw because"*: *100 Years of Al Hirschfeld: A Celebration Marking the Rededication of the Martin Beck Theatre as the Al Hirschfeld Theatre*, June 23, 2003, Call No. NCOV 2737, Theatre on Film and Tape Archive, New York Public Library for the Performing Arts.

221 *"has his finger in the public rectum"*: Judith and Gabriel Halevi, interview with the author, March 21, 2012.

222 *"Up to the mines"*: Harris, interview with the author, November 21, 2011.

222 *"C'mon, Dolly"*: Gabriel Halevi, interview with the author, March 21, 2012.

222 *"My childhood idol"*: Barab, interview with the author, November 10, 2011.

222 *"I could not believe"*: Feiffer, interview with the author, March 5, 2012.

222 "This is not happening": Jules Feiffer, *Backing into Forward* (Chicago: University of Chicago Press, 2010), 273.

222 *"Ach, the stories"*: Lisa Aronson, interview with the author, November 11, 2011.

223 *"HIRSCHFELD'S PÂTÉ"*: Recipe dictated by Hirschfeld to the author, April 10, 1987.

223 *"we're all trying to sit"*: Kaufman, interview with the author, October 26, 2011.

223 *"She was always on the stage"*: Foy, interview with the author, April 23, 2012.

223 *"She had an Isadora Duncan"*: Riva, interview with the author, October 10, 2011.

223 *"She enjoyed being"*: Barab, interview with the author, January 8, 2015.

223 *"I am forced to admit"*: Perelman to Alex and Margie King, July 14, 1958, Box 3, Alexander King Papers, Manuscripts Division, Library of Congress.

223 *"You knew where"*: Lisa Aronson, interview with the author, November 11, 2011.

224 *"Those times were so"*: Ginger Montel, interview with the author, April 3, 2012.

224 *"Generally, he was"*: Feiffer, interview with the author, March 5, 2012.

225 *"It annoyed people"*: Carol Channing, interview with the author, November 8, 2011.

225 *"Uh-huh"*: Riva, interview with the author, October 10, 2011.

225 *"Even if he didn't"*: Paar, interview with the author, March 18, 2012.

225 *"Let's dirty up"*: Gabriel Halevi, interview with the author, March 21, 2012.

225 *"You were expected"*: Hershkowitz, interview with the author, March 20, 2013.

226 *"All of everybody brought"*: Wanklyn, interview with the author, March 15, 2012.

226 *"My father's happiest times"*: Tony Kahn, "Biographical Note on Gordon Kahn," in Hirschfeld, *Speakeasies of 1932*, 93.

226 *"this year"*: Radie Harris, "On the Town," *Newsday*, December 27, 1963.

227 *"You don't have to read"*: Louise Kerz Hirschfeld, interview with the author, October 6, 2011.

227 *"a kind of fiery guy"*: David Hays, interview with the author, November 12, 2012.

227 "Very *difficult"*: Eli Wallach, interview with the author, September 29, 2011.

227 *"I really didn't"*: Harvey Sabinson, interview with the author, April 2, 2013.

227 *"When I first met him"*: Montel, interview with the author, April 3, 2012.

227 *"I sat there"*: Louise Kerz Hirschfeld, interview with the author, October 6, 2011.

227 *"the kid"*: Marvin Siegel, interview with the author, August 13, 2012.

26. GAME OF THE NAME

228 *"Yours for only"*: Arthur Hays Sulzberger to Hirschfeld, April 11, 1960, Al Hirschfeld Foundation.

228 *"It occurred to us"*: Walter Spieth, PhD, to *New York Times*, November 18, 1960.

229 *"to model the effects"*: Calvin F. Nodine to *New York Times*, January 26, 1992.

229 *"a national insanity"*: Hirschfeld, *Hirschfeld: Art and Recollections*, 71.

229 *"As kids, we were"*: Riva, interview with the author, September 29, 2011.

229 *"I thought it demeaned"*: Feiffer, interview with the author, March 5, 2012.

230 *"The engraving department"*: Hellman, "Caricaturist."

230 *"I saw the typesetters"*: Guy Flatley, interview with the author, February 23, 2012.

230 *"Santa Claus sittin' there"*: Whoopi Goldberg, interview with the author, November 17, 2011.

231 *"That's Hirschfeldland"*: Roz Chast, email to the author, August 5, 2014.

232 *"Dear Mr. Hershfield"*: Robert M. Leylan to Hirschfeld, April 21, 1965, Hirschfeld Papers.

232 *addresses him as Herschfeld*: Victor Hammer to Hirschfeld, October 11, 1961, Hirschfeld Papers.

232 *thanks Harry Hirshfeld*: Richard Halliday to Hirschfeld, October 23, 1954, Hirschfeld Papers.

232 *to Mr. Albert Hischfeld*: Mrs. Marc A. Rose to Hirschfeld, March 26, 1970, Hirschfeld Papers.

232 *"you and Alfred"*: Lenya to Haas, April 28, 1969, Hirschfeld Papers.

232 *"Are you sure you got"*: Leo Hershfield to Hirschfeld, November 13, 1967, Al Hirschfeld Foundation.

232 *"He's sitting in his office"*: Hirschfeld, interview with Heller, August 12, 1988.

232 *"Somehow I never thought"*: Walter Kerr to Brooks Atkinson, telegram, December 16, 1959, *T-MSS 1968-001, box 4, folder 27, Atkinson Papers.

233 *"Manhattan's Thoreau"*: John Mason Brown, *As They Appear* (New York: McGraw-Hill, 1952), 38.

233 *"a plow boy"*: O. O. McIntyre, *The Big Town* (New York: Dodd, Mead, 1935), 111.

233 *"If it weren't for this gala"*: Al Hirschfeld birthday tribute to Brooks Atkinson, incomplete text, Al Hirschfeld Foundation.

233 *"Certainly not!"*: Al Hirschfeld, "Valentine for Brooks (a Retiring Fellow)," *Times Talk*, May 1965.

27. BEHIND THE SCENES

234 *"It is, without a doubt"*: Nina Hirschfeld to Liza Kronenberger, July 3, 1960. Courtesy of Liza Kronenberger Wanklyn.

234 *"I made the trip up"*: Hirschfeld to Atkinson, July 25, 1960, *T-MSS 1968-001, box 4, folder 10, Atkinson Papers.

234 *"We got to the second floor"*: Hirschfeld, oral history memoir, October 1974.

235 *"She was getting into"*: Champion, interview with the author, November 14, 2011.

235 *"Something kind of went"*: Cronyn, interview with the author, January 22, 2013.

235 *"All of a sudden she started"*: Barab, interview with the author, November 10, 2011.

235 *"Dolly did not discuss"*: Riva, interview with the author, October 10, 2011.

236 *"I think it has a lot to do"*: Popper, interview with the author, April 9, 2012.

236 *"He was such"*: Rosenblum Halevi, interview with the author, December 9, 2011.

236 *"with a young man"*: Kaufman, interview with the author, October 26, 2011.

236 *"He couldn't stand"*: Harris, interview with the author, November 21, 2011.

236 *"I would have thought"*: Riva, interview with the author, October 10, 2011.

237 *"It's in a long tradition"*: Long, interview with the author, February 10, 2015.

238 *"A swift line here"*: Martha Swope, interview with the author, August 21, 2013.

238 *"To get an Al Hirschfeld"*: Sabinson, interview with the author, April 2, 2013.

238 *"I think he must have come"*: Walton, interview with the author, April 5, 2012.

239 *"I want you to send me the* real*"*: Carrie Robbins, interview with the author, July 11, 2013.

239 *"The lines don't join"*: Hirschfeld, oral history memoir, March 17, 1987.

240 *"I had a bit of a gut"*: John McMartin, interview with the author, June 6, 2012.

240 *"He brings out"*: Jeremy Irons, interview with the author, December 14, 2012.

240 *"It's something to hang on to"*: Allen, interview with the author, January 18, 2013.

240 *"Wish I could think"*: Hirschfeld, interview with Heller, August 12, 1988.

240 *"Bring me the rabbit's foot"*: Kaufman, interview with the author, April 30, 2012.

241 *"I can't recognize who that is"*: Herbert Mitgang to Al and Dolly Hirschfeld, June 20, 1988, Al Hirschfeld Foundation.

242 *"I couldn't have gotten"*: Wanklyn, interview with the author, March 15, 2012.

242 *"Kids liked him"*: Paar, interview with the author, March 18, 2012.

242 *"One of the joys"*: Judy Goetz Sanger, interview with the author, February 22, 2012.

242 *"Gordon never said"*: James Kahn, interview with the author, March 18, 2013.

242 *"My father was a very"*: Adam Perelman, interview with the author, October 23, 2012.

243 *"He was like"*: Abby Perelman, interview with the author, November 11, 2012.

243 *"Obviously, he held"*: Chan Lowe, interview with the author, November 26, 2012.

243 *"If you really"*: Carol "Sumishta" Brahm, Al Hirschfeld tribute, https://www.sumishta.com/pages/alhirschfeld.html.

244 *"where you sent your"*: "Rock 'n' Roll High," *Spin*, September 2005.

244 *"After the initial"*: Judith Rosenblum Halevi, interview with the author, December 9, 2011.

244 *"We realize, of course"*: Hirschfeld to Nina Hirschfeld, July 21, 1964.

244 *"The important, essential quality"*: Hirschfeld to Nina Hirschfeld, July 31, 1964.

245 *"He had a car crash"*: Nina Hirschfeld, interview with the author, June 28, 2011.

246 *"I always thought"*: Rosenblum Halevi, interview with the author, December 9, 2011.

246 *"She always had boyfriends"*: Rosenblum Halevi, interview with the author, March 21, 2012.

246 *"It was a little"*: Rosenblum Halevi, interview with the author, December 9, 2011.

28. HOW MANY NINAS?

247 *"She's captivating"*: Hirschfeld, interview with Terkel, November 14, 1997.

247 *"He gets what I'm* thinking": Carol Channing, interview with the author, April 23, 1987.

247 *"I remember meeting her"*: Paar, interview with the author, March 18, 2012.

247 *"She was* invented": Tune, interview with the author, October 1, 2012.

247 *"Dolly told me"*: Channing, interview with the author, November 8, 2011.

248 *"The door was opened"*: Hirschfeld, *World of Hirschfeld*, 40.

249 *"Last Tues. he and Dolly"*: Margie King to her uncle Dale [n.d.], box 2, King Papers.

249 *"During Hirschfeld's visit"*: Claudia Anderson, email to the author, April 13, 2015.

249 *"flying wastes a glorious ocean"*: Brooks Atkinson, *Brief Chronicles* (New York: Coward-McCann, 1966), 18.

250 *"Almost got* Exodus": Nina Hirschfeld, interview with the author, June 27, 2011.

250 *"Jessica Tandy lent Nina"*: Harris, interview with the author, November 21, 2011.

250 *"My father came"*: Nina Hirschfeld, interview with the author, June 27, 2011.

251 *"I realized what a tough time"*: Dolly Hirschfeld to Nina Hirschfeld, July [n.d.] 1966, Al Hirschfeld Foundation.

251 *"I Am Well"*: Dolly Hirschfeld to Nina Hirschfeld, November 3, 1966, Al Hirschfeld Foundation.

251 *"I, for one"*: Hirschfeld to Nina Hirschfeld [n.d.], 1967, Al Hirschfeld Foundation.

252 *"We are delighted"*: Dolly Hirschfeld to Beauford Delaney, April 17, 1968, Beauford Delaney collection, ScMG59, Schomburg Center for Research in Black Culture, Manuscripts, Archives and Rare Books Division, The New York Public Library.

252 *"gorgeous"*: Harris, interview with the author, November 21, 2011.

29. A PIECE OF WORK

253 *"Let's just say"*: John Canaday, "Art: Shimmering Treasures of Peru," *New York Times*, May 7, 1966.

253 *"I thought the exhibition"*: Atkinson to Hirschfeld [n.d.], Al Hirschfeld Foundation.

254 *"When I'm old enough"*: Margo Feiden, interview with the author, July 21, 2015.

254 *"I was listening"*: Bruce Stark, interview with the author, March 8, 2012.

255 *"She had no hesitation"*: Margo Feiden, interview with the author, July 21, 2011.

255 *"Granted, I saw"*: Elisabeth Sussman, interview with the author, September 22, 2014.

255 *"Wow!"*: Jeff Rosenheim, interview with the author, July 20, 2016.

256 *"I dragged her with me"*: Feiden, interview with the author, July 21, 2011.

256 *"What are you talking about?"*: Rosenblum Halevi, interview with the author, March 21, 2012.

257 *"job that most"*: Dolly Hirschfeld to Nina Hirschfeld, September 3, 1969, Al Hirschfeld Foundation.

257 *"Each week it was a new job"*: Popper, interview with the author, April 9, 2012.

258 *"tortured soul"*: Isaiah Sheffer, interview with the author, April 24, 2012.

258 *"I said, 'I'm very pleased'"*: Feiden, interview with the author, January 7, 2015.

258 *"the artist who was designing"*: James Rosenquist, *Painting Below Zero* (New York: Alfred A. Knopf, 2009), 256.

258 *"What he did"*: Alexandra Goodstadt, interview with the author, November 6, 2013.

30. WHEELING, DEALING

260 *"He didn't say a word"*: Feiden, interview with the author, July 21, 2011.

260 *"I know that Victor"*: Nancy Wicker, interview with the author, February 13, 2012.

261 *"She's such a self-promoter"*: Harris, interview with the author, November 21, 2011.

261 *"It was miserable"*: Lisa Aronson, interview with the author, November 11, 2011.

261 *"When he drove"*: Lane, interview with the author, October 6, 2011.

261 *"He drove like"*: Champion, interview with the author, November 14, 2011.

261 *"Like a madman"*: Riva, interview with the author, October 10, 2011.

261 *"You left your wife"*: Chan Lowe, interview with the author, November 26, 2012.

262 *"Al's secret ways"*: Stamm, interview with the author, April 2, 2012.

262 *"And then we look"*: Adrian Bryan-Brown, interview with the author, May 20, 2013.

262 *"He was not quite Mr. Magoo"*: Rachel Rome, interview with the author, May 22, 2013.

262 *"was terrifying"*: Vicky Traube, interview with the author, November 19, 2012.

262 *"Must have been a pothole"*: Paar, interview with the author, March 18, 2012.

262 *"He would drive"*: Jerry Tallmer, interview with the author, March 28, 2012.

263 *"a whole van of his art"*: Feiden, interview with the author, July 21, 2011.

264 *"He was a populist"*: Feiden, interview with the author, July 13, 2016.

264 *"I will happily ship"*: Hirschfeld to Mr. Olson, May 10, 1972, Al Hirschfeld Foundation.

264 *"not only the largest"*: Alan Rich, "Sunday Punch," *New York*, October 14, 1974.

265 *"If* The New York Times*"*: Nat Hentoff, "William Honan vs. the Arts," *Village Voice*, December 30, 1974.

265 *"She gave him"*: Howard Kissel, interview with the author, September 19, 2011.

265 *"There hasn't been anything going on"*: Hirschfeld, oral history memoir, March 17, 1987.

265 *"archaic"*: Heller, interview with the author, April 12, 2012.

265 *"I thought, What goddamn"*: Prince, interview with the author, August 7, 2012.

265 "The Times *has to resume*": Atkinson to Hirschfeld, November 20, 1974, Al Hirschfeld Foundation.

265 *"He would* never *have had the guts"*: Gelb, interview with the author, April 17, 2012.

266 *"I was not a party"*: Max Frankel, email to the author, March 24, 2014.

266 *"it was getting"*: Louise Kerz Hirschfeld, interview with the author, April 13, 2015.

266 *"does not wish"*: Frankel to Arnold Weissberger, September 8, 1975, Hirschfeld Papers.

266 *"The* Times *stopped"*: Feiden, interview with the author, August 7, 2014.

267 *"He knew a lyric of mine"*: Harnick, interview with the author, May 25, 2012.

267 *"He had not drawn"*: Jo Sullivan Loesser, interview with the author, December 14, 2012.

267 *"I engaged him"*: James Earl Jones, interview with the author, July 12, 2012.

268 *"Even though I could feel"*: Chris Curry, interview with the author, February 16, 2012.

268 *"Sure"*: David Leopold, interview with the author, December 8, 2014.

269 *"I never got"*: Feiden, interview with the author, June 4, 2015.

269 *"Once Hirschfeld came"*: Heller, interview with the author, April 12, 2012.

269 *"The drawing could never"*: Linda Brewer, interview with the author, December 5, 2012.

269 *"Hirschfeld had a lot"*: Eric Seidman, interview with the author, February 24, 2012.

270 *"I have two or three"*: Heller, interview with the author, April 12, 2012.

270 *"I've got a lot of them"*: Bryan-Brown, interview with the author, May 20, 2013.

271 *"She'd call the second"*: Bryan-Brown, interview with the author, May 20, 2013.

272 *"in the picture you see"*: John Clark to Feiden, March 13, 1975, Hirschfeld Papers.

31. LONE STAR

274 *"She was drop-dead gorgeous"*: Mike Russell, interview with the author, March 25, 2013.

274 *"You need to drive"*: Nina Hirschfeld to Al and Dolly Hirschfeld, [n.d.].

275 *"I'll get you a job"*: Russell, interview with the author, March 25, 2013.

275 *"Was your grandson"*: Atkinson to Hirschfeld, September 18, 1975, Al Hirschfeld Foundation.

275 *"There I was"*: Nina Hirschfeld, interview with the author, June 29, 2011.

276 *"We had a huge kitchen"*: Steven Tyler, *Does the Noise in My Head Bother You?*, 282.

276 *"It was very important to him"*: John Berg, interview with the author, July 1, 2013.

277 *"What are you"*: Rosenblum Halevi, interview with the author, March 21, 2012.

277 *"Just now I hear"*: Dolly Hirschfeld to Nina Hirschfeld, July 14, 1977.

277 *"the whole effect"*: Hirschfeld to Nina Hirschfeld [n.d.], 1977.

277 *"Gay as a grig"*: Perelman, *Entertainers*, unpaginated.

277 *"There wasn't another"*: Nina Hirschfeld, interview with the author, June 28, 2011.

278 *"I was so much younger"*: Ben Brantley, interview with the author, October 1, 2013.

279 *"She was very much around"*: Victor Navasky, interview with the author, June 10, 2013.

279 *"The curvaceous Mrs. Kerz"*: Perelman to Mel Calman, July 26, 1978. Permission of Abby Perelman.

280 *"I didn't go to one"*: Nina Hirschfeld, interview with the author, June 27, 2011.

280 *"I always felt"*: Feiffer, interview with the author, March 5, 2012.

280 *"Matthew would be hiding"*: Louise Kerz Hirschfeld, interview with the author, October 12, 2011.

32. OUT OF LINE

281 *"They slept together"*: Feiden, interview with the author, February 21, 2014.

282 *"a sort of nest"*: Paul Richard, "Eggstra Special," *Washington Post*, April 12, 1982.

282 *"I feel that, in a sense"*: Leo Lerman, *The Grand Surprise: The Journals of Leo Lerman* (New York: Alfred A. Knopf, 2007), 531.

282 *"she gave him the kind"*: Riva, interview with the author, October 10, 2011.

283 *"Your son needs"*: Nina Hirschfeld, interview with the author, June 27, 2011.

283 *"You have no idea"*: Gonzales, interview with the author, December 19, 2014.

283 *"You are the one!"*: Susan Dryfoos, interview with the author, February 8, 2013.

284 *"We could hear the piano"*: Shari Thompson, interview with the author, June 11, 2015.

284 *"It was falling apart"*: Hershkowitz, interview with the author, March 20, 2013.

284 *"It was dim"*: Foy, interview with the author, April 23, 2012.

284 *"Just dismal"*: Piedy Lumet, interview with the author, June 11, 2012.

284 *"He was completely helpless"*: Riva, interview with the author, October 10, 2011.

284 *"I need somebody"*: Lynn Surry, interview with the author, October 25, 2011.

285 *"Right"*: Feiden, interview with the author, July 27, 2016.

285 *"you're not likely"*: Review of *The Calorie Factor*, *Library Journal*, June 15, 1989.

286 *"I looked and I thought"*: Charles Busch, interview with the author, February 13, 2013.

286 *"They were bootlegged"*: Bryan-Brown, interview with the author, May 20, 2013.

287 *"Opening nights"*: Prince, interview with the author, August 7, 2012.

287 *"When I was with Julius"*: Feiden, interview with the author, February 17, 2014.

288 *"I know that he"*: Will Barnet, interview with the author, September 12, 2012.

288 *"Oh, no!"*: Stanley Goldmark, interview with the author, March 27, 2015.

288 *"She was Elaine Kaufman"*: Joel Kaye, interview with the author, April 23, 2012.

289 *"they didn't even notice me"*: Feiden, interview with the author, July 6, 2011.

289 *"as though I lived there"*: Feiden, interview with the author, July 6, 2011.

290 *"I went from the"*: Nina Hirschfeld, interview with the author, June 27, 2011.

290 *"a wild look"*: Herbert Sanders, interview with the author, October 22, 2012.

290 *"beside himself"*: Rosenblum Halevi, interview with the author, March 21, 2012.

290 *"He was fat"*: Teresa Gonzales, interview with the author, December 19, 2014.

290 *"I think Danny"*: Feiden, interview with the author, July 21, 2011.

291 *"It was a beautiful dress"*: Harris, interview with the author, November 21, 2011.

292 *"maybe because"*: Matthew Russell, interview with the author, June 28, 2011.

33. CHANGING *TIMES*

293 *"Forgive me, please"*: Paul Goldberger to Hirschfeld, October 26, 1990, Al Hirschfeld Foundation. Permission of Paul Goldberger.

293 *"I thought it was the stupidest"*: Gelb, interview with the author, August 8, 2012.

294 *"to everyone's horror"*: Frank Rich, interview with the author, December 12, 2015.

294 *"Have they personally acknowledged"*: Hirschfeld to Ken Fallin, November 28, 1990. Courtesy of Ken Fallin.

294 *"What did the contract say?"*: Feiden, interview with the author, January 14, 2015.

295 *"Where are the"*: Terry McCaffrey, interview with the author, November 14, 2013.

295 *"Mr. Hirschfeld"*: Surry, interview with the author, October 25, 2011.

296 *"It looks like it was all done"*: Eric Goldberg, interview with the author, July 27, 2013.

297 *"It was very hush-hush"*: John Kascht, interview with the author, March 11, 2015.

298 "*just* awful": Brewer, interview with the author, December 5, 2012.

298 *"It looked a little muddy"*: Barbara Richer, interview with the author, December 5, 2012.

299 *"If he witnessed"*: Riva, interview with the author, October 10, 2011.

299 *"Al was a force of life"*: Wanklyn, interview with the author, March 15, 2012.

299 *"The doctor says"*: Nina Hirschfeld, interview with the author, June 27, 2011.

299 *"She was just too sick"*: Barab, interview with the author, November 10, 2011.

299 *"No, darling"*: Louise Kerz Hirschfeld, interview with the author, May 30, 2012.

299 *"She motioned for us"*: Kaufman, interview with the author, October 26, 2011.

300 *"She never showed up"*: Aaron Shikler, interview with the author, November 12, 2012.

300 *"No tear was shed"*: Feiden, interview with the author, May 3, 2011.

300 *"Bizarre and rude"*: Sirgay Sanger, interview with the author, March 5, 2012.

300 *"Who's going to take"*: Frances Kazan, interview with the author, August 14, 2012.

300 *"She knew that was"*: Gonzales, interview with the author, December 19, 2014.

34. SING OUT, LOUISE!

302 *"That's the attic"*: Feiden, interview with the author, July 21, 2011.

302 *"Better than any"*: Nina Hirschfeld, interview with the author, June 28, 2011.

303 *"They came out of"*: Riva, interview with the author, October 10, 2011.

303 *"the ladies with casseroles"*: Kaufman, interview with the author, October 26, 2011.

303 *"a posse"*: Lane, interview with the author, October 6, 2011.

303 *"the widder ladies"*: Barab, interview with the author, November 10, 2011.

303 *"Suddenly he was* old*"*: Baker, interview with the author, June 26, 2012.

304 *"She must be all attention"*: Gonzales, interview with the author, December 19, 2014.

304 *"decided to devote herself"*: Ann Gussow, interview with the author, March 6, 2012.

304 *"You drive"*: Louise Kerz Hirschfeld, interview with the author, October 12, 2011.

304 *"He hadn't been alone"*: Stephen Pascal, interview with the author, March 14, 2013.

305 *"It seemed that"*: Louise Kerz Hirschfeld, interview with the author, April 13, 2015.

305 *"She described to me"*: Feiden, interview with the author, February 21, 2014.

305 *"a real entrepreneur"*: Feiden, interview with the author, August 7, 2014.

305 *"He made a"*: Louise Kerz Hirschfeld, interview with the author, October 12, 2011.

306 *"There was no question"*: Gelb, interview with the author, August 8, 2012.

306 *"I was the only person"*: Edward Sorel, interview with the author, February 10, 2012.

306 *"Never thought of it"*: Louise Kerz Hirschfeld, interview with the author, August 15, 2012.

306 *"Oh, darling!"*: Louise Kerz Hirschfeld, interview with the author, August 15, 2012.

307 *"When do you want to do this?"*: Louise Kerz Hirschfeld, interview with the author, August 15, 2012.

307 *"The fact that"*: Nina Hirschfeld, interview with the author, September 28, 2011.

307 *"that* was *the main course"*: Kissel, interview with the author, September 19, 2011.

309 *"I didn't know"*: Louise Kerz Hirschfeld, interview with the author, October 6, 2011.

309 *"I used her a lot"*: Enid Nemy, interview with the author, October 20, 2011.

310 *"I got some"*: Louise Kerz Hirschfeld, interview with the author, October 6, 2011.

35. POINTING FINGERS

311 *"Boy, he sure knew"*: Channing, interview with the author, November 8, 2011.

311 *"He was so happy"*: Lumet, interview with the author, June 11, 2012.

311 *"She was amazing"*: Rosenblum Halevi, interview with the author, December 9, 2011.

311 *"He adored her"*: Surry, interview with the author, October 25, 2011.

311 *"Please, please, please"*: Baker, interview with the author, June 26, 2012.

311 *"The food improved"*: Walton, interview with the author, June 11, 2012.

311 *"I'm right on the next block"*: Kazan, interview with the author, August 14, 2012.

313 *"Margo had an English"*: Leopold, interview with the author, October 19, 2011.

313 *"the minute I met him"*: Feiden, interview with the author, June 4, 2015.

313 *"an* incredible *amount"*: Louise Kerz Hirschfeld, interview with the author, August 28, 2013.

314 *"When we got the painting"*: Arthur Hochstein, interview with the author, October 5, 2012.

315 *"You can't do that"*: Hochstein, interview with the author, October 5, 2012.

315 *"a real lawn-ornament-type thing"*: Warren St. John, "Why Al Hirschfeld's Drawing of Louis Armstrong Never Made It onto Time Magazine's Cover," *New York Observer*, June 8, 1998.

315 *"If you do a* Ne-gro*"*: Jones, interview with the author, July 12, 2012.

315 *"As I recall it"*: Daniel Okrent, interview with the author, December 1, 2014.

315 *"This portrait is based"*: Hochstein, interview with the author, October 5, 2012.

316 *"Al didn't do"*: Morgenstern, interview with the author, January 20, 2015.

317 *"the cost would have been"*: Eric Goldberg, interview with the author, July 27, 2013.

317 *"an outgrowth"*: Hirschfeld to Feiden, September 15, 1999, Al Hirschfeld Foundation.

318 *"Horrible"*: Leopold, interview with the author, October 19, 2011.

319 *"was the event"*: David Wolf, interview with the author, December 9, 2013.

319 *"she did not work for him"*: Complaint, *Al Hirschfeld, Plaintiff, v. The Margo Feiden Galleries Ltd., Margo Feiden, and The Margo Feiden Galleries, Defendants*, Index, No. 00/602067, Supreme Court of the State of New York, County of New York, May 16, 2000.

319 *"he was my 'boss'"*: Affidavit, Al Hirschfeld, Plaintiff and Counterclaim Defendant, against The Margo Feiden Galleries Ltd., Margo Feiden, and The Margo Feiden Galleries, Defendants and Counterclaim Plaintiffs, Index No. 00/602067, Supreme Court of the State of New York, County of New York, June 5, 2000.

319 *"She has also called me"*: Judith H. Dobrzynski, "Al Hirschfeld Sues Gallery, Asserting It Cheated Him," *New York Times*, May 17, 2000.

319 *"a multimillionaire"*: Feiden, interview with the author, June 4, 2015.

320 *"Yes"*: Feiden, interview with the author, August 7, 2014.

320 *"The only time I was mad"*: Harris, interview with the author, November 21, 2011.

320 *"my broomstick"*: Tony Kerz, interview with the author, November 15, 2013.

321 *"We said big hellos"*: Prince, interview with the author, August 7, 2012.

321 *"very much the same"*: Celestine Bohlen, "Al Hirschfeld Drops Suit and Resumes Ties with Gallery," *New York Times*, October 14, 2000.

321 *"dramatically different"*: "Signed, Al Hirschfeld," Letters to the Editor, *New York Times*, October 20, 2000.

322 *"I'm the one that handles"*: Feiden, interview with the author, August 7, 2014.

36. END OF THE LINE

323 *"It's a religious war"*: Louise Kerz Hirschfeld, interview with the author, August 15, 2012.

323 *"He wasn't hard to make"*: Carl Reiner, interview with the author, March 13, 2013.

324 *"complete with newly bleached"*: Louise Kerz Hirschfeld, interview with the author, December 14, 2015.

325 *"If you live long"*: Eileen Mason, interview with the author, September 29, 2011.

325 *"What are you"*: David Leopold, lecture, Society of Illustrators, April 11, 2012.

325 *"I usually do things in nines"*: Hirschfeld, interview with the author, April 30, 1987.

325 *"Tranquil"*: Sirgay Sanger, interview with the author, March 5, 2012.

325 *"I thought it was an outrageous request"*: Louise Kerz Hirschfeld, interview with the author, April 13, 2015.

325 *"Do you know how this* killed *him?"*: Feiden, interview with the author, October 30, 2013.

326 *"I just knew I wanted a place"*: Louise Kerz Hirschfeld, interview with the author, May 30, 2012.

326 *"There's something otherworldly"*: Louise Kerz Hirschfeld, interview with the author, July 3, 2012.

37. EVER AFTER

328 *"Al's drawing had become"*: *100 Years of Al Hirschfeld.*

330 *"I knew we had a lot of things in common"*: Louise Hirschfeld and Lewis Cullman marriage announcement, *New York Times*, December 17, 2010.

330 *"When Al died"*: Hays, interview with the author, November 12, 2012.

BIBLIOGRAPHY

Abbott, Berenice, and Elizabeth McCausland. *New York in the Thirties*. New York: Dover, 1973. Photographs by Abbott; text by McCausland.

Abbott, George. *"Mister Abbott."* New York: Random House, 1963.

Adler, Richard. *"You Gotta Have Heart."* With Lee Davis. New York: Donald I. Fine, 1990.

Albrand, Martha. *Desperate Moment*. New York: Random House, 1951.

Allen, Fred. *Much Ado About Me*. Boston: Little, Brown, 1956.

Allen, Frederick Lewis. *Only Yesterday*. New York: Perennial Library, 1964.

Amick, George. *Linn's U.S. Stamp Yearbook 1991*. Sidney, OH: Linn's Stamp News, 1992.

Arbus, Diane. *Revelations*. New York: Random House, 2003.

Armitage, Shelley. *John Held, Jr.: Illustrator of the Jazz Age*. New York: Syracuse University Press, 1987.

Atkinson, Brooks. *Brief Chronicles*. New York: Coward-McCann, 1966.

———. *Broadway*. Rev. ed. New York: Macmillan, 1974.

———. *East of the Hudson*. New York: Alfred A. Knopf, 1931.

———. "Off Stage and On." In *We Saw It Happen: The News Behind the News That's Fit to Print*, edited by Hanson W. Baldwin and Shepard Stone. New York: Simon & Schuster, 1938.

———. *Tuesdays and Fridays*. New York: Random House, 1963.

Atkinson, Brooks, and Albert Hirschfeld. *The Lively Years*. New York: Da Capo Press, 1973.

Atkinson, Oriana. *Manhattan and Me*. Indianapolis: Bobbs-Merrill, 1954.

Aylesworth, Thomas, and Virginia L. Aylesworth. *New York: The Glamour Years (1919–1945)*. New York: Gallery Books, 1987.

Bach, Steven. *Dazzler: The Life and Times of Moss Hart*. New York: Alfred A. Knopf, 2001.

Bader, Robert S., ed. *Groucho Marx, and Other Short Stories and Tall Tales*. Milwaukee: Applause Theatre & Cinema Books, 2011.

Baedeker, Karl. *The United States*. New York: Charles Scribner's Sons, 1909.

Bainbridge, John. *The Wonderful World of Toots Shor*. Boston: Houghton Mifflin, 1951.

Bair, Deirdre. *Saul Steinberg*. New York: Nan A. Talese/Doubleday, 2012.

Baker, Jean-Claude, and Chris Chase. *Josephine: The Hungry Heart*. New York: Cooper Square Press, 2001.

Baldwin, Hanson W., and Shepard Stone, eds. *We Saw It Happen: The News Behind the News That's Fit to Print*. New York: Simon & Schuster, 1938.

Barrett, James W. *"The World," the Flesh, and Messrs. Pulitzer*. New York: Vanguard Press, 1931.

———. ed. *The End of "The World."* New York: Harper & Brothers, 1931.

Beebe, Lucius. *The Lucius Beebe Reader*. Edited by Charles Clegg and Duncan Emrich. Garden City, NY: Doubleday, 1967.

Behrman, S. N. *Portrait of Max*. New York: Random House, 1960.

Bell, Clare. *Hirschfeld's New York*. New York: Harry N. Abrams, in association with the Museum of the City of New York, 2001.

Berg, A. Scott. *Goldwyn*. New York: Alfred A. Knopf, 1989.

Berle, Milton, with Haskel Frankel. *Milton Berle*. New York: Delacorte Press, 1974.

Bernard, Emily. *Carl Van Vechten and the Harlem Renaissance*. New Haven, CT: Yale University Press, 2012.

Bessie, Simon Michael. *Jazz Journalism*. New York: E. P. Dutton, 1938.

Bishop, Jim. *The Mark Hellinger Story*. New York: Appleton-Century-Crofts, 1952.

Blumenthal, Ralph. *Stork Club*. Boston: Little, Brown, 2000.

Bodenheim, Maxwell. *My Life and Loves in Greenwich Village*. New York: Bridgehead Books, 1954.

Bogard, Travis, and Jackson R. Bryer, eds. *Selected Letters of Eugene O'Neill*. New Haven, CT: Yale University Press, 1988.

Bok, Sissela. *Lying*. New York: Pantheon Books, 1978.

Bordman, Gerald. *American Musical Theatre*. New York: Oxford University Press, 1978.

Bosworth, Patricia. *Anything Your Little Heart Desires*. New York: Touchstone, 1997.

———. *Diane Arbus*. New York: Alfred A. Knopf, 1984.

Bricktop, with James Haskins. *Bricktop*. New York: Welcome Rain, 2000.

Brinkley, Alan. *Voices of Protest*. New York: Alfred A. Knopf, 1982.

Brooks, Louise. *Lulu in Hollywood*. New York: Alfred A. Knopf, 1983.

Broun, Heywood. *Seeing Things at Night*. New York: Harcourt, Brace, 1921.

Brown, John Mason. *As They Appear*. New York: McGraw-Hill, 1952.

———. *Still Seeing Things*. New York: McGraw-Hill, 1950.

Broyard, Bliss. *One Drop*. New York: Little, Brown, 2007.

Calder, Alexander. *Calder: An Autobiography with Pictures*. New York: Pantheon Books, 1966.

Callow, Simon. *Orson Welles: Hello Americans.* New York: Viking, 2006.

———. *Orson Welles: The Road to Xanadu.* New York: Viking, 1996.

Carrick, Edward. *Art and Design in the British Film.* London: Dennis Dobson, 1958.

Channing, Carol. *Just Lucky I Guess.* New York: Simon & Schuster, 2002.

Chaplin, Charles. *My Autobiography.* New York: Simon & Schuster, 1964.

Charyn, Jerome. *Gangsters and Gold Diggers.* New York: Four Walls Eight Windows, 2003.

Chilton, John. *Sidney Bechet.* Boston: Da Capo Press, 1996.

Clark, Colin. *My Week with Marilyn.* New York: Weinstein Books, 2011.

Cohen, Rachel. *A Chance Meeting.* New York: Random House, 2004.

Colby, Michael Elihu. *The Algonquin Kid.* Albany, GA: BearManor Media, 2015.

Considine, Bob. *The Remarkable Life of Dr. Armand Hammer.* New York: Harper & Row, 1975.

Covarrubias, Miguel. *Island of Bali.* Singapore: Periplus, 1973.

Cox, Beverly J., and Denna Jones Anderson. *Miguel Covarrubias Caricatures.* Washington, DC: Smithsonian Institution Press, 1985.

Crawford, Cheryl. *One Naked Individual.* Indianapolis: Bobbs-Merrill, 1977.

Crowther, Prudence, ed. *Don't Tread on Me: The Selected Letters of S. J. Perelman.* New York: Viking, 1987.

Cullen, Frank, with Florence Hackman and Donald McNeilly. *Vaudeville Old and New.* Vol. 1. New York: Routledge, 2006.

Cullman, Marguerite. *Ninety Dozen Glasses.* New York: W. W. Norton, 1960.

———. *Occupation: Angel.* New York: W. W. Norton, 1963.

David, Eunice. *Hal David: His Magic Moments*. Pittsburgh: Dorrance Publishing Co., 2016.

Davis, Ronald L. *Mary Martin, Broadway Legend*. Norman: University of Oklahoma Press, 2008.

Delaney, Edmund T. *New York's Greenwich Village*. Barre, MA: Barre Publishers, 1968.

Delaney, Edmund T., and Charles Lockwood. *Greenwich Village: A Photographic Guide*. With photographs by George Roos. New York: Dover, 1976.

Dietz, Howard. "Public Relations." In *Behind the Screen*, edited by Stephen Watts. New York: Dodge, 1938.

Doctorow, E. L. *The Book of Daniel*. New York: Random House, 1999.

Dolkart, Andrew. *Touring the Upper East Side*. New York: New York Landmarks Conservancy, 1995.

Dos Passos, John. *Manhattan Transfer*. Boston: Houghton Mifflin, 1925.

Dregni, Michael. *Django*. Oxford, UK: Oxford University Press, 2004.

Drennan, Robert E., ed. *The Algonquin Wits*. Secaucus, NJ: Citadel Press, 1968.

Du Maurier, George. *Trilby*. London: J. M. Dent & Sons, 1977.

Edwards, Anne. *The DeMilles: An American Family*. New York: Harry N. Abrams, 1988.

Eig, Jonathan. *Luckiest Man: The Life and Death of Lou Gehrig*. New York: Simon & Schuster, 2005.

Eliot, Valerie, and John Haffenden, eds. *The Letters of T. S. Eliot*. Vol 3. New Haven, CT: Yale University Press, 2012.

Engel, Lehman. *The American Musical Theater*. New York: Collier Books, 1975.

Epstein, Joseph. *Partial Payments: Essays on Writers and Their Lives*. New York: W. W. Norton, 1989.

Eyman, Scott. *Ernst Lubitsch: Laughter in Paradise*. Baltimore: Johns Hopkins University Press, 2000.

Fabre, Michel. *From Harlem to Paris*. Urbana: University of Illinois Press, 1991.

Feaver, William. *Masters of Caricature*. Edited by Ann Gould. New York: Alfred A. Knopf, 1981.

Feiffer, Jules. *Backing into Forward*. Chicago: University of Chicago Press, 2010.

Finch, Christopher, and Linda Rosenkrantz. *Gone Hollywood*. Garden City, NY: Doubleday, 1979.

Fisher, Charles. *The Columnists*. New York: Howell, Soskin, 1944.

Fitzgerald, F. Scott. *Babylon Revisited and Other Stories*. Edited by Matthew J. Bruccoli. New York: Scribner, 2003.

———. *The Crack-Up, with Other Uncollected Pieces*. Edited by Edmund Wilson. New York: New Directions, 1956.

———. *The Great Gatsby*. New York: Charles Scribner's Sons, 1925.

Fitzpatrick, Kevin C. *The Algonquin Round Table New York*. Guilford, CT: Lyons Press, 2015.

Flanner, Janet. *The Cubical City*. New York: G. P. Putnam's Sons, 1926.

Fordin, Hugh. *The World of Entertainment!* Garden City, NY: Doubleday, 1975.

Frankel, Max. *The Times of My Life and My Life with "The Times."* New York: Dell, 1999.

Freeman, Don. *Come One, Come All!* New York: Rinehart, 1949.

———. *Norman the Doorman*. New York: Viking Press, 1969.

Fruhauf, Aline. *Making Faces*. Cabin John, MD: Seven Locks Press, 1987.

Gelb, Arthur. *City Room*. New York: G. P. Putnam's Sons, 2003.

Gelb, Arthur, and Barbara Gelb. *O'Neill: Life with Monte Cristo*. New York: Applause, 2000.

Gilbert, James. *Whose Fair? Experience, Memory, and the History of the Great St. Louis Exposition*. Chicago: University of Chicago Press, 2009.

Gill, Brendan. *Late Bloomers*. New York: Artisan, 1966.

Gish, Lillian, with Ann Pinchot.. *The Movies, Mr. Griffith, and Me*. Englewood Cliffs, NJ: Prentice-Hall, 1969.

Goat Hill Neighborhood Association History Book. New York: Goat Hill Neighborhood Association, 2010.

Goetz, Ruth, and Augustus Goetz. *The Heiress*. New York: Dramatists Play Service, 1948.

Gold, Michael. *Jews Without Money*. New York: Carroll & Graf, 2004.

Goldstein, Malcolm. *George S. Kaufman*. New York: Oxford University Press, 1979.

Goodman, Wendy. *The World of Gloria Vanderbilt*. New York: Abrams, 2010.

Goodrich, David L. *The Real Nick and Nora*. Carbondale: Southern Illinois University Press, 2001.

Gottfried, Martin. *Jed Harris: The Curse of Genius*. Boston: Little, Brown, 1984.

Gottlieb, Polly Rose. *The Nine Lives of Billy Rose*. New York: Crown, 1968.

Grauer, Neil A. *Remember Laughter*. Lincoln: University of Nebraska Press, 1994.

Green, Abel. *The Spice of "Variety."* New York: Henry Holt, 1952.

Grosswirth, Marvin. *The Art of Growing a Beard*. New York: Jarrow Press, 1971.

Groth, Janet. *The Receptionist*. Chapel Hill, NC: Algonquin Books of Chapel Hill, 2012.

Gubernick, Lisa Rebecca. *Squandered Fortune: The Life and Times of Huntington Hartford*. New York: G. P. Putnam's Sons, 1991.

Guridy, Frank Andre. *Forging Diaspora: Afro-Cubans and African Americans in a World of Empire and Jim Crow*. Chapel Hill: University of North Carolina Press, 2010.

Hamburger, Philip. *Curious World*. San Francisco: North Point Press, 1987.

———. *Friends Talking in the Night*. New York: Alfred A. Knopf, 1999.

———. *Mayor Watching and Other Pleasures*. New York: Rinehart, 1958.

———. *The Oblong Blur, and Other Odysseys*. New York: Farrar, Straus, 1949.

———. *Our Man Stanley*. Indianapolis: Bobbs-Merrill, 1963.

Hammer, Armand, with Neil Lyndon. *Hammer*. New York: G. P. Putnam's Sons, 1987.

Hansen, Arlen J. *Expatriate Paris*. New York: Arcade, 2012.

Harris, Jed. *Watchman, What of the Night?* Garden City, NY: Doubleday, 1963.

Hart, Kitty Carlisle. *Kitty*. New York: Doubleday, 1988.

Hay, Peter. *MGM: When the Lion Roars*. Atlanta: Turner, 1991.

Hayward, Brooke. *Haywire*. New York: Alfred A. Knopf, 1977.

Hearn, Michael Patrick. *The Art of the Broadway Poster*. New York: Ballantine Books, 1980.

Held, John, Jr. *Grim Youth*. New York: Vanguard Press, 1930.

Heller, Joseph. *Now and Then*. New York: Alfred A. Knopf, 1998.

Hellman, Lillian. *Pentimento*. Boston: Little, Brown, 1973.

———. *Scoundrel Time*. Boston: Little, Brown, 1976.

———. *An Unfinished Woman*. Boston: Little, Brown, 1969.

Hemingway, Ernest. *The Letters of Ernest Hemingway*. Vol. 2, *1923–1925*. Edited by Sandra Spanier, Alfred J. Defasio III, and Robert W. Trogdon. Cambridge, UK: Cambridge University Press, 2013.

———. *A Moveable Feast*. New York: Charles Scribner's Sons, 1964.

———. *On Paris*. London: Hesperus Press, 2012.

———. *The Sun Also Rises*. New York: Charles Scribner's Sons, 1926.

Henderson, Mary C. *Broadway Ballyhoo*. New York: Harry N. Abrams, 1989.

———. *The City and the Theatre*. New York: Back Stage Books, 2004.

Herrmann, Dorothy. *S. J. Perelman*. New York: G. P. Putnam's Sons, 1986.

Herwood, Gary, and Robert Stevens. "A Life in Art: Victor Thall." [unpublished]

Hirschfeld, Al. *The American Theatre as Seen by Hirschfeld*. New York: George Braziller, 1961.

———. *The Entertainers as Seen by Hirschfeld*. London: Elm Tree Books, 1977.

———. *Hirschfeld: Art and Recollections from Eight Decades*. New York: Charles Scribner's Sons, 1991.

———. *Hirschfeld by Hirschfeld*. New York: Dodd, Mead, 1979.

———. *Hirschfeld on Line*. New York: Applause, 1999.

———. *Hirschfeld's British Aisles*. New York: Glenn Young Books, 2006.

———. *Hirschfeld's Harlem*. New York: Glenn Young Books, 2004. Expanded edition of *Harlem as Seen by Hirschfeld*. New York: Hyperion Press, 1941.

———. *Hirschfeld's World*. New York: Harry N. Abrams, 1961.

———. *Manhattan Oases: New York's 1932 Speak-Easies, with a Gentleman's Guide to Bars and Beverages by Gordon Kahn*. New York: E. P. Dutton, 1932.

———. *Show Business Is No Business*. New York: Da Capo Press, 1979.

———. *The Speakeasies of 1932*. Text by Gordon Kahn and Al Hirschfeld. New York: Glenn Young Books, 2006. Rev. ed. of *Manhattan Oases*.

———. *The World of Hirschfeld*. New York: Harry N. Abrams, 1970.

Holroyd, Michael. *On Wheels*. London: Chatto & Windus, 2013.

Houdini, Harry. *The Right Way to Do Wrong*. Brooklyn: Melville House, 2012.

Houseman, John. *Run-Through*. New York: Simon & Schuster, 1972.

Huddleston, Sisley. *Back to Montparnasse*. Philadelphia: J. B. Lippincott, 1931.

Hutchens, John K., and George Oppenheimer, eds. *The Best in "The World."* New York: Viking Press, 1973.

Jablonski, Edward. *Gershwin*. New York: Doubleday, 1987.

Jamison, Kay Redfield. *Touched with Fire*. New York: Free Press, 1993.

Josephson, Barne, with Terry Trilling-Josephson. *Café Society*. Urbana: University of Illinois Press, 2009.

Joshi, S. T., ed. *Mencken on Mencken*. Baton Rouge: Louisiana State University Press, 2010.

Kahn, Gordon. *Hollywood on Trial*. New York: Boni & Gaer, 1948.

Kammen, Michael. *The Lively Arts: Gilbert Seldes and the Transformation of Cultural Criticism in the United States*. New York: Oxford University Press, 1996.

Kanin, Garson. *Do Re Mi*. Boston: Little, Brown, 1955.

———. *Hollywood*. New York: Viking Press, 1974.

Kardish, Laurence. *Weimar Cinema, 1919–1933*. New York: Museum of Modern Art, 2010.

Katz, Harry, ed. *Cartoon America: Comic Art in the Library of Congress*. New York: Abrams, 2006.

Kaufman, Bel. *Up the Down Staircase*. Englewood Cliffs, NJ: Prentice-Hall, 1964.

Kazan, Elia. *Elia Kazan: A Life*. New York: Alfred A. Knopf, 1988.

Kazin, Alfred. *New York Jew*. New York: Vintage Books, 1979.

Kellner, Bruce. *Carl Van Vechten and the Irreverent Decades.* Norman: University of Oklahoma Press, 1968.

———. *The Last Dandy, Ralph Barton.* Columbia: University of Missouri Press, 1991.

Kerr, Walter. *The Decline of Pleasure.* New York: Simon & Schuster, 1962.

———. *Journey to the Center of the Theater.* New York: Alfred A. Knopf, 1979.

———. *Pieces at Eight.* New York: Simon & Schuster, 1957.

Kevles, Bettyann Holtzmann. *Naked to the Bone.* New Brunswick, NJ: Rutgers University Press, 1997.

Kimbrough, Emily. *Better Than Oceans.* New York: Harper & Row, 1976.

———. *We Followed Our Hearts to Hollywood.* New York: Dodd, Mead, 1943.

King, Alexander. *I Should Have Kissed Her More.* New York: Simon & Schuster, 1961.

———. *May This House Be Safe from Tigers.* New York: Simon & Schuster, 1960.

———. *Mine Enemy Grows Older.* New York: Simon & Schuster, 1958.

Kinney, Harrison, ed., with Rosemary A. Thurber. *The Thurber Letters.* New York: Simon & Schuster, 2002.

Komisarjevsky, Theodore. *Myself and the Theatre.* New York: E. P. Dutton, 1930.

Kronenberger, Louis. *Company Manners.* Indianapolis: Bobbs-Merrill, 1954.

———. *Kings and Desperate Men.* New York: Alfred A. Knopf, 1942.

Kunkel, Thomas. *Man in Profile.* New York: Random House, 2015.

Kurnitz, Harry. *Reclining Figure.* New York: Random House, 1955.

Lanier, Henry Wysham, and Berenice Abbott. *Greenwich Village Today and Yesterday*. New York: Harper & Brothers, 1949. Text by Lanier; photographs by Abbott.

Lanoux, Armand. *Paris in the Twenties*. New York: Golden Griffin Books/Essential Encyclopedia Arts, 1960.

Lauder, Sir Harry. *Roamin' in the Gloamin'*. Philadelphia: J. B. Lippincott, 1928.

Lawrenson, Helen. *Stranger at the Party*. New York: Random House, 1975.

Lawson-Peebles, Robert, ed. *Approaches to the American Musical*. Exeter: University of Exeter Press, 1996.

Lee, Jennifer, ed. *Paris in Mind*. New York: Vintage Books, 2003.

Lee, Lawrence, and Barry Gifford. *Saroyan*. New York: Harper & Row, 1984.

Leeming, David. *Amazing Grace: A Life of Beauford Delaney*. New York: Oxford University Press, 1998.

Leggett, John. *A Daring Young Man: A Biography of William Saroyan*. New York: Alfred A. Knopf, 2002.

Leider, Emily W. *Myrna Loy: The Only Good Girl in Hollywood*. Berkeley: University of California Press, 2011.

Leopold, David. *Hirschfeld's Hollywood*. New York: Harry N. Abrams, in association with the Academy of Motion Picture Arts and Sciences, 2001.

Lerman, Leo. *The Grand Surprise: The Journals of Leo Lerman*. Edited by Stephen Pascal. New York: Alfred A. Knopf, 2007.

Levant, Oscar. *The Memoirs of an Amnesiac*. New York: G. P. Putnam's Sons, 1965.

———. *The Unimportance of Being Oscar*. New York: G. P. Putnam's Sons, 1968.

Lewine, Richard, and Alfred Simon. *Songs of the American Theater*. New York: Dodd, Mead, 1973.

Lewis, Jerry D., ed. *Great Stories About Show Business*. New York: Coward-McCann, 1957.

Liebling, A. J. *The Press*. New York: Ballantine Books, 1975.

Lowe, Sue Davidson. *Stieglitz: A Memoir/Biography*. New York: Farrar, Straus and Giroux, 1983.

Lumet, Sidney. *Making Movies*. New York: Alfred A. Knopf, 1995.

Lynn, Kenneth S. *Charlie Chaplin and His Times*. New York: Simon & Schuster, 1997.

Lyons, Eugene. *Assignment in Utopia*. New York: Harcourt, Brace, 1937.

Malina, Judith. *The Piscator Notebook*. London: Routledge, 2012.

Maney, Richard. *Fanfare*. New York: Harper & Brothers, 1957.

Mansfield, Irving. *Life with Jackie*. With Jean Libman Block. Toronto: Bantam Books, 1983.

Martin, Hugh. *Hugh Martin: The Boy Next Door*. Encinitas, CA: Trolley Press, 2010.

Martin, Mary. *My Heart Belongs*. New York: William Morrow, 1976.

Marx, Arthur. *Goldwyn*. New York: W. W. Norton, 1976.

Marx, Groucho. *Groucho and Me*. New York: Bernard Geis Associates, 1959.

———. *The Groucho Letters*. London: Pocket Books, 1967.

———. *Memoirs of a Mangy Lover*. New York: Bernard Geis Associates, 1963.

Marx, Harpo, with Rowland Barber. *Harpo Speaks . . . About New York*. New York: Little Bookroom, 2001.

Marx, Samuel. *Mayer and Thalberg: The Make-Believe Saints*. New York: Random House, 1975.

———. *Queen of the Ritz*. Indianapolis: Bobbs-Merrill, 1978.

Matthau, Carol. *Among the Porcupines*. New York: Turtle Bay Books, 1992.

Maurer, David W. *The Big Con*. New York: Anchor Books, 1999.

McHugh, Dominic. *Loverly: The Life and Times of "My Fair Lady."* New York: Oxford University Press, 2012.

McIntyre, O. O. *The Big Town*. New York: Dodd, Mead, 1935.

———. *White Light Nights*. New York: Cosmopolitan, 1924.

McKay, Claude. *Home to Harlem*. Boston: Northeastern University Press, 1987.

Meade, Marion. *Lonelyhearts: The Screwball World of Nathanael West and Eileen McKenney*. Boston: Mariner Books, 2011.

Meredith, Scott. *George S. Kaufman and His Friends*. Garden City, NY: Doubleday, 1974.

Merwin, Ted. *Pastrami on Rye*. New York: New York University Press, 2015.

Mielziner, Jo. *Designing for the Theatre*. New York: Bramhall House, 1965.

Miller, Alice. *The Drama of the Gifted Child*. New York: Basic Books, 1997.

Miller, Donald L. *Supreme City*. New York: Simon & Schuster, 2014.

Miller, Frank. *MGM Posters*. Atlanta: Turner, 1994.

Milne, Christopher. *The Enchanted Places*. New York: E. P. Dutton, 1974.

Mitchell, Joseph. *My Ears Are Bent*. New York: Pantheon Books, 2001.

Monsaingeon, Bruno. *Mademoiselle: Conversations with Nadia Boulanger*. Manchester, UK: Carcanet Press, 1985.

Mordden, Ethan. *Anything Goes*. Oxford, UK: Oxford University Press, 2013.

———. *Love Song*. New York: St. Martin's Press, 2012.

Morgan, Ted. *Maugham*. New York: Simon & Schuster, 1980.

Morgenstern, Dan. *Living with Jazz*. New York: Pantheon Books, 2004.

Morgenstern, Soma. *The Son of the Lost Son*. New York: Rinehart, 1946.

———. *The Third Pillar*. New York: Farrar, Straus and Cudahy, 1955.

Morris, Jan. *Manhattan '45*. New York: Oxford University Press, 1987.

Morris, Sylvia Jukes. *Rage for Fame: The Ascent of Clare Boothe Luce*. New York: Random House, 1997.

Mott, Frank Luther. *A History of American Magazines*. Vols. 3 and 5. Cambridge, MA: Belknap Press of Harvard University Press, 1968.

Murray, Ken. *The Body Merchant*. Pasadena, CA: Ward Ritchie Press, 1976.

Nathan, George Jean. *Passing Judgments*. New York: Alfred A. Knopf, 1935.

Nelson, Nancy. *Evenings with Cary Grant*. New York: William Morrow, 1991.

Newman, Danny. *Tales of a Theatrical Guru*. Urbana: University of Illinois Press, 2006.

New York City Guide. Prepared by the Federal Writers' Project of the Works Progress Administration in New York City. Guilds' Committee for Federal Writers' Publications, 1939. Reprint, New York: Octagon Books, 1970.

The New Yorker. The 40s: The Story of a Decade. Edited by Henry Finder with Giles Harvey. New York: Random House, 2014.

"New York in the 1920s: Supreme City." Special issue of *American Heritage*, November 1988.

The New York Times. The Newspaper: Its Making and Its Meaning. New York: Charles Scribner's Sons, 1945.

Nightingale, Benedict. *Fifth Row Center*. New York: Times Books, 1986.

North, Joseph, ed. *New Masses: An Anthology of the Rebel Thirties*. New York: International Publishers, 1969.

O'Brien, Pat. *The Wind at My Back*. Garden City, NY: Doubleday, 1964.

Osato, Sono. *Distant Dances*. New York: Alfred A. Knopf, 1980.

Paar, Jack. *P.S. Jack Paar*. New York: Doubleday, 1983.

Palmer-Smith, Glenn. *Murals of New York City*. Photographs by Joshua McHugh. New York: Rizzoli, 2013.

Parascandola, Louis J., and John Parascandola. *A Coney Island Reader*. New York: Columbia University Press, 2015.

Parker, Douglas M. *Ogden Nash: The Life and Work of America's Laureate of Light Verse*. Chicago: Ivan R. Dee, 2005.

Patinkin, Sheldon. *"No Legs, No Jokes, No Chance."* Chicago: Northwestern University Press, 2008.

Paul, Elliot. *Hugger-Mugger in the Louvre*. New York: Random House, 1940.

Pen and Sunlight Sketches of Saint Louis. Chicago: Phoenix, 1898.

Perelman, S. J. *Acres and Pains*. Short Hills, NJ: Burford Books, 1995.

———. *The Beauty Part*. New York: Simon & Schuster, 1963.

———. *Crazy Like a Fox*. New York: Random House, 1944.

———. *Eastward Ha!* New York: Touchstone, 1977.

———. *The Most of S. J. Perelman*. New York: Simon & Schuster, 1958.

———. *The Rising Gorge*. New York: Simon & Schuster, 1961.

———. *The Road to Miltown*. New York: Simon & Schuster, 1957.

———. *The Swiss Family Perelman*. New York: Lyons Press, 2000.

———. *Westward Ha!* New York: Simon & Schuster, 1948.

Perelman, S. J., and Ogden Nash. *One Touch of Venus*. Boston: Little, Brown, 1944.

Pollack, Howard. *George Gershwin*. Berkeley: University of California Press, 2006.

Prince, Hal. *Contradictions*. New York: Dodd, Mead, 1974.

Raabe, Meinhard, with Daniel Kinske. *Memories of a Munchkin*. New York: Back Stage Books, 2005.

Raphaelson, Dorshka. *Morning Song*. New York: Random House, 1948.

Raphaelson, Samson. *The Human Nature of Playwrighting*. New York: Macmillan, 1949.

Reaves, Wendy Wick. *Celebrity Caricature in America*. New Haven, CT: National Portrait Gallery, Smithsonian Institution, in association with Yale University Press, 1998.

Reichman, Stella Jolles. *Great Big Beautiful Doll*. New York: E. P. Dutton, 1977.

Reiner, Carl. *My Anecdotal Life*. New York: St. Martin's Press, 2003.

Rittner, Don. *Then and Now Albany*. Charleston, SC: Arcadia, 2002.

Riva, Maria. *Marlene Dietrich*. New York: Knopf, 1993.

Robinson, David. *Hollywood in the Twenties*. London: A. Zwemmer, 1968.

Robinson, Ray. *Iron Horse: Lou Gehrig in His Time*. New York: HarperPerennial, 1991.

Rodgers, Richard. *Musical Stages*. New York: Jove/HBJ, 1978.

Rogers, W. G., and Mildred Weston. *Carnival Crossroads*. Garden City, NY: Doubleday, 1960.

Roiphe, Anne. *1185 Park Avenue*. New York: Free Press, 1999.

Rorem, Ned. *The Paris Diary and the New York Diary*. New York: Da Capo Press, 1998.

Rosenblum, Constance. *Gold Digger*. New York: Metropolitan Books, 2000.

Rosenquist, James. *Painting Below Zero*. With David Dalton. New York: Alfred A. Knopf, 2009.

Ross, Lillian. *Moments with Chaplin*. New York: Dodd, Mead, 1980.

Rudel, Anthony. *Hello, Everybody! The Dawn of American Radio*. Orlando, FL: Harcourt, 2008.

Runyon, Damon. *Guys and Dolls, and Other Writings*. New York: Penguin Books, 2008.

Sabinson, Harvey. *Darling, You Were Wonderful*. Chicago: Henry Regnery, 1977.

Sachs, Joel. *Henry Cowell*. New York: Oxford University Press, 2012.

Sachs, Maurice. *The Decade of Illusion: Paris, 1918–1928*. New York: Alfred A. Knopf, 1935.

Salerno, Marie, and Arthur Gelb, eds. *The New York Pop-Up Book*. New York: Universe, 1999.

Sardi, Vincent, and Richard Gehman. *Sardi's*. New York: Henry Holt, 1953.

Sardi, Vincent, Jr., and Thomas Edward West. *Off the Wall at Sardi's*. New York: Applause Books, 1991.

Saroyan, Aram. *Last Rites*. New York: William Morrow, 1982.

Saroyan, William. *The Beautiful People and Two Other Plays*. New York: Harcourt, Brace, 1941.

———. *Places Where I've Done Time*. New York: Praeger, 1972.

———. *Sons Come and Go, Mothers Hang In Forever*. New York: McGraw-Hill, 1976.

———. *The Time of Your Life*. New York: Harcourt, Brace, 1939.

Schapiro, Steve, and David Chierichetti. *The Movie Poster Book*. New York: E. P. Dutton, 1979.

Schoenstein, Ralph. *My Year in the White House Doghouse*. New York: David White, 1969.

Schultz, William Todd. *An Emergency in Slow Motion*. New York: Bloomsbury, 2011.

Secrest, Meryle. *Somewhere for Me*. New York: Alfred A. Knopf, 2001.

Seebohm, Caroline. *The Man Who Was "VOGUE."* New York: Viking Press, 1982.

Selznick, Irene Mayer. *A Private View*. New York: Alfred A. Knopf, 1983.

Shaffer, Mary Ann, and Annie Barrows. *The Guernsey Literary and Potato Peel Pie Society*. London: Bloomsbury, 2008.

Shaw, Irwin, and Ronald Searle. *Paris! Paris!* New York: Harcourt Brace Jovanovich, 1977.

Shawn, Allen. *Wish I Could Be There: Notes from a Phobic Life*. New York: Viking, 2007.

Simon, Howard. *Cabin on a Ridge*. Chicago: Follett, 1970.

———. *Primer of Drawing for Adults.* New York: Sterling, 1953.

Skolsky, Sidney. *Times Square Tintypes.* New York: Ives Washburn, 1930.

Smith, Linell Nash. *Loving Letters from Ogden Nash.* Boston: Little, Brown, 1990.

Snow, Carmel. *The World of Carmel Snow.* With Mary Louise Aswell. New York: McGraw-Hill, 1962.

Snyder, Robert W. *Crossing Broadway.* Ithaca, NY: Cornell University Press, 2015.

Solomon, Deborah. *American Mirror: The Life and Art of Norman Rockwell.* New York: Farrar, Straus and Giroux, 2013.

Spurling, Hilary. *Matisse the Master.* London: Hamish Hamilton, 2005.

Stagg, Jerry. *The Brothers Shubert.* New York: Ballantine Books, 1968.

Stein, Gertrude. *The Autobiography of Alice B. Toklas.* New York: Literary Guild, 1933.

———. *Paris France.* New York: Liveright, 1970.

Stevens, Robert. "A Forgotten Abstract Expressionist." [unpublished]

Stevens, Walter. *St. Louis: History of the Fourth City, 1763–1909.* Chicago: S. J. Clarke, 1909.

Strunsky, Simeon. *No Mean City.* New York: E. P. Dutton, 1944.

Sussmann, Elisabeth, and Doon Arbus. *Diane Arbus: A Chronology.* New York: Aperture, 2011.

Swan, Claudia, ed. *1939: Music and the World's Fair.* New York: Eos Music, 1998.

Tauranac, John. *Elegant New York.* New York: Abbeville Press, 1985.

Taylor, Robert. *Fred Allen: His Life and Wit.* Boston: Little, Brown, 1989.

Teachout, Terry. *Duke: A Life of Duke Ellington.* New York: Gotham Books, 2013.

———. *Pops: A Life of Louis Armstrong*. Boston: Houghton Mifflin Harcourt, 2009.

Teichmann, Howard. *George S. Kaufman*. New York: Atheneum, 1972.

Teicholz, Tom, ed. *Conversations with S. J. Perelman*. Jackson: University Press of Mississippi, 1995.

Thomas, Bob. *Walt Disney*. New York: Fireside, 1976.

Thomson, David. *Showman*. New York: Alfred A. Knopf, 1992.

Thurber, James. *The Beast in Me and Other Animals*. New York: Harcourt, Brace, 1948.

Thwaite, Ann. *A. A. Milne*. New York: Random House, 1990.

Toklas, Alice B. *What Is Remembered*. New York: Holt, Rinehart and Winston, 1963.

Tunick, Susan. *Terra-Cotta Skyline*. New York: Princeton Architectural Press, 1997.

Tyler, Steven. *Does the Noise in My Head Bother You?* New York: HarperLuxe, 2011.

Van Nimmen, Jane. *Lightest Blues: Great Humor from the Thirties*. New York: Imago Imprint, 1984.

Van Riper, Guernsey, Jr. *Lou Gehrig: Boy of the Sand Lots*. Indianapolis: Bobbs-Merrill, 1949.

Van Vechten, Carl. *Parties*. New York: Avon Books, 1977.

Vreeland, Diana. *D.V.* Edited by George Plimpton and Christopher Hemphill. New York: Vintage Books, 1984.

Wainwright, Loudon. *The Great American Magazine*. New York: Alfred A. Knopf, 1986.

Walker, Danton. *Guide to New York Nitelife*. New York: G. P. Putnam's Sons, 1958.

Walker, Stanley. *The Night Club Era*. New York: Frederick A. Stokes, 1933.

Wallach, Eli. *The Good, the Bad, and Me*. Orlando, FL: Harcourt, 2005.

Wearing, J. P., ed. *Bernard Shaw and Nancy Astor*. Toronto: University of Toronto Press, 2005.

Whelan, Richard. *Alfred Stieglitz: A Biography*. Boston: Little, Brown, 1995.

Wilk, Max. *And Did You Once See Sidney Plain?* New York: Coalition of Publishers for Employment, 1985.

———. *OK! The Story of "Oklahoma!"* New York: Grove Press, 1993.

Williams, Adriana. *Covarrubias*. Austin: University of Texas Press, 1994.

Williams, Ellen. *Picasso's Paris: Walking Tours of the Artist's Life in the City*. New York: Little Bookroom, 1999.

Wintz, Cary D., and Paul Finkelman, eds. *Encyclopedia of the Harlem Renaissance*. Vol. 1. New York: Routledge, 2004.

Wolfe, Thomas. "The Lost Boy." In *The Hills Beyond*. New York: Harper & Brothers, 1941.

Woollcott, Alexander. *Long, Long Ago*. New York: Bantam, 1946.

———. *While Rome Burns*. New York: Viking Press, 1934.

Woolrich, Cornell. *Times Square*. New York: Horace Liveright, 1929.

Woon, Basil. *The Paris That's Not in the Guide Books*. New York: Brentano's, 1926.

Worden, Helen. *Discover New York with Helen Worden*. New York: American Women's Voluntary Services, 1943.

———. *Here Is New York*. New York: Doubleday, Doran, 1939.

Wynn, Neil A., ed. *Cross the Water Blues: African American Music in Europe*. Jackson: University Press of Mississippi, 2007.

ACKNOWLEDGMENTS

My tip-top thanks to Al Hirschfeld, who, with tongue in cheek and pen in hand, designated me his biographer one April afternoon in his studio. As we sat together there, little did we know we'd wind up together here.

This book could not have been written without the access extended to me by Louise Kerz Hirschfeld Cullman and David Leopold. Our many conversations and the treasures they shared from the Al Hirschfeld Foundation—letters and ledgers, scrapbooks and sketchbooks, artifacts and ephemera—were invaluable.

Nina Hirschfeld welcomed me to Texas, where she and her son and daughter reminisced about Al the father and grandfather, life on Ninety-fifth Street, and the mixed blessing of wearing a famous name.

Nearby and far-flung, I am indebted to many archivists and mappers, librarians and curators for their expertise and perseverance:

In Arkansas: Catherine Wallack, architectural records archivist at the University of Arkansas Libraries, Fayetteville.

In Hollywood: Stacey Behlmer, coordinator of special projects and research assistance; Ellen Harrington, museum collections curator at the Academy Museum; Kristine Krueger, NFIS coordinator; Jenny Romero, research archivist; and Faye Thompson, photograph department coordinator, all at the

Academy of Motion Picture Arts and Sciences. And Edward (Ned) Sykes Comstock, senior library assistant at the Cinematic Arts Library, University of Southern California.

In London: Georgia Clemson, archives and special collections assistant at the University Archives and Special Collections Centre, London College of Communication.

In New England: Karen Nangle, public services assistant at the Beinecke Rare Book & Manuscript Library, Yale University; Barbara Zabel, professor emeritus, art history, at Connecticut College; Kimberly Reynolds, curator of manuscripts at the Boston Public Library; and Dale Stinchcomb, curatorial assistant in the Harvard Theatre Collection at the Houghton Library, Harvard University.

In New York: Isaac Gewirtz, PhD, curator at the Henry W. and Albert A. Berg Collection of English and American Literature, New York Public Library; Ira Goldberg, executive director of the Art Students League; John Coyne, manager, and Davida Deutsch, in-house historian of the Osborne; Laurence Kardish, former senior curator of the film department at the Museum of Modern Art; Phyllis Magidson, Elizabeth Farran Tozer Curator of Costumes and Textiles at the Museum of the City of New York; Gino Francesconi, museum director and archivist at Carnegie Hall; Norman Brouwer, maritime historian; Ray Wemmlinger, curator and librarian at The Players; and archivists Hermann Teifer and Michael Simonson at the Leo Baeck Institute.

In St. Louis: Patricia Boulware, collections documentation assistant at the Saint Louis Art Museum; Terry Leon Garrett, archivist with the City of Saint Louis Recorder of Deeds (and Barbara Renfrow and Dusty Reese, too); Adele Heagney, reference librarian at the St. Louis Public Library; Jason Stratman, assistant reference librarian at the Missouri History Museum; Miranda Rechtenwald, curator of local history at the University Archives and Special Collections, Washington University; and Debbie Kittrell at Ittner Architects.

In Texas: Dr. Russell Marin III, director, and Terre Heydari, operations manager, at the DeGolyer Library, Southern Methodist University, Dallas; and Claudia Anderson, supervisory archivist at the LBJ Presidential Library, Austin.

In Washington, DC: Martha Kennedy, curator of popular and applied graphic art and poster acquisitions, Prints and Photographs Division, Library of Congress; Wendy Wick Reaves, curator of prints and drawings at the National Portrait Gallery, Smithsonian Institution; and James H. Lesar, Esq.

For their generosity in sharing interviews and outtakes from their own projects, I thank Karen Goodman and Michael Kantor. Ted Chapin, too, for the screener of *Main Street to Broadway*, Marshall Akers for the tape of Nina Hirschfeld on *To Tell the Truth*, and Lynne Kirste, special collections curator in the film archive at the Academy of Motion Picture Arts and Sciences, for enabling me to view Hirschfeld's home movies. In another context, I was deeply moved by Tony Kahn's *Blacklisted*, the personal history of his family's Hollywood nightmare, produced as a six-part radio series on NPR.

On the New York home front, Margaret Bay, Jeffrey Brown, Philip Germano, and Denise and Paul Lachman opened their doors to give me tours of Hirschfeld's former digs on East Fifty-fourth Street, the Osborne roof, and East Ninety-fifth Street. Outside, Shari Thompson, the Hirschfelds' next-door neighbor on Ninety-fifth, ushered me up and down the block. And uptown, Bob Isaac and Rachel Chodorov walked me around Washington Heights.

On other Hirschfeld terrain, Paul Finkelman, PhD—historian, law professor, co-sleuth—drove me through Albany, to the sites of Marcus Hirschfeld's tailor shops and dwellings and to the cemetery where he and his family repose. Behind other wheels, Adrienne and Mark Hirschfeld, Barbara Singer, and Bruce Yampolsky with the Board of Public Service met me in St. Louis and showed me the town. In Austin, Nina Hirschfeld's friends Shirley Beeman and Becky Davis were truly Texas darlin's. In

Paris, Deena Schnitman enthusiastically accompanied me on the quest for Hirschfeld's bohemian hangouts from 1925, and Liza Kronenberger Wanklyn translated my brief but belligerent interview with the proprietor of Hirschfeld's 1929 gallery on the Boulevard Montparnasse.

For their love of the chase, I thank the indefatigible Kenneth R. Cobb, assistant commissioner, New York City Department of Records and Information Services; Jane Klain, manager of research services at the Paley Center for Media; John Tauranac, author and historian; and Sandra L. Levine, architectural historian and sharpshooter.

For facilitating and finessing, I am grateful to Katherine Eastman, Paul Chapman, and Bridget Hallowell at the Al Hirschfeld Foundation in Bedminster, Pennsylvania; Phyllis Westberg at Harold Ober Associates; Josh McKeon with the Berg Collection at the New York Public Library; Frank Collerius at the Jefferson Market branch of the New York Public Library; Ally Malinenko with the Brooklyn Collection at the Brooklyn Public Library; Phyllis M. Mingione, Joe Van Nostrand, and Bruce Abrams in the New York County Clerk's Office; Naomi Kuromiya, administrative assistant of the department of painting and sculpture, Museum of Modern Art; Joan Paley at Congregation Beth Emeth in Albany; Nina Rolfs at Cedar Park Cemetery in Emerson, New Jersey; Corey Stewart, archivist at the National Personnel Records Center; Beth Kleber, founding archivist at the Milton Glaser Design Study Center and Archives and the School of Visual Arts Archives; Michelle Mavigliano at the Schuyler Mansion in Albany; and Richard Barry at the South Station of the Albany Police Department. Thanks, too, to Maggie Tauranac for her transcription tutelage.

A sumptuous bouquet to the following for their anecdotes and leads, *Times* tales, and Broadway melodies: Emanuel Azenberg, Ella Baff, Seymour Barab, Tom Beebe, Clare Bell, Joe Benincasa, Dr. Anna Bruni Benson, Walter Bernard, Shirley Claire, Douglas Colby, Michael Colby, Prudence Crowther,

Virginia Dajani, John Darnton, Jamie Donnelly, Victor Elmaleh, Joe Feczko, Stella Ferrer, Paul Finkelstein, Richard Frankel, Peter Funt, Paul Gardner, Barbara Gelb, John Lawrence Githens, Grace Glueck, Fred Goldberg, Carol Frueh Gourley, Frank Granat, Neil Grauer, Richard Hamburger, Jeff Harnar, Halley Harrisburg and Michael Rosenfeld, Kathy Hayes, Gary Herwood, Darryl Herzon, Matt Hirschfeld, Nina Hirshfeld [*sic*], Tony Hiss, Ann Hould-Ward, Holly Hynes, Walter Isaacson, Bill and Janet Jacklin, Al Jaffee, Stephen Jones, Jim Kelly, Everett Raymond Kinstler, Max Klimavicius, Robert Klein, Hilary Knight, Carol Stock Kranowitz, John Kronenberger, Joe LaRosa, Elliot Lawrence, Matthew Levine, David Levering Lewis, Lynn Lewis and Dr. Francis Perrone, Samuel ("Biff") Liff, Margo Lion, Dr. Cynthia MacKay, Sheri Mann, Mel Maron, Lynne Meadow, Michael Montel, Lee Moskof, Mike Naumann, Dr. Bettina Simon Niederer, Norton Owen, Gail Papp, Stephanie Plunkett, Joel Raphaelson, Lee Roy Reams, Michael Riedel, Ray Robinson, John Rockwell, Madeline Rogers, Ned Rorem, Marie Salerno, Emerlinda Sanchez, Joyce Schiller, Julian Schlossberg, Barbara Kahn Schwartz and Bob Schwartz, Daniel Selznick, Jay Shaw, Keith Sherman, Brooke Shields, Hazel Shore, Rabbi Scott L. Shpeen, Jan Simpson, Lee Snow, Louise Sommers, Karen Sperling, Gary Springer, Robert Stevens, Elaine Stritch, Michael Strunsky, Nicolas Surovy, Bob Ullman, Diane Englander Underberg, Michael Valenti, Pamela Vassil, Jac Venza, Mort Walker, Naomi Warner, Louis Webre, Samuel White, Michael Witte, JoAnn Young, and Suzanne Schwarz Zuber.

Learning Hirschfeld has been a splendid adventure. Thanks to Mark Gompertz and Caroline Russomanno at Skyhorse for taking the reins and riding my book to the finish line. Thanks, too, to my agent Robin Straus, a harbinger of spring and new beginnings, and to Judith Bass Esq., an advocate in every sense. And for sustenance throughout, my love to Peter Stern, Charley Stern, Katie Stern, Kyle Martin, Daisy Martin, and Murphy May at home.

INDEX